Bernard Ward

**History of St. Edmund's College**

Bernard Ward

**History of St. Edmund's College**

ISBN/EAN: 9783337326661

Printed in Europe, USA, Canada, Australia, Japan

Cover: Foto ©ninafisch / pixelio.de

More available books at **www.hansebooks.com**

St. Edmund's College and Chapel.

# PREFACE.

It is much to be wished that some one would have taken in hand the work of writing a history of St. Edmund's College, whose literary and other qualifications would have fitted him for the task better than my own. I can only hope that what is wanting from a literary point of view may be made up for by the intrinsic interest of much of the material, and by the care and trouble which have been bestowed upon its collection.

At the present day Old Hall stands alone as a Catholic school which existed during the time of the Penal Laws, and has been carried on in the same place from day to day without intermission ever since. Its history forms a complete connecting link between the days of persecution and the present time. Before the breaking up of Douay and St. Omer it was, indeed, of much less importance than it afterwards became; but even then, when it was a private school, the property of Bishop Talbot, it was the chief—almost the only—place of education for the sons of the Catholic nobility and gentry on this side of the Channel, and as such it had connections with almost all the Catholic families of note. When Douay came to an end in 1793, however, and "Old Hall Green Academy" grew into "St. Edmund's College," it assumed a position and importance of a much higher kind. It is true that it did not become, as Bishop Douglass had hoped, a general College for the whole of England, and therefore it never replaced Douay in the full sense of the term; but it took up the work of Ecclesiastical education so far as the London district was concerned, and for many generations nearly all the priests of the South of England came out from its walls.

St. Edmund's College has for a long time past ceased to hold its ancient position as the chief place of education for the Catholic laity. The lay students are still there; but they no longer form the majority, as they once did, and the spirit of the place is chiefly Ecclesiastical. The latter element has steadily increased down to the present day, notwithstanding the fact that the Church students are now those for the Archdiocese only, instead of for the whole London District, as formerly. In following the change which has come about, we have brought before us the gradual growth of Catholicity in England during the present century. A hundred years ago twenty Church students were sufficient for the wants of the whole of the South of England; to-day, the Diocese of Westminster alone requires four times that number.

The work of looking through old letters and documents has been necessarily long and tedious; but the results of the searches have exceeded my most sanguine expectations. The "Iron Room" at St. Edmund's has been a safe receptacle for letters and papers, which seem to have been indiscriminately thrown into it, and although heaped up in utter disorder, have at least been saved from destruction.

A considerable number of these papers were found to be of the greatest possible value. Some of them must have been brought from Douay by Dr. Poynter, or some other of the priests who came over during the French Revolution; amongst others a MS. which seems to be the original Douay Rules, drawn out in the year 1600; a packet of letters written by the Venerable Thomas Maxfield, the martyr, to Dr. Kellison, President of Douay, within a few days of his execution in 1616; several copies of the Theological "Dictates," printed Theological Theses, and some valuable old transcripts. Among the papers of value which did not come from Douay may be mentioned a document dating from the middle of last century, entitled the "Rules and Customs of Standon School;" a complete set of Ordos and Catholic Directories from 1765 down to the present day; the Architect's plans for the proposed College of St. Edmund, submitted to Dr. Gregory Stapleton in 1795; the "Diary of St. Edmund's College," beginning the same year; the old account books, and a large number of miscellaneous letters. These have now been sorted and arranged, and those of value have been bound up into volumes.

Considerable material was obtained also in looking through the Westminster Diocesan papers in London. At the Archbishop's house, in Canon Johnson's possession, is a large two-volume Diary, in Bishop Douglass's writing, containing many details connected with the foundation and early days of St. Edmund's; and at the Oratory, among the Westminster Archives, numbers of letters were found from the various Presidents and others to the Bishops of the London Districts, describing the progress of the building of the College at the end of last century, and many other things connected therewith. The work of looking through these was rendered comparatively easy by the admirable manner in which they have been sorted and arranged by the Oratorian Fathers. By the kind permission of His Eminence the late Cardinal Manning, an exchange was effected between the Oratory and St. Edmund's, by which we gave up all letters and other documents on purely Diocesan affairs, and received in return all those bearing on the history of the College. These are now bound up with the other papers in the College *archivium*. My special thanks are due to Father Stanton, the custodian, not only for affording me every facility for searching through all the old papers, but also for proposing and helping to carry out the exchange alluded to, to the mutual advantage, it is hoped, of both collections.

From these and other minor sources a fairly complete history of St. Edmund's College, from its first establishment in 1793, is now produced, together with a short account of the parent establishments of Douay and St. Omer Colleges on the one hand, and Twyford and Standon Schools, and "Old Hall Green Academy" on the other. The chief difficulty in obtaining a continuous record concerns the period before the Relief Act of 1791, when all Catholic schools kept in England were illegal and their masters liable to heavy penalties. Although these penalties were rarely enforced, as a matter of precaution the destruction of all papers connected with the working of such schools was deemed advisable. We are not, however, entirely in the dark about the early history of Old Hall. A few papers of accounts, lists of students, marginal notes on the old Ordos, and some letters have survived from this period; and relating to the earlier time when the school was conducted as originally established by Bishop Challoner at Standon Lordship, we have, in one single document already alluded to, a full and detailed description of the "Rules and Customs" of the community there.

From the date of the passing of the Act of 1791 records are plentiful enough, and a connected account is for the first time presented of the negotiations which succeeded the fall of Douay in 1793, and led to the establishment of the Colleges in England. Here a remark of some importance must be made. It has sometimes been stated that St. Edmund's was a filiation or successor of St. Omer College rather than of Douay. Such has never been the tradition at St. Edmund's itself, but it has been asserted comparatively lately by one or two who wished to prove that Ushaw is the only modern representative of Douay. Bearing on this a large amount of new matter will be found in the following pages, and the documents and letters reproduced will, it is hoped, remove a good deal of misconception, and place the facts of the relation between Old Hall and Douay in a clear light. I have endeavoured simply to quote these letters as I found them, and have left the reader to form his own conclusions. There has always been a cordial feeling between Ushaw and St. Edmund's, and there is every reason why this should be so. Dr. Newsham wrote very strongly in this sense as early as the year 1833, in a letter to Dr. Newell, then Vice-President of St. Edmund's, from which I am glad to be able to quote. ".I assure you," he said, "it gives me infinite pleasure to communicate to you [our Holy Week music] *Nonne fratres sumus?* for we are both children of the same old Alma Mater, Douay College; and I should be ashamed of any one educated at Ushaw who did not feel an interest for Old Hall Green." This feeling has always been shared by Edmundians. It is impossible for any Old Hall student, especially one who remembers the College before the departure of the Divines, to visit Ushaw without noticing the great resemblance between the Colleges and their systems, and I may be allowed to add my personal testimony as to the kindness and hospitality I received when visiting Ushaw about ten years ago, as Prefect of St. Edmund's.

The later part of the history of St. Edmund's will chiefly interest those who have been students during the time, and it has been curtailed as far as seemed compatible with completeness. With the opening of the "new chapel" in 1853 it breaks off. For many reasons it seemed undesirable to enter too fully into events of more recent date; but a short chapter has been added, consisting of a few personal recollections during the Presidencies of Dr. Weathers, Dr. Rymer, and Mgr. Patterson, which will serve to point out sufficiently the chief changes which have taken place since that time.

My grateful thanks are due to several friends for reading the MS. and for making suggestions. In particular, I may mention Mr. Joseph Gillow, author of the "Biographical

Dictionary of English Catholics," who has given me very valuable assistance, which will be found acknowledged in its place. I have also derived much information from sources indicated to me by the Rev. Raymund Stanfield, and more than one chapter has been re-cast according to suggestions made by the Rev. Edmund Nolan, to whom I am specially indebted.

With respect to personal recollections, I have been less fortunate than with the documents. By the death of the Rev. Bernard Jarrett, S.J., the last of those who had been students under the old state of affairs, before the reconstitution of the College by Dr. Griffiths, passed away, and I have been unable therefore to obtain a personal description of it at an earlier date than the Presidency of Dr. Griffiths. Canon Last, who came in 1819, was able to add a certain amount about the old state of things, as his recollections dated back to within a few months of the change, when the traditions of the circumstances which led to it were still fresh. Moreover, his memory, which for recent occurrences had become weak, seemed to revive wonderfully when he talked about what happened seventy years ago. Only a fortnight before his death he entered into an animated conversation about old times at St. Edmund's. I have learnt some things also from the Rev. Henry Telford, who came to the College in 1827. In addition to his own reminiscences, he has been able to recall a good deal which he heard from those who visited the College when he was Prefect about fifty years ago. Among such may be mentioned Mr. John Butler, who was a boy at Bishop Talbot's school in 1771, and Mr. Robert Archbold, M.P., who was at St. Edmund's under Dr. Stapleton and Dr. Poynter. For details of the College during the last half century I am likewise indebted to Bishop Weathers, whose name seems more than any other identified with St. Edmund's; to the Rev. Frederick Rymer, D.D., with whom as Vice-President, and afterwards as President, my own earliest recollections are bound up ; to the Rev. William I. Dolan, Mr. William H. Bower, and others.

The pictures at St. Edmund's of the Vicars Apostolic of the London District, nearly all of whom were connected with Old Hall, have been reproduced throughout the book. They form an interesting collection which many Edmundians have hitherto hardly appreciated. It is much to be regretted, however, that Bishop Talbot is not among them, and every search for a picture of him elsewhere has so far proved fruitless. The other plates have been taken chiefly from the photographic negatives of the late Rev. Victor Soenens, D.D., for many years Professor of Philosophy. The rough sketches of the "Ship" and the "School in the Garden" have been drawn by Albert Revillon, a student in the class of Grammar.

St. Edmund's College, Old Hall, Ware.
*Feast of St. Edmund, November 16th, 1892.*

## POSTSCRIPT.

Since the bulk of this work has been in proof, several changes have taken place at the College, and it has been impossible to make the alterations in the allusions consistently throughout. I have therefore left it in the same form in which it went to the printer last November. Its appearance has been somewhat delayed by the additional work thrown on my shoulders by my appointment as President of the College, and I am afraid that the correction of the later proof-sheets may have suffered. I shall be very glad to have any errors pointed out by those who observe them.

A few fresh documents have been found since the book

went to press, but the additional light thrown on any part is not of great importance. The chief of them is the original draft of the College rules, partly in the Rev. John Potier's writing and partly in Dr. Poynter's. They confirm my surmise on page 138 that the copy we already had is practically identical with the first set drawn up.

*February 21st,* 1893.

# CONTENTS.

## CHAPTER I.

### TWYFORD SCHOOL.

#### 1685—1745.

Description of St. Edmund's College—Its origin—Twofold ancestry—On its purely English side descended from Twyford—England under the Vicars Apostolic—School established at Silkstead in reign of James II.—Early masters—Removal to Twyford—Bishop Leyburn—Alexander Pope a student at Twyford—Bishop Giffard—State of Catholics in the London District in 1733—Their schools—Twyford under Father Fleetwood—Bishop Petre, Vicar Apostolic—Twyford in financial difficulties—Rev. J. P. Betts the last master—Rev. Turberville Needham, F.R.S., his assistant—Jacobite Rising in 1745—Twyford temporarily closed . . . . . . . . . . . 1

## CHAPTER II.

### THE SCHOOL AT STANDON LORDSHIP.

#### 1753—1767.

Twyford School re-assembled at Standon Lordship—History of Standon Lordship—Sir Ralph Sadler—His descendants—The estate passes to the Aston family—Catholic chapel opened—The Astons persecuted at the time of Titus Oates's Plot—Death of the last Lord Aston—Standon Lordship let to Bishop Challoner for a school—Outline of Bishop Challoner's life and works—State of Catholics in England at that time—The Rev. Richard Kendal, Chief Master of Standon School—Its rules and customs—Standon Lordship sold in 1767—Subsequent history of the building . . . . . . . . 17

## CHAPTER III.

### "OLD HALL GREEN ACADEMY."

#### 1769—1793.

The School temporarily at Hare Street—Establishment at Old Hall Green by Bishop Talbot in 1769—The Rev. James Willacy master—Other professors and students—Reported multiplication of "Popish seminaries"—Last trials of priests under the xiv *Contents.*

PAGE

Penal Laws—Relief Act of 1778—Gordon Riots—Death of Bishop Challoner—Death of Bishop Talbot—Bishop Douglass appointed Vicar Apostolic—Relief Act of 1791—New Chapel built at Old Hall—The Rev. John Potier master—Early advertisements of the "Academy"—Arrival of the first refugees from Douay . . . . . . . . . . . 34

## CHAPTER IV.

### THE ENGLISH COLLEGES OF DOUAY AND ST. OMER.

#### 1568—1793.

Douay College founded by Cardinal Allen—Scope, object, and early history—Description of its state about the beginning of the eighteenth century—Rebuilding of the College—Its condition at the time of its fall in 1793—The College at St. Omer founded by Father Parsons, S.J., in 1592—Expulsion of the Jesuits in 1762—The College handed over to the secular clergy of Douay—Alban Butler second President—Gregory Stapleton fourth President—Daniel O'Connell a student—Prospectus of the College—Its state at the breaking out of the Revolution . . 50

## CHAPTER V.

### THE IMPRISONMENT OF THE ENGLISH COLLEGIANS.

#### 1793—1795.

The French Revolution—The Douay Clergy and the "Civic Oath"—Disturbances at Douay—Attack on the College—Death of Louis XVI.—War with England—National guards take possession of Douay College—Secret burying of the plate and valuables—The English expelled from the town—The collegians recalled a few weeks later—Seizure of the College and imprisonment of the students—Removal to Doullens—Escape of the Rev. W. H. Coombes and others—The "Trente-deux"—Dr. Stapleton and the other professors and students at St. Omer imprisoned—Behaviour of the boys under the schismatical priests—Removal to Arras—Thence to Doullens—Death of Robespierre—Its effect on the treatment of the collegians—Return to St. Omer and Douay—Dr. Stapleton goes to Paris, and obtains the liberation of the collegians—Return to England March, 1795 . . . 68

## CHAPTER VI.

### ARRIVAL OF THE FIRST DOUAY STUDENTS AT ST. EDMUND'S.

#### 1793—1794.

News of the fall of Douay reaches England—Discussions between the Vicars Apostolic—Preparations at Old Hall for the reception

*Contents.* xv

of the Douay refugees—St. Edmund's College established by
Bishop Douglass on November 16th, 1793—Description of its
state—First ordination—Arrangements for the divines—The
" Hermitage "—Proposal to remove the College to the north—
The idea temporarily abandoned—The "Ship"—Further proposals by Bishop Gibson for a general college in the north—
The project again given up—Disputes between northern and
southern divines—Bishop Gibson opens a college at Crook Hall,
and recalls his students from St. Edmund's—Changes at Old
Hall in consequence—Oscott College established—Landing of
the collegians from Douay and St. Omer . . . . . 96

## CHAPTER VII.

### RECONSTITUTION OF ST. EDMUND'S UNDER DR. STAPLETON.

#### 1795.

Discussions as to the foundation of a general college—Letter from
Dr. Milner—Bishop Douglass's circular to the Vicars Apostolic
—Proposal to set up an Eccclesiastical College in the north and
to continue Old Hall as a lay school—Interview of Bishop
Douglass with Pitt and the Duke of Portland—Their promises
of assistance—Mr. John Sone gives 10,000*l.* for founding a
college—Mgr. Erskine Papal Envoy in London—Dr. Stapleton
goes to Crook Hall to meet Bishop Gibson and Rev. John
Daniel—Rev. John Daniel returns to London and waits on Mgr.
Erskine—Old Hall decided on for the college—Dr. Stapleton
appointed temporary President—Death of Mr. Sone—Constitutions drawn out for St. Edmund's—College rules—Course of
studies—Foundation stone of the new college . . . . 122

## CHAPTER VIII.

### BUILDING OF THE NEW COLLEGE.

#### 1795—1800.

Plans for new college—Dispersion of the "Trente-deux"—The
Benedictines at Acton Burnell—Meeting of Northern clergy at
Preston—Memorial to Bishop Douglass in favour of a general
college in the north—His answer—Letter from Bishop Gibson—
Pitt promises government grant for St. Edmund's—Correspond-
ence between Mgr. Erskine and Bishop Gibson—Rev. John
Daniel appointed by Propaganda President of St. Edmund's—
He begs off—Proposal to unite Crook Hall and St. Edmund's—
Also to send Dr. Lingard to Old Hall—Meeting of northern
clergy at Fernyhalgh in 1798—Decision to build a college in the
north and not to join in St. Edmund's—Progress of Old Hall—
Visit of Colonel Harcourt, who gives the great clock—Mr. Sone's
will disputed—Further financial difficulties—Building stopped—
Dr. Stapleton appointed Rector of the English College at Rome
—Events at Rome prevent his going—Mr. Sone's will case

decided in favour of the College—Building resumed—Sacrilegious robbery—Chapel of Reparation—Visit of Bishop Moylan of Cork—Opening of new college . . . . . 148

## CHAPTER IX.

### ST. EDMUND'S COLLEGE UNDER DR. POYNTER.

#### 1800—1813.

Dr. Stapleton called to Rome—He is appointed Vicar Apostolic of the Midland District—Dr. Poynter succeeds him as President—Meeting of Bishops and Douay Seniors—Decision not to re-establish Douay College—Bishop Stapleton, Mr. Daniel and others go to France to reclaim the colleges—Death of Bishop Stapleton—Dr. Coombes presented with an honorary degree—New chapel and refectory built at Old Hall—College medal struck—Rev. John Potier leaves—His death—Reports against St. Edmund's—Its gradual decline as a lay college—Dr. Coombes goes on the mission—Rev. Francis Tuite Vice-President—Rebellion amongst the students—Its consequences—Departure of the Rev. Francis Tuite—Rev. Joseph Kimbell Vice-President—Death of Bishop Douglass—Enumeration of distinguished Edmundians of this period . . . . . . 178

## CHAPTER X.

### THE TRANSITION PERIOD.

#### 1813—1818.

The decline of St. Edmund's continues—Its causes—Most of them traceable to the loss of the Douay funds—Dearth of missionaries—Bishop Poynter's efforts on behalf of Ecclesiastical Education—Further changes at St. Edmund's—Rev. Thomas Griffiths, Vice-President—He builds the Parish Chapel—Resignation of Rev. Joseph Kimbell—Appointment of Dr. Bew—Establishment of "Ecclesiastical Seminary" at the Old House under Mr. Griffiths—Resignation of Dr. Bew—Critical state of the College 210

## CHAPTER XI.

### THE PRESIDENCY OF DR. GRIFFITHS.

#### 1818—1834.

Dr. Griffiths appointed President—The Lay Students at the Old House—A year later they are transferred back to the College—Institution of the "Lay Bounds"—St. Edmund's once more in a flourishing state—List of the chief students—Description of the

*Contents.* xvii

PAGE

College under Dr. Griffiths—Visit of Ambrose Lisle Phillips and Kenelm Digby—"Mores Catholici" written at Old Hall—Death of Mr. Cleghorn—Consecration of Bishop Bramston—Death of the Rev. John Daniel—Fate of the Colleges of Douay and St. Omer and final loss of the Douay funds—Rev. F. Tuite last titular President of Douay—Death of Dr. Poynter—Catholic Emancipation—Standon Inclosure Act—Dr. Griffiths appointed Coadjutor of London District—He succeeds Bishop Bramston as Vicar Apostolic . . . . . . . . . . 224

## CHAPTER XII.

ST. EDMUND'S COLLEGE DURING THE EPISCOPATE OF BISHOP GRIFFITHS.

### 1833—1847.

Dr. Newell, Rev. John Rolfe and Dr. Cox successive Presidents—List of students—The *Edmundian* magazine—Welcome given to the Queen when passing the college in 1843—Plans for new Chapel—Visit of Pugin—His answer to the Address presented to him—Foundation stone of the new Chapel—Oxford converts—Canon Oakeley and Dr. Ward—Society of St. Vincent of Paul established at the College—Charles Lynch drowned skating—Philip Weld drowned at Rye House—The "Weld Ghost Story"—Death of Bishop Griffiths . . . . . . . . 242

## CHAPTER XIII.

### THE NEW CHAPEL.

Negotiations for the restoration of the Hierarchy—Bishop Walsh appointed first Archbishop of Westminster—He dies before the arrangements are completed—Dr. Wiseman becomes Cardinal Archbishop—Dr. Weathers President of St. Edmund's—The "New Rules"—Description of the new Chapel—Consecration and opening in 1853—Additions since the opening—The Windows—The Lady Chapel—The Scholfield Chantry—Church plate and furniture—Names of Donors . . . . . 264

## CHAPTER XIV.

### LATER REMINISCENCES.

This chapter not a continuous history—Three main events—Establishment of St. Thomas's Seminary by Archbishop Manning in 1869, and consequent changes at St. Edmund's—Fourth Provincial Council of Westminster held at St. Edmund's College in 1873—Pilgrimage to the shrine of St. Edmund at Pontigny in 1874—Sermon by Archbishop Manning—His last gift to St. Edmund's sixteen years later—His death—The third Archbishop of Westminster, Dr. Vaughan, formerly Vice-President of St. Edmund's—Conclusion . . . . . . . . 281

a

## APPENDIX A.

RULES AND CUSTOMS OF STANDON SCHOOL . . . . . 300

## APPENDIX B.

NARRATIVE OF THE ESCAPE FROM FRANCE OF THE REV. WILLIAM HENRY COOMBES, PROFESSOR OF DIVINITY IN ST. EDMUND'S COLLEGE, OLD HALL GREEN . . . . . . . 305

## APPENDIX C.

EXTRACTS FROM THE LAST DOUAY DIARY . . . . . 311

## APPENDIX D.

FIRST ATTEMPT TO RECLAIM THE FOREIGN COLLEGES . 316

## APPENDIX E.

RESULT OF THE DELIBERATIONS OF THE VICARS APOSTOLIC, IN A SYNOD AT WINCHESTER AND OLD HALL . . . . 319

## APPENDIX F.

LETTER OF DR. POYNTER TO DR. BEW, PRESIDENT OF OSCOTT, ADVOCATING A UNION AMONG THE DISTRICTS TO FORM A SINGLE GENERAL COLLEGE . . . . . . . 321

## APPENDIX G.

EXTRACT FROM BISHOP POYNTER'S MEMORIAL TO THE BRITISH COMMISSIONERS ON THE DOUAY CLAIMS . . . . 324

## APPENDIX H.

PRESIDENTS OF DOUAY AND ST. OMER COLLEGES, CHIEF MASTERS AT TWYFORD, STANDON AND OLD HALL, AND PRESIDENTS OF ST. EDMUND'S COLLEGE . . . . . . . 331

INDEX . . . . . . . 337

# LIST OF ILLUSTRATIONS.

|  | PAGE |
|---|---|
| St. Edmund's College and Chapel | *Frontispiece* |
| Bishop Giffard | 8 |
| Standon Lordship (XVIIth Century) | 17 |
| ,,      ,,      Ground Plan | 20 |
| ,,      ,,      Elevation | 21 |
| Bishop Challoner | 24 |
| Standon Lordship (Modern) | 32 |
| "Old Hall Green Academy" | 34 |
| Bishop Douglass | 45 |
| Cardinal Allen | 50 |
| Douay College (Front) | 59 |
| St. Omer College (Front) | 61 |
| Douay College (Back) | 68 |
| St. Omer College (Bird's-eye View) | 88 |
| Old Hall and Douay (Sketch by George Leo Haydock) | 96 |
| The "Hermitage" | 106 |
| The "Ship" | 108 |
| The "School in the Garden" | 117 |
| Bishop Stapleton | 122 |
| Mgr. Erskine | 130 |
| The New College, Elevation | 148 |
| ,,      ,,      Ground Plan | 171 |
| Bishop Poynter | 178 |
| College Medal | 190 |
| John Talbot, sixteenth Earl of Shrewsbury | 207 |
| St. Edmund's College, from the *Catholic Gentleman's Magazine*, 1818 | 210 |
| ,,      ,,      from the *Catholic Miscellany*, 1826 | 224 |
| William Bernard, twelfth Lord Petre | 230 |

## List of Illustrations.

| | PAGE |
|---|---|
| Bishop Bramston | 235 |
| Bishop Griffiths | 242 |
| St. Edmund's College, with proposed new Chapel | 249 |
| "Old Hall House" (now St. Hugh's Preparatory School) | 254 |
| Choir of the New Chapel | 264 |
| Bishop Walsh | 266 |
| New Chapel High Altar | 268 |
|     ,,    Rood Screen | 269 |
| Cardinal Wiseman | 271 |
| St. Edmund's College (Modern) | 281 |
| Shrine of St. Edmund, Pontigny | 289 |
| Cardinal Manning | 291 |
| Cardinal Vaughan | 298 |

# HISTORY

OF:

# ST. EDMUND'S COLLEGE,

## *OLD HALL.*

---

### CHAPTER I.

#### TWYFORD SCHOOL.

#### 1685—1745.

Description of St. Edmund's College—Its origin—Twofold ancestry—On its purely English side descended from Twyford—England under the Vicars Apostolic—School established at Silkstead in reign of James II.—Early masters—Removal to Twyford—Bishop Leyburn—Alexander Pope a student at Twyford—Bishop Giffard—State of Catholics in the London District in 1733—Their schools—Twyford under Father Fleetwood—Bishop Petre, Vicar Apostolic—Twyford in financial difficulties—Rev. J. P. Betts the last master—Rev. Turberville Needham, F.R.S., his assistant—Jacobite Rising in 1745—Twyford temporarily closed.

THE College of St. Edmund, Old Hall Green, is situated in a pleasant part of Hertfordshire, twenty-six miles from London and five from Ware, on the road to Cambridge. The country around is what is commonly called a "rolling country," made up of ridges of hills and alternate valleys, and is mostly under tillage. On one of these ridges the College is built, with a wide prospect all round. It forms, with St. Hugh's School, the farmhouse and servants' cottages, the hamlet of Old Hall Green. The main building, begun in 1795, containing the principal rooms, is very plain in style. In the south wing is the refectory. The north wing is formed by Pugin's beautiful chapel, in which is a rood screen and east window of which he was justly proud. The college stands well, and has a broad terraced front, before which stretches a well-wooded park, with spreading oaks and an avenue of chestnut trees leading to the lodge gates. South of the south wing, hidden by a belt of trees, is St. Hugh's School, a house originally designed by Pugin for the Ward family, who lived in it for many years. Behind the main building are several acres of old-fashioned garden, where the professors take their recreation. A shady path leads through it to the "Old Hall," a quaint, low, red-brick house, where was established the "Old Hall Green Academy," by Bishop Talbot, as early as 1769. Near it are the "Hermitage," the "Ship," and the "School in the Garden," which were all inhabited by students when the Douay men, on the suppression of their college during the Reign of Terror, came to the Old Hall, whither a few of their number, noting the signs of the times, had already preceded them.

The Old Hall itself is now tenanted by different servants of the college, and all around are cottages for other dependents. These are the farm bailiff's house, the laundry, the carpenter's and tailor's workshops, the gas-works, and a large old-fashioned farm yard and farm buildings, the whole indicating such a community as was grouped around a mediæval house of religion and education.

The meeting of Old Hall and Douay serves at the outset to point out the character of the history of St. Edmund's. This involves some points which must be explained here, in order to make clear many of the stages of the story which is now to be told.

To begin with, the College has a twofold work to do: to train both ecclesiastical and lay students. The ecclesiastical students wear a cassock and Roman collar, rise earlier than the others for meditation, and have special conferences and retreats to prepare them for their holy calling. In other ways, they share the same studies and playgrounds as the lay students. All alike go through the established course of classics, mathematics, modern languages and natural science. In due time they are prepared for the matriculation examination of the London University, and, if they wish, they may proceed to take degrees. Moreover, a full theological course was given until the year 1869, when this particular work of the college was transferred to St. Thomas's Seminary, Hammersmith. But a course of philosophy is still carried on at St. Edmund's, for the ecclesiastical students who have completed their school work.

In the next place, this twofold function reminds us of the twofold ancestry which must now be described. The following table will bring it home to the reader's mind :—

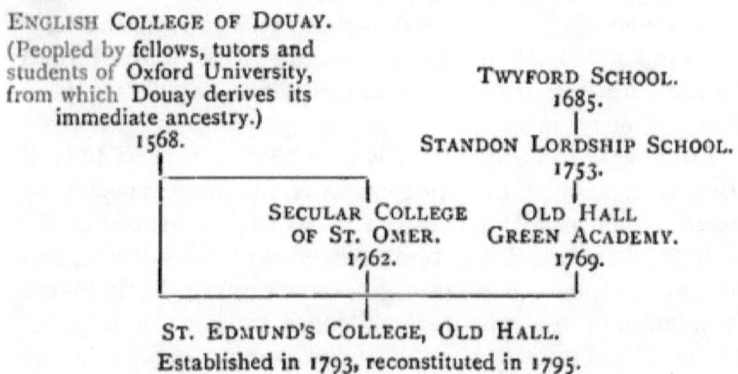

ST. EDMUND'S COLLEGE, OLD HALL.
Established in 1793, reconstituted in 1795.

A school was opened at Silkstead, near Winchester, in the reign of James II., and shortly afterwards was removed to Twyford, where it rested more than half a century. It was purely a lay school. In 1745 it was suspended, but revived at Standon in 1753, and removed to Old Hall in 1769. Meanwhile, the English College of Douay, which had been founded by Cardinal Allen in 1568, principally for the education of the clergy, had, with its offshoot, the Secular College of St. Omer,[1] been confiscated and closed during the French Revolution. The two lines met when the professors and students of Douay and St. Omer came to seek hospitality at

---

[1] Out of the several different ways in which St. Omer is spelt, the one here chosen is that which is used in the prospectus and other official documents of the Secular College there. It also corresponds with the modern spelling. The spelling chosen for Douay is that which occurs most frequently in the letters and papers in the archives at St. Edmund's.

Old Hall in 1793 and 1795. The result of their meeting was St. Edmund's College.[1]

It follows from this that there are some marks peculiar to St. Edmund's among the Catholic schools of England, and its history has a distinct colouring. In its purely English foundation, at Twyford, or even dating from Standon, it is older than any other Catholic school by many years, and is the only one that can be said to have had a long and trying experience of the Penal Laws.[2] As the direct heir of Douay, it inherits the history and the spirit of that famous college; so much so, that although, as will be seen, the rules of Standon School are still extant, they were quite overlaid by the substitution of a new constitution, based chiefly on that of Douay, in 1795.

From what has been said it is clear that, so far as Old Hall itself is concerned, the lay element is the more ancient by nearly a quarter of a century. In writing a history of the College, therefore, it is natural to begin with the lay side, and in order to trace this to its origin, we are taken back to the foundation of the school at Silkstead, during the reign of James II. The exact year of its commencement is not known; but it must have been very shortly after the revival of regular episcopal government in England, and a few words on this subject is a necessary prelude to the history of Silkstead and Twyford.

The ancient Catholic Hierarchy came to an end with the death in Rome, in 1585, of Thomas Goldwell, Bishop of St. Asaph, the last Bishop of Lincoln, Dr. Watson, having died

---

[1] It is well known that Ushaw College also claims descent from Douay, as will appear in the sequel. It is not included in the above table, because we are only concerned here with tracing the ancestry of St. Edmund's.

[2] The last priest to die in prison under the Penal Laws was the Rev. Matthew Atkinson, who was confined in Hurst Castle from 1699 till his death in 1729. The date of his imprisonment corresponds with a great part of the existence of Twyford School. The last priest tried under the same laws was Bishop Talbot. He was tried more than once, the last time being in 1771, two years after he had opened his school at Old Hall. He only escaped imprisonment on account of the insufficiency of the evidence. He was again threatened with prosecution three years later, on account of his school at Old Hall, but it does not appear that the threat was carried out.

in Wisbech prison about six months before. No regular ecclesiastical authority was for some time re-established. As long as Cardinal Allen lived he had jurisdiction over the whole of England. After his death, the country was ruled by "archpriests," for some five-and-twenty years, until in 1623 a Vicar Apostolic was created and England became a single vicariate. This state of things continued nominally for sixty-five years; but the first Vicar Apostolic, Dr. Bishop, died the year after his appointment, and the second one, Dr. Smith, was compelled to pass most of his episcopal life in Paris, and governed England by his Vicar-General. On his death in 1655, the vicariate remained vacant, and England was again without a bishop, this time for thirty years.

When James II. came to the throne in 1685, better times seemed in store for the Catholics, and Dr. Leyburn, formerly President of Douay, a member of an old Westmoreland family, was forthwith appointed Vicar Apostolic. In 1688 three other vicariates were erected, and England became divided into four "districts," the London, Northern, Western and Midland, an arrangement which lasted till about fifty years ago. At the same time, Catholics began to open schools in different parts of the country. The most important of these, and one of the few which survived the Revolution, was at Silksteed, or Silkstead, a little hamlet in the neighbourhood of Winchester, about two miles west of Twyford. The first master was the Rev. Augustine Taylor,[1] a native of Herefordshire, who had been educated at St. Omer and Rome. He had been a missionary in Hampshire since 1670, and we learn from the records of the "Old Chapter"[2]

---

[1] For the biographical details concerning the masters of Silkstead and Twyford, I am indebted to Mr. Joseph Gillow, author of the Biographical Dictionary of English Catholics, who has kindly placed at my disposal his elaborate lists of priests and missions of that time. It is only by examining his catalogues and notes that one is able to realize the care and trouble with which he has traced out the biographies of almost every priest in England in past times, and the history of every mission. Some of the details he has now furnished have been brought to light since the publication of the first volume of his Dictionary; hence there are occasionally slight discrepancies between these and his previous accounts.

[2] The Old Chapter was created by Dr. Bishop, first Vicar Apostolic

that "he resided mostly at Winchester, and laboured hard in the Catholic school at Silksteed." He was assisted by the Rev. Thomas Brown, *alias* Weatherby, a Yorkshireman, who had been a student at Douay. Mr. Weatherby had already been on the mission in the north, and Bishop Leyburn wrote to Bishop Smith, Vicar Apostolic of the Northern District, on August 12th, 1688, asking for his services, either at the coming Michaelmas, or in the spring of the following year, as might be most convenient. Referring to Mr. Weatherby, he says :—

"We look upon him as one verie proper and indeed necessarie to assist a friend of ours who hath employment for him near Winchester. I made some overture of the business to Mr. Weatherby himself when he gave me a visit in my former lodging, and discovered no adverseness in him to the undertaking it. . . . I need not tell you how much it imports that a fitt person be not wanting in that place, and especially since he for whom an assistant is desired doth not enjoy a strong habit of health. I, therefore, recommend the care of it as a

---

of England, immediately after his arrival in 1623, and was confirmed by his successor, Dr. Richard Smith. On the death of the latter, when England was left without a bishop, the government of the Catholics devolved on the Chapter. They were duly organized, and consisted of a dean, a treasurer, a secretary, archdeacons and canons. After the erection of the four vicariates, some doubt was thrown on the right of the Chapter to exercise the same powers as heretofore, and they ceased for the time to take any active part in ecclesiastical government; but it was not dissolved. Their succession of deans continued uninterruptedly, and whenever a vacancy occurred in their number they elected a new member. This continued until the restoration of the hierarchy in 1850, by which their *raison d'être* ceased to exist. They therefore no longer claimed to be a Chapter; but being unwilling to destroy what had so long played an important part in the history of Catholicity in England, and to break with the traditions of the past, they reconstituted themselves, styling themselves the "Old Brotherhood of the Secular Clergy," the Dean of the Chapter becoming President of the Old Brotherhood. They are the possessors of considerable funded property, out of which the expenses of two annual meetings in London are paid, and what is left is distributed year by year to different charities. The present president is Canon Bans, who succeeded Canon Last in 1892; the treasurer is the Rev. Joseph Wyatt, and the secretary the Rev. Frederick Rymer, who has kindly furnished me with the above particulars. All the offices are now held by Edmundians, and it may be added that several of the Presidents of St. Edmund's, including Mgr. Crook, the present president, have been members of the Old Brotherhood.

thing I take much to heart, and which, on that account, I make my parting request."

A few months after this came the Revolution, and on December 11th Bishop Leyburn set out in company with Bishop Giffard of the Midland District for Dover, with a view to escaping from the country. They were arrested on their way and brought back to London, Bishop Giffard being sent to Newgate and Bishop Leyburn to the Tower. After two years' imprisonment the latter was released and received an informal permission to dwell privately in London, where he spent the remaining fourteen years of his life unmolested.

Mr. Taylor, the master of Silkstead, who had been in failing health for some time, died about the year 1692, and was succeeded by the Rev. William Husband, *alias* Bernard, who, like Mr. Weatherby, was a Yorkshireman educated at Douay. He had been on the mission since about 1680. According to the Rev. John Ward, Secretary of the Chapter, he governed Silkstead school "with great applause and public benefit." He was assisted by the Rev. Edward Taverner, *alias* Banister, who had been ordained at Valladolid on March 26th, 1692, and came straight thence to Silkstead.

About this time the school migrated to Twyford, where it rested for about half a century. The exact date of its removal is uncertain; but it was before 1696, in which year Alexander Pope, the future poet, was sent there as a boy. Mr. Taverner had by this time become head-master, and under his care Pope made great progress in his studies. "By a method very rarely practised," writes Dr. Johnson, "he taught him the Greek and Latin rudiments together. He was now first regularly initiated in poetry by the perusal of Ogilby's Homer and Sandy's Ovid."[1] Before he left he

---

[1] "Lives of the Poets," p. 58. Pope's biographers usually represent him as having been placed under Mr. Taverner first, and afterwards removed to Twyford. This probably arises from ignorance of the fact that Banister was an *alias* of Taverner. There was no other priest of the latter name, so far as can be ascertained. Pope was only eight years old when he went to Twyford, and there seems little doubt that the Mr. Taverner whom he used to speak of as having taught him so well was the same man as the head-master of that school. See Gillow's Dictionary, vol. i. p. 123.

is said to have translated about a quarter of the Metamorphoses and a great part of Statius, who, after Virgil, was his favourite Latin poet in later life. In 1698 he composed a satire on one of his masters at Twyford, as a result of which he was so unmercifully thrashed that his parents removed him and placed him at another Catholic school, near Hyde Park Corner, kept by a Mr. Deane,[1] where, according to his own account, he lost much of what he had learnt under Mr. Taverner. It is said that some of Pope's verses were to be seen scratched on a window at Twyford as lately as fifty years ago.

Mr. Taverner ruled Twyford for many years, till well on in the eighteenth century. Eventually he removed to Warkworth Castle, the seat of the Holmans, who possessed property near Winchester, and were very probably amongst the school's principal benefactors and patrons. Here he died in 1745.

Bishop Leyburn died in 1702, and Bishop Bonaventure Giffard was translated from the Midland District to succeed him. The Giffards of Chillington were an old Staffordshire family, distinguished for their loyalty to the house of Stuart, in defence of whose interests Andrew Giffard, father of the Bishop, lost his life during the Civil war. Bishop Giffard was appointed to the Midland District in the reign of James II., who almost immediately afterwards named him President of Magdalen College, Oxford. From this post he was shortly afterwards deposed by the Bishop of Winchester, in his quality of Visitor of the College. To this decision, says Macaulay,[2] "James did not yield till the Vicar Apostolic Leyburn, who seems to have behaved on all occa-

---

[1] Thomas Deane, M.A., University Coll., Oxon, became a Catholic early in 1685, and subsequently kept a school, first in Marylebone and afterwards at Hyde Park Corner, at both of which places Pope was under his charge, previous to going to Bromley's school in or about 1700. John Bromley was also a convert, and had his school in Devonshire Street, near Bloomsbury, where Pope only remained about four months. According to some of the poet's biographers, it was from this school that he was removed in consequence of the thrashing he received for writing a lampoon on his master. See Gillow's Dictionary, vol. i. p. 310, and vol. ii. p. 36.

[2] " History of England," fifth edition, vol. ii. p. 263.

BISHOP GIFFARD,
Vicar Apostolic of Midland District, 1688-1703; and of London District, 1703-1734.

sions like a wise and honest man, declared that in his judgment the ejected President and Fellows had been wronged, and that on religious as well as on political grounds, restitution ought to be made to them."

When the Revolution came, Bishop Giffard set out from London in company with Bishop Leyburn, and they were arrested together on their way to Dover, as has already been stated. After nearly two years' confinement in Newgate, Bishop Giffard was set at liberty and allowed to return to his district, where he lived for a time in peace. The respite was only temporary, however, and after his translation to London, he had to undergo almost continuous persecution for the remaining thirty years of his life. The law entitling "informers" to a reward of 100*l*. had recently been passed, and several apostate Catholics and others tried to earn the sum by following him about wherever he went. The following description given by himself, in a letter dated October 7th, 1714, is worth quoting in full [1]:—

"Since the 4th of May I have had no quiet. I have been forced to change lodgings fourteen times and but once have I lain in my own lodging. Besides the severe proclamation which came out on the 4th of May, three private persons have been, and still are, the occasion of my troubles. The first, some fallen Catholic, who, in hope of the great reward of 100*l*., informed and procured warrants for me, Mr. Joseph Leveson and some others. The second is Mottram, who, being expelled the University of Cambridge for his immoralities, got into Spain, there was entertained by the good Fathers at Seville, and in a very short time made a convert and a priest; but no sooner in England than he became as loose and immoral as ever, and now, to gain money for his wicked courses, is turned priest-catcher and has got warrants for me and others. The third is one Barker, turned out of Douay for his ill-behaviour, received at Rome, made priest and sent hither; but always of so scandalous a life that no persuasions or endeavours could reclaim him. Nay, with much expense we sent him to our good community

---

[1] See the *Catholic Miscellany*, vol. vii. p. 170.

in France, where he was presently so infamous, especially for being frequently drunk, that they turned him out, and now being returned, he follows Mottram's tread. A few days ago he took up Mr. Brears, and has been in search of me and others, so that I am forced to lie hid as well as I can. I may truly say what was said by St. Athanasius, " Nullibi mihi tutus ad latendum locus," whence I am obliged often to change my habitation. I have endeavoured to procure a little lodging in the house of some public minister, where I could be secure from the attempts of these wretches, but I could not effect it. My poor brother,[1] though much indisposed, was forced, by the threats of an immediate search by Mottram, to retire into the country, which so increased his fever that in seven days he died. An inexpressible loss to me, to the whole clergy and to many more.

"My service to Mgr. Bianchini and Marcolini. They saw my little habitation, poor and mean, and yet I should think myself happy if I could be permitted to lodge there. However, 'gloriamur in tribulationibus.' I may say with the Apostle, 'in carceribus abundantius.' In one I lay on the floor a considerable time; in Newgate almost two years; afterwards in Hertford gaol; and now daily expect a fourth prison to end my life in. I have always envied the glory of martyrs; happy if God in His mercy will let me have that of a confessor. Mottram took up Mr. Saltmarsh, but, by a good providence, he got from him. The continual fears and alarms we are under is something worse than Newgate. It is also some mortification for an old man, now 72, to be so often hurried from place to place. God grant me eternal rest.

"I am, yours,
"B.G."

Notwithstanding these trials and hardships, Bishop Giffard lived to the age of ninety-two. Within a few months of his death, a pamphlet was published containing what professed to be a translation of a letter " written in Italian by a Romish divine in London to a cardinal at Rome, wherein he gives his

---

[1] The Rev. Andrew Giffard.

eminence an exact account of the state of Popery in England." Whoever its real author may have been, there seems no reason to doubt the accuracy of the picture given of the state of Catholicism at that time, and a few quotations from it will be to our present purpose.

Speaking of Bishop Giffard and his district, the writer says[1] :—" This worthy pastor and faithful servant of the Lord has gone through several persecutions and confinements since he came into this mission, with exemplary piety and constancy. Some years ago, on account of his great age, Dr. *Peters*,[2] otherwise known by the name of *White*, another worthy missionary, was made his coadjutor, having before served as chaplain to the late Earl of *Derwentwater*,[3] who suffer'd martyrdom for his attachment to the Catholic faith and loyalty to his unfortunate king. These two prelates take special care that no Catholic family in their jurisdiction shall want the assistance of missionaries, for they constantly recommend chaplains to them, to read prayers on Sundays, holy days, and other particular days of devotion ; they also preach to them very frequently, and though all this is carried on with the greatest privacy in the world, yet fails not of producing wonderful good effects, and brings a vast sight of strayed sheep into the pale of the true church and to the light of the Catholic faith. They also recommend chaplains to all the Catholic Embassadors who reside here, under whose protection they enjoy vast privileges to our great advantage, and the freedom of exercising publickly all their functions without comptroul." A little later on, he commends certain convert ladies, who "bestow large sums of money yearly towards maintaining several poor Catholic families in this city, and send several considerable charities to colleges,

---

[1] "The Present State of Popery in England," p. 16.
[2] Benjamin Petre, great grandson of the first Lord Petre.
[3] A curious tradition existed many years ago at St. Edmund's, that a woman at Colliers' End was still alive at the beginning of the present century, who had seen the body of the Earl of Derwentwater, which passed near Old Hall on its way to the north in 1716. This tradition has recently received unexpected confirmation by the discovery among the Funeral Registers of Standon Parish, the name of Margaret Backhouse, who died on April 9th, 1807, and is described as "a Catholic from Colliers' End, aged 105 years."

seminaries, and nunneries, founded for this nation in foreign countries."

The writer then mentions some of the schools which were being carried on. "Father Harvey," he says, "has also set up a school for the benefit of Catholic children, where he instructs them in all the principles of our holy religion; and though the laws are very severe against us on this head, yet for the reasons already mention'd, he practises, in this double capacity, without any disturbance. The success this pious father's undertakings have been attended with, and the applause so deservedly given him by our zealous Catholics, induced several other missionaries to set up schools also, and to preach with more constancy than had been hitherto done. These schools have render'd themselves so famous already, through the good management and strict discipline observed by their governors, but particularly on account of the practice of our holy religion, that besides the children of our Catholic gentry (such of them as are not sent abroad to be educated from their infancy), and those of rich merchants and tradesmen, which are instructed in them, the Catholic merchants of *Maryland, Barbadoes*, etc., send their sons to *England* to be educated by those fathers." The writer then alludes to Twyford in the following terms:—"Among all our schools, however, none comes up to that of *Winchester*, a city in the west of *England*, where we have at present upwards of one hundred pensioners or boarders; it is now chiefly under the care and direction of one Father *Fleetwood*."

The Rev. Francis (*alias* John Walter) Fleetwood belonged to a younger branch of a Lancashire family, who had settled at Colwich, in Staffordshire. He was born in London in 1699, and was brought up at the court of St. Germains, where his father was in attendance on the exiled royal family. From there he went to the English College at Valladolid about the beginning of the year 1719: soon after his ordination he came to England, and was appointed "chief master" of Twyford, the date being about 1726. Under his direction the school spent its most prosperous time. Among the more noted of its scholars at that period, and later, may be mentioned the two Bishops Talbot, the elder of whom afterwards founded Old Hall, and their brother, the fourteenth Earl of Shrewsbury, the Earl of Fingall, one of the Blounts of Maple Durham, and the Rev. Peter Browne.

About the year 1732 Father Fleetwood left Twyford, and, after serving the mission of Paynsley for a short time, he went to Liège, and there joined the Society of Jesus on June 30th, 1735. His retirement from the mastership was a great loss to the school at Twyford, and has been assigned as one of the principal causes of its subsequent decline. His interest with the scholars and their parents was supposed to have been transferred to the Society, and to have made it difficult, as Bishop Stonor says, to supply his place. Whether or not this was the cause, it is certain that soon after his retirement Twyford was in financial difficulties, and applied to the Dean and Chapter for help. The chief master at this time was the Rev. Joseph Gildon, son of Joseph Gildon, of Witham Friary, Somerset. He had been educated at Lisbon, and taught philosophy there for a time. Being obliged to leave on account of his health, and coming to England in 1707, he was appointed assistant master at Twyford. Here he lived the remainder of his days. He succeeded Father Fleetwood as head-master, in 1732, and survived his appointment four years. His death is thus recorded by the Very Rev. Thomas Berington, Dean of the Chapter:—"We have lately had a great loss. Good Mr. Joseph Gildon, master of the school at Twyford, dyed on July 26, 1736."

The last chief master of Twyford was the Rev. John P. Betts,[1]

---

[1] It has sometimes been stated that Mr. Betts, who had been at Twyford several years as assistant master, succeeded Father Fleetwood as head-master in 1732. This is, however, difficult to reconcile with what has been gathered about the Rev. Joseph Gildon. The mistake probably arises from the fact that the bill of sale on the household goods at Twyford to Mr. John Shepherd, treasurer of the Chapter, dated February 15th, 1734, N.S., was signed by Mr. Betts. But it is easy to account for this on the supposition that he was trustee or responsible proprietor of the school before the time when he became head-master. Possibly it was considered advisable, in view of the possibility of the penal laws against schoolmasters being suddenly enforced, that the head-master and the proprietor should be two different men.

son of Dr. John Betts, physician-in-ordinary to Charles II. The Betts family were connected with the locality, where they probably held property, for Dr. Betts was a native of Winchester, and received his education at the college there. He was a staunch Catholic, and it is most likely that he was one of the chief patrons and supporters of the school.

During Mr. Betts's mastership, he had under him for several years an assistant who became afterwards famous in the scientific world, and had the honour of being the first priest ever elected a Fellow of the Royal Society. This was the Rev. John Turberville Needham, a member of an ancient Catholic family, who was born in London in 1713, and educated at Douay College. After his ordination he remained for a time as Professor of Philosophy, but came to England in 1740, and taught at Twyford for about three years. At the end of that time he went to the English College at Lisbon, but the climate not suiting his health, he soon returned home, and became a travelling tutor to young gentlemen of position. He resided alternately at London and Paris. In the meantime his scientific reputation was growing so much as to win public favour, even in those intensely bigoted times, and he was elected successively a Fellow of the Royal Society and of the Society of Antiquaries; and in 1768 the French Academy of Sciences elected him a corresponding member. The following year he was invited by the Government of the Low Countries to assist in the formation of the Academy of Sciences and Belles Lettres of Brussels, founded by Maria Thérèse, of which he was rector at the time of his death in that city, on December 30th, 1781. Mr. Needham greatly distinguished himself by his experimental labours and speculations concerning the formation of organized bodies. He was an unflinching antagonist of Voltaire, and combated his views on miracles. Voltaire retaliated by ridiculing Needham's microscopical discoveries, and continued his sarcasms to the end of his life.

Twyford School did not survive long after Mr. Needham's departure. The immediate cause of its downfall was the Jacobite Rising of 1745, and the consequent revival of the

"No Popery" cry. "Though [Charles Edward] was neither invited nor encouraged by any considerable number of Catholics," writes Dr. Milner,[1] "yet merely because he was of their religion the same was made use of as a pretence for sharpening the edge of the penal laws against them. Their houses were constantly disturbed by legal visitors, under the pretence of searching for arms; their houses were taken away from them; and, above all, their schools and chapels, which in some places had been winked at, were now everywhere shut up. The most celebrated of the Catholic schools that were ruined and dissolved at this period," he adds, "was that of Twyford, near Winchester, the head-master of which was the Rev. Mr. Betts."

After the closing of the school Mr. Betts came to London, and took up his residence in Gray's Inn, where he had the charge of the Clergy Library. He had been a member of the Chapter for many years. Throughout his life he maintained his connection with Winchester, where he was a frequent visitor. He was trustee for St. Peter's House, the seat of the mission, and had the management of its funds, the missionary work being performed by a curate paid by him. His old account book is still preserved at St. Edmund's, and is continued in his own handwriting till within a few months of his death, which occurred on March 28th, 1770.

At the time Twyford was closed Bishop Petre was Vicar Apostolic of the London district, and he had recently obtained Dr. Challoner as his coadjutor. To both of these prelates the fall of the chief Catholic school of England must have been a source of grief, and they watched carefully the signs of the times, for the chance of reviving so important an establishment. Dr. Challoner especially, then in his full vigour, determined to devote his energies to the cause of Catholic education. His labours and anxieties bore double fruit. Twyford School was revived at Standon in 1753, and ten years later was established the famous school of Sedgley Park, which continued for more than a century bound up with the Catholic history of this country. Sedgley Park

[1] "Life of Challoner," p. 16.

itself is now no more; but when it was closed its inmates moved to Cotton Hall, Staffordshire, where the " Associated Society of Parkers " still hold their annual meeting, and where the " Park " traditions and customs have been perpetuated to this day.

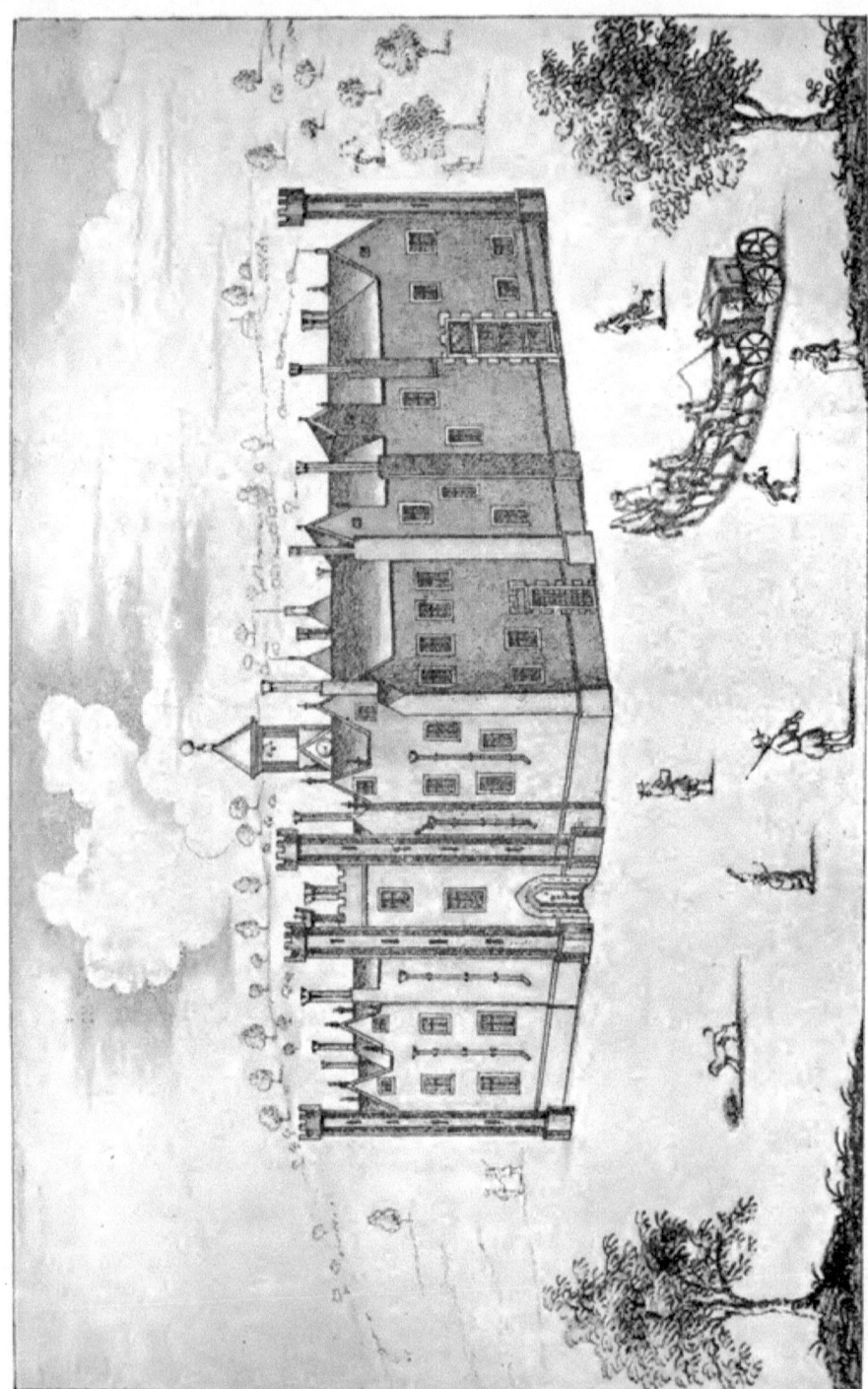

## CHAPTER II.

### THE SCHOOL AT STANDON LORDSHIP.

#### 1753—1767.

Twyford School re-assembled at Standon Lordship—History of Standon Lordship—Sir Ralph Sadler—His descendants—The estate passes to the Aston family—Catholic chapel opened—The Astons persecuted at the time of Titus Oates's Plot—Death of the last Lord Aston—Standon Lordship let to Bishop Challoner for a school—Outline of Bishop Challoner's life and works—State of Catholics in England at that time—The Rev. Richard Kendal, Chief Master of Standon School—Its rules and customs—Standon Lordship sold in 1767—Subsequent history of the building.

WE have it on Dr. Milner's authority that the school opened at Standon Lordship in 1753 was regarded as a revival of Twyford. In a letter dated May 21st, 1794, at which time he was priest at Winchester, and addressed to Bishop Douglass, Vicar Apostolic of the London District, he writes as follows: "I cannot help adhering to the opinions I have stated by word of mouth, that there ought to be a good classical school in the south,[1] because such an one is wanted. ... Let it also be remembered that at the time when our colleges abroad were in their full strength and splendour, there always has been such a school under the direction of the clergy in the south. The situation of the said school until the year 1745 was Twyford, near this city, where Pope, the Bishops Talbot, Lords Shrewsbury and Fingall, and Mr. P. Browne, etc., were educated. It was after that removed to Standon."

Before speaking about the school itself, a brief outline of

---

[1] At the time this was written Douay College had recently been seized, and the question of reconstructing our colleges in England was being discussed. It then seemed probable that a single college in the north would be decided on. See Chapter VI.

the history of the venerable mansion where it found a temporary home will not be out of place.

Standon Lordship owes its existence to Sir Ralph Sadler, who was born in 1507, and lived to the age of eighty, his life being interwoven with most of the chief events of the country's history during that period. He was secretary to Thomas Cromwell, Earl of Essex, and afterwards member of the Privy Council, and he rose in a few years to be one of the secretaries of state. Among other rewards for his services, he was presented by Henry VIII. with a "parcel of the possessions of the Knights of St. John of Jerusalem," in the parish of Standon, Herts.[1] Here he built himself a mansion, in which he lived in splendour many years. A stone is still to be seen in one of the old gables bearing his initials, with the date "1546." His father had resided some time at Great or Much Hadham, so that he was familiar with the neighbourhood. During Mary's reign Sir Ralph disappeared from public life, but again came to the front on the accession of Elizabeth, during whose reign he filled, among other offices, that of jailer to Mary, Queen of Scots. Queen Elizabeth herself spent some days at Standon Lordship in the year 1578. She was on her way to Norfolk, and after making her first halt at Hunsdon House, near Widford, the seat of her cousin, Lord Hunsdon, she proceeded to Standon, where she was entertained, together with a large retinue. Sir Ralph died in 1587, and was buried in the nave of Standon Church, and his tomb, representing him lying down in full armour, remains one of its chief features.

Sir Ralph was succeeded by his son Thomas, of whom we read in Chauncy,[2] that " he splendidly entertained King James I. and his royal train for two nights in his progress from Scotland to London, anno 1603, and died on the 5th of January, 1606, leaving issue Ralph and Gertrude, which Ralph was his heir, and did succeed him." Ultimately the

---

[1] A considerable amount of land in this neighbourhood belonged at that time to the Knights of St. John, who were patrons of the living of Standon.

[2] "Historical Antiquities of Hertfordshire," second edition, vol. ii. p. 430.

property passed to the Astons, concerning whom we may again quote Chauncy:—

"In the 8th year of [King James] Sir Walter Aston of Tixall in the County of Stafford (who was invested knight of the Bath at the Coronation of King James I.) came hither to furnish himself with Horses, against the time that Prince Henry was to be created Prince of Wales. Who as 'tis reported was so taken with the Beauty and Deportment of the said Gertrude, that he shortly after made her his wife.... [Ralph, her brother] died on the 12th Day of February, 1660, without Issue; whereupon this manor descended to Walter Lord Aston the Son and Heir of Gertrude his Sister."

In this way Standon Lordship passed into Catholic hands; a mission was established there, and a little Catholic colony grew up around it. The Astons had not always been Catholics; but Sir Walter, afterwards the first Lord, son of Sir Edward Aston of Tixall, Staffordshire, was received into the Church at Madrid about the year 1620, when on an embassy to negotiate a marriage between the Prince of Wales and the Infanta of Spain.

Like most English Catholics of that period, the Astons suffered more than once for their religion. On one occasion what is described as a "Standon mob" came to plunder the Lordship. Their coming having been anticipated, all the plate and jewellery, etc., had been packed in boxes and hidden at the bottom of the river Rib, which runs through the grounds, while Lord Aston himself was concealed in the dove-house. In this way most of the valuables were saved, and the "mob," finding their way into the cellar, made themselves so intoxicated that they did no further damage.[1]

This probably took place at the time of the Titus Oates Plot, when popular feeling ran very high against Catholics.

---

[1] The authority for this story is a Mrs. Watts, of Puckeridge, who was still alive in 1863. She had been a servant to a Mrs. Cozens, also of Puckeridge, who died about the year 1820, at the age of eighty-two, and who was just able to remember the last Lord Aston. She used, said Mrs. Watts, to describe the incident mentioned as a traditional story among the Astons. She used also to say that when young she had danced with the Duke of Norfolk at Standon Lordship. She had two sons at Old Hall under Mr. Willacy, and one at Sedgley.

A short time previously Lord Aston had been prosecuted for recusancy; and a little later, on an indictment for high treason, he was sent to the Tower, where he remained a prisoner four years. At the end of this time he was subpœnaed, together with his nephew, Sir Edward Southcote,

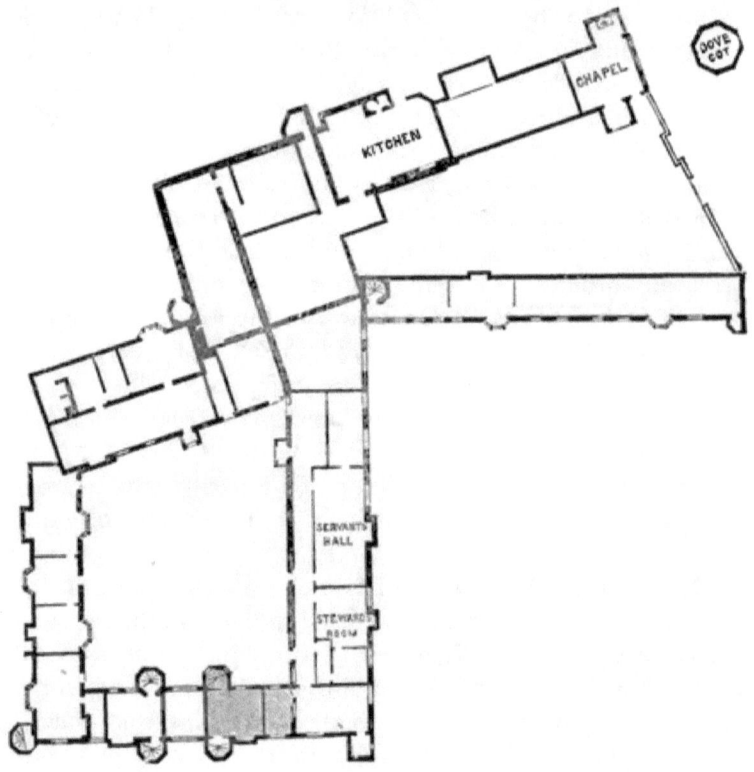

STANDON LORDSHIP—GROUND PLAN.[1]

as a witness against Oates, his evidence showing that Father William Ireland, S.J., afterwards martyred, had been with

[1] The shading shows the part of the old front now standing. The remainder of the front exists as far as the first floor only. The wing building opposite the chapel is likewise still standing; but all the rest of the old mansion has been pulled down.

him at Standon Lordship and elsewhere at the very time that Oates had sworn to having seen him in London.[1]

The general arrangement of the building may be seen by the accompanying plan, drawn up from excavations recently made of the old foundations. The original mansion was a quadrangle. The other part was added later, including the chapel, which is situated at the extremity of the servants' offices, close to the river. The Catholics of the neighbourhood were allowed access to it on Sundays; but no one

STANDON LORDSHIP—ELEVATION.[2]

was ever admitted unless personally known—a necessary precaution in those days against "informers." The first name with which we are acquainted as resident priest at Standon, is that of the Rev. P. Southcote, O.S.B., a relative of the Astons, who was there from 1705 to 1717.

Standon Lordship remained the property of the Aston

[1] See "Troubles of our Catholic Forefathers," First Series, by the Rev. John Morris, S.J., where many further details of Standon Lordship and the Astons are given.
[2] By comparing this with the picture from Chauncy at the beginning of the chapter, it may be easily seen that the proportions of the latter are quite at fault.

family till the middle of last century. A curious codicil to the will of Walter, the fourth Lord Aston, has been preserved, dated August 11th, 1747. It is in the form of a letter to his son James, and he leaves 100*l.* "for prayers for his soul, viz. 50*l.* to the two Bishops in London, Mr. White and Mr. Challence, to give to the most pious and wanting of their clergy to pray for me. . . . And as I believe it will not cost much, and that your sister Margaret will expect to have a service for me at her house, I would have you to pay her what is usual on that occasion, and let her know it is my desire."[1] This James succeeded his father as fifth Lord Aston in 1748, but only lived to hold the title a short time, and died on August 20, 1751. At his death, there being no male issue, the peerage became extinct. His two infant daughters, Mary and Barbara, aged seven and five respectively, became co-heiresses to the property, and as soon as they came of age they sold the mansion. During their minority they lived at Tixall, and Standon Lordship was let. In this manner it came to be available when Bishop Challoner was looking for a site with a view to the re-establishment of Twyford School. The Rev. Richard Kendall, a priest of some fifteen years' standing, was chosen to make a beginning. He went to Standon as missionary priest in 1752, and probably opened his school the following year.

The new undertaking is thus alluded to in Dr. Milner's Life of Challoner[2]:—

"We have now to mention different pious establishments of which our Prelate was the chief, if not the only author, though other persons were employed to carry them into execution. In the first place, within ten years after the dissolution of the celebrated school at Twyford, another was established on the same plan, being chiefly calculated for the sons of the nobility and gentry in their tender age at Standon Lordship, in Hertfordshire. Of this the Rev. Richard Kendal was appointed chief Master."

[1] See "Records of the English Catholics of 1715," by John Orlebar Payne, p. 22. "White" was an alias for Bishop Petre, Vicar Apostolic of the London District, and by "Challence" Dr. Challoner is intended.
[2] p. 33.

Dr. Challoner was at this time coadjutor to Bishop Petre; but the latter was advanced in years, and the chief part of the work devolved on his assistant. The name of Challoner is so universally known and venerated by English Catholics that it is unnecessary here to say much about his life. He was born at Lewes, in Sussex, in 1691, and lived to be more than ninety years old. Though his parents were Protestants, he was received into the Church as a boy by the Rev. John Gother, and was educated entirely at Douay College, where he afterwards held the office of Vice-President for ten years, from 1720 to 1730. On his return to England he went on the London mission, and laboured with indefatigable zeal for another period of ten years before being chosen by Bishop Petre as his coadjutor. The election was confirmed by Rome, but not before a determined attempt had been made to secure him as President of Douay, in succession to Dr. Witham, then lately dead. Dr. Petre's wishes, however, prevailed, and Dr. Challoner was consecrated Bishop of Debra on January 29th, 1741.

Bishop Challoner's new dignity made little difference in his way of living, either at this time or when he succeeded Bishop Petre as Vicar Apostolic. The following sketch of his daily life, given by the Rev. James Barnard, his biographer, refers to the period of his Episcopate:—

"Summer and winter, he rose at six . . . he then employed a whole hour in Meditation, on one or other of the pious subjects set down in his Meditations. . . . And this was succeeded by his immediate preparation for, and celebration of the Eucharistick Sacrifice, which he always began at eight o'clock; but on Sundays and Holydays he began it at nine o'clock, and always made it his practice on those days to preach on some Text contained in the Gospel of the day. This being finished and his usual prayers said, to return thanks to God for having partaken of the precious body and blood of his Son in this divine Sacrament; if it was not a Fast day he took his breakfast at nine o'clock; after which he recited with great recollection, attention, and devotion, the little

[1] "Life," pp. 130-133.

hours of the Divine Office. . . . After which he was ready to attend to any business concerning which any person might want to apply to him. But if no one wanted him, he then sat down to write something for the instruction and edification of his flock, or to answer Letters which he had received from different parts. . . . At one o'clock he used to say the evening part of the Divine Office; which finished, he used either to say some vocal prayers, or else employ himself in Meditation till Two, when, with his Chaplains, he sat down to dinner: at which time he unbent a little his mind from that close application; and was always very chearful and agreeable, discoursing with them on different subjects, and endeavouring to inspire them likewise with a spirit of Christian chearfulness. . . . Dinner being finished, and about half an hour's more conversation; if the weather was fine, or permitted it, he would usually take one of his Chaplains with him, either to go and visit some friend, or to take a walk in the fields for the benefit of the air. But he made it his invariable practice, before ever he quitted his house, to say a short prayer to beg that the protection and blessing of God might attend him in his excursion. His time of returning home was between five and six o'clock, when he was ready to attend those who wanted him : and from thence till supper-time, which was at nine o'clock, he employed his time in giving spiritual advice to those who applied to him, in reading, Meditation, and saying the Divine Office, and in doing what other business he had in hand. After Supper and a little conversation, he said his prayers, examined his conscience concerning the manner in which he had discharged the duties of that day ; endeavoured by lively acts of the Theological Virtues to put himself into the condition in which he desired to be found at the hour of his death, lest he should not live to see the morning ; resigned himself into the hands of God, and then composed himself to rest under his divine protection."

For a long time Dr. Challoner kept no house of his own, but lived in lodgings, partly to save expense and to have more money to distribute to the poor ; but partly also because it

BISHOP CHALLONER,
Vicar Apostolic of London District, 1758-1781.

was sometimes necessary for him to keep out of the way, in order to avoid persecution under the Penal Laws. Nevertheless, says Dr. Milner,[1] "he never omitted even in the worst of times, while an obscure retreat was to be found to shelter his poor audience," to preach to them every Sunday; "and, indeed, to such obscure retreats has he at times been driven to comply with this essential obligation that the catacombs where the ancient Christians held their assemblies in times of persecution were elegant and commodious compared with them."

But by far the greatest part of his work, so far as he is known to posterity, was done with his pen. From the time when in 1728, as Vice-President of Douay, he brought out the little book entitled "Think well on't," scarcely a year passed for nearly forty years without his completing one or other of the works which he had in hand. Among the many books which he wrote or edited may be mentioned: "The Memoirs of Missionary Priests," which remains to this day the chief authority on the English Martyrs; "Britannia Sancta, or the Lives of the most celebrated English, Scottish, and Irish Saints;" "Daily Meditations;" "Lives of the Fathers of the Desert;" "Life of St. Theresa;" a new edition of the "Douay Bible;" translations of the "Imitation of Christ;" "St. Augustine's Confessions;" and the "Introduction to the Devout Life," of St. Francis of Sales; the "Garden of the Soul;" the "Grounds of the Old Religion;" etc., etc.

Dr. Challoner's own copy of "Britannia Sancta" is at St. Edmund's, with an inscription in an old handwriting: "This book is that which the Right Revd. Dr. Challoner, Bishop of Debra, used to peruse himself." His cassock and manteletta are likewise in the museum, and an original painting, taken when he was sixty-eight years of age, hangs in the parlour,

---

[1] "Funeral Oration," p. 12. It should perhaps be explained that although mass was allowed at the chapels of the various embassies, under the protection of the Catholic ambassadors, no sermons were permitted, and hence, in order to preach the word of God, Bishop Challoner had to assemble his hearers in private houses, or sometimes in an out-of-the-way tavern. The "Ship Ale House," near Lincoln's Inn Fields, and another public house, the "Windmill," were frequently the scenes of Bishop Challoner's sermons.

and, according to Mr. Barnard, it was an excellent likeness.

The state of Catholics in England at the time when the school was established at Standon Lordship was still one of great depression. It is true that the older generation used to congratulate their juniors on the improvement brought about since half a century earlier; but when this improved state is examined, it only serves to bring into stronger light the persecutions which our forefathers went through, even after the days of the martyrs. In a memoir of Bishop Challoner, published in the *Catholic Spectator* in 1824,[1] Mr. Charles Butler speaks of the state of things during the reign of George I. as follows :—

"The punishment of recusancy was penal in the extreme; and persons objecting to take the oaths of allegiance and supremacy might be subjected to all the penalties and horrors attendant on recusancy, merely by refusing to take the oaths of allegiance, abjuration, and supremacy, when tendered to them. It added to the penal nature of this law, that the oath might be tendered at the mere will of two Justices of the Peace, without any previous information or complaint before a magistrate or any other preliminary proceeding. This statute had a silent but dreadful operation. It left Catholics at the mercy of every one who wished to injure or insult them. Frequently they were withheld by it from asserting the rights which the law had left them: and even from urging pretensions which were not subjects of legal cognisance. It depressed them so much below their legitimate rank in society, that they hardly entered with the look or attitude of freemen into the meetings of their Protestant neighbours. 'Such was their situation,' to avail myself of Mr. Burke's strong but just expressions, 'that they not only shrunk from the frowns of a stern magistrate, but were obliged to fly from their very species; a kind of universal subserviency that made the very servant behind their chair the arbiter of their lives and fortunes.'"

[1] p. 315. The memoir was afterwards reprinted in the *Catholic Magazine* for 1831. Mr. Charles Butler was a nephew of Alban Butler.

Though, in the latter part of Dr. Challoner's life, things were to some extent improved, and the penal laws were not consistently enforced, yet even then prosecutions under them were by no means unknown. The following extracts from the *Universal Museum* supply examples of the treatment which Catholics had often to undergo :—

"1765. October 21. Two Romish priests were taken out of a private mass house, near Moorfields, to be dealt with according to law.

"1767. February 6. Wednesday, a private mass house, at the back part of a house near Saltpetre Bank, was suppressed.

"1767. February 7. Another private mass house has this week been suppressed in Kent Street.

"1767. February 17. Friday, John Baptist Moloney, a popish priest, was taken up for exercising his function in Kent Street, several Sundays, contrary to law. He is bound over in 400*l.* penalty to appear at the next Kingston assizes.

"1767. March 20. A private popish mass house in the park, Southwark, where four young couples had assembled to be married, was visited by the peace officers, on which the parties got off, and the apartments were padlocked and shut up. The priest was dressed as an officer.

"1767. March 27. Another private mass house was shut up in Black Lion Court, St. Giles.

"1767. July 17. By an account taken this week, it appears that there are near 10,000 Papists, most of them poor miserable people, who live in the purlieus of St. Giles and the neighbourhood thereof. A number of Papist priests lurk in this part of the town, who chiefly support themselves by marrying poor papists for a few shillings.

"1767. August 23. Last Friday, at the assizes at Croydon, John Baptist Moloney was tried for unlawfully exercising the functions of a popish priest, and administering the sacrament of the Lord's Supper to divers persons, after the manner of the Church of Rome, where he was convicted and received sentence of perpetual imprisonment."

Mr. Butler says that it was ascertained about the time of the first Relief Act that one firm of solicitors alone, Messrs. Dyneley and Ashmall, of Gray's Inn, had defended more than twenty prosecuted priests, for the most part gratuitously; and he proceeds, "The double land tax continued to be levied; the laws which deprived Catholics of their landed property for the sake of religion, were sometimes enforced; and in other respects the Catholics were subject to inconceivable hardships and contumely."

"In all these transactions," he adds, "Doctor Challoner conducted himself with great prudence and firmness. Scanty as was his income, he was the chief refuge of the persecuted priests. The expenses attending the prosecutions of them, their imprisonments, removals, concealments, and other vexations were almost always discharged by him; he defrayed them with kindness, and in a manner that showed how greatly he honoured the sufferers in their sufferings and wants."

Of the "chief master" of Standon, the Rev. Richard Kendal, we do not know very much. He was born in 1709, and was the younger brother of the Rev. Hugh Kendal, who afterwards became the first President of Sedgley Park on its establishment in 1763. Both were educated at Douay, and several members of the family gave endowments for ecclesiastical education, some of which exist to the present day.

With respect to the mode of life and customs at Mr. Kendal's school, we are happily better informed. Among the archives of the college, a document has been handed down to us entitled "The Rules and Customs of Standon School," from a perusal of which we can form a very complete idea of the manner of life there, and obtain an insight into Catholic life and Catholic practices in the middle of the last century. This document is printed in full in the Appendix,[1] but may be briefly summarized here.

The school year was divided by four vacations—at Christmas, Shrovetide, Easter, and Whitsuntide respectively—the

[1] See Appendix A.

last of which, evidently corresponding with our Midsummer, was preceded by general examinations, and lasted four weeks. The Christmas vacation was a fortnight; but for the other two studies were only interrupted for a few days. In each case "holiday tasks" were provided for.

The following was the order of the day[1]:—

    6.0. Rise.
    6.15. "Washing and combing" in the lavatory.
    6.30. Morning prayers. Mass.
    7.15. Breakfast.
    8.0. Study. (Catechism at first; then Latin or Greek.)
    10.0. Recreation.
    10.15. Study
    12.0. Dinner. Recreation.
    2.0. Study. (Writing or geography, or the like.)
         (At 4 o'clock in summer, "small beer.")
    6.0. Evening prayers.
    6.30. Supper. Recreation.
    8.0. Bed time. (In summer "small beer," at 8, and bed-time 8.30.)

Tuesdays and Thursdays were half play-days. On Sundays and holidays, the order of the day was as follows:—

    7.0. Rise.
    7.30. "Washing, combing, and powdering" in the lavatory.
    7.45. Morning prayers.
    8.0. Breakfast.
    9.0. Spiritual reading.
    10.0. Mass.
    11.0. Study.
    12.0. Dinner. Recreation.
    2.30. Vespers and Compline. Recreation.
    6.0. Supper. Remainder as on school days.

In the above it will be seen that the "combing" was an important feature in the toilette of the students. It was performed by the housekeeper and housemaids every morning, whilst the scholars learnt their catechism in silence. On Sunday they were "powdered" in addition, and had to wear their best suits. They were directed to sit upright at their studies, always to walk with their toes out, and to make a bow before speaking to the head-master or any stranger or visitor.

The devotional exercises are laid down at length. In the morning as soon as they were dressed they came down to

---

[1] In a few instances the exact hour is not stated in the rules, and has been filled in approximately from the context.

morning prayers and mass; in the evening there was the Litany of the Saints, Rosary, or Bona Mors, with "Ye night exercise and reflection or meditation for ye following day," which were to "be read leisurely and distinctly by ye ablest readers among ye scholars in their turns (ye whole family being present)." A short private prayer was likewise provided for before retiring to rest. On Sundays the congregation were present at the ten o'clock mass, at which a sermon was preached. Before mass the boys had an hour's spiritual reading, the nature of which is thus specified: "The first lecture should be out of some book yt contains an exposition of ye Catholic doctrine in a catechistical way. The second should inculcate and enforce morality, such as the "Instructions of Youth." The third may be historical, such as the "Life of our Lord Jesus Christ," "Ye History of ye Bible," "Ye Saints' Lives," etc. No more than ye last half hour ought to be spent in reading ye above mentioned or like pious history."

Vespers and Compline were recited at half-past two, followed by the Litany of the Saints, Ave Maris Stella and Exaudiat, all in English. On the first Sunday of the month, and on great feasts, there was Benediction of the Blessed Sacrament. The service concluded with an explanation of the Douay Catechism for half an hour, after which there was recreation till supper time. It was, however, strictly laid down that there should be no noise on Sundays, for fear of scandal; "for which reason, nine pins and drawing ye cart about are forbid, as also whistling or singing."

The diet of the "children" consisted of boiled milk and milk pottage for breakfast; meat, bread, and beer for dinner; and bread and butter or cheese, with milk, for supper. In the summer time there were two "small beers," in addition, at four and eight o'clock respectively. Three times during the winter months mince pies were provided for the "children," and on the Twelfth Night plum cake; but with the proviso "they paying for it." In all cases it is laid down that "as it is ye chief master's duty to see nothing comes to table but what is wholesome and good in its kind, so neither are ye scholars to be suffered to refuse eating what is sent them, under pretence of natural antipathy or aversion, without very good proofs of this or that kind of food disagreeing with them, etc.—one of the ends of sending children to school being to break them of nicety in their diet."

The boys' recreations seem to have consisted chiefly in drawing each other in 'ye cart,' and this was prohibited in the hot weather. No games are mentioned, except nine pins, but it seems that a walk was customary on all half play-days, provided that the weather was fine. In the summer they used also to bathe in the river Rib.

Regulations for the health of the children abound. They were not to lie on the grass in any month containing an *r* in its name, those being supposed to be the winter months; they were never to be out without a hat, nor to snowball in the snowy weather; and whenever it was cold enough for fires indoors, they were to wear their great coats outside.[1] The penances for disregarding these or other rules were forfeiting a half-penny to the poor, having some of their pocket money stopped, being served last at table, and in extreme cases "ye rod." On the other hand, special industry was to be rewarded by extra pocket money, additional play-days, and other such privileges.

Bishop Petre died in 1758[2] at the age of eighty-one. Bishop Challoner succeeded as Vicar Apostolic, and continued to watch over the school at Standon, till it came to a forced termination by the sale of the Lordship. This took place, as explained above, as soon as the Aston heiresses attained their majority,[3] and in 1767, therefore, Mr. Kendal

---

[1] It is curious to find that the custom at Old Hall of beginning fires on November 1st dates back to Standon Lordship School, nearly a hundred and fifty years ago.

[2] Apparently no portrait of Bishop Petre exists. The only memorial of him is a picture at Thorndon of his favourite dog, which once saved his life when he was attacked by robbers in the Lime Walk, Ingatestone.

[3] The two Miss Astons married Sir Walter Blount, Bart., and Hon. Thomas Clifford, a younger son of the fourth Lord Clifford, respectively. The former lived till 1804, when she was burnt to death. The Hon. Mrs. Clifford died in 1786. Her son, Arthur Clifford, was at Douay College at the time of its fall, and after going through the imprisonment, came to St. Edmund's, under Dr. Stapleton.

received notice to quit. The estate was bought by Mr. R. Plumer, of Blakesware, near Widford.[1] After it passed into his hands the Lordship gradually fell out of repair. Towards the end of the century it was fitted up as a temporary court house, and about the same time a proposition was entertained of repairing it throughout, instead of building the present college at Old Hall, but this idea was not carried out.

STANDON LORDSHIP—MODERN.

During the years which followed a great part of it was pulled down at various times, in order to supply tiles, bricks, lead, and old timber for repairs on the estate. In 1828 all the

---

[1] It is a somewhat remarkable coincidence that Standon Lordship eventually passed to the family of the late Dr. W. G. Ward, of Northwood Park, Isle of Wight, who was for many years so closely associated with St. Edmund's. The granddaughter of Mr. Plumer, Mrs. Plumer Lewin, became by a second marriage Mrs. Plumer Ward. At her death the property, including Standon Lordship, passed to her husband, Mr. Robert Plumer Ward, at that time one of the Lords of the Admiralty and M.P. for Haslemere, a great uncle of William George Ward. He was succeeded by his son, Sir Henry Ward, G.C.M.G., sometime governor of Madras, who sold the Standon estate to the Duke of Wellington. In 1850 he also sold Blakesware, the purchaser being Mr. Martin Hadsley Gosselin, whose son, the present owner, is a Catholic. Mass is now said there every Sunday.

valuables were removed by Mr. Plumer Ward, whose property it then was, to his residence at Gilston, and the west and south fronts were taken down. Fifteen years afterwards it was sold to Arthur, first Duke of Wellington, but nothing was done to put it in repair till 1872, when his son, the second duke, fitted up what was left of it as a shooting-box. At the present day it is let as a country residence. The old gateway remains and a great part of the north front, but most of the rest is destroyed.

## CHAPTER III.

### "OLD HALL GREEN ACADEMY."

#### 1769—1793.

The School temporarily at Hare Street—Establishment at Old Hall Green by Bishop Talbot in 1769—The Rev. James Willacy master—Other professors and students—Reported multiplication of "Popish seminaries"—Last trials of priests under the Penal Laws—Relief Act of 1778—Gordon Riots—Death of Bishop Challoner—Death of Bishop Talbot—Bishop Douglass appointed Vicar Apostolic—Relief Act of 1791—New chapel built at Old Hall—The Rev. John Potier master—Early advertisements of the "Academy"—Arrival of the first refugees from Douay.

WHEN compelled to leave Standon Lordship, Mr. Kendal seems to have had great difficulty in finding a suitable place to which he might transfer his school. In the end a house was obtained which had belonged to a Mrs. Brand,[1] a Catholic, at a hamlet called Hare Street, on the Braughing road to Cambridge, about five miles distant from Old Hall. The hamlet still exists, but the house which was used for the school was pulled down many years ago. The date of the transfer from Standon Lordship to Hare Street is given in Clutterbuck's "History of Hertfordshire" as 1767. We have few particulars of the state of Mr. Kendal's community at that time beyond the fact that the house which they were in afforded them scant accommodation. The old account book shows that the numbers were very low, and in all probability it became a question whether the school would survive.

At this stage Bishop James Talbot came to the rescue, and by his exertions the school was saved. We have already

---

[1] Mrs. Dorothy Brand, of Hare Street, in the parish of Hormead Magna, widow of Thomas Brand, gent, registered as a Catholic non-juror in 1717, a freehold and life estate then of the annual amount of 73*l*. 8*s*. 2*d*., a considerable income in those days.—Payne, Eng. Cath. Non-jurors, p. 83.

"Old Hall Green Academy."

come across his name among the list of Twyford boys, together with those of his two brothers, one of whom became fourteenth Earl of Shrewsbury, and the other was afterwards Vicar Apostolic of the Midland District. After leaving Twyford they all had together the advantage of a year's travel with the learned Alban Butler. Shortly after their return the two younger ones, James and Thomas, declared their vocation to the priesthood, and went to Douay College. The elder of the two, James Talbot, with whom we are now concerned, became a "senior" in 1750, and taught philosophy and then theology. A year or two later he was chiefly instrumental in the establishment of a preparatory school at Equerchin, three miles from Douay, where boys were received previously to entering the college. Having taken his licentiate, he returned to England in 1755. Four years later he was chosen by Bishop Challoner as his coadjutor, and was consecrated Bishop of Bertha on August 24th, 1759. Throughout his episcopate, which lasted more than thirty years, he was well known for his great charity to the poor, and for the self-denial of his life, which earned for him the common title of "The Good Bishop Talbot."

Having determined, therefore, to spend his own money in the cause of Catholic education, Bishop Talbot looked about for a suitable site which might permanently receive the school from Hare Street. According to tradition, two localities were proposed, one of which was Hammel's Park, and is familiarly known to Edmundians of recent years as "Miss Mellish's." The other site proposed was Old Hall Green, sometimes called Odey Green, and this was eventually decided on.

The "Old Hall" was an old house in the manor of Milkley, otherwise Mentley, erected about the year 1640, and was the property of Hale Young Wortham, Esq., of Furneux, Pelham, Herts. Behind the house was a large old-fashioned garden and orchard covering about eight acres of ground. In addition to this, Mr. Wortham had about as much land again under tillage, together with a cottage commonly known as "The Hermitage," of which we shall hear again. Bishop

Talbot began by renting the Hall, but two years later he bought it, and built considerable additions to it.

In effecting the purchase he had recourse to an expedient not unusual in the time of the Penal Laws. A Catholic was unable to acquire land validly by purchase, and it was therefore advisable, as a matter of precaution, to find a friend to act as an intermediary. Mr. John Hollingworth, a surveyor or land agent of Puckeridge, undertook to do so. The estate was accordingly sold to him on July 11th, 1771. The following day he in turn sold it to Bishop Talbot.[1] The price in each case was 800*l.*, and the total quantity of land a little more than twenty acres.

The deeds having been signed, it was also necessary, in order to effect the transfer, for Bishop Talbot to appear before the Manor Court, as Mr. Hollingworth had already done, the property being copyhold. Again, as a matter of prudence, this formality was postponed, and Mr. Hollingworth therefore remained the ostensible owner; for which reason, no doubt, he describes himself in his own purchase deeds as a schoolmaster. By this artifice the double land tax, which was still often levied from Catholic owners, was evaded. Matters were complicated three years later by the death of Mr. Hollingworth, but no serious difficulty resulted. The court sat on July 18th, 1775, when Bishop Talbot himself appeared and produced the deeds of purchase, which were duly recognized, and he was formally put in possession.

If we refer to the illustration, we can easily see the "Old Hall," which is the middle part, bounded by the two gables. The north and south wings, which are of unequal size, are Bishop Talbot's additions. They formed the study place and kitchen respectively, with a dormitory above in each case. The chapel was in the loft over the south dormitory, and was so arranged as not to be observable from outside, in

---

[1] Bishop Talbot's covenant to purchase is dated July 12th, 1771; but as Mr. Hollingworth himself did not enter into legal possession till after the session of the Manor Court on October 1st, he could not actually sell the land till after that date. The actual purchase by Bishop Talbot is dated August 5th, 1772.

order to avoid attracting notice as far as possible.[1] At the present day it remains practically as it was when Bishop Talbot last said mass there a hundred years ago. It has never been used for any other purpose, being small and inconvenient.

Everything being ready, the students moved from Hare Street to Old Hall in the autumn of 1769. Mr. Kendal stayed behind, and spent the rest of his days in the village where his school had found a temporary shelter. He was by this time an elderly man, and very possibly felt unequal to the labour and energy required to make a new beginning, and to work up Bishop Talbot's school properly. He was elected Dean of the Chapter in 1771, and died in London [2] nine years later, his death being hastened, it is said, by the anxieties caused by the Gordon Riots.

The first master of the new establishment at Old Hall Green was the Rev. James Willacy, a relative of Mr. Kendal's, and a native of Lancashire. He was educated at Douay, where his name first occurs in the Fourth of Rudiments [3] at the time when the future Bishop Talbot was a "senior." He was ordained priest in 1762, and stayed on as Professor, first of Poetry and then of Rhetoric, being reckoned, says Dr. Kirk, of Lichfield,[4] a good classical scholar. He left Douay July 23rd, 1764, and not improbably went straight to the Standon Lordship school. After three years at Standon and two at Hare Street, he was appointed to the management of the new "Academy" at Old Hall Green, as has been stated.

---

[1] The curve in the roof of the south dormitory which covered the left can be seen in the illustration.

[2] Whether he was on a visit to London at the time of his death, or whether he had by this time left Hare Street, is uncertain. The last letter of his which has been preserved is dated Hare Street, November 25th, 1775.

[3] This "Fourth of Rudiments," disappears after 1751, which is about the date when Dr. Talbot founded the Preparatory School at Equerchin.

[4] The Rev. John Kirk, sometime President of Sedgley Park died at Lichfield on December 21st, 1851, aged 91. He was a learned antiquarian and at one period of his life he devoted much time to putting together biographical collections, etc., with a view to writing a continuation to Dodd's "Church History of England." These he afterwards handed to the Rev. Mark Tierney, and they are now among the Westminster archives.

The list of all the new students from 1769 to 1782 has been preserved, and gives us a fair idea of how Bishop Talbot's school prospered. At its opening there seems not to have been more than twelve or fifteen boys, though this cannot be known with certainty, as no complete record has been kept of those who came from Standon or Hare Street. Later on, they averaged from twenty-five to thirty-five, and at one time there were more than forty. The first two new boys to arrive, according to the list, were William and Charles Mawhood. Their father, Mr. William Mawhood, of Finchley, kept a diary, which is now in the possession of Mr. John Corney, the son of the late Mr. Charles Corney, an old Edmundian, who was one of the founders of the Edmundian Association, and for thirty years its Treasurer. The following entries in this diary concern the period of the foundation of Old Hall :—

"Saturday, July 9th, 1769. Called on Bishop Talbot, settled at £22 per annum for my boys, got his letter to ye master.

"Monday, October 9th, 1769. Called on Mr. Talbot, who says Mr. Willacy will be in town this day and return Friday or Saturday next. . . .

"Monday, October 16th, 1769. Set out for Old Hall Green with Mr. Palmer; dined with Mr. Willacy; left ye two boys; went from thence to Baldock. . . .

"Wednesday, November 8th, 1769. Mr. Willacy, of Old Hall Green, called; our boys very well.

"Thursday, November, 9th, 1769. Mr. Willacy dined with us at Finchley; went with him in ye even to show him the way. . . .

"Wednesday, May 9th, 1770. Paid Mr. Willacy in full for my two boys' schooling half a year due ye 16 April last, Wm., £12 13s. 1½d; Charles, £12 16s. 9½d. Total £25 9s. 11d."

The next students mentioned are John and Thomas Butler, afterwards wine merchants of Austin Friars, uncles of the late Arthur Butler, the well known Secretary of the Benevolent Society. One of these used to visit the College when quite an old man, seventy years later, and is remembered by some still living.

The list which follows is thoroughly representative, and includes members of all the principal Catholic families of that time. We find, for example, amongst others, such names as Arundel, Bedingfield, Blount, Charlton, Clifford, Dormer, Giffard, Heneage, Howard, Jerningham, Langdale, Riddell, Petre, Salvin, Stapleton, Stonor, Talbot, etc.

In addition to looking after the school, Mr. Willacy also had charge of the Catholics of the district, which at that time included the whole of Hertfordshire and more besides. In a list of the "Standon Congregation," made out in 1780, we find mention of Catholics living at Royston, Buntingford, Puckeridge, Walton, Ware, Stanstead, Magdalen Lervis, (Essex) and Standon itself. There were about seventy Catholics all told, of whom some thirty lived at Standon, including several members of the family of Sedcote, who were descended from the steward of the last Lord Aston. There is no record or tradition, however, of mass having been said at Standon after the sale of the Lordship, and the probability is that all came to Old Hall Green from the time that the school was opened there.

Mr. Willacy's chief assistant at first was the Rev. Henry Postlethwaite. He was succeeded about the year 1785 by the Rev. John Potier, of whom we shall speak presently. It is probable that there were other priests in addition to these; at any rate such seems to have been the impression of the author of the following very curious anonymous letter which Bishop Talbot received six years after the establishment of the school, and which is preserved among the College archives:—

"My Lord Bishop,—A Friend to the roman Catholicks begs leave to inform your Lordship that the number of Roman Catholick schools which of late have been set up in this nation, have given cause of complaint, and there are several informations lodged which are supposed to take place soon, among the rest your Lordship and two or three Chaplains at Odey Green,[1] near Puckridge, in Hertfordshire. Your

---

[1] "Odey Green" was a common abbreviation for "Old Hall Green."

Lordship is left to make what use you please of this friendly admonition, but its great pity you could not be satisfied with one or two Schools which have always been winked at, without drawing on yourselves the just odium of all, by establishing Popish seminaries all over the kingdom. Real Charity has induced me to give you this intelligence, begging you would take care of yourself not only in the Country, but also in London where dilligent search will soon be made for you.

"Doctor's Commons, March y° 8, 1775."

"To Lord Bishop Talbot, at his School, Odey Green near Puckerige, Hertfordshire."

Here we have an instructive example of the state into which Catholics had fallen at this time in the estimation of their fellow countrymen. The writer of the letter was professedly a "Friend to the Roman Catholics," and the best he can wish for them is that they should have a few schools "winked at" by the authorities; and he regards the setting up of new schools of any importance, as drawing down on themselves the "just odium of all."

The reported multiplication of "Popish seminaries," however, had no existence in fact. The Rev. Joseph Berington, in a description of the state of Catholicism in England in the year, 1780,[1] calls it "a groundless rumour, which lately prevailed, that Catholics were opening schools in all parts of the kingdom, whereby the rising generation of Protestants were all to be perverted to the errors of Popery." He proceeds to enumerate the Catholic Schools then existing, and, leaving out of account a few day schools in London, they do not in all, he says, exceed three. Of these he describes one near Wolverhampton, which must be Sedgley Park, as the largest, but for a lower class of boys. The other two, one of which is clearly Old Hall, and the other a small establishment near Birmingham,[2] number each about twenty or thirty scholars, he says, who do not stay beyond the age of fourteen.

[1] "The State and Behaviour of English Catholics from the Reformation to the Year 1780," p. 168.
[2] The school here referred to was founded at Osmotherly, in Yorkshire, about the year 1672, and removed to Edgbaston in 1723, or soon afterwards.

Whether this anonymous letter had any effect on Bishop Talbot's mind, we cannot say, but it is known that on more than one occasion it was deemed necessary to suddenly close the school and send the "children" to their homes. Dr. Talbot was not a stranger to this kind of persecution. He has the honour of being the last priest tried for saying mass in England, which happened in the very same year that Old Hall was first established. He was likewise tried for exercising Episcopal functions in 1771. He was acquitted each time for want of evidence; but the judge, Lord Mansfield, was plainly on his side. The *Catholic Spectator* for 1824, in the same memoir of Bishop Challoner which we quoted from in the last chapter, tells us[1] that at that time "the Lord Mayor and the Bishop of London discountenanced [such] proceedings, and juries were with great difficulty induced to find the bills. After they were found warrants were obtained against the persons indicted, and they were taken into custody." Bishop Challoner was accused in this way by one Payne, an apostate, who spent all his energies about this time in trying to revive the penal practices against priests and Catholics. Bishop Challoner escaped, as Bishop Talbot did, from want of evidence; but the partiality of the same Lord Mansfield was again evident. This was brought out still more clearly in the case of the Rev. James Dillon, who was acquitted on the plea that although it was established that he had said mass, no proof had been brought that he was a priest. "All the twelve judges have been consulted," said Lord Mansfield, "and they have all agreed in opinion that the statutes are so worded that in order to convict a man upon them, it is necessary that he should be first proved to be a priest, and secondly that it should be proved that he has said mass."

In the year 1778 came the first Catholic Relief Act, and it

---

Dr. Milner received the early part of his education there. (See Husenbeth's "Life of Milner," page 6.) In 1792 it was transferred to Baddesley Green, where it continued for about forty years before being finally closed. Bishop Weathers was at the "Baddesley Green Academy" from 1823 to 1828, when he came to St. Edmund's.

[1] p. 316.

is worth while to remark in passing that one of the most active members of the committee then formed to agitate on behalf of the Catholics[1] was Lord Petre, whose two sons were at Old Hall at that time, and whose grandsons and great-grandsons were afterwards educated there. The new Act passed into law at the end of May, 1778, and though it did not repeal by any means all the penal statutes, the relief given, according to Father Amherst, was precisely that which was most necessary at the time.[2] Indirectly also the condition of Catholics was much improved by the Act. "It shook the general prejudice against them to its centre," writes Mr. Butler; "it disposed their neighbours to think of them with kindness; it led the public to view the pretensions to further relief with a favourable eye; and it restored to them a thousand indescribable charities in the ordinary intercourse of social life which they had seldom experienced."[3]

With respect to its bearing on Old Hall, it should be noted that the school was not legalized; but the penalty to which Catholic schoolmasters were liable was reduced from imprisonment for life to imprisonment for a year. A more important point was the abolition of the reward for "informers," so that henceforth prosecutions could only be initiated by the Government, and were, therefore, rarely if ever instituted. Thus the position of Bishop Talbot and Mr. Willacy was undoubtedly greatly improved. The laws against the colleges abroad, however, remained in full force. It was still a criminal offence for parents to send their children "beyond the seas" to be educated as Catholics, and any one who informed of such a case remained legally entitled to the reward of a hundred pounds.

The effect of the new Act was sufficient to produce a temporary reaction on the public mind, and a renewal of the "No Popery" cry, culminating two years later in the dis-

---

[1] The committee of 1778 must not be confused with the "Catholic committee" formed about ten years later, which gained for itself an unenviable notoriety. Lord Petre was, however, a member of both committees.

[2] See "History of Catholic Emancipation," vol. i., p. 107.

[3] "Historical Memoirs," vol. iii., p. 194.

turbances known as the "Gordon Riots." A monster petition was signed for the repeal of the new Act, and this was borne to the House of Commons by a procession of the people, headed by Lord George Gordon. The mob, once assembled, were not so easily dispersed, and for several days they ran wild over London. Bearing large banners with "No Popery" painted thereon, they pillaged and set fire to most of the Catholic places of worship and other institutions. The Sardinian chapel at Lincoln's Inn Fields was burnt, and those in Warwick Street, Virginia Street, and Wapping all suffered severely. The school at Moorfields was likewise set on fire, as well as Newgate prison and many other places. On the night of Friday, June 2nd, news reached Dr. Challoner that his own life was in danger; but he was able to escape in time, and found a refuge at Finchley, in the house of Mr. Mawhood, the father of the two first Old Hall boys. The anxiety and worry, however, told on him at his advanced age, and he survived only a few months, dying at his house in London on January 12th, 1781.

Bishop Talbot survived him nine years, during which time he ruled the London district as Vicar Apostolic without any coadjutor. He died at Hammersmith, on January 26th, 1790, and lies buried in the parish churchyard. A brass to his memory has recently been erected at St. Edmund's, bearing the following inscription:—

Orate pro anima clarissimi viri, Episcopi maxime venerabilis
IACOBI TALBOT S.T.D.
Pii domus nostrae conditoris
Veterrima in familia atque illustrissima
Et quod plus est honoris Ecclesiae Dei semper studiosissima
Natus A.D. MDCCXXIV
Homo spectatissimae virtutis ad Episcopatum provectus ad tit Berthae
Simul Ricardo Challoner S.T.D. Ep. Debrensis Regionis Londinensis
Antistiti
Viro summa pietate nobilissimo
A sacris adiutor sociusque additur
Quo tempore, Anno nempe Incarnationis MDCCLXIX
Cum Parentes Catholici amplioribus ex Ordinibus qua erudirentur nati conquirerent
Ipse suam in villam vulgo Old Hall ut in proprium ovile
Pastor aeque de agnis ac de ovibus sollicitus liberos congregat
Ibidem munificentia sua Collegii futuri fundamenta iacet.
Obdormivit in Domino A.D. MDCCXC.
R.I.P.

In his will Bishop Talbot left all his property to his brother, Bishop Thomas Talbot, as the safest way to ensure the carrying out of his wishes. These he explained in detail in the following " private instructions " :—

" DEAR BROTHER,—Whereas by my will, dated 1st of March, 1784, I have left you my sole executor and residuary legatee, it was in full confidence that you would dispose of the residue of my effects as hereby directed :—

" 1st. 300*l.* to Douay College, and 100*l.* each to Valladolid, Lisbon, and St. Omer's ; in all 600*l.*

" 2nd. One guinea to each of the priests [1] having faculties in my district at the time of my death, whether secular or regular, native or foreigner.

" 3rd. To my successor, if a secular priest, all that was left to me by my predecessor ; as also my little farm and all my property in Herts ; as also all my furniture, books, papers, and other effects in town or in Hammersmith. But in case my successor should be a regular, the whole of this article is to devolve to our Chapter, to be managed by them till a secular bishop succeeds.

" 4th. The rest, as you can't want it, I leave to the poor, as witness my hand.

" (Signed)     JAMES TALBOT."

The new Vicar Apostolic was the Rev. John Douglass, a Scotchman by descent, but born in England, and educated at the English College at Douay. In accordance with the above instructions, being a secular priest, he became the proprietor of the "little farm and property" at Old Hall. At the time of his appointment he was stationed at York, and was forty-eight years of age. He lived another twenty-one years, the early part of which was perhaps as critical as any period in the history of the Church in this country. After more than two centuries of persecution Catholics were slowly emerging from the state to which they had been reduced. Emancipation was yet far off; but the first step towards it had been taken, and the troubles connected with

---

[1] No doubt for masses for his soul.

BISHOP DOUGLASS,
Vicar Apostolic of London District, 1790-1812.

the "Catholic Committee," which were at their height at this time, showed that it would not be reached without difficult and delicate work. Within a few months of Bishop Douglass's consecration the second Relief Bill passed through Parliament. As is well known, the defeat of the committee was accomplished by the energy of Dr. Milner, at that time priest at Winchester, whom Bishop Douglass had already learnt to value, and to whom, both then and afterwards, he constantly applied for advice.

Hardly was this question settled, when further troubles of a different nature arose. The great Revolution had already commenced, and the appearance of France and the Netherlands, where so many of our convents and colleges had been established since the days of persecution, was already menacing. The worst apprehensions were more than realized during the next few years, when nearly all the English Catholic establishments on the Continent had to be broken up, and the communities disbanded. One after another they arrived in England in a state of destitution, and had to be received and housed temporarily while provision was made for their future. The English colleges of Douay and St. Omer suffered with the rest. The buildings and property were confiscated, and the students and professors imprisoned for more than a year before they were allowed to return to England, and it became a matter of urgent necessity to found new establishments for the education of the clergy, lest the supply of missioners should fail.

With all these difficulties to confront, Bishop Douglass put his heart and soul into his work, and the early years of his Episcopate were years of energy and activity, during which the foundations were laid for the "Catholic revival" of this century. He had the assistance of many of the French clergy, who had come to England as a place of safety while the revolution ran its course, and some of these helped in the regular missionary work of London and elsewhere. From the nature of the case, however, such assistance could be only temporary, and the establishment of a regular college for the training of the clergy, to replace fallen Douay, was an immediate necessity. The foundation of St. Edmund's College was the most important, as it was the most necessary of the works of Bishop Douglass, and he is justly considered its chief founder. His portrait hangs in the college parlour, and a bust stands in the library. He is described as a tall thin man, of a healthy appearance, with a lively and good-natured expression, and wearing a little close white wig. In his own house at Castle Street, Holborn—or "the Castle," as it was commonly called—he wore his pectoral cross over his coat; but even this was considered bold in those days, when a cassock was never worn except in church.

Dr. Douglass was a methodical man, and kept his letters and papers in excellent order. We owe it to him that so many of the details of the few years which succeeded the founding of St. Edmund's have been preserved. He kept a diary, which he headed "A chronicle or register of events relating to the history of the Church in England, particularly that of the London District," and in this there are many entries concerning the early days of the college, which will be quoted hereafter. It is a large book, in two volumes, and is filled in from 1793 to within a few months of his death, in 1812. A number of his other papers and letters are at St. Edmund's, including a collection of sermons, three for each Sunday in the year, all arranged in order, and indexed. Many of these seem to have been written while he was a student at Douay.

Mr. Willacy was still chief master of Old Hall, when, on the death of Dr. Talbot, it became the property of the London district. A few months later, by the Relief Act of 1791, Catholic schools became at last recognized by the law, and an advertisement of "Old Hall Green Academy" appeared in the Laity's Directory. At the same time the prohibition against Catholic places of worship was removed, the only proviso henceforth being that they should be registered before the quarter sessions; that there should be no bell or steeple outside, and that they should not be "locked, barred, or bolted," during service time. The "Old Hall" was duly registered as a place of Catholic worship on January 9th,

1792. The register certificate is still preserved, signed by Benjamin Rooke, Clerk of the Peace.

Bishop Douglass regarded this as a favourable opportunity for raising and extending the work of the school, having doubtless already in his mind the precarious condition of the English colleges in France, owing to the breaking out of the Revolution and the possibility of Old Hall being required to receive some of the students from Douay or St. Omer, should it be deemed advisable to temporarily close those establishments. He determined, therefore, to spend a considerable amount of money on his school, and a new chapel was forthwith commenced, which was to serve in place of the loft previously used. Before its completion Mr. Willacy retired from the mastership, after filling the office for twenty-three years. Of his subsequent history we do not know very much. He was a member of the Old Chapter, and held the titular Archdeaconries of Gloucester, Worcester, and Leicester. The last years of his life were spent at Canford House, Wiltshire, where he acted as chaplain to the Theresian nuns, who had settled there when driven from the continent by the French Revolution. He died on September 25th, 1805, aged sixty-seven.

The new master of Old Hall was the Rev. John Potier, the son of James Potier, of Low Walworth, Durham. He was born on September 22nd, 1758. When eleven years of age he went to Equerchin, the preparatory school for Douay, at which latter place he went through his full course of twelve years, and was ordained priest in 1782.[1]

After his ordination he spent two or three years on the London mission[2] before coming to Old Hall as an assistant

---

[1] In the Prefect of Studies' lists his name is entered throughout as John Jenison, the latter being his mother's maiden name. It was not uncommon, even as late as this, to take an *alias* either to escape identification when coming to England on the mission, or to avoid the penalties still legally due to any parents sending their children abroad to be educated Catholics. In the "Douay Diary" Mr. Potier's proper name is given.

[2] According to a family tradition. Mr. Alfred Rymer, the father of Dr. Rymer, afterwards president at Old Hall, was baptized by Mr. Potier in 1785.

master, probably in 1785. He succeeded as chief master in the early autumn of 1792. The new chapel was ready for use by the middle of the December following, and was blessed and opened by Dr. Douglass on the second Sunday of Advent. It stood at the back of the "Old College" in what is now the farm-yard, projecting eastward, and was about thirty-five feet long by twenty broad, the altar being at the east end. It served as the loft had done, both for the students of the school and for the country congregation. The mark of where the roof joined on to the "old college" is still visible, a little below the southern gable, as also the blocked-up doorway which used to lead into it; but the building itself was demolished more than seventy years ago, at the time when the present "parish chapel" was built.

The following advertisement of Old Hall is taken from the Catholic directory for 1793 [1] :—

## "OLD HALL GREEN ACADEMY, PUCKERIDGE, HERTS.

"1. For a yearly pension of twenty-five guineas young gentlemen will be furnished with board, lodging, washing, and taught reading, writing, arithmetic, book-keeping, geography, and the use of the globes, English, Latin, Greek, and French, which last they will be obliged to speak in their familiar conversation on certain days. A strict attention will be given to cleanliness, civility, and, above all, to their morals and religion.

"2. The young gentlemen will contend for precedency several times in the year, and before the vacation, which begins on the 24th of June and continues to the end of July, when all are expected to be at home or pay according to the time. The most advanced will give public exhibitions of their improvement, and all undergo a public examination,

[1] The advertisement is here copied from the *Edmundian*, a college magazine, for 1843. It has been torn out of the Ordo at St. Edmund's. Hence there are possibly slight verbal errors in copying. The advertisement is substantially the same as that which appeared the following year.

when the first in each class will be rewarded with a suitable premium.

"3. At dinner, two good dishes besides vegetables. Breakfast: milk, milk pottage, or tea and bread and butter, if parents desire it. Supper: milk, bread and butter and cheese, or sometimes tarts, besides a piece of bread at eleven and four o'clock. None admitted after the age of twelve, but may continue after that age as long as parents choose.

"N.B.—The situation is one of the most pleasant and healthy in all England."

At the time of Mr. Potier's appointment the students were already, one or two at a time, beginning to leave Douay, and several found their way to Old Hall. The first two to arrive were Edward and James Tichborne. They were above the ordinary age for admission, but Lady Tichborne petitioned Dr. Douglass in a letter dated August 24th, 1792, that an exception might be made in consideration of the circumstances of the case. "They went to Douay three years ago," she wrote, "and would have remained there but for the troubles and disturbances in France, which rendered their situation extremely perilous. . . . After making many inquiries, we found no school that we so much approved of as yours at Old Hall Green. . . . I should hope you would have the goodness to waive that single objection of my sons being above the age prescribed." As the eldest was not more than thirteen, it need hardly be added that Dr. Douglass had no scruple in accepting them.

The next Douay refugee was Thomas Cook, who came as a master a few months later. John Devereux arrived in the October of the following year, and these were all that had come before the memorable St. Edmund's day, 1793, when Dr. Douglass formally inaugurated the ecclesiastical side of Old Hall. Here, then, we will leave Mr. Potier and his boys, while we speak of the history of the two English colleges of Douay and St. Omer, and of their dissolution at this time, which had so great an influence on the destinies of Old Hall.

## CHAPTER IV.

### THE ENGLISH COLLEGES OF DOUAY AND ST. OMER.

#### 1568—1793.

*Douay College founded by Cardinal Allen—Scope, object, and early history—Description of its state about the beginning of the eighteenth century—Rebuilding of the College—Its condition at the time of its fall in 1793—The College at St. Omer founded by Father Parsons, S.J., in 1592—Expulsion of the Jesuits in 1762—The College handed over to the secular clergy of Douay—Alban Butler second President —Gregory Stapleton fourth President—Daniel O'Connell a student —Prospectus of the College—Its state at the breaking out of the Revolution.*

THE English College at Douay was founded by Cardinal Allen in 1568, and came to an end in 1793, during the Reign of Terror. We do not propose to enter into the details of its history, but only to recall those facts of its foundation and development which throw a light on its actual state at the time of its fall, and thus enable us to form an idea of its effects and influence on the history of Old Hall, where a large proportion of its last students found a new home.

The establishment of St. Edmund's in 1793 is described by Bishop Douglass as that of a "New College," a "substitute for Douay." This accurately expresses the relation between the two colleges. When Douay came to an end those of its inmates who had not already taken flight were imprisoned for more than a year before they were allowed to return to England. To use the words of the Rev. Lewis Havard, one of the students, "Some of the scattered remains . . . . were collected at St. Edmund's College." Others came together at Crook Hall, near Durham, and there founded the college from which Ushaw took its rise. At a meeting of Bishops held at Old Hall in 1801, it was decided not to attempt the re-establishment of Douay

CARDINAL ALLEN,
President of Douay, 1568-1588.

College, and Crook Hall and St. Edmund's remain its sole descendants. A list of the last *alumni* of Douay will be found in the Appendix.[1] From this list it seems that about half were collected in England to resume their studies; that these were nearly equally divided between Crook Hall and St. Edmund's; but that of the last professors of Douay, the only four[2] who continued their teaching work at all came to St. Edmund's.

There was also a considerable connection between Old Hall and the English College at St. Omer about which we shall have to speak. Dr. Stapleton, its last president, became President of St. Edmund's, and was followed there by two professors[3] and several of the students, though they were fewer in number than those who came from Douay. By Edmundians the connection with Douay, the venerable parent of their own customs and traditions, the school of martyrs, missionaries, and many generations of the best Catholic blood, is looked on as far more worthy of their affectionate remembrance. The secular College at St. Omer had but a short existence, and though the list of its presidents includes some distinguished names—notably that of Alban Butler—it had few traditions of its own, and these were borrowed from Douay, of which it was an affiliation. Douay, on the other hand, the connecting link between Catholic England and the Catholicity of modern times, had traditions and associations the inheritance of which was regarded by the founders of St. Edmund's as among their most valued possessions. The Douay students themselves always shared this feeling. "There was a sort of prestige," writes one of them, "acting silently but efficaciously in the breasts of all the inmates when they reflected that their house had been the home of so many eminent men who had done honour to religion by their learned and voluminous writings; that it had been the *Alma Mater* of at least one hundred and sixty pious and devoted priests who had laid down their lives in

[1] See Appendix C.
[2] These were the Revs. William Poynter, William Wilds, William H. Coombes, and John Lee.
[3] The Rev. Francis Tuite and Mr. Cleghorn.

defence of religion; and of a more numerous body still, who, having received their education at that College, abided the loss of lands and liberty sooner than forsake their religion. Surely this was a home to live in. No one ever left it without reluctance; no one ever recollected it without delight."[1] In the same strain the Rev. Lewis Havard, speaking of his superiors at Douay and their behaviour during the imprisonment, says: "We always believed them to be—what we then knew from daily ocular evidence—men worthy to be the successors of those glorious martyrs and confessors, who had imbibed the spirit of primitive fortitude on the same spot, within the same walls, and who had there been endued with virtue from on high, to offer their lives in testimony of the faith once delivered to the saints. Hail, sacred asylum!" he continues, "with recollections of indelible gratitude I hail thee, most venerated College of Douay! May my tongue cleave to the roof of my mouth if ever I forget thee, most happy seat of religion, virtue, piety, and unruffled contentment."[2]

With this introduction, we proceed to a brief outline of the history of the foundation of the English College at Douay.

William Allen was born at Rossal, Lancashire, in 1532. At the age of fifteen he went up to Oriel College, Oxford, and took his degree as Bachelor of Arts in 1550, and Master of Arts in 1554. Two years later he was chosen Principal of St. Mary's Hall, and was likewise presented with a canonry of York. Soon after the accession of Elizabeth, and the subsequent reappearance of Protestantism, he found himself compelled to resign these offices and to leave England. After spending a short time in Flanders, he returned, and, though not yet in priest's orders, laboured as a missionary in his native county of Lancashire and elsewhere for several years, before being forced to quit the country a second time in 1565. Two years later he went on a pilgrimage to Rome, in company with Dr. Vendeville, Professor of Canon Law in the University of Douay, afterwards Bishop of Tournay.

[1] Gillow, "Haydock Papers," p. 100.
[2] "Funeral Sermon on Bishop Poynter," p. 11.

It was during this journey that the idea of founding a college on the continent first occurred to him. His original scheme was simply to collect together such English Catholic young men as were living in exile, the majority of whom were Oxford men, and to give them the facilities for continuing their university studies. At the same time he hoped that it would be the means of educating priests for the future, who might be able to restore the Catholic faith in England when the opportunity should arise. This was, of course, a very different thing from sending over missionaries in defiance of the law while England was still in the hands of Protestants, which was apparently quite an after-thought. But when once the college was founded, this soon became its chief work, and for more than two hundred years the Faith was almost entirely kept alive in this country by missionaries who came over continuously from Douay.

A beginning was made in a hired house on Michaelmas Day, 1568, with four English students and two Belgians. "Douay was chosen," as the Rev. Edmond Nolan has recently pointed out,[1] "because it was already under Oxford influences. It was a new university, founded in 1560. Its first Chancellor was Richard Smith, Fellow of Merton, and Regius Professor of Divinity at Oxford. The Principal of the Marchiennes College was Richard White, Fellow of New College, and Regius Professor of Civil and Canon Law. The Professor of Canon Law at Douay University was Owen Lewis, formerly Fellow of New College"

"By 1574," he continues, "it may be said that Allen had fully formed an English college of the University of Douay. At that date he had with him Morgan Philips, tutor of Oriel; Richard Bristow and John Howlett, Fellows of Exeter; John Marshall and Thomas Stapleton, Fellows of New College; Thomas Ford, Fellow of Trinity; Thomas Dorman, Fellow of All Souls'; Gregory Martin and Edmund Campion, Fellows of St. John's; with other graduates and students. Naturally they formed their college on the model of those of their own university, and it became the continuation of Catholic Oxford."

[1] See *Pastoralia*, August, 1892.

There was at first no fixed income beyond Allen's private means, and the College was supported chiefly by the alms of Catholics in England. A few years later this was supplemented by a monthly pension of 100 gold crowns granted by Pope Gregory XIII., and it was then established on a permanent basis as a pontifical college, subject directly to the jurisdiction of the Holy See. It was the first regular seminary established in accordance with the decrees of the Council of Trent.

The number of students rapidly multiplied, and Douay soon became a general centre for all English Catholics exiled from their country. All those who came were received with open arms, and no one was ever refused admittance, so that the number of students was often in excess of what the regular income would warrant. "For," Cardinal Allen explains,[1] "they cannot wait till a vacancy occurs, as is usual in colleges which belong to places at peace, seeing that they have come to these foreign parts forlorn and stripped of everything, often too with debts contracted for the journey, so that they cannot live a day without aid, much less return home to the heretics through so many dangers and across such tracts of land and sea." "Besides," he adds, "if we sent back or rejected only one such person who was otherwise worthy to be received, none would ever come afterwards."

The following account of the College seven years after its foundation is taken from a letter from the the Rev. Gregory Martin, one of the earliest students, by then a priest, to Blessed Edmund Campion, already on the English mission [2]:—

"It was a beautiful sight which I beheld when I was lately there. In that refectory, where in our time we sat down about six at one table, nearly sixty men and youths of the greatest promise were seated at three tables, eating so pleasantly a little broth, thickened merely with the commonest roots, that you could have sworn they were feasting on

---

[1] "Historical Introduction to the Douay Diaries," p. lxxvi.
[2] Ibid., p. xxxvi.

stewed raisins and prunes, English delicacies. Meanwhile, the reader from the pulpit reads aloud the portion of the Old Testament which occurs in the Roman Breviary at the time, adding the parts omitted, so that the whole Bible is easily gone through in one year. Twice a day, at the end of each meal, they still have the usual explanation of a chapter; only it is done more perfectly than formerly, not merely on account of the pains which Richard Bristow takes, and his knowledge, which was always very great, but also of the increased authority and maturity which is implied in the degree of doctor in divinity lately conferred on him. But there is one thing new, and an admirable novelty it is. Every Saturday and vigil of a Saint's day at one o'clock, a sermon or rather exhortation is delivered in the refectory, to which all our country people come from their lodgings in the town."

The first four Douay priests were ordained in 1573, one of whom was the above named Gregory Martin. The following year six were ordained, and in 1575 ten. Two years later the annual number had risen to over twenty. Nearly all these went on the English mission, and not a few ended their days by martyrdom. We may quote the following statistics from the introduction to the "Calendar of the English Martyrs," published in 1876 [1] :—

"The Douay registers regularly record each year the names of the newly ordained priests. The lists of 1581 give the ordination of 43 priests. Of these 15 are marked with the letter M, as subsequently martyred. In 1583 the martyrs are 10 out of 29. Next year they are 9 out of 30, and in 1585, 10 out of 24. During the last six months of a single year, 1588, there were no less than 33 martyrs, 22 of whom were priests. Yet the stream of missionaries did not slacken. The report of each fresh martyrdom was celebrated at the College by a Mass of thanksgiving and a solemn *Te Deum*, and only served to stimulate the zeal and fervour of those who were longing to share the same labours and win the same crown. From calculations furnished in 1596 it is

[1] p. 6.

estimated that in that year there were already above 300 priests from the seminaries at work on the English mission, assisted by about 50 survivors of the old Marian clergy and 16 priests of the Society of Jesus. At this time the catalogue of martyrs already numbered 101 secular priests and 4 Jesuits, while more than 100 priests had been sent into banishment."

Ten years after its foundation the College had to be temporarily transferred to Rheims, owing to political troubles, but possession of the old house at Douay was retained, and all returned thither in 1593. The well-known edition of the New Testament was published while the College was at Rheims, but owing to want of funds, the Old Testament was not printed till later, and did not appear till after the return to Douay.

Dr. Allen was created Cardinal in 1587. The following year he resigned the presidency of Douay, and retired to Rome, where he spent the rest of his life. He was already in failing health, and he breathed his last on October 16th, 1594. He was buried in the Church of the Holy Trinity, which at that time adjoined the English College.[1]

The second President of Douay was Dr. Richard Barratt, who brought the students back from Rheims. Previously to this time the studies had been purely theological; Dr. Barratt now received students in Philosophy, and later on also those who had not yet completed their "Humanities." Thus the College gradually grew to the form in which it existed latterly and in which it is usually known.[2]

It will not be necessary to follow in detail the vicissitudes of the next two hundred years. The following extract may be taken as giving a general idea of the state of the College about the beginning of the eighteenth century. Edmundians will recognize in it an interesting resemblance

---

[1] Cardinal Allen's crosier was presented to Dr. Griffiths at St. Edmund's in October, 1845. It is now kept at Archbishop's House, Westminster.

[2] The old Douay rules, kept among the archives at St. Edmund's, are of about this date. They are in Latin, and occupy about forty-five pages, giving a very complete idea of the constitution of the College at that time. See Historical Introduction to the Douay Diaries, p. lxxix., foot note.

to the St. Edmund's they know. The account from which this is taken was published in pamphlet form by "R.C.," who describes himself as a Protestant army chaplain taken to Douay in the course of his duties at the time of the siege in 1710; in reality, he was no other than the Rev. Hugh Tootell, better known as "Dodd," the author of the "Church History of England." He writes as follows:—

"The College as to the building is very mean and low (excepting the refectory, or room where they dine, which is a large, cheerful structure), but this defect is abundantly recompensed with other conveniences of chambers and offices for servants, with a large extent of ground, employed in gardens, of which there are four in number. A private one for the President's use, a common one for the scholars, another for the students in Divinity and masters, a fourth for the use of the kitchen.

"The Church is but small, proportioned to the rest of the College, 'tis dedicated to Thomas Becket, whom the Papists number amongst their saints, as having lost his life in defence of the immunities of the Church. It is beautified with a fine organ; and (as I was informed) not many years ago, they did not want several very able musicians; but of late they have very much laid that study aside, upon pretence that it called the scholars from applying themselves to things of greater moment. The Church is not unprovided with relics of Saints (as they esteem them), whereof there are two most remarkable, Thomas Becket's hairshirt, and Charles Borromaeus, the Archbishop of Milan's Cardinal's cap, which upon more solemn days are placed upon the altar in silver cases.

"The College has two libraries, one for the students in Divinity, the other is chiefly made up of classic authors. I was amazed to see such a number of books of controversy about religion, chiefly published by members of this College, which shows how indefatigable their ancestors were in endeavouring to make up the breaches of Henry VIII. and stemming the tide of the Reformation. But what I mostly admired was that the greatest part of these works were printed when the authors laboured under the very extremity of poverty; and yet more money was never wanting to carry on the press. .... Every scholar (excepting they are very young) has a private chamber to himself, notwithstanding which several prefects and superiors have an arbitrary access to by means of a common key. There is a very decent infirmary for the sick, at some distance from the College, with a prefect and servants to attend them, a physician and an apothecary.

"I had not the opportunity to be an eye witness to the order of their studies and the economy of the house; the siege having driven away most of the masters and scholars, and interrupted the usual course; but, by the relation I had from them their way of living appeared very edifying, and the order of their schools very methodical. I have frequently heard some in our universities repine at their happiness in this respect, and earnestly wish something of that regularity might be established amongst us. They don't run headlong upon their studies. The progress they make is slow and gradual, and by consequence must be solid. They are obliged to hear nine different masters before they can complete their studies. Five masters are allotted for what they call Humanity; two for Philosophy, and two for Theology. What we call the Accidence they call Figures,[1] which they divide into two years, one for the lower, the second for the higher, the third for Grammar, the fourth for Syntax, the fifth for Poetry, the sixth for Rhetoric, which with two years Philosophy and four years Theology make up twelve years.

"They have different rooms for their schools, which they every year remove into, according as they advance in their studies. They have daily, monthly, and yearly exercises, or experiments of learning, both private and public, which provokes the scholars with laudable emulation to run with

---

[1] The two classes of "Figures" were changed very shortly after this into three classes of "Rudiments," and this term has survived at St. Edmund's to the present day. At Ushaw the older title of "Figures" is now in use, though at Crook Hall the term "Rudiments" was used. The name of the other classes, Rhetoric, Poetry, Syntax, and Grammar, still survive at both places.

Douay College, Front (Modern).

courage through the tedious paths of learning. They are obliged to about an hour's devotion every morning, and every day is in like manner finished by public prayer; and as I take it, their hours of rising and going to bed are five and nine.

"This College entertains no foreigners, yet there are a mixture of English in it; some designed for the Church, other persons of figure and plentiful fortunes in their country; some of mean parentage, others of the prime nobility; and yet the discipline of the College runs so that there is not the least distinction observable, either in dress, diet, or apartment. If there is any preference or partiality, it is only when a singular progress in their studies recommends them. The house is governed by a President, who is constantly named by the Pope. He enjoys his place for life, and his power is arbitrary in punishing or rewarding, though he governs according to the standing rules of the College, and seldom acts in matters of moment without the advice of a counsel of Seniors. The next in dignity was the Vice-President, a Procurator, a General Prefect, a Prefect of the Infirmary, a Prefect of the Wardrobe, a Prefect of the Kitchen, and (as I said before) nine masters. All these offices depend entirely upon the President. Besides they have a Gardener, Cook, Brewer, Baker, Tailor, &c., all within the precincts of the college, and maintained by yearly salaries. Their dress is uniform, black cossacks, surtouts plated upon the shoulders and collar-bands. They eat thrice a day. Their breakfast is bread and butter; at dinner they have half-a-pound of meat; at supper the same; with double the quantity upon Sundays and holidays. Their bread and beer is of the best sort, and of this they may have a discretion."

The inconvenience arising from the small size of the College and the want of accommodation alluded to above continued till 1770. About that time, during the presidency of the Rev. William Green, a collection was made throughout England for the rebuilding of Douay.[1] The new College was

[1] See letter of Bishop Challoner, in Rev. J. F. Gordon's "Catholic Church in Scotland," p. 64.

solidly constructed of white stone, and may now be seen, forming one side of the " Place des Grands Anglais." The chapel, which stands at one extremity of the front, has a plain exterior, but was richly adorned inside.

Both the College and the chapel were confiscated by the French Revolutionists within twenty-five years after their erection, and nearly all the ornaments, etc., perished. Among the few that have been preserved is the marble Tabernacle, richly sculptured by Lowell, of London, which may be seen at the present day in the Church of St. Jacques, Douay, on the Altar of the Blessed Sacrament.

Of the state of the College during the last years of its existence we have contradictory accounts. On the one hand, the Rev. Thomas Smith, one of the last "Seniors," when afterwards Vicar Apostolic of the Northern District, used to say that under Dr. Gibson, his predecessor, who was President at Douay from 1781 till 1790, it had been as flourishing as at any period of its existence. "Never greater harmony prevailed among the superiors," he said, "never was greater zeal and ability displayed by the various professors, never was better conduct, greater attention to their studies, nor a more willing observance of the College discipline than was to be found in the different grades of students at [this] time."[1]

On the other hand, Bishop James Talbot was so firmly persuaded of the very reverse, that he was with difficulty persuaded to send any students to the College. Much correspondence passed between him and Dr. Poynter, then prefect of studies, and a subject of the London district. Most of the letters are preserved among the Westminster archives. Dr. Poynter was a personal friend of Dr. Gibson, and he maintained that the reports about the want of discipline, and the rumours current of the financial embarassment of the College, were alike without foundation. He himself signed a formal certificate that the studies were in good order, and he sent a similar document with respect to the discipline signed by the prefect.

[1] "Haydock Papers," p. 100.

St. Omer College (Modern).

## The English Colleges of Douay and St. Omer. 61

A short time after this, Dr. Gibson was made Vicar Apostolic of the Northern District, and his post at Douay was filled by the Rev. Edward Kitchen. The latter ruled the College for less than two years, when he resigned, and a few months later he died. The Rev. John Daniel succeeded to the office of president, which he held when the College came to an end in 1793, as will be presently described.[1]

We must now turn our attention to the other English college in the north of France, which was likewise confiscated during the Revolution, and the fall of which had considerable bearing on the future of Old Hall. The College at St. Omer was founded originally by Father Parsons, S.J., in 1592, and remained a Jesuit college till 1762. In that year the French Government determined on the expulsion of the Society from France, and, although the Jesuits of St. Omer were British subjects, it was soon ascertained that they would not be exempted from the decree. In order to frustrate the design as far as possible, the professors and students moved secretly across the frontier in the month of August with such of their effects as they were able to carry, and the establishment was transferred bodily to Bruges. Here it remained eleven years till the suppression of the Society by Clement XIV. in 1773. On being dispersed from Bruges, a number of the students took refuge at the old-established Jesuit College at Liège, which the Prince Bishop had allowed to continue, and they were followed by one or two of their old superiors. When in turn driven from Liège by the Revolution in 1794, the community took refuge in England, and Mr. Weld, a former student at Bruges, placed at their disposal the mansion of Stonyhurst, in Lancashire, where the College has been ever since. Stonyhurst can therefore trace a descent from the St. Omer College, founded by Father Parsons.

After the departure of the Jesuits, the College at St. Omer

---

[1] Mr. Daniel was the last acting president. The last nominal president was the Rev. Francis Tuite, who was elected so that there might be a legal representative to claim the funds from the French Government after Mr. Daniel's death. For a complete list of Presidents of Douay, see Appendix H.

was handed over to the English secular clergy of Douay, and by a decree of the French Government, dated September 7th, 1762, the Rev. Thomas Talbot, brother of Bishop James Talbot, was appointed president. Two years later, on March 24th, 1764, the new constitutions were formulated by "Letters Patent" of the King of France, who formally declared it to be "**our** will that our said College continue to be **even in time of war under our** royal safe-guard and protection, **and that it remain supported and** confirmed, as we do support **and confirm** it by these presents, in all rights, exemptions and priveledges, which it hath, might or ought to have enjoyed to this day."[1]

A long and heated **discussion afterwards took place as to** the conduct of the secular **clergy in accepting the College.** With this we need not here concern ourselves, beyond remarking that the case was sufficiently **complicated to** present a difficulty to Alban Butler when he was appointed to succeed Mr. Talbot in 1766. According to his nephew and biographer,[2] "doubts were suggested to him on the justice or propriety of his accepting the presidency of a college which in fact belonged to others." He adds, however, that "He advised with the Bishop of Amiens and the Bishop of Boulogne upon the point, and they both agreed in opinion that he might safely accept it." He acted on this advice, and retained the post till his **death in 1773.** His successor was Dr. Wilkinson, who managed **the College** for fourteen years, and then retired in favour of **Dr. Gregory Stapleton,**[3] who **was** afterwards so intimately connected with St. Edmund's.

---

[1] An old copy of the "Letters Patent" is at St. Mary's College, Oscott. A more recent one is among the archives at St. Edmund's. It may be noted that this document gives the date of the original foundation as 1594.

[2] "Life," p. 103.

[3] Gregory Stapleton was the seventh son of Nicholas Stapleton, of Carlton Hall, Yorkshire. He was educated at Douay College, where he arrived from Equerchin Preparatory School in 1762. Ten years later, being then a deacon, he was appointed professor of music, and took rank as a "Senior." On his ordination a year afterwards, he became Procurator, which post he retained more than twelve years. After this he travelled for a time with young Mr. Stonor, and on his return from Italy in 1787 he was appointed President of St. Omer.

The new College at St. Omer—for such it really was—was carried on under considerable disadvantages at first. It is true that the royal pension of 250*l.* a year, which had been paid by the King of France since 1594, was continued; but this was itself the cause of a good deal of trouble, for it left the authorities in a great measure dependent on the French Government. They were obliged to have a "Council of Administrators," consisting of the President, Vice-President, General Prefect, and the Professors of Rhetoric and Poetry, and this Council frequently interfered greatly with the internal affairs of the College: for though the President was one of the Council, he was liable to be outvoted or even deposed when at variance with the other members. It became a matter of difficulty to obtain professors, and the administrators had sometimes to fall back on men who were not fit for their work. Moreover, it was not easy to fill the College with students. The boys who had been there under the Jesuits had all, or nearly all, accompanied their old masters to Bruges, and there was no demand for another college at the time. By article VI. of the Constitution, no student was admitted "unless he be English by birth or by issue of English and Catholic parents, and unless he profess the Roman Catholic religion;" and though this rule was not strictly adhered to, and both foreigners and Protestants were sometimes taken, the number of students under the new *regime* at no time reached the figure it had stood at under the Jesuits. Notwithstanding the disadvantages, however, the secular presidents managed to form a school, and within four years of their undertaking it they had fifty boys. This appears from the following letter from "An English gentleman on his travels" dated Paris, March 21st, 1766:—

"DEAR SIR,—

In compliance with your request, I have made it my business to inquire into the present state of popish seminaries in Flanders and along the coast from Boulogne. . . . At St. Omer's there is a stately college which belonged to the English Jesuits before the Jesuits were expelled from France. On their expulsion a party of secular priests from Douay obtained leave to settle in that College. These priests are partly Irish, but the majority of them English; they have under their care about 50 boys. . . . Their brethren at Douay have near 150 boys at their College."[1]

Later on, the numbers showed a further increase, and in spite of all its difficulties, the College succeeded in gaining for itself a fair reputation. Piers,[2] in fact, states definitely that it was as successful under the new administration as it had been before, and instances in proof of what he says the names of such people as Daniel O'Connell, Bishop Milner (sic), Bishop Walsh, the Rev. Joseph Birch, and others who were educated there. Cavrois,[3] a more recent writer, speaks in the same sense. The following certificate[4] gives testimony from those who were not likely to be predisposed in favour of the College :—

"We the Administrators of the Directory of the District of St. Omer certify and declare that we regard the establishment of the English College of St. Omer very useful to this town, and that it is within our knowledge that the persons who are charged by the state with the education of the youths entrusted to their care there discharge their duties with the greatest possible exactitude. In witness whereof, at their request, we have given these presents under the seal of our directory, and signed by our registrar."

An old prospectus of St. Omer, no doubt brought over by Dr. Stapleton himself, is among the archives at St. Edmund's. The following is a copy :—

---

[1] *Gentleman's Magazine*, May, 1766.

[2] "Notice Historique sur le Collége Anglais de Saint-Omer," par H. Piers. Aire, 1846. His words are (p. 25), " Sa réputation loin de faiblir dans cette seconde periode, sembla grandir encore par les brillans sujets qui sortirent de son sein."

[3] Le Collége Anglais à Saint-Omer, par Louis Cavrois, Arras et Saint-Omer, 1867.

[4] This is a translation of an undated document, kept among the archives of the Department at Arras, whither all the papers belonging to the English College of St. Omer were removed by virtue of an " Arrête," dated January 6th, 1804.

## AT THE ENGLISH COLLEGE OF ST. OMER.

### I.

YOUNG GENTLEMEN are admitted from nine to eleven years of age. They are expected, at least, to read currently; and, such as have been at other schools, to bring with them from thence a Certificate of their good behaviour.

### II.

THE terms are Twenty-five Pounds a year; one quarter of which to be always advanced. Each Student to pay one Guinea entrance, and to bring with him two good suits of clothes, six shirts, four pair of stockings, four pocket handkerchiefs, and two pair of shoes; otherwise, whatever may be deficient will be procured and charged to account.

### III.

FOR the above sum, the Latin, Greek, English and French languages, Writing, Arithmetic, and Geography are taught. Table, Bed and Clothes, Washing, Fire, Candle, School-books, Pens, Ink and Paper are provided; also Physician, Surgeon and Drugs, in all slight disorders; and every student is allowed sixpence French a week, for pocket-money.

### IV.

DRAWING, Music, Dancing and Fencing may be learned, in the hours of recreation; but these are charged apart; as are Consultations of Physicians and Surgeons extraordinary, Nurses and Remedies in serious diseases, and also the Clothes with which the Students quit the College, after one year's residence.

### V.

NO particular privileges nor exemptions are granted to any of the Students: all are without distinction bound to observe the established Rules of the College. They are not permitted to receive any money unknown to the Superiors.

### TERMS FOR LEARNING.

|   | s. | d. |   |   |
|---|---|---|---|---|
| Drawing | 4 | 6 | a month. | |
| Dancing | 2 | 9 | ,, | |
| Harpsichord | 5 | 4 | ,, | |
| Flute | 5 | 4 | ,, | |
| Singing | 5 | 4 | ,, | |
| Violin | 3 | 9 | ,, | exclusive of broken strings. |
| Fencing | 3 | 9 | ,, | exclusive of broken foils. |

Agent for the College,
MR. HORRABIN,
No. 4, Castle Street, Holborn, London.

During the last two years of the existence of the College Daniel O'Connell and his brother Maurice were students, and it was here that the former made the acquaintance of the future Bishop Walsh, with whom he afterwards became so intimate. Dr. Stapleton, who is said to have been a specially good judge of character, wrote the following remarkable forecast of O'Connell's future in a letter dated January, 1792, addressed to his uncle, Maurice O'Connell :—

"You desire to have my candid opinion respecting your nephews, and you very properly remark that no habit can be worse than that of the instructors of youth who seek to gratify the parents of those under their care by ascribing to them qualities which they do not really possess. You add that being only the uncle of these young men, you can afford to hear the real truth respecting their abilities or deficiencies. It is not my habit to disguise the precise truth in reply to such inquiries as yours. You shall, therefore, have my opinion with perfect candour."

After a short account of Maurice, the younger, he proceeds:—

"With respect to the elder, Daniel, I have but one sentence to write about him, and that is, that I was never so much mistaken in my life as I shall be unless he be destined to make a remarkable figure in society."

O'Connell was removed from St. Omer in 1792, and sent to Douay; but he only stayed there a few months, when, being alarmed at the progress of the Revolution, he returned to Ireland, just in time to escape the general imprisonment.

The Colleges of Douay and St. Omer were both confiscated by the Revolutionists in 1793—St. Omer in August, Douay in October. In each case the communities had to undergo a long and trying imprisonment before they were allowed to return to England. The first establishment of St. Edmund's as a substitute for Douay took place a month after the fall of the College; but for more than a year after this the men who were most required at Old Hall as professors and superiors, as well as some of the most promising ecclesiastical students, were in confinement at Doullens and Arras. In order to understand matters connected with the foundation of St. Edmund's, therefore, it will be necessary first to make ourselves acquainted with the circumstances under which Douay came to an end, and the various stages of the imprisonment. We owe it, moreover, to the memories of Dr. Stapleton, Dr. Poynter, and others of the "Confessors of Doullens," the transmitters to St. Edmund's of Douay customs and traditions, to record the trials and hardships which they went through for the sake of religion, in meeting which they showed a courage and devotion worthy of the best days of the College. The history of their sufferings in prison will form the best introduction to their work for St. Edmund's.

## CHAPTER V.

### THE IMPRISONMENT OF THE ENGLISH COLLEGIANS.

#### 1793—1795.

*The French Revolution—The Douay clergy and the "Civic Oath"—Disturbances at Douay—Attack on the College—Death of Louis XVI.—War with England—National guards take possession of Douay College—Secret burying of the plate and valuables—The English expelled from the town—The collegians recalled a few weeks later—Seizure of the College and imprisonment of the students—Removal to Doullens—Escape of the Rev. W. H. Coombes and others—The "Trente-deux"—Dr. Stapleton and the other professors and students at St. Omer imprisoned—Behaviour of the boys under the schismatical priests—Removal to Arras—Thence to Doullens—Death of Robespierre—Its effect on the treatment of the collegians—Return to St. Omer and Douay—Dr. Stapleton goes to Paris, and obtains the liberation of the collegians—Return to England March, 1795.*

FOR some time before the execution of Louis XVI., at the beginning of the year 1793, the position of the English collegians in the north of France had become far from pleasant. Douay, as a town, suffered less at first than St. Omer, and during the early period of the Revolution, England and France being nominally at peace, and the British ambassador still at Paris, the College seemed fairly safe. At the time when the National Assembly decreed the suppression of the French establishments of education, and appropriated their property, the superiors of the English College at Douay claimed exemption on the score of its being British property. Their claim was allowed, but in order to establish it they permitted the title deeds to be taken to Paris and examined, which led some years afterwards to most unfortunate results.

Towards the end of the year 1791 the question arose as to the professors taking the "Civic Oath," and again they claimed exemption on account of their nationality. By the

DOUAY COLLEGE (BACK).

Treaty of Navigation and Commerce of September 26th, 1786, all foreigners had been excused from any obligation of attending the public ceremonies of Divine worship in the churches or elsewhere; and on the strength of this the superiors of all the British establishments at Douay claimed the privilege of performing the exercises of religion in their own houses without molestation. In order to make good their claim, the heads of each of the five houses[1] had to appear before the Directory. They contended that being foreigners, they were not to be classed with the "Prêtres assermentés," or with the "Prêtres non-assermentés," being at the most "Fonctionaires Publics" of their respective countries. After they had been heard, they were politely dismissed, with an assurance that due regard should be paid to their remonstrances, and the next morning a favourable message was sent to each of the houses.

So far the town had been comparatively quiet. The first serious disturbance occurred a few months later. It was witnessed by two students of the College,[2] from one of whom the following particulars were afterwards obtained:—

"They were returning from a walk in the country, when, on entering the gates, they saw in every direction too evident signs of some extraordinary and alarming proceeding. Women standing in groups at the doors of houses were wringing their hands, collecting in parties and as quickly separating, some with terror, but more with menace painted on their countenances, and all tending in one way or other towards the great square. Alarm, not less than curiosity, led the two students in the same direction, and they soon found

---

[1] The English, Scotch, and Irish colleges, and the English Benedictine and Franciscan monasteries. These particulars are taken from a memorial addressed by Dr. Poynter and Mr. Daniel to the British Commissioners in Paris more than twenty years later. See Appendix G.

[2] Thomas Penswick, afterwards Bishop, and Thomas Gillow, subsequently missionary rector of North Shields, who escaped together when the others were taken to prison. Both came to Old Hall for a time, but afterwards went to Crook. The details here given are taken from the rough notes made from the latter's description by the Rev. John Gillow, D.D., his nephew, vice-president of Ushaw. They are printed here by kind permission of Mr. Joseph Gillow, who is a great-nephew of the Douay student.

themselves in the midst of a serious *émeute*. Before them was a multitude of upwards of 10,000 men, a promiscuous mob of soldiers and citizens, entirely filling the great square. Not far off was a body of troops waiting the orders of their captain, who was in anxious conversation with one of the civil authorities. The mob seemed to be waiting the issue of their discussion, evidently prepared to resist should orders be given for their dispersion. After a short time the magistrate retired into the court house, and the captain withdrew his troops, leaving the town at the mercy of the insurgents. Some officers were indeed seen making ineffectual efforts to withdraw the soldiers, but it was only by persuasion; for a great part of the garrison had joined in the tumult, and none of the authorities, either civil or military, dared to interfere by compulsory measures.

"This was the first successful outburst of the spirit of anarchy at Douay; for, notwithstanding all the attempts of the ruling Jacobin party to seduce its good faith, Douay had still stood by the side of loyalty and order longer than any of the towns of the northern departments. This unfortunate beginning of real troubles was occasioned by two of the orators of the National Assembly, who had been sent from Paris to spread the spirit of their faction. Taking advantage of the scarcity arising from the late bad harvests, from which the poor of Douay had grievously suffered, they harangued the people in their accustomed licentious tone, attributing their miseries to the rapacity of the rich, and by their violence they succeeded in inflaming their worst passions. In their fury the excited populace fell on the good and loyal citizens, one of whom, Derbaix, was the printer employed by the College, and had become obnoxious to the orators by the loyal tone of his press; and the other was an extensive baker, whom they charged with starving the people for the gratification of his avarice. They hung them up to the lamp post as victims to the cause of liberty, and then spent the night in dragging their dead bodies in tumultuous procession through the streets. Having thus publicly committed these two murders, the town became implicated, and the influence of the well-disposed was crushed beneath the triumph of popular tyranny."

The first attack on the College is also described by Mr. Gillow:—

"It was a short time before ten o'clock, and at the moment when the community was leaving the chapel to retire to rest. Their attention was first caught by the mingled sounds of many voices, as of a riotous crowd filling the street before their doors. Then followed tremendous knocks at the door with the butt ends of their muskets, accompanied with menacing demands of immediate admission. Dr. Poynter and a large body of the higher students were at the moment passing the door. Perceiving that resistance would be worse than useless, he opened the door, while the students stood in the open passage to see the cause of this visit. Immediately four or five of the soldiers in a state of intoxication entered, and pushed forward through the porch and inner door into the corridor. They called out for the young men to be led out into the streets to go along with them. Dr. Poynter attempted to remonstrate, saying that the students were many of them in bed, and the rest were now retiring, and begged that they would not disturb them. 'Where are your prisons? open your prisons,' they exclaimed. 'We have no prisons,' replied Dr. Poynter, and would have added that the young men were free and happy, but the soldiers grew furious. One drew his sword, and the consequences threatened to become serious, when, in an instant, Messrs. Gillow, Silvertop, Riddell, and one or two more, as if moved by a common influence, rushed forward, and taking each of the soldiers by the arm, cried out 'Vive la nation!' and so drew them out into the streets. The doors were closed, and the crowd moved away to the cry of 'Vive la nation! vive la liberté!' The students were carried in a sort of triumphal procession through the streets of Douay, and were out most of the night; and in this manner the College was temporarily saved."

In the meantime the state of France was beginning to tell on the numbers at the College. Most of those who were able to do so were returning to England, and no new students arrived to take their places. The diary gives the total of those in the house on October 1st, 1790, as 140, exclusive of servants. The following year it had fallen to 126, and in 1792 to 103. During the next few months many more returned to England, and it became a serious question as to the best course to pursue. The Irish College had already been broken up, and Mr. Farquharson, the Rector of the Scots' College, likewise sent his students away; while he himself, with a few others, stayed to keep possession of the house. A similar course had been pursued by the Anglo-Benedictines; the main body of the community were disbanded, while Prior Sharrock with five others remained behind in charge of the monastery. The question was whether the English collegians should follow their example.

In the difficult situation in which they were placed some hesitation was shown. "Perhaps," wrote Mr. John Penswick,[1] "there was a deficiency of energetic resolve about our very worthy President (Mr. Daniel). . . . Great allowances must be made for his indecision. . . . Could he have surmised that the College had been lost through his own want of perseverance, that imagination, slender and groundless though it might be, would have been fatal to his peace, and perhaps to his life." This was the motive that decided them to remain. Were they now to retreat to England, it seemed that the College would at once be confiscated, and such an event seemed almost fatal to the prospect of Catholicity in England. Hence they made up their minds to remain, trusting partly to their being less than twelve miles from the frontier, over which they could escape if necessary. "To their honour, be it said," adds Mr. Penswick, "that they never faltered in their determination for a single moment. To one final resolve they arrived, and from it they never swerved. The College must be retained at all hazards."

After the execution of the king on January 21st, 1793, war was declared with England, and the troubles began in

---

[1] "Haydock Papers," p. 115. Rev. John Penswick was the brother of Bishop Thomas Penswick, and lived to be the last survivor of the Douay collegians. He died on October 30th, 1864.

earnest. The following letter from one of the students, dated February 21st, 1793, describes the beginning of the end :—

"On the morning of Monday last, the 18th of the present month, a body of national guards was ordered to assemble in the market place, without being informed of the design of their expedition. They were no sooner assembled, and their commissaries from the district arrived, but they filed off to the five British establishments which are settled in our town. We had not been informed of their coming till a few moments before their arrival, when some people, with countenances bespeaking their fears, ran to inform us that the guards were assembled to expel us from our habitations. I leave you to judge of our alarms at this information. They arrived soon after, and summoned the president and some others into the parlour. There an apostate priest and monk of Marchiennes, as a member of the district, read over a warrant which authorized them to impose the national seals upon the goods and papers of the College as also those of the superiors. On leaving the parlour the guards dispersed themselves in the different places on the different gal.eries, some few excepted, who attended the commissaries in the different places where they laid the seals. The guards in general formed a despicable collection; they were seemingly the scum of the town. The commissaries were equally unknown to us. The places on which the seals are to be seen are the president's and procurator's chests and papers, the divines' library, the curiosity room, the street doors of the bakehouse, infirmary, and church. The sacristy was left untouched. The refectory plate in part was seen, but nothing taken. We are indeed apprehensive that when they come to erase the seals an entire inventory of our goods will be taken, after which term they will be said to be no more at our disposal. The pretended motive of these proceedings was to put our property in security, as a storm, they said, seemed to be gathering against us from people of inferior conditions, among whom several rumours, unfavourable to us, had been spread. The imposture, though trimmed with a good deal of *finesse*, was too palpable to gain any credit among impartial reviewers. We have observed the first proceedings in regard to every religious community from the beginning of the Revolution down to the present times, and we always discovered them to begin with deceit and end in robbery; so that to think that we should trust to their outward sincerity was the meanest compliment that could be paid to our understandings. The real cause was unknown to us for some time, but a letter received from Paris seems to unravel the whole mystery; at least to throw such light upon it as to direct our determinations. . . .

"The letter clearly discovers to you the reason of our goods being sealed, and shows the cause traced up to the National Convention. The decree of the 9th last August mentioned is a decree by which all incorporate bodies, without exception, were declared suppressed. On hearing this we were not alarmed, because we did not suppose it regarded strangers, but we were deceived. The decree of the 14th instant, February, declares that English, etc. etc., colleges should receive the pay of their funds till the expiration of the six first months in 1793, ordering the Committees of Instruction, Surveillance, and that of Alienation to prepare the final decree. . . . There is no one amongst us who discovers reason for hope, but I suppose we shall linger on a month or two longer. Remember me in a particular manner to all friends, informing them that I shall perhaps be very soon with them. . . . If I can send you any information of the precise time we are to depart, I will.

"P.S.—We have had two or three guards in the house since Monday last, the most ill-looking fellows you ever saw, so that we are obliged to have one or two to sit up to guard them."

The above letter was printed in England for private circulation, and on the back was added an extract from another dated Paris, February 18th, 1793, giving further particulars about the decree alluded to. From this it appears that it concerned the colleges only, the English convents being considered as already suppressed by a decree of the previous August. The writer, whose name is not known, urges that

Dr. Stapleton should come to Paris on behalf of the Colleges of Douay and St. Omer, which, he says, are the most concerned in the matter, and obtain the best conditions possible, such as leave to dispose of their property and go elsewhere. "It may be proper," he says, however, "to consider the probabilities of things continuing to go on for any long time, and whether it may not be most prudent to linger on till it be seen what will be the final event." This latter was the course adopted.

In the meantime steps were taken by some of the more daring of the students to elude the jailers and rescue some of the College property. One boy let himself down by a rope from a room on the second floor to the window of the physical science room, and having taken some of the best instruments, again let himself down from the first floor to the ground. Another climbed up one chimney, down another which communicated with it, and so gained access to the president's room. In this way some of the plate and other valuables were secured and carried out by four philosophers, who after scaling the walls reached a safe spot outside the town and buried the treasures.[1] Another portion was

---

[1] The four philosophers were Richard Thompson, John Clarkson, William Lucas, and Thomas Penswick. For the information of those who may not be accustomed to the terms in use at our Catholic colleges, it may be as well to explain that those who studied Philosophy were then, as now, called "Philosophers." Similarly, students in divinity were known as "Divines," or "Theologians."

The plate and valuables buried outside the walls were dug up again eighteen months later, on the return of the collegians from Doullens, and sold to defray their expenses. The part which was buried inside the College, however, remained under ground for a very long time afterwards. It was recovered in the year 1863 by the late Mgr. Searle, an old Ushaw student, and one of the trustees of St. Edmund's, who having obtained permission from Napoleon III. to search for it, found it by means of descriptions previously given of the hiding-place. It was brought to England and most of it was divided between Ushaw and Old Hall, as the heirs of Douay. The two Giffard goblets were presented to Oscott. The portion that fell to St. Edmund's included a mounted salver, the gift of the Duke of Norfolk in 1701, six special goblets, given by old Catholic families, with their names inscribed, ranging in date from 1694 to 1753, a number of ordinary goblets, salt dishes, mustard pots, forks and spoons. In addition to this, Mgr. Searle, on his death, left to St. Edmund's the large drinking goblet which had been given by the Norfolk family in 1744, and which he reserved to himself during his lifetime.

buried inside the college, as were also the relics, including the hair shirt of St. Thomas à Becket, and the red biretta of St. Charles Borromeo.[1]

The next turn of affairs showed the collegians that they were all prisoners, for leave to quit the city was refused. A few managed to escape, among them the Rev. Edward Peach and Robert Freemont. Others tried, failed, and were put in prison. "Thus situated," writes the Rev. Joseph Hodgson,[2] "we deemed it less dangerous to abide all consequences by a peaceable demeanour in our own house than to attempt an escape. Superiors were not wanting in every possible exertion to procure protection and safety. Everything was done to keep up our spirits and to remove despondence; and, strange as it may appear, never do I remember a more cheerful flow of spirits, in the generality, than what was manifested during the whole time. We literally cheered away the gloom of thoughtful reflections and pining wishes, by singing whole hours at a time. 'God save the King' and 'Rule Britannia' bespoke our hearty wishes for success to his Majesty's arms; and the Latin song, made by a scholar at Winchester School, 'Dulce Domum,' was a fond wish once more and soon to see our friends and home. It was, however, soon found prudent to be careful in singing 'God save the King,' so that 'Dulce Domum' remained our standing song. Such a behaviour astonished every one. Friends and enemies wondered alike how we could sing in such circumstances; and sometimes heaved a sigh of concern to tell us we did not know what we had still to expect."

---

[1] The body of the Ven. John Southworth, the martyr, was also one of the Douay treasures; according to the *Orthodox Journal* for 1817 (p 446), it was removed to a place of security on May 4th, 1793. No trace was discovered by Mgr. Searle of this or any other of the relics. Even if he had known exactly where to look—and it seems that, owing to changes in the internal structure, there was in some cases considerable difficulty in identifying the precise spot—it is more than doubtful whether anything would have been left of them after seventy-five years under ground.

[2] The Rev Joseph Hodgson, last Vice-President of Douay, wrote a long account of the seizure of the College and the imprisonment at Doullens, which was published in the *Catholic Magazine* for 1831. The original is among the Westminster archives.

Meanwhile, the defeat of the French general, Dumourier, brought the seat of war to the neighbourhood of Douay, and several times the fighting was near enough to be heard by the college students. At the beginning of August matters came to a crisis. A siege appeared imminent, and the order was given to expel all British subjects within twenty-four hours. A list of English residents was appended, and in it were included the professors and students of the English College, and the monks of the Benedictine Monastery. An exception was made in favour of Mr. Daniel, the president, who was allowed to stay and take care of the College, and two students who were too ill to be moved.[1]

It was necessary for all those who were expelled to provide themselves with passports, on which their destinations were written. Those of the English collegians were made out to Lens, a small town in the Department Pas de Calais; but they never reached there. Mr. Daniel obtained leave for them to stop the first night at their country house at Equerchin, and there they remained unmolested for nearly two months. The English Benedictines likewise had a house in the same village, where they also remained without being disturbed.

Early in the month of October, when the danger of siege had passed, a sudden order was given for all to come back to Douay. "The order to return," writes Dr. Gillow, "had a pacific appearance. It was represented to them at Equerchin that the seat of war being removed further into Flanders, and Douay being no longer in danger of a siege, the community might come back without inconvenience or danger to the town. This pretext was put forth to prevent their attempting to escape. . . . Hence may be conceived their consternation, when they found on their arrival in the town by the edict which had been issued, and which they saw placarded on the walls, ordering the English students to go as prisoners to the Scotch College, that they had been deceived and ensnared."

The edict referred to was dated Saturday, October 13th,

[1] John Eldridge and Thomas Brady. Eldridge afterwards recovered, but Brady died of a decline the following year.

and contained three articles, which were to the following effect:—

1. That all subjects of the King of Great Britain be arrested till peace be established.
2. That they be treated with tenderness.¹
3. That all their property be confiscated.

No preparations had been made at the Scotch College for the reception of the English students. When they arrived, late in the evening, they were simply given the refectory as a sleeping room and allowed to make the best of it. The next day was Sunday, October 13th, the Feast of St. Edward the Confessor, but no mass was possible. Prayers were read in English, morning and afternoon. The same day gendarmes arrived with some captives from Equerchin. Among these was the Rev. William H. Coombes, in whom Edmundians will take a special interest on account of his long connection with St. Edmund's. He was professor of Rhetoric at Douay, and is described by a contemporary as an accomplished scholar and an excellent linguist. Comparatively a young man, his impetuous disposition sometimes carried him beyond the limits of prudence, and it is said that much of the animosity displayed by the Revolutionists against the College arose in the first instance from an article written by him the previous year in a Royalist newspaper.

Mr. Coombes was one of those who, at the time of the imprisonment, succeeded in escaping to England. Some years afterwards he was asked to write an account of his adventures, which appeared in the " Catholic Directory " for 1800.² Most of those who escaped had similar experiences to recount, and that of Mr. Coombes may fairly be taken as a specimen of the rest.

It appears that he first came to the determination of trying to get away as soon as he saw the proclamation at Douay. Having managed to get out of the town without mishap, he was found the same evening at the country house at Equerchin,

---

¹ This second article, according to Dr. Douglass's Diary, was shortly afterwards cancelled.
² See Appendix B.

by the officer who was sent there to take possession of it as British property, according to the same proclamation. He tells us that he was mistaken for the president and was made to attend the sealing up of the various rooms. The next morning he was brought back to Douay and placed in the Scotch College with the others, his first attempt thus ending in failure.

In the meantime, the English College was left at the mercy of the people. "The doors were thrown open for three days," writes Dr. Poynter, "during which part of the furniture was sold, and the rest of the goods that could be easily moved and carried off was plundered by the mob." On the Wednesday following, an order was given for the collegians to be taken to Doullens, a town in Picardy, to be there imprisoned in the citadel. We are told that "Mr. President was indulged with a coach," and the others, including Prior Sharrock and five Benedictine monks, followed in a train of eight waggons, under the escort of dragoons and gendarmes. They set out soon after one o'clock, and a long afternoon's drive followed, as they had to reach Arras, a distance of some twenty miles, that evening. The guards allowed those who chose to get down from their waggons and walk, and most of them profited by the permission. This was advantageous for any that had thoughts of escaping; but the road between Douay and Arras being of the common French type, straight and without hedge or fence, and the country quite flat, such a proceeding was not easy. In the case of Mr. Coombes, the shortness of his sight formed an additional obstacle, and though he made frequent attempts to slip away unobserved, walking from one waggon to another, and conversing with the different guards in turn, he was for a long time unsuccessful, and was beginning to despair, when a favourable opportunity presented itself, of which he at once took advantage. He describes it as follows:—

"It was evening. The waggons were at some distance from each other, and the attention of the guards was, of course, more divided, or, what is more probable, their vigilance was considerably relaxed. We had just entered a village situated at the bottom of a considerable declivity; while some of the waggons advanced and by the irregularity of the road were soon out of sight, the rest were gently proceeding down the hill. I embraced this happy moment; alone and unperceived retired to a poor habitation on the side of the road and begged the favour of enjoying the comfort of a fire. A poor honest woman, the wife of a day labourer, and her aged parent gave me a kind reception; the door was shut, and I seated myself by the fire.

"Here I remained in some agitation, while the prisoners and guards were passing by the door; fortunately, no one entered the house at this critical moment, when I might have been easily discovered. The name of this village is St. Laurent; it is but a small distance from Arras, at which place the prisoners soon arrived. The gates of that town were shut at an early hour and I was relieved from the apprehension of being pursued."

The most difficult part of Mr. Coombes' undertaking was now accomplished; but he had still before him the task of getting across the frontier. In order to effect this, he set out from St. Laurent at about ten o'clock the same night and walked to Equerchin, and thence to a little village two miles further on, called Flers, which he reached the following morning. Whilst here, he heard that two others[1] had escaped between Douay and Arras, and had arrived at a farm-house hard by. He joined them, and the three together started to cross the frontier the next evening. Their first attempt was not successful. The canal which flows from Lille to Douay lay between them and the frontier and the bridges were all guarded. They tried a place where formerly a boat used to be stationed, but it had been removed, and they returned to their farm-house before daybreak. Nor were their troubles over yet. The next day it was reported that "emigrés" were taking refuge in the village, and, in anticipation of a search, Mr. Coombes and his companions were advised to take refuge in a small barn, where they hid themselves behind a pile of straw. Here they spent

[1] John Devereux and John Rickaby.

what Mr. Coombes describes as a "long and tedious day, in silence, darkness and sorrow." Evening came at last, and again they set out. This time they were more successful. By means of an old ladder, which they fixed to the remains of a broken bridge, they managed to climb across the canal, and after walking all night, at four o'clock on the morning of the 20th of October, they were pronounced to be in a place of safety.

Of Mr. Coombes's subsequent movements we are only briefly informed. He arrived at Tournay on Sunday, October 20th, and went thence to Brussels and Louvain to visit some friends, who were much astonished to see him. He arrived in London a few weeks later.

We must now return to the narrative of what happened to the rest of the students and professors after Mr. Coombes left them. The first part can be given in the words of Richard Thompson, who himself escaped about a month later, and was at Old Hall by the end of the year. He wrote to Dr. Douglass from Louvain on December 11th, as follows :—

"Mr. Coombes, I presume, informed you of everything till his happy escape, soon after which we arrived at Arras and had the soldiers' barracks assigned to us for our night's repose. But an alarm arising that the soldiers had left behind them a garrison of vermin, we reposed as well as we could in the open court, in carts, coaches or wherever we could please ourselves the best. Mr. President, for example, in a coach, Mr. Vice-President walking in the court, Mr. Prefect in an open cart. Arriving the following evening at the citadel of Doullens, we were drawn up in battle array and marched into a sally-port under the ramparts—a ci-devant necessaries for the soldiers—covering the ground with a little straw, which the generous republic granted us at eight sous a bundle, after a booty of all our beds and other possessions. Here you would naturally conclude that we passed a long and unhappy night ; long indeed, but not miserable, for never, I am persuaded, did either our superiors or the boys pass a more merry and sportful night at Equerchin, neither will they ever forget the night in the black hole. Having remained there till about eleven the next morning, we were removed thence into a garret, from one extremity into another; for as we were that night placed on the bare ground, so the next we were on the top of the chateau, as it is termed, where we remained for a fortnight, exposed on every side to wind and rain. The extent of the garret was just sufficient to contain straw for forty-seven of us, each about a foot in breadth. If the wind blew, we were forced, as I may say, to hold fast our blankets, for these our generous district had allowed us, or rather overlooked in the common hurry. If we wished to enjoy daylight, which they could scarce deprive us of, we had to open little square wooden doors, for those were our windows, and as the building was lately raised, the wind burst in on every side by the chinks, slates and other such places. Such was our church, such our dormitory, study-place and refectory; which last was least wanted, for regular meals we had none for some few days at first, but ate whenever we could beg or buy a little bread, without regard to the colour, white, brown, black, or purple, for we ate all sorts indifferently.

"In this lodging we passed our time from the 18th of October till St. Charles' day, when we changed our apartment for another below stairs, not indeed exposed to the inclemency of the weather, but less commodious as it was of less extent. But you must remark that all these disadvantages are not without some advantages, for we have a court to play in, not less than our garden at Douay. We have likewise lately obtained, by repeated petitions to the Department and District of Douay, Department, District and Committee of the Public of Dourlens, and to Citizen Dumont the Commissary in those parts, an allowance of bread, viz. a loaf of six pounds every four days to . . . .[1] not of the best sort, nor is it distributed regularly, for we do not receive it oftener than every six or seven days. Other allowances they likewise expect to be granted very shortly. But I fear they have too good an opinion of French generosity. At present they generally procure, but at an excessive rate, a little meat for dinner, and hope that may not fail them, as most other things have

[1] Here a few words are torn off.

already failed the town. Such, indeed, are the difficulties and hardships they have to encounter, but they have wherewith to gain the victory, for, so far are they from yielding by discontent and grief, they show a courage and alacrity able to subdue every enemy they may meet."

For the first six weeks of the imprisonment nothing of importance occurred to break the monotony, but the finances were gradually getting low, and they were beginning to be in great straits. Some were already selling their watches and other valuables, when a curious coincidence brought them relief.

Among some prisoners who were being marched through the town was an old servant of the English College of St. Omer, who recognized Mr. Wilds, one of the Douay professors (afterwards a professor of St. Edmund's), having seen him once when he was on a visit to St. Omer. An opportunity was thus afforded of communicating with Dr. Stapleton, then imprisoned in that city in the French College. It was not considered safe to talk to this man for any length of time, but a hurried note was written by Mr. Daniel, and afterwards safely delivered, in which the difficulties in which they were placed were described. On receipt of this letter Dr. Stapleton lost no time in communicating with friends in England, which he was fortunately able to do without much difficulty, his confinement being at that time less strict; and after this they were kept supplied with money at regular intervals.

During the early part of the imprisonment it had not been considered safe to attempt the celebration of Mass. After a time, when they became more accustomed to their situation, they became at the same time bolder, and began to think of venturing on a secret Low Mass. The necessary appurtenances had been brought by the Benedictines.[1] To serve for an altar, one of the windows was unhinged and supported horizontally. On it was placed the altar stone. For fear of creating suspicion, they did not rise any earlier than usual, but at the accustomed time all knelt as quietly as possible on

---

[1] The chalice used on these occasions is now at St. Gregory's, Downside, the lineal descendant of St. Gregory's, Douay.

their straw beds, and the Holy Sacrifice was offered by Prior Sharrock.

Mass was said in prison for the first time on the Feast of All Saints. There was still, however, no possibility of confession, as Doullens, being in a different diocese from Douay, the priests had now no longer any faculties. To remedy this, an escape party was formed, to endeavour to communicate with the Bishop of Amiens, in whose diocese Doullens was situated, and who was at that time living in exile at Tournay. Four of the students[1] volunteered to undertake the errand, and a word was agreed upon to be communicated, as a signal that the necessary permission was granted.

The ramparts at Doullens are easily accessible from the interior, but the wall is some forty or fifty feet high outside. For their escape, therefore, it was first necessary to elude the sentinels so as to reach the ramparts. This was successfully accomplished on November 24th about dusk by the assistance of the main body of students, who managed to form themselves into a temporary screen between the sentinels and the fugitives ; and when it was dark a rope, which they had obtained from a French gentleman, was securely fixed at the top of the wall. They all descended successfully except Mr. Blakoe, who slipped, and fell a distance of more than twenty feet. He did not lose his hold completely, and managed to guide himself as he fell, but was severely hurt, and unable to accompany the others. Having left him at the house of a hospitable neighbour, therefore, they went on their way, and crossed the frontier in safety a day or two later. Mr. Blakoe followed by easy stages, and could not have been very long delayed, as we hear of him calling on Dr. Douglass in London on December 11th.

The letter from the Bishop of Amiens containing the word agreed upon was safely delivered to Mr. Daniel on Christmas Eve, and the afternoon was spent by all in preparing for the Sacraments. On Christmas Day Mass was again celebrated

---

[1] Robert Blakoe, Richard Thompson, John Clarkson, and William Lucas.

with a general Communion, which order was afterwards observed every Sunday till the end of the captivity.

Early in the year 1794 there were some further escapes. On the 15th of January two students[1] got away in a similar manner to the previous party, but were assisted from the top by Thomas Cock. After fording the river breast-deep near Doullens on a cold winter's night, they walked on for about twenty-four hours without stopping, and succeeded in reaching Equerchin on the evening of the 16th.

Mr. Stout, the prefect, was much distressed when he heard that they were gone, as he thought that those who stayed behind would be made to suffer for it. He said, however, that they would probably suffer as much for the escape of two as for twenty, and urged on any who had thoughts of going that now was their time. Eight others, therefore, went the following night.[2] Some of their number were very young, and for this reason they had been previously dissuaded from trying to escape. One of them, Thomas Cock, in order to prove his own powers of endurance, had for several days walked for five or six hours consecutively about the citadel, and he now became the leader of the party of adventurers.

Having been provided with bread, wine, and brandy in as great plenty as possible, they set out soon after sunset, and succeeded in descending the rope without any accident. Guided by the light of the moon, which was nearly at the full, they walked on all night across ploughed fields, not wishing to trust themselves to the road. The moon set at about five o'clock, and when daybreak arrived they found that one of their party, Thomas Storey, was missing. It was evidently useless to stay and search for him, and they therefore continued their journey, coming in sight of Arras just as the clock was striking twelve. Getting past Arras was the most difficult part of their undertaking. They accomplished it in safety by means of directions previously obtained from a French fellow-prisoner at Doullens, but it took them more

---

[1] Charles Thompson and Stephen Philips.
[2] John Canning, Thomas Lupton, John Bates, John Eldridge, John Bradley, Thomas Storey, William Veal, and Thomas Cock.

than three hours. Once on the other side they went on more briskly, and some reached Equerchin that night. One or two missed their way, and when the sun rose again found themselves close to Douay; but now they were in a country they knew, and they did not take long to reach Equerchin, where they found Thompson and Philips. At ten o'clock Storey also arrived, and they were all reunited.

After resting that day, they set forward again at nightfall, accompanied this time by guides who were to conduct them over the frontier. These men demanded exorbitant pay, and as there was nothing for it but to give what was asked, several of the students had to part with their watches. After walking several hours they were pronounced to be on the "neutral ground," between the outposts of the two armies, and an hour or two later they were practically safe. Their subsequent adventures are thus recorded by Dr. Douglass in his diary:—

"The aforesaid gentlemen on arriving at Tournay were recommended by the governor to Mr. Nill, English commissioner, who gave them four guineas for their journey to Ghent, and a letter of recommendation to Mr. Matt, who introduced them to the Duke of York, whose headquarters were then at Ghent. The Duke made each of them a present of ten pounds to help them on their journey to England. The aforesaid young men looked well in the face and appeared to be in good health, but were truly *sans culottes* in dress. They confirmed the account given by Mr. Clarkson and others that our friends at Doullens have money enough, and that when they have been straitened in food that evil arose from the general scarcity of provisions."

Twenty-four hours elapsed before the escape of the ten boys became known to the authorities at Doullens. The *commandant*, when he heard of it, was very angry, and tried to frighten those who were left with a story of the fugitives having been captured and taken to Bethune. Though few believed what he said, anxiety as to their fate continued for some days. The high road to Arras was visible from the citadel, and anxious watch was kept for fear of seeing them return under escort. As day after day passed away these fears were gradually dispelled, and before long news arrived of all having reached England in safety. Henceforward, however, the vigilance of the guards was much increased, and the liberty of the prisoners so far curtailed that further escapes were impossible. Their number was by now brought down to twenty-six, together with six Benedictines, making up the "Trente-deux," by which name they were in future known. Their names were frequently called out, and they were warned that if any were missing the others would suffer.

Nothing further of importance happened till the unexpected arrival of Dr. Stapleton and the other prisoners of St. Omer about the middle of the following May, and we must interrupt our narrative in order to say something of the former sufferings of these men. The only connected account extant of what they went through is in a letter from a former student, which was in the possession of the late Mr. Charles Corney. The letter has already been published in full,[1] and is the chief authority for what here follows.

It seems that the pretext for the first attack on the English College at St. Omer was a forged letter, alleged to have been written by one of the College professors, and the arrest made on the strength of this came without warning of any sort. There were at that time eleven professors and about fifty boys. Two hundred soldiers entered the College on August 1st, 1793, and, taking the president and professors, led them off to the French College, which was adjacent to their own, and there imprisoned them. A fortnight later three commissaries from the National Convention arrived at St. Omer, and the professors were brought up before them one by one and examined, their answers being taken down in writing. The Rev. Francis Tuite, the procurator, used in after life at St. Edmund's to relate with tears in his eyes his cross-examination at this interview.

*Q.* "Have you ever been to Paris?"
*A.* "Yes."
*Q.* "More than once?"

[1] "Haydock Papers," pp. 143—161.

*A.* " Yes, several times."

*Q.* " What was your object in going ? "

*A.* " Sometimes business, sometimes pleasure."

*Q.* " You must have been at times, then, amongst the enemies of the nation. What was then your conversation ? "

*A.* " I spoke as became a Christian."

Here he made the sign of the cross.

" Then you may go."

" I left," he would add, " with my heart in my mouth, not knowing whether I was to go back to prison or to the guillotine."

In the meantime the boys had been confined in their college, and five French priests were sent in to teach them. These priests had taken the constitutional oath, and were therefore schismatical, so that the boys did not feel bound to obey them, and they seem to have regarded this as an opportunity for playing all sorts of pranks. The following is the description given in Mr. Corney's MS. :—

"The same day the French masters entered the house bustle and tumult began to break forth. Their behaviour was exceedingly obliging, but the French and English characters constitute a distinction which can never be combined, never act in concurrence. We had agreed when they were first introduced to study regularly two hours every school day, but in those two hours very little was done; some ran out of the study place, others remained idle, all was bustle and confusion. On recreation days the boys used to form into different parties and run all over the house; when the masters were at one end of a gallery, run to the other, and abuse them in the most insulting and contemptuous language. Whenever a bustle became serious, the sentinels were immediately called forth. . . . One morning they were determined to punish us and deprive us of our breakfasts, but all their endeavours would have proved ineffectual, had not the guards come forward to their assistance and driven us from the refectory, who repented afterwards for their interference, and assured us that they would never come forward again on a similar occasion. We found afterwards from experience that they kept their word. As soon as we were expelled the refectory we ran all together into the garden and formed into two ranks. The master was parading before us, quite pale with fury; the Marseillaise

ENGLISH COLLEGE, ST. OMER—BIRD'S-EYE VIEW.
From an engraving in the Bibliothèque Nationale, Paris.

hymn was struck up, and those parts where liberty came in, such as "Liberté, liberté, chérie," were sung in the most extravagant and exulting strain. Whenever the master turned his head he was kindly saluted with a stone or two, whilst the guards were well acquainted with all that passed. At last the boys thought proper to break up.

"When our masters in the French College were allowed to walk in the garden we spoke to them over the wall that separated the two colleges,[1] and Mr. Stapleton exhorted us to continue these tumults, and encouraged us in our insubordination. . . . All the time that we were under [the] jurisdiction [of the French masters], scarce a day passed without some new scene of disorder . . . . so that the municipality was obliged to dismiss them and return us some of ours, whom we received, after we had heard their voices, with the loudest expressions of satisfaction. These few were restored to us about two months after the first imprisonment. From that time till we were all united in the French College, one whole month intervened, which we spent in the greatest quiet and subordination, so great was the change occasioned by the difference of masters and dispositions."

Throughout the winter the prisoners were fairly well treated, and we have already seen that Dr. Stapleton had sufficient means of communication with England to be of substantial service to those who were at Doullens. This state of things was not destined to last. Early in the month of January an order arrived that they were to be transferred to Arras, which was known to be one of the towns where the Revolution was raging most violently. The transfer was made, as usual, in waggons. One or two escaped during the journey, but this was by no means so easy for them as it had been for the Douay students, owing to the greater distance from the frontier.

The imprisonment at Arras lasted rather more than four months, during which they were confined to three different places in succession, and endured very great hardships. Such, indeed, was the distress they suffered that Mr. Hodgson speaks of their subsequent situation at Doullens as being liberty and happiness by comparison. During the early part of the time, Dr. Chester, of St. Omer, who had himself succeeded in getting safely back to England, reported that they

[1] That is, the wall on the right-hand side of the garden in the picture.

were confined in the house of the Orphelins, "distressed for clothing, ill-fed, and had only straw to lie on." He added that a cargo of cheese, which he and Mr. Brown Mostyn had sent to them from St. Omer, was received; but that a hamper of wine despatched at another time had been seized by the guards, and the bearer of it menaced with imprisonment.

According to Mr. Corney's MS., on one particular night it was actually intended to massacre all of them, and this would have been done but for the friendly assistance of the jailer, who testified to their being orderly and well-behaved. Mr. Cleghorn used to tell a story which probably refers to the same occasion. According to his account, some of the collegians were condemned to be guillotined, and the usual red mark which used to be affixed overnight was painted on the doors of several, including his own and those of Dr. Stapleton and Mr. Tuite. In some way this came to his knowledge, or he strongly suspected it, and he thought within himself what he should do. He had already succeeded once before in getting out of his cell, by what means is not exactly known. It is said that he was able to remove the receiver of his bolt; but it is more probable that he had some understanding with the jailer. On this occasion he again succeeded in getting out, and by means of a liberal offer of money he again secured the assistance of the jailer, who spoke on their behalf as already stated above.

The imprisonment at Arras came to an end in May, when an order arrived for all the St. Omer prisoners, collegiate or otherwise, to be transferred to Doullens. This was very acceptable to Dr. Stapleton and his students. Their arrival at Doullens took place at ten o'clock at night, and came as a pleasant surprise to the Douay collegians. We are told that, dark as it was, old friends recognized each other, and all that was possible at that late hour was done to refresh and comfort them.

During the time which followed, the prisoners from the two colleges were kept in separate quarters, and went through their daily routine separately. They were, however, allowed to see each other in the daytime and cheer each other in their troubles. In the hours of recreation things seem to have become wonderfully lively, considering all the circumstances of the case, and we read of daily games of Leap-frog and Prisoners' Base, to the no small astonishment of the French prisoners and guards.

The Revolution was now at its height. The country was daily drenched in blood, and massacres in different towns were of continual occurrence. When things seemed at their worst came the sudden fall of Robespierre. The relief was at once perceptible. Those in power became more moderate and humane, and the English prisoners were treated with some consideration. The use of the upper citadel was granted almost at once, the advantage of which was much appreciated; for several of the more elderly, including Mr. Daniel and Prior Sharrock, had begun to feel the effects of the hardships they had undergone, and sickness was making its appearance. One of the St. Omer professors, the Rev. Richard Brettargh, sank under it, and died on July 24th, 1794. This was the only death among the collegians in prison, and the facilities now granted, together with improvement in their lodgings, did much to drive away sickness.

The following anecdote concerning Dr. Poynter, relating to about this time, taken from a letter of the Rev. John Penswick,[1] will be of interest to Edmundians:—

"When our restrictions in matters of space and recreation ground, which had been imposed on account of the escape of so many of our companions, and to prevent the flight of more, had been somewhat relaxed, and a wider circuit had been conceded for air and exercise, Mr. Poynter, profiting by this indulgence, ascended the walled ramparts which separated the two citadels, and in full view of both, calmly, quietly, and composedly recited there for a time, almost daily, the divine office. His purpose appeared to us to be twofold, viz. to testify by this noble demonstration his obedience to God in almost the worst times, his adherence to his own personal duties, irrespective of consequences to himself, and to

[1] "Haydock Papers," p. 123.

console and reanimate the faltering courage of so many French captives, to whom hope had become almost an entire stranger. If such were his object, he succeeded. When better times followed, they often expressed to us their great admiration of his noble conduct, and their grateful thanks for the well-timed edification he had given them."

As time went on the situation of the prisoners continued to improve; and petitions were ventured on to the authorities of Douay and St. Omer respectively, to permit the students to return to their own towns, this being considered the first step towards getting back to England. Towards the middle of October the St. Omerians received a favourable answer, and on the morning of the 20th of that month Dr. Stapleton, with his ten professors and fifty boys, mounted their waggons outside the wicket gate of the citadel, and with joyful hearts took leave of Doullens. As they started off they gave a loud cheer, in which the "Trente-deux," who were still kept back, heartily joined. As they disappeared from view they were heard singing the psalm "In exitu Israel de Ægypto." On arriving at St. Omer they were still kept prisoners, and were in the French College, where they had been before, but they were better treated, and their condition was in every way much improved.

A month later similar orders came from Douay for the "Trente-deux" to return, and on the 24th of November they set out from Doullens Citadel, where they had been confined for a period of thirteen months. After sleeping the first night at Arras as before, on the following evening they were once more at Douay. This time the Irish College was allotted to them, but the Benedictines were allowed to return to their own house. Although still prisoners, they were no longer treated with any great severity. All had mattresses to sleep on instead of straw, each was provided with a new suit of clothes, books were more plentiful, and mass was said daily.

This state of things lasted about a month. At the end of that time a further relaxation was obtained under a curious pretext, one which will command the sympathy of all boys.

It was no more nor less than a skating play-day. The frost had lasted some days, the ice was strong, and it was well known at Douay how fond the English boys were of the pastime of skating. Leave was granted them, therefore, to go out, on the express promise, which was readily given, that no advantage should be taken of it to attempt to escape. On the 21st of December, 1794, therefore, the students were once more at large, and probably no day's skating was ever more appreciated. This permission to leave the College was never afterwards withdrawn, and the students were allowed to go out for walks daily.

All were now looking forward to the time when they might be set at liberty, and be allowed to return to their country, but in the then state of France it was no easy matter to obtain such a permission. The overcoming of difficulties in the way was nearly three months' work, and was due to the energy and perseverance of one man, the Rev. Gregory Stapleton. This we learn from the sequel to Mr. Hodgson's narrative, which appeared in the *Catholic Magazine* for August and September, 1831,[1] without any signature, but supposed to have been written by Dr. Poynter:—

"All these difficulties were surmounted," he says, "by the ability and address of the Reverend Gregory Stapleton, President of St. Omer's College. In the beginning of the following year, 1795, this gentleman obtained leave to go to Paris, to present to the men in power a petition[2] for the release of the two colleges. After many repulses, he at length succeeded in his object. By remonstrance, by entreaty, and by the more powerful influence of money, he obtained from the Directory an order addressed to the magistrates of St. Omer's and Douay, empowering them to release from imprisonment the citizens, ex-members of the two *ci-devant* English colleges, and to furnish them with passports to return to England. Prior Sharrock and his five companions were included in the Douay list.

[1] p. 461.
[2] This petition had been drawn up by him at Doullens, and was signed by all the members of the two colleges and by the Benedictine monks.

"We shall never forget the impression made on our minds," he continues, "by the unexpected arrival of Mr. Stapleton at the door of our prison at Douay, on his return from Paris. During the hesitation and delay of the turnkey to admit Mr. Stapleton, we had nearly all heard of his arrival, and had assembled in the court to meet him. It was a moment of the most intense anxiety. He soon relieved us from our suspense. 'Good news, my boys,' said he; 'thank God, we are going to England.' I believe we never in the whole course of our lives experienced such lively emotions of joy; many of the collegians gave loud cheers of applause."

The next day Dr. Stapleton left for St. Omer, and on February 26th the "Trente-deux" bade their final farewell to Douay, and left in the usual train of waggons. After sleeping a night at Bethune, they arrived the next evening at St. Omer. Here they remained till Sunday, March 1st, when after hearing an early mass, they resumed their journey together with Dr. Stapleton and his party, reaching Calais the same night. The following day they crossed the Channel in an American vessel, and, after a somewhat rough passage, landed safely at Dover on the afternoon of Monday, March 2nd, 1795.

## CHAPTER VI.

### ARRIVAL OF THE FIRST DOUAY STUDENTS AT ST. EDMUND'S.

#### 1793—1794.

News of the fall of Douay reaches England—Discussions between the Vicars Apostolic—Preparations at Old Hall for the reception of the Douay refugees — St. Edmund's College established by Bishop Douglass on November 16th, 1793—Description of its state—First ordination—Arrangements for the Divines—The "Hermitage"—Proposal to remove the College to the north—The idea temporarily abandoned—The "Ship"—Further proposals by Bishop Gibson for a general college in the north—The project again given up—Disputes between northern and southern Divines—Bishop Gibson opens a college at Crook Hall, and recalls his students from St. Edmund's—Changes at Old Hall in consequence—Oscott College established—Landing of the collegians from Douay and St. Omer.

IN the diary of Bishop Douglass we find the following entries:—

"On the 9th of August, 1793, Mr. Daniel and all his subjects were expelled the College and banished to Equerchin. . . . . On the 12th of October they were recalled to town by the municipality to re-enter their college, under the pretext of preserving it from being turned into a barracks. They were immediately arrested and confined in the Scotch College, together with the Prior, Sub-Prior, and six of their subjects.[1] . . . On the 16th of October they were conveyed in waggons to Doullens, in Picardy. . . . Thus is *Alma Mater* lost, our property all confiscated, and our gentlemen under confinement. May our Father in heaven be their comfort and support! How will they be treated? . . . . We have not any communication or correspondence with them, *proh dolor!*"

[1] Bishop Douglass made a slight error here. The six Benedictines *included* the prior and sub-prior.

OLD HALL AND DOUAY COLLEGE IN 1793.

*Sketch drawn by George Leo Haydock, one of the earliest students who came from Douay to Old Hall, at the head of a letter to his brother.*

The following references are appended:—1, Fire School. 2, Dormitory. 3, Study-place. 4, Hall. 5, Boys' Dormitory. 6, Kitchen. 7, Chapel. 8, Highway. 9, Douay College.

Such is Bishop Douglass's short record of the news of the fall of Douay as it reached London. Its gravity could not be disguised. Few Catholics, indeed, regarded the College as finally lost to the English Mission; but for the time it was at an end, and Bishop Douglass saw plainly that if a supply of missioners was to be kept up, it would be necessary to take instant and immediate steps to provide a substitute and successor to the fallen College.

Already, during the summer months of 1793, many of the Douay students who left before the imprisonment had arrived in England. Others followed, having escaped either from Douay itself, or, like Mr. Coombes, on the road to Arras; and later on, again, those who succeeded in getting away from the citadel of Doullens reached London. Their first act was to call at Castle Street, and report themselves to Bishop Douglass. Thus the Rev. Thomas Varley, Dean of the Chapter, writes on November 13th, 1793:—

"The latter end of last month arrived Messrs. Monk, Rickaby, Penswick, Gillow, Devereux, Lancaster, Lee, Saul, Law, Worswick, and Coombs. Mr. Coombs stayed at Louvain, but is safe. They left behind them 43, all of which were arrested and sent to prison at Doullens, in Picardy. Pray God preserve them! Mr. Daniel had too much faith in the French about him; he has now time to repent for not sending all away." [1]

In anticipation of these arrivals, Bishop Douglass had already communicated with the other Vicars Apostolic. Of these, Bishop Gibson, of the Northern District, was the most important, owing to the comparative numerical strength of Catholics in Lancashire and Yorkshire, and apparently the first idea was to find a temporary shelter for the refugees in his part of the country. Writing on May 15th, 1793, to the Rev. Thomas Eyre, who was afterwards President at Crook Hall and Ushaw, he says: "Douay College is almost empty, as I hear, and students in philosophy and divinity are coming over every day. I am advised to take Flass Hall immediately

---

[1] "Haydock Papers," p. 168.

and begin. Bishop Douglass will pay half the rent. Unless we begin all will be dispersed."[1]

Bishop Walmesley, of the Western District, at first took the opposite view, and was against a college of any sort being started in England. The following are his words, in a letter to Bishop Douglass, dated January 4, 1793 :—

"In answer to your query, my opinion is that it will be more advantageous to the cause of religion to keep the colleges where they are than to remove them to England. In the first place, it will save a great expense, as they are in actual possession of houses properly fitted up for colleges, and may probably remain undisturbed, though alarmed; and if French Flanders should pass into the hands of the Austrians, perhaps it may fare better with the English colleges. Furthermore, studies would never be carried on so well in England as they are in their present situation— theological studies in particular, which are there publicly discussed; nor are the students called away by their parents to pass away part of their time with them, which would be the case were the colleges in England."

When Douay College was actually seized on the 12th of October of the same year, such considerations as the above ceased to have any force. The negotiations for Flass Hall had by this time fallen through, and Dr. Douglass determined to make a start immediately at Old Hall. At the same time he offered to receive as many of Dr. Gibson's students as he could find room for, and his offer was temporarily accepted. This we gather from a letter from the Rev. Henry Rutter to the Rev. Thomas Eyre, dated November 11, 1793, alluding to a previous communication. "It appears from your letter," he wrote, "that his lordship has not yet informed you that Flass is given up for Old Hall Green, which Bishop Douglass considers a more eligible place for our emigrant students. I think so, too, for the present moment, because everything is now ready to receive them; but if the plan is to establish a permanent college, the

---

[1] "Chapels of Ushaw," by the Rev. Henry Gillow, Historical Introduction, p. 22.

bishopric [Durham] seems a far more preferable situation."[1]

The advantages of Old Hall at that moment were several. The school was in full working order, and within easy reach of London; hence the refugees could resume their studies with less delay, and the junior students might join the classes already existing. But Bishop Douglass had also in his mind the idea of a future college there, to be engrafted on the school already in existence, so that a permanent substitute for Douay might be provided. He therefore communicated with Mr. Potier, who answered, on October 20th, that he was prepared to receive a dozen Douay students at a day's notice. A week later he wrote to say that he had got the north dormitory over the study place, which was at that time unoccupied, prepared for the new divines, as well as the attic above; while he added that Mr. Devereux, who was expected, was to have a room to himself, as, according to reports, he was "very large." "The garden and pleasure grounds may be appropriated for their place of recreation without any difficulty," he said, but he regretted that the Hall was too much broken by doors, etc., to admit of long tables, and that therefore the divines would not be able to be placed all together, as he would have liked.

On the question of the formation of a staff of professors greater difficulties presented themselves. "I am very glad to hear that so many have escaped from Douay," he wrote; "I wish one of the superiors had come with them. Mr. Hodgson or Mr. Poynter might have taught them divinity, and at the same time have acted as their immediate superior. This would have been a great means of keeping them separate from the children, etc., which, as your Lordship is aware, is absolutely necessary." Though the seniors were still in prison, however, two of the professors had escaped; the Rev. John Lee, a deacon, professor of Syntax, and the Rev. W. H. Coombes, whose adventures were described in the last chapter. The former was a subject of Bishop Douglass, and there was no difficulty in securing his services.

[1] Ibid, p. 24.

Mr. Coombes, on the other hand, belonged to the Western District, and his bishop, Dr. Walmesley, when he heard of his escape, had marked him out for the Plymouth mission, which was just then vacant. As he seemed the only man capable of teaching theology whilst the others were in prison, Bishop Douglass wrote an urgent letter to Bishop Walmesley on his behalf, and, after some demur, the latter consented to part with him, if he himself wished it. "I am very sensible," he wrote, "of your reasons for having Mr. Coombes for master to your young divines, and we ought to be ready to help one another.... On that account I have left him to settle the affair with your Lordship." Mr. Coombes therefore arrived at Old Hall before the end of the year.

Dr. Douglass did not wait for the northern students before making a commencement, but himself proceeded to Old Hall on the 12th of November, exactly one month after the fall of Douay, and there got together the first four Edmundian church students. The inauguration of the new work is thus described by him, in his diary:—

"1793. On the 12th of November I took Messrs. William Beauchamp and John Law to Old Hall, and on the 16th, the Feast of St. Edmund, Archbishop of Canterbury, we commenced studies or established the new College there, a substitute for Douay. Mr. Thomas Cook, who had been at Old Hall Green half a year, employed in teaching the children, and Mr. John Devereux joined the other two.

"These four communicated at my hands. I said Mass, and after Mass exposed the Blessed Sacrament; and these four, with Mr. Potier, sang the 'O Salutaris,' 'Pange Lingua,' 'Deus misereatur nostri' and 'Laudate Dominum omnes gentes,' ad finem.

"Thus was the new College instituted under the patronage of St. Edmund, Archbishop of Canterbury, the aforementioned students recommencing their studies in divinity. Felix faustumque sit!"

Here we have the foundation of St. Edmund's as an

ecclesiastical college to succeed and carry on the work of the fallen College of Douay. It was a small and humble beginning, and in one sense far less worthy of the occasion than the more solemn reopening nearly two years later, when the priests from Douay and St. Omer had arrived. But the earlier occasion is the more interesting of the two, simply because it was the beginning of a new state of things. For more than two hundred years no ecclesiastical training had been attempted in England, all those who aspired to the priesthood being sent for their education to a foreign country. The establishment of St. Edmund's was the first sign of better times, and the unpretending Benediction service in the little chapel behind the "Old Hall" was the beginning of the restoration of colleges and seminaries throughout England.

What Bishop Douglass's precise ideas were at this time as to the future of Old Hall we can only conjecture. The fate of the prisoners at Doullens was as yet full of uncertainty. "The Seniors will not attempt to escape," he writes, "being determined to abide with the President," and he must have felt that nothing very permanent could be settled till their release—if, indeed, they were fortunate enough ever to be released. Mr. Potier therefore continued at the head of St. Edmund's as a temporary arrangement, pending the further development of affairs in France.

Fresh students continued to arrive during November and December, and in the early part of the following year. Mr. Coombes did not come until nine days before Christmas, for he wished to visit his relations in the West of England, and, moreover, it was necessary for him to see his bishop, Dr. Walmesley, before he could arrange to accept the post at St. Edmund's. On returning to London he called on Bishop Douglass on the 11th of December, and his affairs having been satisfactorily settled, they drove down together five days later.

By the end of February, 1794, there were twenty-one Douay men at St. Edmund's, of whom six belonged to the northern district. The names of these, the first church students and professors of St. Edmund's, deserve to be recorded :—

Rev. William H. Coombes (late Professor of Rhetoric at Douay).

Rev. John Lee, deacon (late Professor of Syntax at Douay).

Rev. John Law, deacon.

Messrs. William Beauchamp, James Delaney, Robert Freemont, Francis Bowland, Edward Peach, John Devereux, Charles Saul, Richard Thompson, John Clarkson, Thomas Gillow, Thomas Cook, Edward Monk, Thomas Penswick, George Leo Haydock, William Lucas, Thomas Pitchford, John Eldridge, and William Veal. There was also one church student (Mr. Frene) from Rome, and one from Lisbon. The total, therefore, including Mr. Coombes and Mr. Lee, was twenty-three, which, added to some thirty lay boys of Mr. Potier's, made a community of over fifty.

An interesting account of the beginning of this new period has been handed down to us in a letter from George Leo Haydock, dated Old Hall Green, December 19th, 1793, and addressed to his brother,[1] from which the following is a quotation :—

"The regulations we here observe are not quite settled on a firm foundation, so that I can only inform you of some particulars. We rise at 6 o'clock, go to church at ye half hour, and meditate out of Bp. Challoner in ye same manner as during ye retreat at Douay. At 7 study divinity till 8 when we all repair to hear prayers or mass[2] with the boys, who do not bear us company in ye aforesaid meditation. At a quarter to 9 breakfast of milk and bread (tea on fasting days), study till 1, when a dinner equal to what we had at Douay *saltim* is served up. I had forgot that at half-past 11 we are to repair to school after ye Epiphany, Mr. Coombs, our master, who only came down with the bishop last Monday, having a desire to go as far as Bath to see his rela-

---

[1] "Haydock Papers," p. 164.
[2] The custom of calling mass "prayers" still survived at that time, a relic of days when it was not safe to use the word mass openly.

tions. This day he and Bp. Douglass examined us all on ye gospel of St. Matthew, but in fact rather answered himself than asked us questions. He is a person of ye most amiable character and seems to deserve ye love of everyone. He informed us that Mr. Potier (a man as good and agreeable as himself) was to be our head superior, and Mr. Coombs ye second in authority and respect. After dinner we play till 3, go to school at 5 till 6, common prayers for half an hour, supper at 8, music for half an hour to prepare for ye church, where we have sung ye offices and masses since our arrival here, to ye great satisfaction of ye auditors. At 10 we go to bed in ye dormitory, for we have no better accommodations, and indeed we may think well to have so good, when we consider ye sufferings our friends undergo at Doullens, where they have only a little straw to sleep on, and are forced to cover themselves with their old tattered coats, which now scarce defend them from ye injuries of ye weather."

The postscript is written in college language: "You'll excuse all inaccuracies and defects in this letter, considering that I am forced to write in ye hurry and confusion of a rumgumtious fire school."

In one page of this letter Mr. Haydock sketched side by side, in full contrast, the two Colleges of Douay and Old Hall Green in 1793. This drawing, here produced by kind permission of Mr. Joseph Gillow, cannot fail to be of great interest to Edmundians. Those who know the "Old College" will recognize it as practically unchanged outside at the present day. Under the sketch is an explanation of what the different rooms were used for at that date. The name "fire school" corresponds with what we should now call the play-room. The other names are clear enough, and will be seen to agree with what has been given in Chapter III. The road at that time passed near the building, as on the picture.

A few further details about these early days at St. Edmund's may be gathered from the marginal notes of the old Ordos. From these we learn that High Mass was sung on all great festivals, a solemnity then comparatively rare in

England; that on Christmas night there were Matins and Lauds at half-past ten, followed by Midnight Mass; that there were periodical solemn votive masses for the Douay collegians imprisoned at Doullens, and other such details. We learn also that even at this early date the feasts of St. Thomas of Canterbury, St. Gregory, and St. Charles Borromeo were observed as High Mass days, as they used to be at Douay. The annual retreat is mentioned as beginning on the Thursday of Passion week. We read also in an old letter that the Douay divines were strong fellows, and "took long walks to Bishop Stotford and Hartford," where chocolate was to be obtained.

On Monday, December 16th, Dr. Douglass paid the visit to Old Hall to which allusion has been made, and on Friday, December 27th, the Feast of St. John the Evangelist, he held his first ordination at which Mr. Lee was ordained priest and Messrs. Beauchamp, Bowland, and Peach subdeacons. A retreat was no doubt made by the *ordinandi*, which was a further reason for postponing the beginning of the theological classes till after the holidays. A commencement was then formally made, in presence of the Bishop, Mr. Coombes giving his first lecture on the sixth chapter of St. John's Gospel.

In the early part of January, 1794, difficulties arose between the new comers and Mr. Potier's boys. The former seem to have been a little rough, and as they were all together in the "fire school" during the hours of recreation, there was a certain amount of bullying, and gradually some ill feeling between the two sections. The following quotations, again from letters of Mr. Haydock,[1] are a little difficult to understand:—

"Being at ye fireside with us, Mr. Saul jokingly talked about cats, that one could pull a man through a pond. Thomas [Pitchford] would bet none could do so with him, so there was a trial, and with a little foul play ye cat was victor."

And again:—

[1] "Haydock Papers," p. 175.

"A cat with a rope fastened round ye middle of Thomas Pitchford, who had Clarkson for a friend, giving him a pinch of snuff on one side of ye shallow pond, while ye rest were holding ye cat on a blanket, and I was ye whipper in on ye other side, actually with some of their help drew him through, while he cried out 'I was not ready,' and for some time did not seem to find out ye trick."

The precise nature of this "trick" is not evident. A cousin of Thomas Pitchford who was at Old Hall at this time, writing half a century later, says, "Of the marvellous history of the cat, *non mi recordor*. If it really occurred, the cat must have been the Samson of his race to have carried away our cousin, who was strong and corpulent;" from which we may gather that he too was puzzled by the description. Whatever it was, to use Mr. Haydock's own expression, "it made Mr. Potier fear his little school would be hurt. He complained to ye Bishop, who next time he came did not visit ye divines as usual. He said, 'I am affronted. It was beneath ye dignity of ye lowest Lancashire lad.' Unlucky expression, as we were five from that county."

It was therefore determined to separate the boys from the divines. This had always appeared the natural course; the difficulty in the way had been want of accommodation. That was now met by clearing out the dormitory on the north side of the College, which with the attic above had been used by the divines, and giving them these two rooms as common room, class-room and refectory, and providing them with sleeping accommodation outside.

A small house existed a few yards north of the Old Hall known as "the Hermitage."[1] It was the property of Dr. Douglass, having been bought by Bishop Talbot with the other property, as stated in a previous chapter. Recently it had served as an infirmary for infectious cases. Here the Douay divines were temporarily lodged. As their numbers

---

[1] The Hermitage is still in existence, and will be known by older Edmundians as Martin Bennett's house, and by a later generation as that of Mr. McLaughlin, the lay professor. It is much more roomy than appears by the picture, as it extends some way at the back.

increased, this also became insufficient, and Mr. Potier wrote in this sense to Dr. Douglass on February 3rd, 1794:—
"Your letter concerning the escape of so many from Dourlens," he said, "put us all into high spirits. But we must now think of providing for them. As we shall not have room in the house, I suppose we shall be obliged to send the students in divinity to the workshop and stables in the Hermitage yard. I have examined them, and have enclosed a plan of what I

"THE HERMITAGE."

think may be done to them. It will be the least expensive thing I can think of. Additions must likewise be made to the chapel, which may be done by bringing a gallery from the tribune to the altar on the epistle side, and raising the sacristy to a level with the chapel, and making a tribune over it for the children, open and railed on each side of the altar."

The work of fitting up the outhouse was not put in hand at once, for it seemed about that time as if the newly founded college might have a very short existence. Bishop Gibson was doing all he could to secure a general college in his district. The chief advantages on which he insisted were, firstly, the cheapness of fuel and provisions, and, secondly, the greater seclusion consequent on the distance from London. Great difficulty was experienced in finding a suitable place in the north ; but at last he wrote saying that he had received an offer that he thought would prove advantageous. A consultation was held between Mr. Potier, Mr. Coombes, and Mr. Lee, and as a result, they reported to Bishop Douglass that they were unanimously of opinion " that we ought to embrace Bishop Gibson's proposal, if his representation of the offer turns out to be founded."

This *if* stood a long time in the way. Bishop Gibson seemed unable to write more definitely. " We cannot collect much from Bishop Gibson's letter," wrote Mr. Potier ; " he certainly ought to be more explicit at a time when everything seems to demand a speedy determination." A month later we find Dr. Douglass and Mr. Barnard drafting a set of rules for St. Edmund's, suited to its new existence ; so that we may conclude that by that time it appeared less likely that the College would be moved.

A few days later Bishop Gibson wrote again to say that his original offer had fallen through. The fitting up of the outhouse was accordingly begun, a work rendered quite necessary, owing to the arrival of other refugees, this time boys from the college of the ex-Jesuits at Liège. The new building supplied in all ten rooms, five on the ground floor and five on the first floor. A plan of it exists in Mr. Potier's writing. When it was ready, the divines moved in. The fact of its being built of wood, and being both small and uncomfortable, earned for it the common designation of " The Ship." About half the " Ship " is still standing, and is easily recognized in a corner of the " pleasure grounds " near the gas works. It has been strengthened by bricking in the lower part of the walls, but the upper portion still consists only of timber, and probably its appearance has not altered much. The other half was destroyed by fire some thirty-five years since.

The accommodation in the " Ship " must have been small

and inconvenient. It is not easy to imagine twenty divines sleeping in a place of this sort, and it speaks well for these the first church students of St. Edmund's that they went through it with so little complaint. They facetiously called the cells into which it was divided their coffins, and some of

"THE SHIP."

them declared in later days that the time they had spent in the "Ship" was the happiest in their lives.

About the beginning of the following May, Mr. Lee, the late Douay professor, left, his place being supplied by the Rev. John Law, then only a deacon. An ordination was held by Bishop Douglass in the month of June, at which Mr. Law was ordained priest, Messrs. Beauchamp, Bowland, and

Peach deacons, and Mr. Devereux sub-deacon. This function seems to have taxed Mr. Potier's supply of ecclesiastical vestments to the utmost. "We have only two surplices," he writes, "but we have four albs, two purple vestments with stoles and maniples belonging to same. There are girdles and amices enough, and a mitre, a mozetta and a rochet."

On May 17th Bishop Gibson wrote again with some further proposals. "I shall be at York," he said, "either on Saturday or Monday next, there to meet Sir John Lawson and some other gentlemen, when we expect to come to an agreement about the place we think will answer the best of any we can find for an establishment at present, till we build or purchase a better for the purpose, where the College may be finally established. Or perhaps we may agree not to purchase at present. I shall write to you during the course of the week on the subject. We do not think of Stella, now, as we cannot get the Hall. I did not mention the name in my last, nor was it mentioned in the paper, because we were not quite sure that it would be let to us. It is called 'Crooked Hall' (*sic*), a retired place about eleven miles from Durham; but it will be needless to mention it till you hear again, and know whether we fix on it or some other. It is in Bishopric."[1]

A month later we find that a further change had been made in Bishop Gibson's plans; Crook Hall had been given up, and in its place Tudhoe, a small school near Durham, kept by the Rev. Mr. Storey, substituted. In order to arrive at a final arrangement, Bishop Gibson went to London and saw Bishop Douglass, when matters were satisfactorily adjusted.[2] A printed appeal for funds was at the same time drawn up in the following terms :—[3]

"The unhappy events which have taken place in a neigh-

---

[1] i.e. Durham county.
[2] See a letter from Bishop Hay quoted in the Rev. J. F. Gordon's "Catholic Church in Scotland," p. 64.
[3] "Recollections of Ushaw," p. 67. One of the originals of this document is also among the Westminster archives, but without a date.

bouring country having deprived the English Catholics of the greater part of those places of education in which hitherto the succession of their clergy has been preserved, and to which also they have been accustomed to send their children for instruction, we, the undersigned Apostolic Vicars, have taken into our most serious consideration the dreadful consequences of such a failure to the rising generation; and we feel it to be our duty most earnestly to exhort and solicit the body at large to concur with us in supplying the said deficiency, by setting on foot a proper place of education in this kingdom from which the ecclesiastical ministry may be supplied, and in which the Catholic youth in general may receive a solid, pious, and learned education.

"An establishment for that purpose will be commenced immediately at Tudhoe, in the county of Durham, which for cheapness of fuel and provisions, healthiness of climate, and other considerations, has been deemed an eligible situation for such an undertaking.

"The plan of studies will be the same as that which was pursued in the English College at Douay. Such alterations only will be admitted as shall appear from circumstances to be advisable.

"To provide and furnish such a school must be attended with a considerable expense, far beyond our resources, without the assistance of the zealous and the charitable. We, therefore, earnestly exhort all Catholics, whom providence has blessed with the means, to concur with us in this plan for the support of our holy religion. And as the greatest part of those foundations on which a considerable number of the clergy have hitherto been gratuitously maintained during their studies is now lost in the general wreck of religious property in France, we are under the necessity of soliciting the zealous and opulent members of our body to remedy that evil, either by new foundations or by annual subscriptions for the important purpose.

"Contributions to the commencement or to the subsequent support of this establishment will be gratefully received at Messrs Wright and Co., bankers, Covent Garden, London, at Sir John Lawson and Co., bankers, Richmond, Yorkshire; and by the undersigned Apostolical Vicars.

"Right Rev. CHARLES WALMESLEY, Bath.
"Right Rev. WILLIAM GIBSON, York.
"Right Rev. JOHN DOUGLASS, London.

"London, June 20th, 1794."

From this it would seem that the scheme of a northern college was definitely determined on; but a little later further difficulties about Tudhoe arose, and gradually Bishop Douglass became less ready to move, and began to set his hopes for the future once more on St. Edmund's. He was strengthened in this frame of mind by letters from Dr. Coombes of Bath and Mr. Potier respectively. The former wrote on March 30th, 1794 :—

"I am happy to hear that your seminary at Old Hall goes on so well, and that my nephew gives satisfaction in his situation; at the same time I must confess to your Lordship that I am not quite so well satisfied with the plan I find in contemplation of removing the establishment into the north."

And again three months later:—

"Your Lordship cannot be ignorant of Bishop Gibson's ill management at Douay, how much he reduced the finances of that house by his extravagant conduct; and your Lordship may rely on it he will waste the small resources yet remaining for the support of the mission. . . . If the idea of continuing theological studies at Old Hall must be abandoned—of which I never could see the propriety—at least before that event takes place let there be a real and visible house procured that has greater advantage than the present. . . . In this view of circumstances, which your Lordship, I confide, must feel to be just, would it not be proper and necessary to prevent these impending evils, to inform Bishop Gibson without loss of time of your intentions of withdrawing your assent to the removal of the students from Old Hall ? No degree of blame or censure can possibly be affixed to your conduct on the occasion. For the conditions on which you gave your assent do not exist; the compact, of course, must be null. When I gave my consent to my nephew's going into the north it was under the conviction that the arrangement met with the perfect approbation of the Bishops, but since I see nothing but confusion and bad consequences likely to be the result of a northern establishment, I certainly wish my nephew to remain at Old Hall."

Mr. Potier in his letter touched on a consideration, the importance of which seems in those days to have been hardly realized:—

"The advantages of having a college in which our subjects may be educated, as it were, under your own eye are not to be forgotten. You may depend upon it, Bishop Gibson has an eye to this last in wishing to have it in the north. And if your Lordship should give up this point with too much facility, I think you will not be easily forgiven by your successors in the bishopric, even if you could ever be persuaded to forgive yourself."

In the end Bishop Douglass followed Dr. Coombes's advice, and withdrew his consent to taking part in founding a general college in the north. It is difficult to fix the precise date at which the negotiations were broken off. On August 16th Mr. Storey wrote from Tudhoe, saying that Bishop Gibson had at last found a house near there, and he hoped that a commencement would soon be made; from which it would appear that up to that time Bishop Douglass had not definitely withdrawn. His doing so must, therefore, have been between then and the date of the beginning made by Mr. Eyre three weeks later at Pontop, two miles from Crook Hall.

In the meantime further difficulties were in store for Mr. Potier. It appears that from the first considerable friction had existed between Bishop Douglass's students at Old Hall and those from the north. The latter were themselves anxious for a college to be opened in their part of the country, feeling that as Lancashire was by far the most Catholic county, they had some right to have it in that district rather than in the south. Nevertheless, the excuse they gave was that they were not well treated where they were. A petition was got up and signed by the northern students, asking Bishop Gibson to remove them to his district. The reasons alleged were the want of accommodation at Old Hall, the insufficiency of the food, both as to quality and quantity, and absence of facilities for continuing their studies. In addition to this, it was pointed out that there was no strict discipline nor regular hours for study, and, as a result, a complete absence of the ecclesiastical spirit. This last they said they felt so strongly that if they stayed there much longer there would be a great danger of their all losing their vocations, as had already happened in the case of two of their number.[1]

There was doubtless some ground for complaint; it could hardly have been otherwise. It had been difficult enough to provide any accommodation at all for the refugees at such short notice, and with the French prisons fresh in the memory of many of them, it might surely have been not unreasonably expected that some readiness would have been shown to put up with such inconveniences as were inevitable under the circumstances. It would seem that such was the case with the majority, and that the discontent was confined to a few; for when Mr. Gillow, as their spokesman, stated to Mr. Potier what they considered their grievances, the latter at once asked the significant question, "Is it the gentlemen of the north or the gentlemen of the south that complain?" Mr. Gillow said it was both; but failing to get what he considered a satisfactory answer, he took advantage of the absence of Mr. Coombes one day, to draw out the petition referred to, which was signed by all the northern students except Edward Monk. Some, however, of those who signed it did so un-

---

[1] William Lucas and Robert Freemont. Of the former, Mr. Potier had said that he had a large share of roughness and a small share of piety, and that he seemed better fitted to be a soldier than a priest. On leaving St. Edmund's he entered the army. Of Robert Freemont, the story goes that he was given as his sleeping apartment a room known as "The Sulphur-room," which had previously been a bath room, and that one day looking round him, and noting the scantiness of his furniture, and the fact that even his bed covering consisted in great measure of his own clothing, he said to himself "Roberte, tolle grabatum tuum et ambula;" and, packing up his few possessions, he went.

willingly, as George Leo Haydock, who afterwards regretted what he had done. "We had too much indulgence and liberty," he wrote. "I was quite content. Some, however, concocted a letter, and Mr. Penswick came and persuaded me to sign it."[1]

Whether this petition or round robin had any effect on Bishop Gibson we can only conjecture, for it is clear that he had already made up his mind to open a college in the north if it could possibly be managed. For this purpose a few students were got together at Pontop Hall, the mission-house of the Rev. Thomas Eyre, who, in a letter to Dr. Poynter thirteen years afterwards, dates the commencement from September 9th, 1794. A month later Crook Hall was obtained, where the new institution rested some fourteen years. At the commencement there was one student in Philosophy, one in Rhetoric, and four in Poetry. Before the end of the year they were joined by the northern students from Old Hall and others, bringing the total up to fourteen, all of whom were Douay refugees. The Rev. Thomas Eyre came with the students to Crook and became its first President, with the Rev. John Lingard, the future historian, then a subdeacon, as Vice-President.

The northern students at Old Hall were recalled at the beginning of November. After signing the petition to be removed, they made no great attempt to settle down, having evidently made up their minds that they could not remain there much longer. Mr. Potier wrote to Bishop Douglass on October 14th: "We have had no news whatsoever from the north. The northern divines are quiet but not contented. . . . The day after the unlucky affair mentioned, Mr. Gillow came to me and wished me to acquaint your Lordship that they could never make themselves happy here, and wished by all means to go to the north." At the same time Mr. Potier also wrote to Bishop Gibson, "entreating for a definite answer, is it your Lordship's intention to leave your subjects at this place, or is it your intention to call them to the north?"

[1] "Haydock Papers," p. 173.

This letter was regarded by the Bishop as an ultimatum, and he forthwith decided to remove his students. Mr. Potier, of course, regretted this decision, and wrote to Bishop Douglass in this sense. "I was sorry to find by Mr. Coombes," he said, "that Bishop Gibson had enforced the necessity of their leaving this place by a palpable misinterpretation of my letter." The decision once come to, however, was soon put into execution. Messrs. Gillow and Haydock left on the 30th of October, and went first to London, where they saw Bishop Douglass. Of this interview we shall speak presently. The other four, namely Messrs. Saul, Monk, Thompson, and Penswick, went straight to the north. They left Old Hall after mass, on All Saints' Day. An old tradition describes their journey as commenced on foot, with a wheelbarrow for their luggage, which they took turns in wheeling. It is not likely that they would have proceeded far in this way, and the following letter from Mr. Saul shows that the last part of their journey at any rate was accomplished in a post-chaise :—

"After escaping from Egyptian slavery, we arrived safe at the land of promise; at the same time I wish I could say it flowed with milk and honey. Crook Hall is a spacious stone building situated in a vale whose adjoining hills are bleak and barren. It has this singularity attending it which few other houses can boast; I mean it has no road to it. We cam in a chaise from Durham, amidst the greatest danger of being overturned. You will be surprised if I tell you we have not everyone a room to himself. We sleep about three in a room, where we have a perpetual fire. When I say fire, I don't mean such as you have at Old Hall; they are but chaufer pots. Our kitchen grate is so large that I don't believe old Stacy with his three horses would be able to draw coals enough to fill it. . . . Besides the fire in our rooms, we the divines, who are distinguished from the vulgar world, are allowed the benefit of a fire in the refectory, so that two can study together by the same fire the whole day without being molested. I hope you will be kind enough not to measure our rooms by the narrow limits of those with you. They are far more spacious in every dimension than the divines' rooms at Douay. More room may be naturally expected as soon as the top rooms are repaired. Mr. Lingard is factotum, a great man with the Bishop. He is professor of Rhetoric and Poetry, and has the care of the cellar. Our regulations are the same as at Douay, but an hour later in everything. Our table is good, especially on meagre days, when fish abounds at two pence half-penny a pound. The Bishop and Mr. Eyre sleep in the same room."

In the meantime Mr. Gillow saw Bishop Douglass in London, and as the latter made numerous inquiries about Old Hall, Mr. Gillow had no alternative but to speak what was in his mind. He therefore recounted his previous complaints, adding, by way of explanation, that Mr. Potier was so much occupied with his boys that he took little or no interest in the divines, and that Mr. Coombes had not the authority to preserve order. At this recital Dr. Douglass, who was now most anxious to keep the college at Old Hall, was not a little astonished and alarmed. He begged Mr. Gillow and Mr. Haydock to go back, promising that he would come down himself and rectify all matters to their reasonable satisfaction.

Messrs. Gillow and Haydock therefore returned to St. Edmund's, and a little later Dr. Douglass came down. After a long conversation with Mr. Potier, he assembled all the Douay divines in their common room, and opened the interview with the same question which the latter had previously asked, "Is it the gentlemen of the north that have complaints to make or is it the gentlemen of the south?" and at the same time he asked them to state publicly their causes of dissatisfaction. By this time, however, four of the northerners having left, less discontent prevailed, and Dr. Douglass waited in vain for an answer of any sort to his question. This Mr. Gillow afterwards attributed to want of courage on the part of the southern divines. The Bishop proceeded to give them a little homily on the duty of accepting the circumstances in which God had placed them, and there the interview ended. Messrs. Gillow and Haydock did not stop at Old Hall long after this. The former arrived at Crook Hall on December 6, and Mr. Haydock followed a few weeks later.

The above events were not without their results. Within a month or so, Bishop Douglass succeeded in securing the services of a former professor of the Sorbonne, the Rev. J. C. R.

"THE SCHOOL IN THE GARDEN."

D'Ancel,[1] one of the many French refugees then in London,

[1] The following details about the Rev. J. D'Ancel have been kindly given me by the secretary to the Bishop of Bayeux :—
John Charles Richard D'Ancel was born at Cherbourg, August 20th, 1761. After achieving brilliant success at his studies at the College of Valognes, he came to Paris, where he joined the little community of Robertins. He took his licentiate in Sorbonne 1786—1788, and was afterwards elected to the chair of philosophy at the College d'Harcourt, Paris. Here he was when the Revolution broke out in 1789. The "Civic Oath" was at this time imposed on all the priests, and M. L'Abbé D'Ancel, without approving of all the details enacted, considered it lawful to take the oath, and wrote a pamphlet to that effect, entitled

who became professor of philosophy at St. Edmund's, and so left Mr. Coombes more time to devote to his theological lectures. At the same time, with a view to providing increased accommodation, the little addition which was afterwards known as "The School in the Garden"—the present carpenter's shop—was begun, but it was not ready for use till the following autumn.

Three students at Old Hall belonged to the Midland District, Edward Peach, Joseph Birch, and Thomas Pitchford. These all stayed on through the remainder of their course; but after the foundation of the College of Oscott no fresh Midland students came to St. Edmund's. It is difficult to fix on the precise date of the establishment of Oscott as a college. As early as November, 1793, Bishop Thomas Talbot wrote to Dr. Bew, late President of St. Gregory's, Paris, inviting him to take charge of a mission there, and at the same time to receive a few candidates for the priesthood, with the view to making it develop into a college or seminary. Dr. Bew received the idea favourably, and wrote to Bishop Walmesley of the Western District, whose subject he was, asking to be allowed to comply with Bishop Talbot's request. The answer he received was in Bishop Walmesley's usual brusque style, and did not promise well. It ran as follows:—

"DEAR SIR,—I received yours of the 29th currt., but as you are so laudably employed in the mission you undertook to serve, I don't chuse to consent to your leaving it.

"Yours, etc.,

"C. WALMESLEY."

"Apologie du serment civique, par un prêtre de la maison et société de Sorbonne, ami de la religion et des lois." He very soon repented of having written it, and retracted publicly even before the decision of Pius VI. arrived. As he himself now refused to take the oath, according to the law of August 26, 1792, he had to leave the country, and he came to England, where he taught at St. Edmund's College for eight years. On returning to France, he was appointed titular Canon of Coutances, and a little later Curé of Valognes, where he remained more than twenty years. In 1827 he was nominated Bishop of Bayeux, and devoted the remaining eight years of his life to the total renovation of his diocese, which had not recovered from the devastation caused by the Revolution. He died April 20, 1836, and is buried in the crypt of the Cathedral.

A month or two later Bishop Walmesley appears to have changed his mind, for Dr. Bew was installed at Oscott in February, 1794, and his accounts begin from that date. The first church student arrived in May, but he had no companion till the middle of July. At any rate, the school was in working order by the early autumn.[1]

We now return to the history of Old Hall. The defection of the northern students reduced the numbers somewhat, and no further recruits arrived for several months. Dr. Douglass sent out a printed appeal for funds some three weeks after their departure, showing that he had now quite determined on keeping to the college at Old Hall. The following is a copy :—

"The persons exercising the powers of government in France, having at Douay, at Paris, and other places seized the property which was devoted to the support of the remains of Catholicity in this country, we have consequently before us the melancholy prospect of spiritual distresses to be entailed on the rising generation and on thousands yet unborn, unless effectual means be instantly put in execution for collecting other sources from which the streams of Religion and Piety may continue to flow amongst us.

"This is an object which must be dear to every breast; an object which has on us, both as men and as Christians, the strongest of all possible claims. On this the preservation of the sacred deposit of Faith which we have happily received from our Forefathers, and the transmitting of it to Posterity; on this the disseminating of moral truth and the maintaining of the peace, the harmony and good order of civil society essentially depend.

"With a view to accomplish this great object, a plan has been formed for providing an establishment at Old-Hall-Green in this district, in order to keep up a succession of ministers of the Gospel, and also to give to our Catholic Youth a virtuous and learned education. But as the execution of this plan must depend on the bounty of Catholics residing in this

---

[1] These latter particulars are taken from the History of Oscott, by the Rev. W. J. Amherst, S.J., which appeared in the *Oscotian* from 1882 onwards.

district, and connected with it, We therefore hope and earnestly desire that all persons who have the ability will emulate the zeal of our Catholic Ancestors in supporting the Seminaries abroad, and according to their respective circumstances contribute cheerfully their pious donations towards promoting so necessary a Foundation ; that we may survive the loss of the establishments in France, and by our united and spirited exertions may obviate all the evils which threaten our holy Religion.

"✠ JOHN CENTURIEN, V.A.L.

"London, November 22, 1794."

No incident of importance is reported during the winter. It was known by this time that the imprisoned collegians had returned to Douay and St. Omer respectively, and that they were now better treated. Still the prospect of their liberation seemed uncertain, and no one could say how long they might still be kept as they were. In the meantime the following little account contained in a letter from Mr. Potier to Dr. Douglass is edifying to read :—

"During this hard weather we have agreed to give up one of our dishes every day to the poor, and have during three weeks fed twelve poor families every day. I hope God Almighty will accept of it, and it will bring a blessing on the house. All do it with a good heart and great cheerfulness."

In the spring of 1795 the communities of Douay and St. Omer were released from prison, and they landed in England on March 2nd. The narrative of what followed shall be taken up in the next chapter. It is sufficient here to state that a few of the " Trente-deux " and several of the St. Omerians went straight to Old Hall ; but most of the prisoners repaired to their homes to rest after their severe trials, and to await the further determination of the Bishops.[1]

[1] Three Douay students, John Bulbeck, Richard Broderick, and Lewis Havard arrived at Old Hall in April ; and Mr. Cleghorn, the Rev. Francis Tuite, and Thomas Walsh, from St. Omer, came about the same time. Dr. Stapleton also came down, but he did not stop at that time, being wanted in London and elsewhere to take part in the negotiations to be described presently. These particulars are gathered from the old account books.

During the remainder of the spring and early summer Mr. Potier and his staff worked on quietly and conscientiously while the arrangements for the future were being discussed. Messrs. Coombes and D'Ancel together prepared the students for their performance on Mr. Potier's last exhibition day, Wednesday, June 24th, which brought the latter's presidency to a close. After the holidays the College was entirely reconstituted, and he retired from its management.

## CHAPTER VII.

### RECONSTITUTION OF ST. EDMUND'S UNDER DR. STAPLETON.

#### 1795.

*Discussions as to the foundation of a general college—Letter from Dr. Milner—Bishop Douglass's circular to the Vicars Apostolic—Proposal to set up an Ecclesiastical College in the north and to continue Old Hall as a lay school—Interview of Bishop Douglass with Pitt and the Duke of Portland—Their promises of assistance—Mr. John Sone gives 10,000l. for founding a college—Mgr. Erskine Papal Envoy in London—Dr. Stapleton goes to Crook Hall to meet Bishop Gibson and Rev. John Daniel—Rev. John Daniel returns to London and waits on Mgr. Erskine—Old Hall decided on for the college—Dr. Stapleton appointed temporary President—Death of Mr. Sone—Constitutions drawn out for St. Edmund's—College rules—Course of studies—Foundation stone of the new college.*

WITH the arrival of the collegians in England we enter on a new phase of the discussion as to the founding of a college. There was now no longer any cause for delay, but every reason that whatever was to be done should be set about as quickly as possible. The effect of the Relief Act of 1791 had already begun to be felt. "The Catholic religion is now beginning to flourish," Bishop Douglass wrote about this time, "and as public services and sermons in the chapels are now permitted, many conversions are the result."[1] Catholic schools were at last recognized by the law, and the experience of the last eighteen months at Old Hall showed that theology might safely be taught in England without fear of molestation or popular outcry. Considering all these things, everyone seemed to feel that the time had arrived for making a great effort to supply in our own country the place of the lost colleges.

Much division of opinion, however, existed as to details.

---

[1] Brady's "Catholic Hierarchy," p. 180.

BISHOP STAPLETON,
President, 1795-1801;
Vicar Apostolic of Midland District, 1801-1802.

Was there to be a single general college, or would it be better to have two, one clerical and one lay? Would Old Hall Green be the best situation for either? if so, for which? and where had the other better be?

The following letter from Dr. Milner, then priest at Winchester, addressed to Bishop Douglass, gives a summary of the chief arguments used:—

"March 23rd, 1795.

"MY LORD,—Shall I take up your Lordship's time and part of this paper with explaining the pressing urgency of the different affairs which have prevented my acknowledging your two last letters earlier? or shall I take it for granted that your Lordship is persuaded that not laziness, but a series of occupations that would admit of no delay, has rendered it morally impossible for me to show that respect to your Lordship that I was desirous of showing? I will adopt the latter measure, and proceed to the subjects of the above-mentioned letters.

"I believe I shall soon set up for a prophet. You recollect I foretold both the detention of our people and their release a very little time before those events took place, and that with a view to specific measures. In the former instance I recommended that our people should be gone in time, with as much of their property as could be secured; in the latter I hinted that it might be better to defer soliciting the [Catholic] body for support until they were collected together and some final measure agreed upon.

"All this is, however, of no consequence now; nor do I see, according to your Lordship's information, that any advice you may even now wish to adopt will be of any service, as the opinion and wishes of the Bishops is so much less attended to than was to have been expected. The gentlemen who are come over seem to have forgotten that they have left their colleges and most of their revenue behind them, and that it can only be by a new foundation, in which the Bishops must necessarily have the chief share, that they can form themselves into colleges on this side of the water.

"To speak plain, I think Mr. Daniel a man of no address, no talents for planning and managing a new college; that he will be laughed at and despised by those whose opinions must be attended to, and, of course, that our expected college will not flourish under him. Mr. Poynter is the man of all others I could wish to see President. If that cannot be, perhaps Mr. Stapleton or Mr. Coombes[1] might be found equal to such a charge.

"Indeed, I adhere to my old opinion, that there ought to be a classical college and a seminary, and if the latter is established anywhere else except at Old Hall, I shall be sorry to see that given up as a place of education. Were Mr. Stapleton, with Lingard and a few others of equal talents, placed at Old Hall, I should be satisfied that at least there would be a proper place of education for the gentry, and properly conducted.

"The seminary might perhaps be better placed at a greater distance from London. Were I to choose, I think I should give the preference to a remote situation in Wales, where food and fuel, etc., are certainly cheaper than in any part of England, and where there would be less dissipation from going abroad and idle visitors. I agree with your Lordship there could not be a more eligible situation in England than Staffordshire, were it not in the middle district. But that circumstance would alone blast the character of our seminary, throw additional weight into that of Stonyhurst, and give a certain Coadjutor[2] an influence which might be abused. I own if Oscott was offered with 1000*l.* per annum, I should be for rejecting the offer. Is not there some missionary house in Wales Messrs. Lindow and Horrabin know with all particulars?

"A situation in the north has been found to be liable to the identical inconvenience I remember mentioning to your Lord-

---

[1] i.e. Wm. Coombes, senior, the uncle of the Wm. Henry Coombes then at St. Edmund's.
[2] Bishop Berington.

ship. A worthy friend of your Lordship's[1] mistakes his talents so far as to think he is fit for nothing so much as managing a College. But all this is but idle speculation on my part. It appears that even your Lordship's wishes are not much attended to. Mr. Daniel, I take it for granted, must be the President, and he will take his own measures. I own he is a good man and a man of good parts, but he will be as much laughed at here as Mr. Richard Southworth.

"I hope your Lordship will not hastily give up Old Hall establishment, at least as a classical school, until you see how the other scheme takes. I make no doubt but in less than twelve months we may have back the walls of Doway College. But though I prefer the other side of the water for a seminary, yet I cannot think we shall ever again have one over there. . . .

"Your most respectful and faithful servant,

"J. MILNER."

The discussions on these points lasted several months. The following circular, drawn out by Dr. Poynter, then staying at Castle Street, in the name of Bishop Douglass, was sent to each of the four Vicars Apostolic:—

"1st. Is it the advice of your Lordship, that considering the present state of things in France, and particularly the situation of the Colleges of Douay and St. Omer, the superiors of the said colleges should unite in undertaking one general permanent establishment in England on the plan of Douay College?

"2nd. Will your Lordship agree that this college shall be on the same footing as Douay College was, with regard to the interference of the Right Rev. Bishops?

"3rd. Will your Lordship send your young men designed to be educated in England for an ecclesiastical state to the said college, as formerly they were sent to Douay?

"4th. Would not your Lordship approve that the house, possessions, and monies belonging immediately to the said

---

[1] Apparently Bishop Gibson.

establishment should stand in the names of the President, Procurator, and Agent?

"5th. That the funds and monies attached to any particular district should stand in the names of the Right. Revd. Bishop of that district, and of the President and Procurator of the said college, who should send an account of these yearly to the said Rt. Revd. Bishops.

"The superiors of the said establishment, and particularly the President, will engage themselves to act with the strictest impartiality to all and every one of the said Rt. Reverend Bishops and their districts, and to take care that studies are diligently attended to, that discipline is regularly observed, that the duties of religion are piously performed, and that all things are conducted in a manner the most conducive to the important end of this establishment."

A rough scheme for the constitution of the proposed new college was drawn out, probably at the same time. It is also in Dr. Poynter's handwriting.

Dr. Gibson was, as before, exceedingly anxious to secure the college for his district, and represented, as he had previously done, the cheapness of fuel and provisions in the north and its distance from the metropolis. By his invitation Dr. Stapleton, himself a Yorkshireman, went over to inspect an old disused residence near Wetherby, in that county, known as Thorpe Arch. Here we find him on March 20th, in company with Sir John Lawson and Rev. Thomas Smith, the Douay "senior," who was a native of Durham. A month later, Dr. Poynter and the Rev. William Wilds, another of the Douay seniors, likewise met Dr. Gibson at this same place, and for a time it seemed that Thorpe Arch would be the spot selected for the new college; but difficulties arose as to the amount of purchase money required, and the project was abandoned.

Even after this it seemed more probable that the "New Douay" would be in the north of England, and it appears that it was determined, in that case, to continue Old Hall; according to Dr. Milner's advice, as a purely lay or classical school. About the details of this scheme we are not informed; but Dr. Stapleton wrote to Mr. Daniel on June 9th saying that he was going to make a start with his "humanity school" at Old Hall Green at once. Mr. Daniel urged him to wait a little, as he was anxious to have one single establishment, and a very little later the whole arrangement was changed, as we shall see presently.

In the meantime it was considered advisable to ascertain the views of the government before embarking on so large an undertaking as building a college; and Dr. Stapleton, together with Bishop Douglass, waited on Mr. Pitt, the Prime Minister, and the Duke of Portland, at that time Home Secretary. The latter was fortunately a personal friend of Dr. Stapleton, who was thus able to state his case more freely. He said that the existence of the English Catholic schools and colleges on the continent was not due to the Catholics themselves, but to the penal laws passed by their adversaries; that for their own part they would rather educate their priests and laymen at home, and let their own country have the benefit of the money which they had for two centuries and more been accustomed to spend in France. No doubt he thought that this argument of pecuniary benefit to the country would be the most efficacious to use to a statesman, and he seems so far to have succeeded; for both Mr. Pitt and the Duke spoke in warm terms of their interest in the proposed foundation, and even gave them hope of a money grant from the public funds. At the same time Mr. Pitt offered some advice and strongly urged them to build at Old Hall rather than elsewhere. He pointed out that should a popular outcry be raised, it might be difficult to repress it: but that if the building was erected at Old Hall people would only hear of it as an enlargement of an existing institution, and would probably not trouble their heads about it. His advice was that the whole thing should be done as quietly as possible, and be made to grow out of the existing school at Old Hall Green.[1]

The result of this interview was therefore to favour the keeping up of St. Edmund's and making it develop into the

[1] See the "Catholic Handbook," Dolman, 1857, p. 93.

new Douay. A more decisive reason in the same direction very soon arose, of which we now have to speak. This was the munificent gift and legacy of Mr. Sone.

It appears that during the spring or early summer Dr. Poynter paid a visit to his relatives, who lived at Petersfield, Hants. During this time he often went over to Havant, where most of the Catholics of that part lived as in a little colony. John Bulbeck, one of the "Trente-deux" already at Old Hall, came from here, and Mr. John Sone of Bedhampton was a connection of his.

The Sones had been Catholics for several generations, and John Sone's father had given large sums of money to the Church. They were millers by trade, and very rich. According to tradition, Dr. Poynter, in Mr. Sone's presence, was lamenting the fall of Douay and the losses the Catholics had sustained, when Mr. Sone said quietly to him, "Sir, would ten thousand pounds help you to meet the difficulty? If so, you shall have it." This announcement must have come in a rather startling manner on Dr. Poynter; but the old man meant what he said, and lost no time in putting it into execution. He made and signed his will and wrote the following letter to Dr. Douglass :—

"HOND. AND REVD. SIR,—I have left in my Will the sum of ten thousand Pounds to Mr. Thomas Wright, of Henrietta Street, Covent Garden, and have directed him to deliver it to you. For prudential reasons I could not mention my intention in the will.

"Now my intention is that the aforesaid Sum be applied to the sole purpose of founding a School, College or Seminary, for the education of Priests and other Catholics, a general one for the four districts, as was heretofore at Doway College. But if a general one cannot be, and each District is to have a separate particular foundation for itself, then in that case my intention is that the above-mentioned money be applied to such a foundation in the London district only; and I trust with confidence that you will be so good as to take care that this my intention be duly carried into execution.

"Being poorly in health and begging your prayers, I remain, Revd. Sir,

"Your ob. hum. servant,
"JOHN SONE.

"Bedhampton, 25th June, 1795.
"Signed by Mr. SONE in the presence of
"RICD. SOUTHWORTH,
"JOHN BUTLER."

The Rev. Richard Southworth, priest at Brockhampton, wrote a couple of days later giving further details, and reporting the fact that the old man was gradually sinking. "Mr. Sone is very poorly indeed," he says; "he begs you and all his friends to pray for him. He frequently inquires of me if I have heard anything about the new college; as likewise how Mr. Talbot has disposed of Brockhampton in his will; but his memory and faculties begin to fail much, as well as strength; and I think he cannot hold long in this condition." And he adds :—" He was very ill when he made his last will; but I hope no difficulty will attend the execution in case of death, though of this I am not sure; and would not have you absolutely depend upon this bequest as a certainty nor alter any determination in consequence till the will be proved, the money made over, etc., there being so many persons about who have pretensions or expectations; and to some of his nearest of kin he has left little or nothing."

The danger thus anticipated was partly met by Mr. Sone paying a portion of the intended legacy during his lifetime, and on July 19th he made over 2000*l*. to Dr. Douglass. "Not knowing how long he may live," wrote Mr. Southworth, "or what may fall out after his death, he wishes to do more good while God grants him time."

These events practically decided the destiny of Old Hall. Dr. Douglass made up his mind finally to continue it as an ecclesiastical college, to spend Mr. Sone's money there, and to do all he could to make it a "New Douay," according to his wishes. From this time onward, therefore, we

K

hear nothing more of his wishing for or consenting to a general college in the north, though great efforts continued to be made by the northern clergy to get him to alter his determination.

Before proceeding further, a word must be said about a dignitary who played an important part in the negotiations

MONSIGNOR ERSKINE.

which followed, and whose influence Dr. Douglass succeeded in securing in favour of Old Hall. This was Mgr. Erskine, a subdeacon, Canon of St. Peter's, Rome. He was an Italian by birth, but of Scotch descent on his father's side. He arrived in London from Rome on November 12th, 1793, the very day that Dr. Douglass had set out with the first church students to inaugurate St. Edmund's, and he remained in England till December, 1801.[1] According to Dr. Douglass's diary, he came commissioned by the Pope "to thank his Majesty and his Majesty's ministers for having taken the ecclesiastical state under protection," and also "secretly to inquire into the state of the English mission and report the same to Rome." It must be remembered that at the time he arrived the disputes between the Bishops and the "Catholic Committee" were still recent, and matters were as yet by no means tranquillized, so that we can well understand the Pope's desire to have a full and impartial report of how matters stood.

Returning now to the negotiations with respect to St. Edmund's, it may at once be said that the importance to Dr. Douglass of Mgr. Erskine's active support could hardly be overrated. Mr. Daniel, as President of Douay, not being subject directly to the vicars apostolic, had not been accustomed to consult their wishes beyond a certain point, and as Dr. Milner remarked in his letter quoted above, he seemed not to realize the necessity of doing so now; while, being himself a Lancashire man, all his sympathies were in favour of the scheme for a northern college. Mgr. Erskine, however, as the Pope's representative, would be able to compel his assent to anything that might be arranged by the Bishops, and of this Mr. Daniel seemed, in the correspondence which followed, to be quite conscious.

Bishop Douglass, therefore, wrote a letter to Mr. Daniel, then with Bishop Gibson in the north, in which he expressed his own sentiments and those of Mgr. Erskine, which he said were shared by the majority of the vicars apostolic. He entrusted it to Dr. Stapleton, who accordingly left for York, where Bishop Gibson and Mr. Daniel were supposed to be, to talk matters over. After his departure the following letter arrived from Mr. Daniel :—

"MY LORD,—Your favour of the 16th inst. was received at Durham a few minutes before we set out for Crook Hall.

---

[1] Since the above was written, Mazière Brady's "Memoirs of Cardinal Erskine" have appeared, to which the reader may be referred for further particulars concerning his mission.

... Mr. Stapleton, in a letter dated the 9th of this month, informed me that he was going to establish immediately a humanity school at Old Hall Green. One from me which crossed his on the road gave him hopes of an advantageous offer to be made us in these parts. Upon the receipt of mine he promised to delay a few days the execution of the plan respecting Old Hall. At the time of my writing to Mr. Stapleton, I did not know the meaning of the aforesaid advantageous offer, and the person who wrote to me in general terms was under secrecy. I have it now in my power to lay the proposal before your Lordship.

"The house at Tudhoe, with all the lands and appurtenances, will certainly be made over instantly to Bishop Gibson, Mr. Thomas Eyre, and Mr. Arthur Storey; all the papers requisite for this purpose are now in the hands of a lawyer, who is drawing up the deeds. Moreover, Sir John Lawson has been so kind as to give a legal and written promise, under heavy penalty in case of failure, for the due discharge of the above mentioned agreement. To come directly to the point in question: Bishop Gibson, Messrs. Eyre, and Storey are willing to make over to us the said house, lands, and appurtenances, for the purpose of establishing a general college. No burthen will be annexed to the donation beside that of allowing an apartment for Mr. Storey, wherein he may remain in his capacity of missionary, to assist and watch over his flock. Mr. Eyre is very ready to resign Crook Hall, so that we may immediately enter these two houses, and thus make a beginning of our general establishment. If we think proper to build (I shall willingly consent), Bishop Gibson, Messrs. Eyre and Storey agree to refund one half of the sum which we expend in building, if we should afterwards either return to Douay and St. Omer, or remove our College to another more eligible situation. There is already drawn an extensive plan for the enlarging of Tudhoe, that could be executed for 900*l.*, according to the estimation of an experienced architect.

"If your Lordship and Mr. Stapleton continue in the same sentiments of settling a school at Old Hall, I do not see anything better for me to do than to begin Douay College at Crook. Tudhoe will be a subsidiary school to it. But I shall not come to any fixed resolution till I have the opinion of your Lordship on this important subject. If this explication do not appear satisfactory to your Lordship and Mr. Stapleton, to whom Alma Mater has such great obligations, Bishop Gibson and myself are ready to meet you and Mr. Stapleton at the place you shall appoint, for the sake of arranging these affairs in the most amicable manner. . . . If Douay College should be established at Crook Hall, I make no doubt of your Lordship's readiness to sign the conditions before agreed upon; with an exception of two articles, the first and the third. Bishop Gibson will do the same.

"Hoping that our final resolutions will be most conducive to the good of religion, I remain with the most sincere respects and deference,

"Your Lordship's most obedient and Hble. servant,

"JOHN DANIEL.

"June 24th, 1795.

"Crook Hall, near Gateshead, North."

The day after the above was written Dr. Stapleton arrived. The following letter from him to Dr. Douglass gives an account of what took place:—

"MY LORD,—I arrived at York on ye Tuesday at eleven o'clock at night, went immediately to Mr. Gillow's[1] to inquire after Mr. Daniel, but I could not get admittance, the whole house was gone to bed, so that I was obliged to stay all Wednesday at York, not being able to get intelligence whether Mr. D[aniel] was in York or at Crook Hall. On Wednesday morning Mr. Worswick[2] told me that Messrs. D[aniel] and G[ibson] had left York on Tuesday, ye 23rd, but that they had not had ye least intelligence from them since they had left them. On Wednesday night I took my

---

[1] The Rev. John Gillow, afterwards President of Ushaw College.
[2] The Rev. John Worswick, son of Thomas Worswick and his wife Alice, daughter of Richard Gillow, of Singleton, had resigned Pontop Hall in favour of the Rev. Thomas Eyre the previous year.

place in the mail to Woodham, where I took a chaise and went to Tudhoe. Mr. Storey informed me that Bp. Gibson and Mr. Daniel were at Crook Hall; I therefore continued immediately my journey to Durham and Crook Hall, where I found them; and I delivered your Lordship's letter. Mr. Daniel, after having perused it, told me that he should certainly comply with ye desire of ye majority of ye Bishops and would return to London. In the meantime, he desired me to forward the enclosed to your Lordship. He is very desirous of our not separating and also of bringing about a perfect union. When your Lordship wishes me to return to London let me know, and I will obey your orders. My brother Miles and Lady Mary desire to be respectfully remembered to you. I remain, with great respect,

"Your Lordship's most obedient and humble servant,

"G. STAPLETON.

"P.S.—I had no conversation with Bp. Gibson about ye contents of your Lordship's letter; I left that to Mr. Daniel. If your Lordship does not write soon, the letter had better be directed to me at Dr. Stapleton's, Preston, as I think that it will be very proper that somebody should go into Lancashire to talk the case over with our brethren there."

Mr. Daniel's letter, which Dr. Stapleton enclosed in his, was as follows:—

"MY LORD,—You know my reasons for giving the preference to the north, the cheapness of certain articles, and the less danger of dissipation. But the least insinuation to the contrary by Monsignor Erskine is amply satisfactory. As Mr. Stapleton is going on farther, I hope to be in London before he returns to town. Believe me to be,

"Your Lordship's most respectful and Hble. servant,

"J. DANIEL.

"Crook Hall, June 25th, 1795."

We have unfortunately no account of Mr. Daniel's interview with Dr. Douglass and Mgr. Erskine in London. We only know that as a result of it the idea of Tudhoe and Crook being formed into a "New Douay" was abandoned;

that Mr. Daniel showed great unwillingness to go to Old Hall; and that he retired to Lancashire to await the further decision of Bishop Gibson.

Dr. Douglass had now practically only one course open to him, and that was to make a beginning with the new college at St. Edmund's, in the hope that when Dr. Gibson saw it rising and everything in working order, he would ultimately consent to join in with the other vicars apostolic and form it into the general college for the whole of England. He therefore arranged with Dr. Stapleton that he should accept the presidency only temporarily, and should be ready to resign, if necessary, should Dr. Gibson afterwards join with them. This he stated in a letter to the Rev. Richard Southworth on August 5th, 1795, to be communicated to Mr. Sone, as follows :—

"I have now to inform you that we in London, with the concurrence of Mr. Walmesley and Mr. C. Berington,[1] have established the College at Old Hall Green as a general College for the whole kingdom. To this end I have made over the house there, with its furniture, the school, playground, and gardens with appurtenances to Messrs. Lindow, Stapleton, and Poynter, to be held by them in trust for the establishment. I also have appointed Mr. Stapleton President, and Mr. Poynter Vice-President. Should Mr. Gibson (who still wishes the College to be in the north) come in to unite with us, Mr. Stapleton has engaged to resign the presidency in that case to the person who may be duly appointed to that charge."

A few days after this, Mr. Sone had a second stroke of paralysis and received Extreme Unction. He lingered on for a time, but breathed his last on October 17th, and was buried in Bedhampton churchyard. The following inscription is on his tomb :—

Sacred to the Memory of
JOHN SONE,
Who departed this life on the 17th of October, 1795,
Aged 79 years.
May he rest in peace. Amen.
Dear friends prepare to die !

---

[1] Vicars Apostolic of the Western and Midland Districts respectively.

In 1876 his tombstone was restored at the expense of the Edmundian Association, and a memorial crucifix was at the same time erected in front of the College. A portrait of him in oil colours hangs over the refectory door, and a solemn requiem mass is sung every year on his anniversary for the repose of his soul.

Before being installed at St. Edmund's, Dr. Stapleton was engaged for some time at Castle Street with Bishop Douglass and Dr. Poynter on the reconstitution of the College. This may be divided into two parts; the first concerning the relations of the Bishop, as proprietor, with the President or administrator; the second concerning the internal regulations of the College.

The former are laid down in the Articles of Agreement which were signed by the parties concerned on August 5th, 1795. These were not drawn out without grave consideration, and a number of different drafts still exist, all in Dr. Poynter's handwriting, from which a very clear idea may be gained of the exact purposes and conditions for which the new college was intended. In all the drafts we find the same general idea. It was to be opened as a general college for the four districts, but as Dr. Gibson had not yet consented to join in the scheme, it was specially agreed that when he did so, Dr. Stapleton, who was appointed President for the time, should resign, so that Dr. Gibson might have a due voice in the election of the permanent President.[1] In the meantime Dr. Stapleton was empowered to spend the sum in his possession belonging to St. Omer College, amounting to about 1100*l.*, on St. Edmund's, with this proviso, that should he return to St. Omer,[2] that College should be refunded by Bishop Douglass.

---

[1] Bishops Berington and Walmesley had both given a provisional consent to Old Hall becoming the general college for the whole of England. The latter wrote on August 12th, 1795, "I fear Bishop Gibson will not join you. He would not like my letter, in which I told him I preferred the south." As in the event these fears were realized, Bishop Berington does not seem to have sent any more students to Old Hall, and it was ultimately decided to keep Oscott up. The Western students remained at St. Edmund's till many years later, but they were few in number.

[2] Dr. Stapleton's return to St. Omer when the Revolution had passed

The following are the Articles of Agreement in the form in which they were signed:—

"ARTICLES OF AGREEMENT.

"1st. The establishment at Old Hall Green is opened for the public, and offered as a general college for the four districts.

"2nd. The house with its present furniture, the playground and gardens, with their appurtenances, are made over to the establishment, and stand in the names of Messrs. John Lindow, Gregory Stapleton, and William Poynter, for the use of the secular clergy.

"3rd. All monies and profits of this College arising from the education of youth, or otherwise coming in, shall be applied to the benefit and purpose of the said establishment.

"4th. The President appointed to govern the College has the same powers for the internal government thereof as the President had in Doway College.[1]

"5th. The Rev. Mr. Stapleton, who is appointed and made President for the present by the Right Rev. Bishop of the London District, takes possession of the premises on this express condition, that when all the secular clergy Bishops shall unite to form a general college at Old Hall Green, he shall resign the said premises and his place as President to the person who shall be duly appointed thereunto.

"London, August 5th, 1795.

"(Were signed by) JOHN DOUGLASS, V.A.L.

"GREGORY STAPLETON, President.

"Witness: JAMES BARNARD.
　　　　　　" THOMAS CLEGHORN."

away, seems to have been expected as probable at this time, and Bishop Douglass describes him in his report to Rome in 1796 as "President of St. Omer's, temporarily appointed over St. Edmund's" (Brady's "Catholic Hierarchy," p. 180). That Dr. Stapleton himself expected St. Omer to be re-established is evidenced by his will, dated April 17th, 1801, which was after his appointment as Bishop over the Midland District. It must have been evident by that time that he, at any rate, would never preside there again. He leaves some of his property to St. Omer College, "should it exist," but the bulk he bequeaths to St Edmund's.

[1] The importance of this proviso becomes evident by comparing the full powers of the President of Douay with the very limited ones of the President of St. Omer.

Besides the above, there were seven "secret articles," which chiefly regarded financial matters. Bishop Douglass was to advance 500*l.* to the new building, to be ultimately refunded out of money which was to be collected for the work. For the present, the Bishop of the London district was to have it in his power to appoint the president or to remove him, with the advice of the vice-president and the "seniors;" and the premises were to be held in lease for 999 years at the nominal rental of five shillings. Other details were arranged, such as the amount of the salaries of the superiors and professors, who, however, agreed for the time only to draw half these amounts, till the finances of the College would admit of their being paid in full. Finally the three possible contingencies were provided for as follows:—(1) If the establishment should not become a general college, it shall be continued as a particular one for the London District. (2) If the College should be broken up, all was to revert to and belong to the Bishop of the London District. (3) If the College should be made a general one, the articles were to be annulled and the president resign.

With respect to the internal administration, we may learn the intentions of the founders from the College rules. No complete copy exists of the original rules, though several extracts are given in the diary of the College. The rules preserved, however, date back at least to Dr. Poynter's presidency and are probably copied from those made when the new building was first used in 1799. Thus in all probability they are substantially identical with those drawn out at this time, and they remained in force till the introduction of what were known as the "new rules" in 1852.

They begin with a statement of the aim and scope of the College. "The College of St. Edmund is instituted for the purpose of promoting the good of religion and society by forming Catholic youth, particularly of the London District, to the duties of the sacred ministry, or of civil life, according to each one's respective vocation. The exercises of piety, the course of studies, and the rules of discipline to be followed for the attainment of these ends, shall be the same as were established for the College at Douay, with such alterations and improvements, as the change of circumstances requires."

An enumeration of the officers of the College follows. Three classes are mentioned. The first are called "seniors," according to the old Douay terminology; the second are professors; and the third prefects. The seniors include president, vice-president, superior of the preparatory school,[1] prefect of studies, general prefect, and procurator. Those who are called prefects correspond with what are now called masters. They are here described as "persons to superintend the students in the dormitories, in the chapel, and in the time of recreation." The conditions upon which a student is received are also laid down, and amongst them a prudent one specified that "no student shall be admitted without sufficient security for the regular payment of his pension."

The order of the day follows:—

$$\begin{array}{ll} 6. & \text{Rise.} \\ 6\frac{1}{3}. & \text{Meditation.} \\ 7. & \text{Mass.} \\ 7\frac{1}{2}. & \text{Study.} \\ 8\frac{1}{4}. & \text{Breakfast.} \\ 9-12\frac{3}{4}. & \text{Study.}^2 \\ 1. & \text{Dinner, recreation.} \\ 3-5\frac{1}{4}. & \text{Study.} \\ 5\frac{1}{4}-5\frac{1}{2}. & \text{Recreation.} \\ 5\frac{1}{2}-6\frac{3}{4}. & \text{Study.} \\ 6\frac{3}{4}-7. & \text{Recreation.} \\ 7. & \text{Supper, recreation.} \\ 8\frac{1}{2}. & \text{Night prayers.} \end{array}$$

With respect to the meditation, it is laid down that all are to assist at it "except the children;" but this was altered in Dr. Griffiths's rules in 1818, and the exception was changed to that of the lay boys in the top dormitory. The following

---

[1] The preparatory school was established at the Old College when the bulk of the students moved to the new building. Before that time "the Hermitage" served for the purpose. See next Chapter. No mention is made in the rules of "pedagogues;" but from letters of Dr. Poynter it appears that they existed at St. Edmund's exactly as they had done at Douay. A "pedagogue" was usually a divine, who was given charge of one or more boys to help them in their preparation work. The system has been long since abolished.

[2] Dr. Poynter introduced the quarter of an hour's recreation from $11\frac{1}{2}$ to $11\frac{3}{4}$ about the year 1801.

regulation about community mass will have a very familiar sound to all Edmundians :—

"The common mass .... will be offered on Sundays, Wednesdays, and Fridays for these particular intentions, viz., (1) In thanksgiving to Almighty God for his past benefits and protection. (2) To pray for the conversion of England and Scotland. (3) To pray for the benefactors of the College and all its members."

High mass on Sundays was to be for the same intentions, and a weekly mass for the benefactors was provided for in addition. The rotation of turns among the priests was then exactly as now, so that one week a priest said community mass and preached at the high mass, while the following week he was celebrant at all the functions. The prefect was exempted from community duties, but was directed to offer one mass each week for the boys, a custom which still survives.

In the evening, after the meditation was read, "the children" were to retire, while the rest stayed for a quarter of an hour's spiritual reading. All lights to be out by ten o'clock. Three half-play days were arranged for, namely, Tuesday, Thursday, and Saturday; and on those days there was recreation not only from dinner till 5¾, but likewise for an hour, nine to ten, in the morning. This latter rule came from Douay, but it was soon changed. At Ushaw it exists to the present day. On Sunday High Mass was at eleven, preceded by an hour's study, and Vespers were at three. The high mass was afterwards put an hour earlier, and followed by the study, as is now the case. The yearly retreat took place in Holy Week. The above order (except that the spiritual reading was put at 6¾ instead of after night prayers) remained without much change till 1852, when it was altered as above stated.

The course of studies was carefully marked out. Dr. Poynter had brought the old Douay prefect of studies' book[1] with him to St. Edmund's, and the Douay course was taken as a

---

[1] We may here correct a rather serious error which has arisen with respect to this book. The *Catholic Magazine* for April, 1831 (p. 147, footnote) states that it was saved from Douay by Robert Gradwell, afterwards Bishop, by him placed at Crook Hall, and transferred thence to Ushaw. A

basis in drawing out a course for Old Hall. One or two important alterations, however, were made. The chief of these concerned the philosophy classes. At Douay two years had

long quotation from it is given in the September number of the same year (pp. 462—465), and it is there called the last Douay diary. This seems to be, moreover, the book referred to in the "Biographical Dictionary of English Catholics," vol. i. p. 552; "Chapels of Ushaw," p. 16; the *Rambler* for August, 1854, p. 108, and elsewhere. In reality, however, the book now at Ushaw is not the original at all, but a copy made from it by the Rev. Thomas Eyre, when President of Crook Hall in 1807. The original was then kept at St. Edmund's, and was lent by Dr. Poynter to Mr. Eyre for the latter to copy. It was accordingly copied out in full; the copy was kept at Ushaw, and the original returned a few months later. This appears from the two following letters, the first of which is at St. Edmund's, and the second among the Westminster archives at the Oratory.

From the Rev. THOMAS EYRE to Dr. POYNTER, dated Crook Hall, January 25th, 1807.

"MY LORD,—Your much esteemed favour of the 5th of December I received the day after Xmas, accompanied with the Pref. Studies Catalogue from 1750, for both which please to accept my most grateful thanks. I make bold to request the loan of it until I can contrive to take a copy of it at leisure hours. In the meanwhile, in case of accidents, I shall leave a memorandum that it belongs and must be returned to Yr. Lp. I am fully convinced that the nearer we approach to the same rules of discipline and to the same order of studies, the more it will conduce to the advantage of both our establishments, especially if these be grounded on the constitutions of Douay, with only such alterations as circumstances seem absolutely to require. A copy therefore of Yr. Lp.'s manuscript regulations will be particularly acceptable. . . .

"Your Lordship's much obliged and most obedient servant,

"THOS. EYRE."

From the same to the Rev. JOSEPH HODGSON, V.G.L.D., dated Crook Hall, Feb. 13th, 1808.

". . . . You will remember to have obtained for me the Prefect of Studies' Book from Bishop Poynter; I thank you kindly for that favour. I copied it out myself, and carefully returned it by the mail, I believe through Keating, with many thanks to Bishop Poynter, in the course of last summer. I have now to request another favour, which is, with my most respectful compliments to Bishop Poynter, to beg he will have the goodness to allow me the loan of his code of rules, such as are observed at Old Hall. I must observe that I had already begged to have them above a year ago; when Bishop Poynter appeared to hint that he would get me a fair copy of that book written out. Let me now, however, entreat that his Lordship will not think of giving himself that trouble; but to allow me to have his copy to transcribe, and I will faithfully return it as soon as the same can be written out. . . ."

The original Douay M.S. is now kept among the Westminster archives at the Oratory, together with the other Douay diaries, etc. It is a small, rather

been given to philosophy, the first to natural and the second to mental. This custom has been kept up at Ushaw, with some slight modification, to the present day. At St. Edmund's the natural philosophy year was abolished from the beginning, and the philosophy course reduced to one year. The theology occupied three and a half years, making the total course, from the the third of rudiments upwards, eleven years and a half. Arrangements were made for monthly disputations and repetitions on the part of the theologians and philosophers. A weekly sermon, after vespers on Sunday, was preached by a divine; and there were to be frequent exhibitions in elocution on the part of the boys, class by class, as at the present day. Special stress was also laid on the church students, all learning plain chant, to which two half hours were devoted every week, as is still the custom.¹

The duties of the different superiors are laid down at length, as well as those of the professors, and also of the

thick book, and there seems no reason to doubt that Dr. Poynter himself took it from Douay in his pocket. At any rate, it was certainly in his possession during the imprisonment at Doullens and afterwards, as the entries of that period are all in his handwriting.

¹ The old plain chant book at St. Edmund's bears the following inscription on its title-page :—

"JOANNES WADE SCRIPSIT ANNO MDCCLX."

It must have come direct from Douay. The John Francis Wade here mentioned was not a student of Douay College, but a man who made his living by copying and selling plain chant and other music. He carried on his business at Douay, simply because it was a great Catholic centre. His death is thus chronicled in the Obituary List of the Catholic Directory for 1787 :— "1786, Aug. 16. Mr. John Francis Wade, a layman, aged 75, with whose beautiful manuscript books our chapels, as well as private families, abound, in writing which and teaching the Latin and church song he chiefly spent his time." The book at St. Edmund's is entirely done by hand, and is remarkable for having all the chant written on five instead of four lines. It contains all the tenebræ offices, matins, lauds, and mass for the dead, and many little pieces such as the Adeste Fideles, Rorate Coeli, the Tantum Ergo commonly known as Webbe's, etc. The book was used regularly until comparatively recently, and is still used occasionally.

Besides the above, there are the old graduals and antiphonals, the former dating to 1779 and the latter to 1792. Both were probably bought for St. Edmund's on its foundation. The edition is Venetian, the common Mechlin version being unknown till nearly half a century afterwards. The Venetian edition remained in use till quite lately, when it was replaced by the Ratisbon.

prefects, or masters. A list of penances which can be imposed is given, limiting corporal punishment to lay students below fourteen years of age. The chief penance used seems to have been what was known later on as the "penance walk," which consists in ordering the delinquent to walk up and down a certain particular walk without a companion during some part of recreation time.

The College continued under the patronage of St. Edmund, according to Dr. Douglass's dedication two years earlier, and from the first a great devotion to their patron saint, as a model of a priest and a scholar, has been a characteristic of the students. While other colleges are usually known by the names of the places where they are built—such as Oscott, Ushaw, Stonyhurst—this College is always known as St. Edmund's, and its students as Edmundians.

The minor patrons were St. Thomas, St. Charles Borromeo, and St. Gregory the Great. There is no special mention of these in the rules, but high mass is recorded on the feasts of the first three in the earliest calendars of the College, even before its reconstitution by Dr. Stapleton. The connection with Douay College is here apparent. For the old Douay chapel was dedicated to St. Thomas of Canterbury, and his hair shirt was among their relics; St. Gregory, as the Apostle of England, was the second patron; and the biretta of St. Charles was also one of the Douay relics, which unfortunately perished at the time of the Revolution. All these three days were kept as high mass days at Douay.[2]

---

[2] See "Douay Diaries," p. 116, and "Le Collége Anglais de Douai," by M. L'Abbe Dancoisne, p. xx.

One other connecting link between Douay and Old Hall deserves a passing mention, namely the game of "Cat," which is played also at Ushaw. Some of the details of the Ushaw game are not the same as in the Edmundian game, and opinions may be divided as to which is the better. At St. Edmund's there is seven-hole and nine-hole cat; at Ushaw only seven-hole. The balls are harder at the latter place, and the style of stroke somewhat different. The chief distinction, however, lies in the method of proceeding with the "crosses." At Ushaw the man who gets the side out always goes to the stroke as his side goes in, and it is therefore a matter of chance who happens to be at the stroke when a "cross" has to be made. The "crosses" have thus to be recorded, and a scorer is needed. At St. Edmund's, on the other hand, the "crosses" are made

In addition to the above, the Venerable Bede and St. Erconwald are minor patrons of St. Edmund's, but their festivals are not observed with High Mass.

Mr. Potier was duly apprised of the change which was to take place in the government and constitution of Old Hall. It was agreed that he should still reside at the College, and take charge of the spiritual interests of the Catholics of the neighbourhood. This arrangement was carried out, and he remained some thirteen years in the capacity of "parish priest," as the office has since been called. He was greatly beloved by the people, and much respected in the neighbourhood; but as a financier he was not successful, and he left the College in considerable debt. The balance sheet made up to the 24th of June, 1795, when he formally ceased to be president, showed a deficit of about 170*l.*, and after it had been examined by Dr. Poynter, Bishop Douglass undertook to pay it. Ultimately, however, the deficit was found to mount up to over 500*l*. In order to inquire into this, Dr. Douglass sent for all the accounts; but in the end there was nothing further for him to say than that he supposed that "ye Bishop must be ye Peter Pay-all."

Dr. Stapleton went to Old Hall on August 5th, after signing the articles of agreement in London. He was accompanied by Mr. Hodgson, who returned to London in a few days. Dr. Poynter arrived within a week, bringing with him several of the old Douay students, and a formal commencement was made on the Feast of the Assumption. On that day the College diary, which was kept by Dr. Poynter all the time that he was vice-president, opens :—

"Diary of St. Edmund's College at Old Hall Green, A.D. 1795.

"The Rt. Rev. John Douglass, Lord Bishop of Centuriæ. and Vicar Apostolic in the London District, desirous of re-

---

by each player in rotation, and the state of the game is at any time evident by the position of the "cross man," who takes his place at the beginning of each innings exactly where he was when the side got out. Which game is more like the "cat" played at Douay is not certainly known; but there is no very great difference between the two.

pairing the losses which England has suffered by the subversion of our Colleges in France, determined to establish without delay a College in the London District, in which the young men who are called to the Ecclesiastical state might be well formed for every part of their duty, and other Children designed for various employments in life might be prepared by a Catholic, and useful education for the discharge of the duties of their respective states. For these purposes his Lordship was pleased to make over the house and gardens of the school at Old Hall Green, near Puckeridge, Herts, belonging to the Bishop of the London District, and to give the said premises to the College which he has intended to establish there. He chose the Rev. Mr. Gregory Stapleton, who was President of St. Omer's College, for the first President of this new College, which he placed under the patronage of St. Edmund, Archbishop of Canterbury."

Here follows a copy of the "Articles of Agreement" which have already been given; and the diary continues:—

" In virtue of this agreement, the Revd. Mr. Stapleton took possession of the Premises and began to govern the College in quality of President on the 15th of August, 1795. The Rev. Mr. John Potier, who was President of the school before established at Old Hall, remains as Pastor of the country congregation, and convictor at the President's table. The Revd. William Poynter, who had been Professor of Divinity, and Prefect of the Studies at Doway College, was appointed Vice-President. The Revd. William Coombes who had taught Rhetoric at Doway College (and Divinity at Old Hall Green, from the time that the Divines who escaped from Doway and Doullens were sent to Old Hall till the establishment of the new College) was appointed Professor of Eloquence. The Revd. William Wilds, who had taught Philosophy at Doway, was appointed Professor of the second Class. The Revd. Francis Tuite, late Procurator of St. Omer's College, was made Procurator. The Revd. John Law, late Master at Old Hall, was made General Prefect and Professor of the Third Class. The Revd. Mr. J. C. R.

D'Ancel, Licentiate in Divinity in Sorbon, late Professor of Philosophy at Paris, was appointed Professor of Philosophy. Mr. Thos. Cleghorn was made teacher of arithmetic."

Four days later, the school year was formally inaugurated by a High Mass *de Spiritu Sancto*, after which the list of students was read out by Dr. Poynter, the Prefect of Studies.[1]

The next entry in the diary records the laying of the foundation stone of the new college:—

"On the same 19th of August, the foundation stone of the new College of St. Edmund was laid in the sandy field by the Revd. John Lindow in the [name] of the Rt. Revd. John Douglass. The following inscription written in Latin, Greek and English, and enclosed in a bottle together with a silver sixpence bearing the date of the year, and the bottle was placed under the South and East corner of the square where the walls meet in the court.

"Hac die 19 Augusti A.D. 1795 hic lapis angularis Collegii Catholici Sti. Edmundi in agro Hartfordensi vulgo dicto Old Hall Green, positus fuit ab Illustrissimo et Reverendissimo Domino Domino Joanne Episcopo Centuriensi, Vicario Apostolico in Districtu Londinensi. Preside Reverendo Domino Gregorio Stapleton."

"Ταύτῃ τῇ ἡμέρᾳ, τῇ ἐννάτῃ τοῦ μηνὸς λήγοντος μεταγειτ-νιῶνος τῷ ἔτει τοῦ Κυρίου αψϟέ οὗτος ὁ λίθος γωνίαιος τοῦ Συλλόγου καθολικοῦ οἰκίας τῷ Ἁγίῳ Ἐδμόνδῳ ἱερᾶς ἐν τῷ τῶν

---

[1] The total number, including a few who came a day or two later, was seventy-three. Of these, twelve were divines or philosophers, all of whom came from Douay. Their names are as follows:—
Revs. William Beauchamp, Francis Bowland, and Edward Peach, deacons.
Rev. John Devereux, subdeacon.
Messrs. James Delaney and Thomas Cook in minor orders.
Messrs. John Clarkson, Richard Broderick, Lewis Havard, Thomas Pitchford, Arthur Clifford, and John Eldridge not in orders.
Of the remaining sixty-one students, three (John Bulbeck and Edward and James Tichborne) had been at Douay, and five are known to have come from St. Omer, including Thomas Walsh, the future Bishop, Joseph Kimbell, afterwards president, and Joseph Birch, some time President of Sedgley Park. There were probably a few others, for Mr. Coombes speaks of ten or twelve all told. This leaves about fifty to be accounted for. Of these the majority were probably boys of Mr. Potier's academy; but a good many were new arrivals; amongst them Robert Varley, afterwards prefect, and then vice-president, who came from Sedgley Park.

'Αρτουρδιενθέων χώρῳ (Βρεττανικῶς Old Hall Green) ἐτέθη ὑπὸ τοῦ ἐνδοξοτάτου καὶ αἰδεσιμωτάτου κυρίου 'Ιωάννου Δούγλαος, 'Επισκόπου τῶν Κεντυρίων, 'Ηγεμόνος αἰδεσίμου τοῦ Κυρίου Γρηγορίου Στάπλετον."

"On the 19th day of August in the year of our Lord 1795 this foundation stone of the Catholic College of St. Edmund at Old Hall Green in the County of Herts was laid by the Right Revd. John Douglass, Bishop of Centuria and Vicar Apostolic in the London District. The Revd. Gregory Stapleton President.

Undersigned.

JOHN LINDOW, representing
the Rt. Revd. John DOUGLASS.

(Signed on the back.)

GREGORY STAPLETON, President.
WILLIAM POYNTER, Vice President.
WILLIAM COOMBES.
WILLIAM WILDS.
J. C. RICHD. D'ANCEL.
JOHN LAW.
JAMES TAYLOR, Surveyor."

# CHAPTER VIII.

## BUILDING OF THE NEW COLLEGE.

### 1795—1800.

Plans for new college — Dispersion of the "Trente-deux" — The Benedictines at Acton Burnell — Meeting of northern clergy at Preston—Memorial to Bishop Douglass in favour of a general college in the north—His answer—Letter from Bishop Gibson—Pitt promises a government grant for St. Edmund's—Correspondence between Mgr. Erskine and Bishop Gibson—Rev. John Daniel appointed by Propaganda President of St. Edmund's—He begs off—Proposal to unite Crook Hall and St. Edmund's—Also to send Dr. Lingard to Old Hall—Meeting of northern clergy at Fernyhalgh in 1798—Decision to build a college in the north and not to join in St. Edmund's—Progress of Old Hall—Visit of Colonel Harcourt, who gives the great clock—Mr. Sone's will disputed—Further financial difficulties—Building stopped — Dr. Stapleton appointed Rector of the English College at Rome—Events at Rome prevent his going—Mr. Sone's will case decided in favour of the College—Building resumed—Sacrilegious robbery—Chapel of Reparation — Visit of Bishop Moylan of Cork—Opening of new college.

THE designs for the new college were prepared by Mr. James Taylor, of Islington, who, about ten years later superintended the building of Ushaw, a fact which explains the resemblance in the main front of the two colleges. Mr. Taylor's son, Mr. James Molyneux Taylor, was educated at Old Hall, and both father and son were great benefactors of St. Edmund's.

Three plans were drawn out to choose from, and they have all been preserved. Neither of them can boast of any architectural beauty, and the name afterwards given to the College by Pugin—the "Priest Factory"—would have been equally applicable to any one of the three designs. The elevation and ground plan of the one selected are here reproduced; but several modifications were afterwards introduced, and a certain part of the plan, including church and refectory,

THE NEW COLLEGE. ARCHITECT'S ELEVATION, 1795.

was never carried out. There seems to have been no contract entered into, but Dr. Stapleton held himself responsible for the whole work and for the payments as they should become due. He had 2000*l*. in hand from Mr. Sone at the commencement, and he knew that there was more to come. Later on he made a collection among the Catholics who had been educated at Old Hall and others. Amongst the contributors we find the Old Chapter down for 250*l*., Mr. Thomas Stonor for 21*l*., Dr. Milner for 20*l*., besides other smaller sums; but the amount raised in this way was not large.

In the meantime it was necessary to supply at once the accommodation requisite for temporarily carrying on the work of the College. The addition begun by Mr. Potier six months before known as the "School in the Garden" (now the carpenter's workshop) were completed in the month of September, and these, together with the Hermitage, the Ship, and the "old college" itself, formed the total accommodation.

Dr. Stapleton, as soon as he arrived, determined to make the "Hermitage" into a preparatory school, and to continue to use the "Ship" for the divines to sleep in. The professors were all accommodated at the old house, except the superior of the preparatory school, who lived at the "Hermitage" and said mass there every morning. The two dormitories in the old college were now both used for their original purpose.[1]

[1] The following enumeration of the buildings is from an old list made out for the window tax:—
"(1) The Principal Dwelling House, which includes likewise Dairy, Store Room, Servants' Offices and our Chambers, &c., 56 windows.
"The Chapel, which is contiguous to the Principal Dwelling House, 6 windows.
"(2) The Granary and other Store Rooms and a working room, together with a room for the Poor to come for their victuals, 6 windows.
"(3) The Schools which stand in the middle of the Garden, 10 windows.
"(4) The wooden habitation formed out of the stable, 20 windows.
"(5) A little separate building called the Hermitage, 10 windows."
The stables were then on the north side of the Hermitage. No. 4 above is the "Ship;" the others explain themselves. There are one or two old inscriptions still to be seen on the walls of the Hermitage. One of them, by the side of the fireplace in the kitchen, runs thus: "Remember me, Francis Neuville, Mr. Baker at Old Hall Green,

By the early autumn of 1795 most of the "Trente-deux" and other Doullens prisoners had settled down in England.[1] Of the former, seven were at St. Edmund's—five students and two priests—and five at Crook Hall. Several of the priests, like the Rev. Joseph Hodgson and the Rev. Thomas Smith, were already on the mission, and the six Benedictines had found a new home at Acton Burnell, the seat of Sir Edward Smythe in Shropshire, where most of the old community of St. Gregory's, Douay, were reassembled, and where they continued till they moved to Downside in 1814. The following letter from Prior Sharrock to Dr. Poynter at St. Edmund's was written soon after the reassembly of the community at Acton Burnell :—

"Acton Burnell, Shrewsbury.
"October 3rd, 1795.

"DEAR SIR,—After different enquiries after yourself and the rest of our Doullens friends, I hear that you and Mr. Stapleton, with some others of our acquaintance, have taken up your quarters, at least for a time, at Old Hall Green. Our former friendship, so well cemented by our common adventures and a long captivity, makes me particularly curious to know what is become of all our fellow prisoners. I have often regretted that our various avocations when we arrived in London allowed us to see so little of one another, and since our separation, though I have been in different parts of England, scarce have I met with one of the celebrated *Trente-deux* or their associates. I hear that several are with you; others in London, others in the North, &c. God be thanked, I do not yet hear that anyone is yet dead. For my part, I am settled, at least for the present, at a seat of Sir Edward Smythe's, my former *elève*, with nearly all my former family. The situation is pleasant, and healthy and retired. We see a newspaper about thrice a week, and have full leisure to contemplate at a distance

Herts, 1798." This man afterwards gained an unenviable notoriety, being suspected of having been concerned in the robbery of the chapel four years later.

[1] It may be noticed that nearly thirty of the Doullens prisoners—about a third of their whole number—were at this time assembled at Old Hall.

the extraordinary circumstances and progress of that awful revolution of which we were once too near spectators. Shall we ever see Douay again is a question which as naturally as frequently mingles itself with our reflections. No doubt the same very difficult problem often presents itself to your thoughts. In the meanwhile, I am very glad to learn that you are determined to attempt something, and if I am rightly informed, you have lain the first stone of a very considerable new building. It is no doubt with a view to continue an establishment which has rendered such eminent services to Religion,[1] and I most sincerely wish it every possible success. You have probably heard me say at different times that certain other losses would not be so severely felt, but the loss of a house like yours, if not replaced, would be irreparable. In these singularly puzzling times, it must have cost you much probably to fix on any plan, and I sometimes apprehended that nothing would have been done as yet. I must own that I think it will be long before any solid religious education can take place in France, if ever. A Revolutionary fever requires at least a century to heal it. Our property may possibly enough be restored at the peace; what then to do with it will be another puzzle. Our Mr. Higginson, who was confined with the Courtrai nuns at Compiegne, tells me that soon after we came over, there appeared another decree concerning us, declaring that our property had been only sequestered, and not confiscated. I wish Monsr. Despres may have seen the decree. I am told he is Mayor of Douay. He might avail himself of it in case our houses should be put up to sale. We are informed, too, that six churches have been opened at Lille for the Orthodox, and that the nuns at Aire perform by permission their offices publickly. They think things are coming round very fast, and feel themselves very happy that they have not been obliged to quit.

"We have lately been favoured with a visit from B. Berington, who was so kind as to make an ordination in our chapel . . . . He gave me some information about you. Mr. Hodgson, he said, was fixed in London, Mr. Smith was in

[1] Douay College.

the North and had pleaded stoutly to have your establishment in his country. This was natural. How is his health since his return to England? If you are building, I presume you and your other friends sometimes collect no little quantity of *mundanus pulvis*. Acton Burnell will be an excellent place to shake it off. Come then by all means to see us in due time. Remember me in the kindest terms to Mr. Stapleton and all our friends.

"I am, Dear Sir, & ever shall be,

"Most sincerely yours,

"J. SHARROCK."

We have seen that Dr. Stapleton was not yet permanently appointed over Old Hall, because it was necessary to await the final decision of Bishop Gibson, as to whether he would unite with the other Bishops at St. Edmund's. The opinion of the northern priests was still opposed to this idea. A meeting of the clergy of Lancashire and Westmoreland was held at Preston, on August 25th, 1795, and a memorial in the following terms was drawn up, signed and sent to Bishop Douglass:—

"Resolved that it is the opinion and the earnest wish of the undersigned priests of the Western Division of the Northern District, that the three Districts, the Northern, Middle and Southern,[1] unite in the establishment of one College, on the plan of that formerly existing at Douay.

"That they see some reasons, on account principally of the comparative cheapness of fuel and provisions, for wishing that the said common establishment should be in the North; in such manner, however, that the Bishop of that district shall not have any more influence in the government and management of the said College than his equals in authority, the Bishops of the Middle and Southern Districts.

"And that if such an establishment can be formed, they will contribute to the utmost of their power to its support."

[1] The Western District was of far less importance, not only because of the fewness of the number of their clergy, but also because the majority of the clergy, including the Bishop, Dr. Walmesley, were Benedictines.

Here follow twenty-two signatures, and the whole was forwarded by Rev. John Orrell. Dr. Douglass answered on September 29th :—

"DEAR SIR,—Friday's post brought me your esteemed favour, the resolves of the meeting held at Preston, on the 25th of last month.

"It is then the opinion and earnest wish of the meeting that the three Districts, viz., the North, Middle, and London, should unite in the establishment of one College, on the plan of that lately existing at Douay ; that if such an establishment can be formed, they will contribute to the utmost of their power to its support ; and that it is wished this one College may be in the North, on account principally of the comparative cheapness of fuel and provisions.

"I beg, Sir, you will be so obliging as to assure the Gentlemen, that their resolves have with me all the weight which is so justly due to the respectable body of our Lancashire Clergy, and that their engagement to contribute to the utmost of their power to the support of this one common College, must be an encouragement to hasten the wished for union of Districts.

"The sole point on which we appear to be divided, is the site which ought to be chosen for such an establishment.

"The Meeting at Preston plead in favour of the North, and found their arguments principally on the comparative cheapness of fuel and provisions. Whereas the Clergy of the Western, Midland, and London Districts, who have been consulted on the business, plead for the South, founding their arguments on the general predilection, which all their friends show for the South, whenever the alternative is proposed ; on the conveniency in procuring, together with the comparative cheapness of a great many articles which are wanted in a College, and on the moral certainty of the Cisalpines relinquishing their school at Oscott, to unite with and support the College of Douay if established in the South.

"For these reasons, and to stop the progress of all the evils arising from our delays, with the concurrence of our clergy in the above mentioned districts, the Establishment at Old

Hall Green has been opened for the public, and offered as a general College for the four districts. . . . His Majesty's Ministers are made acquainted with the design of the new erection, Mgr. Erskine, His Holiness's Agent and confidential friend, approves of it, advised me to begin it on a large scale, and we have the most flattering prospect of support and success in every line.

"When you make our brethren in Lancashire acquainted with the contents of this, my letter, please to inform them that their resolves have been shown to some of their brethren here, who all unite in soliciting their patronage for the College at Old Hall Green, at which College the annual pension will not exceed what is fixed for the North.

"I hold myself much obliged to you, Sir, for the friendly and very handsome manner in which you conveyed to me the resolves of your Meeting. With best compliments to all.

"I remain, &c.,

"JOHN DOUGLASS."

Dr. Gibson's own views at this time are shown clearly in the following letter to Dr. Poynter :—

"York, September 12th, 1795.

"DEAR SIR,—I received your letter sent by Mr. Smith long after he came to ye North, as he forgot to deliver it. I likewise received yours from Old Hall, but had so much business on my return home that required immediate despatch, that I could not find time to thank you for them, nor give an answer. Nor is it easy to know what to say. On account of ye great distance of ye principal clergy from each other in ye North, more time is required in getting through any business of importance than can be imagined, particularly where money is necessary, on account of ye consent of so many being required, and because all these matters are in ye names of so many, who being dispersed and not concentred as in London, greater difficulties arise, as is easy to conceive. And even now I scarce know what to say to you. Mr. Daniel is in Lancashire. I have only seen him once for two or three hours, and most of that time in company, since he left London. I understand you are building fast at Old Hall. Whatever takes place, it may be of great use to that part of ye Kingdom, in some way or other, and I am glad you find yourselves happy together; but if you expect it to be ye general College or what is called Doway, it is not ye opinion of this part of ye Kingdom that it will answer for that purpose : so they do not expect it to answer ye purposes mentioned in yours. The general opinion of ye Clergy in ye North, seems clearly for a College in ye North; and in this case, if you go on with ye idea of having it there, it will not, I fear, answer ye ends of Union of doctrine &c., but perhaps a separation of North and South in regard of a College. The Clergy are of opinion, that union of doctrine by having more together, &c., would have been better preserved by having it in ye North. You say Bishop Douglass was determined by having a majority. There must have been a mistake. The majority is on ye other side; I mean of ye Clergy, as I am persuaded there are more in ye North than in all ye rest of ye Kingdom. Many were and are much displeased at ye manner ye affair was carried on. . . . Application to others, as it were to force Mr. Daniel, was not approved. They do not look on these measures as candid &c. But if the main thing did but answer, these would pass away in time, and be only looked on as ye doings of particulars. But I fear ye main point of Union will not be effected. Not to speak of many other arguments, consider that if they from Liege,[1] ye Monks and Friars, be all established in the North, what influence they must naturally have in ye North; if ye Bishop supports and encourages them in preference to establishments out of ye District, that in a short time there will be little connexion with ye North (the great majority) and South. If he does not prefer those in his own District, what can he expect but disagreements, &c.? The same would not be ye case, if ye General College were in ye North; and a proper convenient establishment made by degrees in ye South, which I do and should always

---

[1] i.e. the members of the suppressed Society of the Jesuits, then recently settled at Stonyhurst.

wish for, thinking it might be very beneficial for ye whole, as some from ye North might wish to be there besides some in ye South. I pray that all may end well at last. What I have written here is with no other motive, but to express to you my desire that all may be done for ye general good of Religion; and, because having been much concerned in these affairs, I have naturally taken them much to heart, and the thought of a separation hurts me more (not to speak of other reasons), than it affects those who do not know any of you personally or have not considered it so much. I beg my best respects to Mr. Stapleton, and all others as if mentioned by name. I have been lately in Lancashire for a short time. I was at Stonyhurst, &c., and returned by ye banks of ye Wharf, and by Thorpe Arch, &c. The country all ye way very pleasant. Am going out again next week, to give Confirmation, &c. Direct to me at York. I believe all or most of the Clergy in ye North have subscribed a petition to have a College[1] in the North for the Secular Clergy. If so, you may understand what ye event may be. Mr. Daniel informed me he had met all ye Clergy Superiors in Lancashire, and they were all for it. I shall be happy to hear from you. I remain, with truest esteem and every good wish, desiring your prayers,

"Yours, &c.,

"WILLIAM GIBSON.

"P.S.—Take all this letter in ye most favourable sense, as I have the greatest regard and most sincere attachment to you all. A difference of opinion in these points generally proceeds from not knowing local situations or different circumstances. I say little on the subject to others. But if a majority petition, what answer? The fixed congregations are mostly in ye North. Four of ye Poor Clares from Rouen are returned to London. The gentleman would not let them

---

[1] Here and elsewhere, Dr. Gibson speaks as if Crook Hall were not in existence, and as if there were as yet *no* College in the North. Probably the explanation is that, at that time, it was uncertain whether it would prove permanent; and moreover, numbering as it did little over twenty students, it could hardly be regarded as a College, or at any rate, such a College as Dr. Gibson wanted, and as Ushaw afterwards became.

have ye house exspected. I hope you keep Mr. Coombes. Compliments to him and Mr. Wilds. Tell Mr. Stapleton all are well at Richmond and Lartington. Pray write. Bishop Douglass did not inform me that he had appointed Mr. Stapleton President."[1]

From the above letter Dr. Gibson's frame of mind, and his determination to have a college in the North if possible, are evident enough. The reason he gives amongst others, of the majority of the Religious Orders being in the North, is at least intelligible. Nevertheless, for a time it appeared as if he would have been forced to give way on account of the money difficulties of Crook Hall. Writing to Bishop Douglass on January 19th, 1796, he said that "although the Haydocks and Gradwell[2] had gone to Crook Hall, they were told that perhaps Crook might be continued only for a short while, but if they chose to risk ye expense of going thither and staying till something was settled, they might take it on themselves."

It seems, then, that Dr. Gibson was making a great effort to keep Crook afloat, but did not feel confident enough of success to give a definite answer at that time. He went to London in December, 1795, and on his way called for a few hours at Old Hall, where he inspected the new buildings and grounds, but did not stay the night. On the 8th of the same month he had an interview with Bishop Douglass at Castle Street, but was very reserved as to his intentions. "Neither Monsignor Erskine nor Messrs. Barnard, Lindow, Horrabin or myself," writes Dr. Douglass, "could prevail to bring him to any determination: he neither would agree to unite with me at Old Hall Green nor say that he would not."

On the 9th of January Dr. Gibson wrote giving an excuse for his delay. He said that Mr. Daniel was proprietor of all Douay moneys, and that the Bishops could not lawfully act without his concurrence, or at any rate if they did so, diffi-

---

[1] No doubt because he hoped that Dr. Gibson would have agreed to have the general College at Old Hall, in which case Mr. Stapleton was to resign. The "Application to others as if to force Mr. Daniel," evidently refers to the part played by Mgr. Erskine.

[2] Robert Gradwell, afterwards Coadjutor Bishop to Dr. Bramston of the London District.

culties might afterwards arise. Mr. Daniel, on the other hand, was waiting for the Bishops to come to a decision, and on the 15th of February, writing from Preston to Rev. James Newsham, he says, " I have heard nothing of the consent of the Bishops respecting a settlement at Old Hall Green, from which circumstance it may perhaps be inferred that the report you mention is not well founded."

In the meantime, the financial prospects of Old Hall received a substantial addition by the promise of a Government grant. The following is the record in the Diary of Bishop Douglass :—

" January 30th, 1796.—The Duke of Portland sent for me and told me that afternoon that Mr. Pitt had agreed to give me towards opening the College £3000, at £1000 per annum for three years, and to make the first payment of £1000 at Lady Day next."

Notwithstanding this promise, Bishop Gibson seems to have gradually made up his mind in favour of keeping up the College at Crook Hall, and he was supported by Mr. Daniel. He wrote to Mgr. Erskine to that effect. The quotations given below from Bishop Douglass's Diary will show the course of the negotiations which followed :—

" 1796. February 13th.—Mgr. Erskine informed me that Bishop Gibson had written to him and said, that the Gentlemen of the North would wish to have united in one general College had it been fixed in the North; but since that is not to be the case, they and also the people of Douay wished to have a College in the North. Mgr. Erskine added that he answered Bishop Gibson that if he would have a College in the North, he would be left to himself; and for the people of Douay, it did not belong to them to choose where to have their College, but to go whither they should be sent. Also that Mr. Daniel should be ordered to Old Hall Green, but that he would wait for another letter from Rome before he would send the order. Moreover he said that he told Bishop Gibson it was not reasonable that three Vicars Apostolic should yield to one, but that one should yield to the three."

" February 23rd.—Mgr. Erskine read me a letter he had received from Bishop Gibson about settling the College, in which he denies that Bishop Berington agreed to it being at Old Hall Green, says Bishop Walmesley being a member of a Religious Order had not a right to vote in the business of establishing a Secular Clergy College &c. &c. Mgr. Erskine expressed much anger against Bishop Gibson, and added, 'I only wait for another letter from Cardinal Gerdil.'"[1]

This letter apparently came in the month of April, for we find the following entries about that time :—

"1796.—April 14th.—Mgr. Erskine sends for Mr. Daniel, the President, to come up to town, and told me he meant to direct him to go to Old Hall Green and employ the Roman pension in the education of youths for the Church."

"May.—On the 13th Mr. Daniel arrives in town from Kirkham, on the next day waits on Mgr. Erskine. Afterwards he called on me, told me Mgr. Erskine desired the Roman pensions might be employed for the purpose for which it was granted[2] and that Mgr. Erskine complained heavily of us

---

[1] Cardinal Prefect of Propaganda.
[2] The Roman pension here referred to was what the Pope allowed to Douay College. It continued to be paid till Pius VI. was taken prisoner in 1798. From the following letters of Bishop Douglass, written in 1796, it appears that half of this, as of other Douay money, was paid to St. Edmund's ; the other half went, presumably, to Crook Hall.

*Bishop Douglass to Dr. Stapleton, dated* 1796 (the rest of the date being torn off).

"DEAR SIR,—Mr. Horrabin tells me that he had not mentioned to you my having informed Mr. Varley that the £500 principal money in the 5 per cents. was to be made over to you. I therefore beg leave to say that the day after our arrival in town, viz., on the 9th inst., I informed Mr. Varley that the said principal money was to be given to you, with the moiety of every remittance from R[ome], and of the annual surplus of the Douay property. I'm sorry Mr. Taylor cannot make any part of the new building convenient to receive you this winter. Remaining with every good wish,

"Dear Sir,
"Your humble servant in J. C.,
"JOHN DOUGLASS."

*The same to the same, November 9th,* 1796.

"DEAR SIR,— .... I must now beg leave to say that Mr. Daniel having determined the application of that money, viz. to be employed in the education of youth, some part of that £500 must be applied to the paying off the bill now standing against me for the education of the young men belonging to this District. 2ndly, that I wish to have Mr. Poynter's opinion on the subject, viz. whether or not it be lawful to employ

Bishops and of the English character, that we are a strange people &c., &c., and that he proposed to him (Mr. Daniel) to go and settle at Old Hall Green."

"Mr. Daniel waits again on Mgr. Erskine on the 16th. Mgr. Erskine settles with Mr. Daniel that the Roman pension be employed, and declares he will meddle no more with our affairs. Ita Mr. Daniel, who takes leave of his excellency, and intends to go down to Lancashire next week. The above is the whole of what Mr. Daniel told me of his two interviews."

"On Monday morning, May 23rd, Mr. Daniel set off for Lancashire by the Manchester coach."

A week later Thomas Haydock wrote from Crook Hall as follows:—[1]

"With regard to news about us and Old Hall, we know next to none. You will no doubt have heard that Bishop Berington intends joining Oscott School with Old Hall. Crook is up to the ears in debt and Mr. Eyre has informed ye Bishop in sundry letters, he would undoubtedly break up immediately after ye defensions in case supplies did not come. The debt amounts to upwards of 400 pounds." He adds, however, "Mr. Gibson has at last answered that he is coming to Crook shortly with plenty of money to defray our debts."

No definite decision about the northern college was come to for two years, during which time the authorities at St. Edmund's were still trying to bring about a union. It seems to have been conceded that if Dr. Gibson sent his students to St. Edmund's, a president should be appointed out of his district; for Dr. Poynter writes in a letter to Bishop Douglass, "If Crook Hall should be transferred hither, would that said money for any other purpose than the pensions of youth &c., as above, since Mr. Daniel's determination, which determination I did not know till a few days ago when the paper was shown to me. Mr. Barnard thinks it cannot be applied to any other purpose. I remain, with every good wish,

"Dear Sir,
"Your humble servant in J. C.,
"J. DOUGLASS."

[1] "Haydock papers," p. 199.

not Mr. Thomas Eyre be at least as proper a person to treat with the Spaniards and to undertake the management of the College as Mr. Smith, who perhaps may be thought necessary by some to act in the recovery of our property in France?"

About that time it was likewise proposed to send Mr. Lingard to Old Hall—for he properly belonged to the London district—and Dr. Poynter was consulted on the matter. He wrote in favour of accepting him. "We should be able to give employment to Mr. Lingard," he said, "if he would be willing to condescend to teach one of our lower classes, and should be happy to have such a professor with us, if we do not an injury to Crook Hall in desiring what they are in possession of . . . . Perhaps if we had one of the Northern District it might be a more evident disposition towards a union."

For some reason this arrangement did not come about, and a little later a definite determination was arrived at by the Northerners to build a college of their own. The following entries in Bishop Douglass's Diary record the decision:—

"July, 1798.—Bishop Gibson informs me by letter from Fernyhalgh that the Lancashire Brethren have held a meeting about the establishment of a College, and that they have resolved to make a purchase and build a College in the North. Before the meeting broke up £4000 was subscribed for the purpose. Thus have they resolved to separate from us at St. Edmund's."

"August, 1798.—The business of purchasing ground for and of building the College in the North is conducted by a committee consisting of Bishop Gibson and Messrs. Barrow of Claughton, Lancashire, Thomas Eyre, President of Crook, Gillow of York and Thomas Smith of Durham."

"December 10th, 1799.—Bishop Gibson tells me by letter this morning that deeds for the purchase of Ushaw in order to build a College &c. were executed."

This decision was a great blow indeed to St. Edmund's, but not a surprise. As a result, it became advisable to curtail the expenditure on the new building as far as possible, as the amount of accommodation required would not now be so great. Dr. Stapleton wrote to Bishop Douglass in this sense. " The contents of Bishop Gibson's [letter] did not in the least surprise me," he wrote ; "it is nothing but what I expected. It will not be possible to contract our new building at present, I fear ; the most we shall be able to do is to continue to make ye kitchen &c. in the building already made." And looking forward to a possible contingency in the future, he adds, "You ask me my opinion about ye Fernyhalgh meeting ; all I can say is that you must take care that ye Doway funds are not spent there. If Mr. Daniel affords any pecuniary assistance to that house, we should certainly have an equal division with them at least, and if the Western and Middle Districts unite with us the foundations destined for them ought to be spent at Old Hall."

Even now, the affair was not finally settled. At the August meeting of the " Lancashire Brethren " great fault was found with the previous decision. We may again quote Bishop Douglass :—

"September, 1798.—The Lancashire Clergy, at their meeting last month, disagreed much about the establishing of a College, and on the subject of ' a meeting of a certain small number of their brethren' at Fernyhalgh, at which public money had been voted away without public concurrence of the Brethren."

As a last chance, therefore, Messrs. Horrabin and Hodgson went to see the Rev. John Barrow of Claughton, one of the most influential members of the Northern Committee, and put before him the disastrous consequences which they said would follow to the Northern District if they spent so much of their mission money on buying land and building a college, besides the difficulty of obtaining a supply of masters or professors and other such considerations. Apparently they succeeded in partially convincing him, "for," writes Bishop Douglass, "after the above meeting of all the Lancashire Clergy [he] drops all his prejudices against Old Hall Green and agrees to come up and see [it] in order to effect a union." He never came, however, but instead asked Mr. Horrabin to send him a statement of the total accommodation at the College. This was duly forwarded on October 18th, 1798.

Mr. Barrow sent his reply on December 16th, and it seems to have been a final negative to all prospect of Old Hall becoming a General College. He gives three reasons. First he says that Bishop Gibson is quite determined to have his own College, and this was probably the chief cause in reality. As a second reason he says—what had been often urged before—that the dearness of provisions and fuel, etc., in the south is against setting up the College there. He estimates the annual saving on this score, by having it in the north, at 2000*l.*, which must surely have been far above the mark. His third reason is the admixture of laity at St. Edmund's. To this last Dr. Douglass answered that it was exactly the same at Douay,[1] and indeed was subsequently the same at Ushaw. However, it was clear that this was now to be regarded as an ultimatum, and Dr. Poynter gave up all further hope of St. Edmund's becoming the College for the four districts. He continued to work for union of forces as far as there was any chance of obtaining it, and his proposition to unite Oscott with Old Hall was discussed for several years, though it was never carried out.[2]

We now go on to record some of the internal events of the history of St. Edmund's, which took place during the progress of the new building, and are all carefully noted down by Dr. Poynter in the College Diary. The first entry of note is as follows :—

"1795.—In the night between the 5th and 6th of November, a violent storm of wind beat down 20 feet of the south-east

---

[1] This was not in fact the case, owing to the absence of the students of the Northern and Midland Districts, which caused the proportion of church boys at St. Edmund's to be very small at that time. Had it become a General College, however, this would have been otherwise.

[2] See Appendix F. It is curious to note, as showing the growth of Catholicism in England during the present century, that Dr. Poynter, in the estimate he made of the expenses and income of the proposed General College, puts the probable number of Church students for the whole of England, including divines, at seventy, a number hardly above what now serves for the diocese of Westminster alone.

corner wall of the new building, and the bottle containing the inscription of the foundation, which was placed under the corner on the 19th of August, was taken up. The wall was soon repaired; but the bottle was not laid again till September 2nd, 1796."

On December 19th, Bishop Douglass confirmed ten students, among whom was the future Bishop Walsh. Nothing further of importance is recorded during the remainder of the year, beyond occasional "exhibitions" and "defensions" of the theologians and others. Among the new students in January we find two nephews of Dr. Stapleton, one of whom afterwards distinguished himself as an officer during the Peninsular War. He used in later life to talk about his days at St. Edmund's, and of his uncle, the President, whom he would often try and put out of temper, he said, in order to see him pull his wig on one side.

During the winter, the want of accommodation at the old College was severely felt, and since no decision had as yet been come to by Bishop Gibson, the resumption of building operations was delayed till late in the spring, when Mr. Daniel had finally declined the presidency; for it was only then that Dr. Stapleton was able to feel settled. As soon as his appointment was made permanent, he wrote to Bishop Douglass, urging the immediate resumption of the work before the holidays should begin. "Otherwise," he said, "[the students] will tell their parents that there are not the least hopes of having it finished this year, which would be a pity." It was determined to get on with the main body of the building and not for the present to attempt the chapel and refectory. A brickfield was temporarily opened in front of the new college, which was a great saving of expense, the first 14,000 bricks having been carted all the way from London. In the course of the summer the farmyard was enclosed and gates put up, and Dr. Stapleton reported with satisfaction that they were now wholly shut out from "ye Green."

The General Exhibition was held on June 21st and 22nd, 1796, and the list of visitors included Dr. Douglass, Mr.

Barnard, his vicar-general, and Mr. Hodgson, who "were pleased to express their satisfaction at the performance." Arthur Clifford delivered a discourse on "The Rise, Progress and Utility of the Mathematics," and in the afternoon Lewis Havard and Thomas Pitchford defended philosophical theses under the direction of the Rev. J. D'Ancel. A set of exhibition verses was written for this occasion by one of the students, and have been preserved, but they are not of any particular merit. The second day was devoted entirely to theological disputations, in which Messrs. Broderick, Peach and Clarkson took part, the whole being prepared under Dr. Poynter's supervision. All the performers on both days were old Douay students.

Schools reopened after the holidays on July 25th, when High Mass *De Spiritu Sancto* was sung by the President. The new year's list of students shows fourteen divines and philosophers and seventy-eight boys, so that there was a considerable increase, and it became of still more importance that the new building should be got ready, at least in part, as soon as possible.

In the month of November, Mr. Taylor brought down a certain Colonel Harcourt, who was not a Catholic, to see St. Edmund's. The purpose of his visit is explained in the following letter, addressed to Dr. Stapleton:—

"DEAR SIR,—I here fulfil the promise made in Mr. Poynter's letter, and take the liberty of acquainting you that Colonel Harcourt[1] intends to make a visit to the College on Tuesday next, and to eat a bit of beef or mutton with you at the usual hour, one o'clock. Mr. Taylor, the surveyor, and self mean to accompany the Colonel. Accordingly Mr. Taylor desires you to set the workmen on the front arches, that those and the whole of the front may, if possible, be finished for 12 o'clock on Tuesday, that is as far as the front is to be finished this year, in order to make the best appearance we can in the eyes of the Colonel. Mr. Taylor does not doubt of the Colonel

---

[1] George William Richard Harcourt, M.P., Colonel of the 12th Regiment, and afterwards Governor of St. Croix, was the second surviving son of John Harcourt, of Ankerwycke Park, Bucks.

making a handsome present towards the building; we have already talked of his giving the great clock.

"He is Mr. Taylor's friend, we dined with him at Mr. Taylor's last Thursday.... Though a Colonel in the army and a brave man, as he showed himself in the West Indies, yet he is young, of a very modest, affable, and genteel behaviour.... He is very friendly to our cause, to our having Colleges &c. So is the whole family. Mr. Taylor expects much from their munificence to the College. The mother of the Colonel has become, by a second venture, Lady Shuldham, and is very desirous of seeing the new building. But Mr. Taylor won't let her ladyship see it till it be completed.

"On Tuesday morning Mr. Taylor is to be at his house at about 8 o'clock; at 9 o'clock they take me up in Castle Street; and if he drive at the rate of ten miles an hour, which Mr. Taylor says is his usual pace, you know when to expect us. I presume you may expect us a little after twelve o'clock at latest. I need not tell you (the frank does it[1]) that he is a member of Parliament. We intend to return after dinner."

The concluding paragraph shows the bishop's worldly wisdom:—

"May I close my letter with a request that your students may be directed to be clean on this occasion, in their Sunday clothes, and be allowed to ask the Colonel for a playday &c.? I daresay he will look at every place and everything, to make a report to his mother and his family.

"I remain, with every good wish, Dear Sir,

"Your humble servant in J. C.

"JOHN DOUGLASS."

The visit seems to have gone off pleasantly enough, for Colonel Harcourt at its conclusion "begged that his name might be put down for fifty guineas towards a tower clock for the College." The rest of the money necessary to buy

---

[1] "Franking" was the privilege of an M.P., who could, by signing his name on the back of a letter, cause it to go post free.

the clock was given by Mr. James Butler, who had been a student at Old Hall twenty years earlier.

At the end of the year, complications arose with respect to Mr. Sone's will, exactly as Mr. Southworth had foretold. Mr. Wright, his brother-in-law,[1] disputed the will, and claimed the whole on behalf of his wife, Mr. Sone's next-of-kin. A long Chancery suit followed, and, until this was concluded, it was not considered safe to continue building. For more than a year, therefore, the walls remained unroofed, and in order to reimburse Dr. Douglass for what he had advanced, it was found necessary to mortgage the old college to Mr. Wright, the banker, on April 8th, 1797, for the sum of 5000*l*. At the same time, Dr. Stapleton addressed a formal petition to the Government, reminding them of their promise of 3000*l*., which was still unpaid. It does not appear, however, that this had the desired effect, and the building was not proceeded with till the lapse of more than a year.

Further difficulties now appeared in the distance. The new war tax, called the "Triple Assessment Act," was passing through Parliament in 1797, the effect of which would be to increase the taxation of the college from about 40*l*. to 160*l*., an addition which it could ill afford to bear. When the time came, an appeal was prepared by the President, on the score of the buildings being all used as a school, and this appeal was heard at Ware on April 4th, 1798, when the assessment was reduced by a half. It was still, however, double what it used to be, and a case was drawn up for counsel's opinion, to know whether there was a chance of a further reduction in case of a second appeal. This was put before Mr. Lowndes of the Inner Temple on August 8th, 1798. The question raised was whether all the buildings were to be regarded as parts of a single college, as the assessors had done, or whether they were not rather to be considered as so many separate and distinct buildings, which would considerably

---

[1] This was not the same man as Thomas Wright the Catholic banker of Henrietta Street, whose name also occurs. The latter was the third son of Anthony White, of Wealside, Essex. The bank failed in 1840.

reduce the sum chargeable. Mr. Lowndes decided in favour of the assessors, and there the matter ended.[1]

Studies were pursued through the year 1797, amidst somewhat dreary surroundings, the new college standing at the other side of the garden with its unroofed walls, without any sign of further work, and with its future completion still full of uncertainty. Dr. Douglass, Mr. Barnard and Mr. Hodgson again attended the General Exhibition, when, in addition to the theological disputation, a debate was performed, followed by some French speeches. After the Midsummer vacations the numbers showed a falling off, and only eighty-one names appear, as against ninety-two the previous year. At a Confirmation the following April, Dr. Douglass administered the sacrament to no less than forty-three students.

In the month of June, an effort was made to reclaim the property of the lost colleges in France. Taking advantage of the temporary peace, Messrs. Tuite and Cleghorn set out for St. Omer on the 19th of June, and they were absent three months. An account of their adventures will be found in the Appendix.[2] They were not successful in getting possession of the college itself, but they recovered a certain amount of the personal property and movables. A similar attempt was planned on behalf of Douay College. According to Bishop Douglass, it was at first proposed that Dr. Poynter should accompany Mr. Daniel there; but as he could not very well be spared, it was arranged that Mr. Smith should go. They

---

[1] The following details, given by Bishop Douglass concerning the taxation of Ecclesiastical Trust money, seem in place here, though the actual date is two years later.

"April 5th, 1799.—Having applied to Mr. Pitt through the Solicitor-General (see answer of the Solicitor-General to William Sheldon, Esq., of Gray's Inn), and to the Chancellor for some clause being inserted in the Income Act to exempt us from discovering our trusts or being obliged to pay the tax for such moneys as we hold in trust, for the support of priests, education of youth, &c., and not meeting with relief on account of the temper of the times (expression of Mr. Pitt and the Lord Chancellor) I on this day gave in, sealed up, my statement of contribution for the prosecution of the war upon the whole of our income arising from the trusts as being my own property, in order to keep concealed the said trusts, which the law considers as Superstitious Purposes. Proh Dolor! But the Gentlemen Commissioners have returned to me the whole tax."

[2] See Appendix D.

met at York on August 17th to arrange details; but it is probable that they never actually started, as war broke out again almost immediately afterwards.

Some three months after the return of Messrs. Tuite and Cleghorn, the misfortunes of St. Edmund's seemed likely to be brought to a climax by the removal of the President. For some years past, the government of the English College at Rome had been in an unsatisfactory state. For about two centuries it had been under the direction of the English Jesuits; but after the suppression of the society in 1773, it was handed over to the care of Italian secular priests, who were anything but fortunate in their administration of it. It was said that the Italian method of government was not suited to the British character, and the advisability of having English students ruled by an English rector was more than once urged. This seemed now on the point of accomplishment. The Cardinal Protector wrote entrusting the selection of a suitable person to Mgr. Erskine, and his choice fell on Dr. Stapleton.

Bishop Douglass's first answer should be noted, namely that Dr. Stapleton was still President of St. Omer College, and must hold himself in readiness to return there when peace was proclaimed. He admitted that this difficulty was not insurmountable, and that if Dr. Stapleton wished it, he could hand over the College of St. Omer to him (Bishop Douglass) by a legal document and that then he would be free. Dr. Stapleton received the idea favourably and promised to come to London to talk the matter over. His loss to St. Edmund's at that time, however, would have been very serious, and it was a matter of thankfulness, so far as Old Hall was concerned, that the disturbed state of Rome in the following spring brought these negotiations to a sudden termination.

With the early months of 1798 better times arrived for St. Edmund's. The law-suit over Mr. Sone's will was decided in favour of the College, and Bishop Douglass wrote at once urging the importance of the immediate resumption of building operations. "All the haste consistent with reason must be made in getting the building up," he said, "for at Rome all our property is confiscated already; and at Lisbon and Valladolid how long shall we have Colleges? Rome is declared an independent Republic. The Pope was still in the Vatican on the 17th of last month, well in health, with a guard of his own people. The arms of the Pope are taken down everywhere, and what authority will be allowed to him is not known. Three magistrates are named to superintend the affairs of Religion. The Municipality consists of five persons called Consuls. Two of them were Prelates. All distinctions are abolished. No more Princes, Cardinals or Prelates, all are equal; no more livery servants. How long is this reign of iniquity to last? May our Father in Heaven look with compassion on His own City, and may He, in His mercy, protect and preserve us." And he ends up with a practical reflection: "These assessed taxes will ruin us all. Yet grieving 's a folly."

The fall of the English College in Rome is thus entered by Dr. Poynter in the College Diary:—

"When the French entered Rome, they took possession of the English College there, sold all the effects and ordered the British subjects to quit the Pope's territories within a fortnight. All the students of the English and Scotch Colleges were sent with passports through France and arrived in London."

The building at St. Edmund's now proceeded briskly enough. The various stages were duly reported at intervals by Dr. Stapleton to Dr. Douglass in letters, which are among the College archives, and which give us a continuous account of how matters progressed. Thus we learn that on March 21st, 1798, the scaffolding was erected, but on account of the frosty mornings a start was not to be made at the brickwork till after Easter. On May 23rd things were going on very satisfactorily, and Dr. Stapleton promised by the Exhibition Day "to have something to show for our money." Six bricklayers were at work and half the timber having arrived, the carpenters were about to commence operations. "Ye barge" had been despatched to London for the remainder of the timber. Two months later, on July 21st, the work was

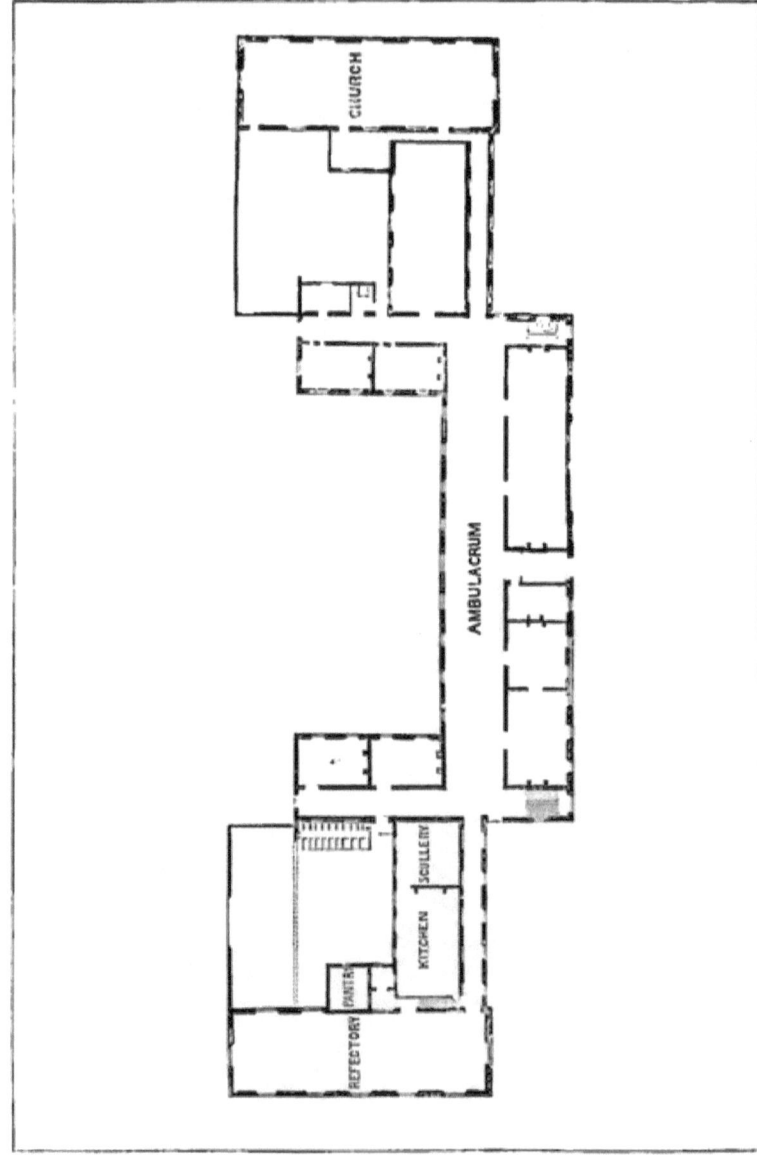

The New College—Ground Plan.

further advanced and the stones were laid in the front, which he said improved the general appearance greatly.

As soon as the holidays had begun, Dr. Stapleton began to consider how the rooms had better be distributed for use. Mr. Taylor had, he said, contrived to make a dormitory in the roof—the present "top dormitory"—and this gave a great deal of extra room in the "top gallery." This was to be used in part for the libraries. The present vice-president's rooms were then one, and were to serve for the divines' library, and two other rooms were put together to form a boys' library, or *Bibliotheca Tyronica*, as it was called. It was proposed to fit up the large room in the "president's gallery," which was ultimately to become the divines' library, as a temporary chapel.[1] The room below this,[2] he destined for a temporary refectory, and the corresponding room[3] at the other end of the ambulacrum was to be used as the study place. The president's and bishop's rooms were in the same place as they are now. The old college was to be the preparatory school, and its chapel to serve also for the Catholics of the neighbourhood under Mr. Potier. It was calculated that the new college would accommodate sixty-five students, and the old one, without the Hermitage or Ship, about fifty.

On September 28th, 1798, Dr. Stapleton wrote that the building was completely roofed in, and the slater had finished his work. The "top dormitory" was floored as well as half the "top gallery," and the window sashes were fast being completed. On October 11th, most of the windows were glazed, and the scaffolding was being taken down. The ground in front of the house was to be cleared, and those who were accustomed to cross the field as a short cut to Puckeridge, were henceforth to be prohibited from doing so. On November 20th, the plasterers had nearly completed their work, and the temporary chapel and president's and bishop's

---

[1] After being used as a chapel for six years, it was devoted to its intended purpose, and was used for the divines' library till their departure in 1869. It is now divided into class rooms.

[2] The present junior study place and physical science room combined.

[3] Now divided into two, and used as parlour and museum.

rooms were being fitted up. A fortnight later the parlours and study place were almost ready, and, moreover, Dr. Stapleton had got very nearly "at ye end of ye building money."

In the following spring, before the new building was ready for use, a sad occurrence took place, which is thus recorded in the College Diary:—

"1799.—March 21st.—In the night between the 20th and 21st, some sacrilegious Robbers broke into the Chapel through the window of the Sacristy, and carried away the Tabernacle with its Divine contents, plundering the Sacristy of everything that had the appearance of gold or silver. In grief and consternation at the loss of the tabernacle &c., many of the Professors, Divines &c. went in search of the lost treasure, thinking it might be thrown into some ditch. In the pond at the north-west corner of the meadow lying before the Front of the New College, near the gate adjoining to the entrance into the new road which leads to the College, were discovered by Mr. Jno. Sedcote, who was coming to Old Hall with Mr. Potier, several small hosts floating on the surface of the water. The tabernacle was found sunk to the bottom, being filled with mud and a large stone. The hosts were carefully taken out of the pond and the tabernacle brought home. The hosts contained in the Ciborium and Remonstrance, which the robbers had carried away, were found for the most part wrapped up in the corporal, laid in the bottom of the tabernacle, and covered with the door, which had been broken off its hinges and put within; on the door was placed a great stone; the tabernacle was filled with dirt and mud, in which many of the sacred hosts were found. All this happened on Maundy Thursday. To make some reparation for this injury offered to the Blessed Sacrament on the very day of the commemoration of its institution, some prayers were said in honour of this Mystery, and it was determined by the President that prayers should be annually said for that intention, after Compline at three o'clock on Maundy Thursday."

The following additional particulars are from a letter

written by one of the priests of the college, probably Dr. Coombes, to Miss Clifford, daughter of Lord Clifford, of Ugbrooke :—

"Old Hall,
"Maundy Thursday,
"March 21st, 1799.

"Last night thieves forced their way into our Chapel and Sacristy, and completely plundered both: from the Chapel they carried off the entire Tabernacle with everything in it. . . . . This morning, on discovering the horrid sacrilege, we immediately made search for the Tabernacle. . . . . We soon found it at the bottom of a pond near the house. You are undoubtedly very anxious to hear how these agents of the devil disposed of your Saviour. Well, they acted thus: finding a Corporal in the Tabernacle, they emptied all the Sacred Vessels into it, folded it up and laid it at the bottom of the Tabernacle: upon it they placed the little door of the Tabernacle which they had torn off. On this door they laid a heavy stone, they then nearly filled it with mud, sank it in the pond, and went off with the booty. These precautions they probably thought necessary to prevent the discovery of the Tabernacle, as the Sacred Species left loose, would rise to the surface of the water. But in their violent hurry they scattered some few Hosts in the water, which appeared this morning very white and floating on the water, which immediately led to the discovery of the Tabernacle. Oh, I can easily anticipate your feelings on hearing this news. Had you and your sisters seen us kneeling and occupied in collecting as well as we could the Sacred Species from a large quantity of mud and water, your little hearts would have been overpowered with grief."

The robbery took place from the chapel of the old college. Two Irishmen were suspected of being its authors. They had been present at Mass on Palm Sunday, and prayed aloud and with unaccountable gesticulations, which attracted suspicion. The same afternoon they were seen prowling about the yard, trying to open some of the doors, and when asked what they wanted, they said that they wished to see

Dr. Poynter, and ask him a question. The following Wednesday two French servants left the college. One was the butler, the other the baker, Francis Neuville, whose name may still be seen cut on the walls of the "Hermitage." As the robbery took place the following night, it was supposed that these Frenchmen had a share in it, and very probably acted in concert with the two Irishmen above alluded to.

The list of articles taken included two chalices and patens, a pair of silver cruets, a thurible and boat, and a monstrance. They were all replaced by the Rev. Thomas Horrabin, the college agent in London, at his own expense. The chalice and monstrance he gave are still in use.

The Act of Reparation in the afternoon, between Compline and Tenebræ,[1] was made publicly in the chapel, and this was repeated annually for many years; and, though it afterwards dropped for a time, it was revived by Mgr. Patterson in 1875, and now takes place every year after the "Mandatum." A little memorial chapel was erected by the Edmundian Association in 1879, outside the end of the "new wing," which is close to the spot where the Blessed Sacrament was found, the pond being now dried up. A mosaic at the back of the chapel represents Our Lord walking on the waters, and the following inscription is underneath :—

<pre>
        A D MD CC XC IX  XII KAL APR
        QUÆ FUIT FERIA V in CŒNA DMNI
        Ss Sacramentum Corporis D N Jesu Xti
        pridie e sacello sacrilego ausu abreptum
        mirabilem in modum fluitans super stagnum
        l passus abhinc orientem versus inventum est
        ita disponente eo qui pedibus super mare
        ambulans Petrum ne mergeretur erexit
        et Paulum tertio naufragantem de profundo
                pelagi liberavit
</pre>

The concluding stages of the building occupied longer than had been anticipated, and the new college was not ready for use till the end of the summer of 1799.

---

[1] The annual Retreat at that time took place, as now, in Holy Week, and therefore Compline was recited in the afternoon, followed by Tenebræ, which was sung.

Shortly before it was opened, Dr. Moylan, Bishop of Cork, visited the college, as we learn from the following extract from Bishop Douglass's Diary :—

"July 29th, 1799.—Dr. Moylan (Bishop of Cork), accompanied me this day to St. Edmund's, Old Hall Green. He expressed much pleasure at the sight of the College, and examining all the conveniences of playgrounds, farmyard, farm &c., relative situation of the College and Seminary, or of the great and small school, he wished Maynooth had the same advantages."

During the month of August the clock was put up in its place, and on September 1st Dr. Stapleton reported the chapel to be nearly ready. Bishop Douglass spent a month at Old Hall in the early autumn, and during his stay the new college was formally opened. The following is his account of the ceremonies used on the occasion :—

"1799.—On this day (September 29th), sacred to St. Michael, we entered the new College. I blessed the College by going to each gallery, praying in each according to the Ritual (*Benedictio domus novae*), sprinkling each with Holy Water, and sang Mass *in Ponticalibus* in the new Chapel; and at Dinner treated the Professors and the Students with wine."

Though the college was now considered open, it was by no means completed, and no one slept in it for several months. The kitchen was not only unfinished, but was to be left in its then state, unplastered and without fittings, owing to the want of funds. A temporary kitchen was fitted up, probably in the room subsequently used as the Lay Library.[1] Moreover there were no proper playrooms for boys or divines, the room intended and afterwards used for the latter purpose being for the present employed as temporary refectory. The "schools in the wing," the present poets' playroom and library, together with the ambulacrum, had therefore to serve as recreation room for both boys and divines. There were two playgrounds, the "Great Bounds," afterwards used as "Church Bounds," and now simply "The Bounds," and

[1] Now the class room of the Second of Rudiments.

the "Little Bounds" at the other end, where the Lay Bounds afterwards were, now forming part of the "Pleasure Ground."

A month or so after the opening of the new college, Mr. Taylor called on Dr. Douglass in London and represented to him the want of room, and in particular his regret that the kitchen and servants' rooms above should be left in so incomplete a state. At the same time he pointed out that what was ultimately intended for servants' rooms might be made into a convenient temporary refectory, and undertook to do this, together with the kitchen and back stairs, for 50*l*. Dr. Douglass agreed to this and paid the money himself.

The required alterations were completed as promised by Christmas, 1799, and at the commencement of the new year, the dormitories being now ready, the students began to move across. Mr. Robert Archbold, when nearly forty years later M.P. for Kildare, visited the college where he had been educated, and said that he was the first boy who moved across, and that he slept in the new college for the first time on January 1st, 1800.

By the end of the month most of the students had moved over, and a little later, as the president's room was not yet ready, Dr. Stapleton took temporary possession of the procurator's room, and wrote on April 13th that they were now all in the new college. The workmen were out of the house by Easter and no further building took place till Dr. Poynter's additions five years later.[1] The cost so far had been a little over 12,000*l*.

The last entry in the Diary in connection with the building of the college is as follows :—

---

[1] It should be observed that the south side of the house was further advanced than the north side. The foundations of the "bounds playroom" were laid, but the walls were not many feet high. It was completed by Dr. Poynter at the same time as his chapel in 1805, and the poets' dormitory on the top of it was built then. This accounts for the fact that the windows of the poets' dormitory do not match the corresponding ones in the passage to the "new wing." The latter agree with Mr. Taylor's plan, which the former do not. There are in fact six windows to the poets' dormitory—exclusive of those in the part added more recently—instead of five.

"1800. June 10th. The Administrators of this College, desirous of expressing their sincere sentiments of esteem for James Taylor Esq. of Islington and their grateful sense of his kindness in surveying, superintending &c. the building of the new College, have this day agreed to educate gratis in this College his sons and all the sons he may have by Mrs. Taylor his present or any future wife, agreeably to the general conditions and terms of education observed in this College. The sum of one hundred pounds shall likewise be remitted to him as soon as conveniently can be done."

## CHAPTER IX.

### ST. EDMUND'S COLLEGE UNDER DR. POYNTER.

#### 1800—1813.

> Dr. Stapleton called to Rome—He is appointed Vicar Apostolic of the Midland District—Dr. Poynter succeeds him as President—Meeting of Bishops and Douay Seniors—Decision not to re-establish Douay College—Bishop Stapleton, Mr. Daniel and others go to France to reclaim the colleges—Death of Bishop Stapleton—Dr. Coombes presented with an honorary degree—New chapel and refectory built at Old Hall—College medal struck—Rev. John Potier leaves—His death—Reports against St. Edmund's—Its gradual decline as a lay college—Dr. Coombes goes on the mission—Rev. Francis Tuite Vice-President—Rebellion amongst the students—Its consequences—Departure of the Rev. Francis Tuite—Rev. Joseph Kimbell Vice-President—Death of Bishop Douglass—Enumeration of distinguished Edmundians of this period.

DR. STAPLETON was not allowed to enjoy the fruits of his labours very long. About a month after he had moved over to the new college, he was called upon to undertake a journey to Rome, described by Dr. Milner as "a deputation of equal secrecy and importance,"[1] which led to his leaving St. Edmund's for good. He set out on the evening of Ascension Day, 1800, in company with the Rev. John Nassau,[2] and was absent rather more than four months. On July 8th he wrote an account of his mission, which he sent to Bishop Douglass, at the same time announcing his intention of starting homewards as soon as he had had another audience with the new Pope, Pius VII. He returned by way of Ancona, Trieste, Linz, Dresden, Hamburgh and Yarmouth, where he landed on October 10th.

In the meantime, the question of the appointment of a new Vicar Apostolic for the Midland District, which office

---

[1] Supplementary Memoirs, p. 108.
[2] The Rev. John Nassau, educated at Sedgley Park and Douay, died in London, January 4th, 1807.

BISHOP POYNTER,
President, 1801-1813;
Vicar Apostolic of London District, 1812-1827.

had been vacant since the death of Bishop Berington on June 11th, 1798, came on for decision ; and, as an indirect result of his visit to Rome, Dr. Stapleton was nominated to fill the post. Many circumstances at that time combined to make it one of peculiar difficulty; but Cardinal Borgia, Prefect of Propaganda, exhorted him to accept it, for the present at least, out of reverence for the Holy See, with the assurance that if after settling the affairs of his district he should prefer to become Coadjutor to Bishop Douglass, he would be permitted to make the exchange as soon as a fit person could be found to take his place.[1]

The return of Dr. Stapleton and his appointment and consecration as Vicar Apostolic are thus entered in the College Diary :—

"1800.—October 13th.—Mr. President returned to the College after his secret expedition to Rome, to the universal joy of all in the College.

"November 7th.—Bulls for the Consecration of Rev. Gregory Stapleton were dated at Rome. . . .

"1801.—March 8th. Right Rev. Dr. Stapleton, was consecrated Bishop of Hierocæsarea by the Right Rev. Dr. Douglass. Right Rev. Dr. Moylan[2] and Right Rev. Dr. Sharrock were assisting Bishops. Bishop Douglass was attended by Rev. William Poynter, and Rev. William Coombes ; Dr. Stapleton by Rev. John Law and Rev. Francis Lycett ; Dr. Moylan by Rev. F. Tuite and Rev. T. Walsh ; Dr. Sharrock by Rev. L. Havard and Rev. John Haly."

This brought the presidency of Dr. Stapleton, which had lasted five and a half years, to a close. The appointment of his successor is next recorded in the Diary :—

---

[1] Husenbeth's "Life of Milner," page 85. Dr. Douglass had applied for a coadjutor a year or two before this ; but the election of one had been delayed by the state of affairs at Rome and the death of Pius VI. Three names had been suggested, Rev. Gregory Stapleton, Rev. William Poynter, and Rev. Thomas Smith. All three were afterwards Bishops, and received their episcopal consecration at Old Hall.

[2] Bishop of Cork. This seems to have been the first occasion that the full number of three Bishops took part in a consecration ceremony. Hitherto it had been customary to use the privilege conceded to England for two priests to assist the consecrating Bishop.

"On the same day Rev. William Poynter was made President of the College by Bishop Douglass, and the Rev. William Coombes was made Vice-President by the President, Rev. William Poynter."

Shortly after his consecration, Bishop Stapleton fell ill, and his state gave rise to much anxiety for some time. Dr. Kirk, in a letter to Dr. Poynter, dated Longbirch, May 6th, says, "I am much concerned to hear from my neighbour, Mr. Roe, that Bishop Stapleton has had a relapse and, when you wrote, was so very ill that you requested he might be remembered in our prayers, and recommended to our congregations. I shall accordingly begin to-night to pray for him in our family prayers, and on Sunday will recommend him to my people. Heaven grant that our prayer may be heard and that our Bishop may yet be spared a little while for the good of his flock. I cannot help adding, however, that from my first hearing of his illness, I have greatly feared that it would be fatal. . . . . You will confer a great obligation on me by giving me information respecting our Bishop's health, and I pray God the tidings may be favourable. The whole district is interested in his speedy recovery; but no one more so than myself."

Bishop Stapleton recovered temporarily, and proceeded to his district early in the summer, taking with him the Rev. Thomas Walsh, then in deacon's orders, as private secretary. According to Husenbeth, his exertions to restore peace were successful as long as they lasted; but the following year his health again began to give way, and he had to take another rest. He temporarily rallied; but being called abroad in May his illness returned suddenly during his travels and ended fatally.

The cause of his journey was connected with the affairs of Douay and St. Omer, which again came to the front towards the end of 1801. On the 17th of September of that year, in virtue of the armistice which preceded the Peace of Amiens, a decree of the French government declared the English Colleges restored to their rightful owners. A Memorial was at once drawn out by Dr. Poynter, and sent to Paris, and a meeting was summoned, first of the Vicars Apostolic and then of the Douay Seniors, to discuss what measures it was advisable to take. The Bishops met first, at Old Hall. The following is Bishop Douglass's minute of the Meeting :—

"1801.—November 26th.—On this day, Messrs. Gibson, Stapleton and self[1] assembled in the President's room at Old Hall Green, and after taking into consideration the present state of our establishments at home and abroad &c. &c. we resolved ;—

"1st. That in the present circumstances it was not proper to attempt the re-establishment of Douay College.

"2ndly. That the moneys belonging to the late Douay College, formerly in the administration of the President thereof, are henceforward to be in the administration of the Bishops."

Four days after this, Mr. Daniel arrived in town from Kirkham, Lancashire, and at the second meeting, which was held at Castle Street on December 4th, besides the above named bishops, the following Douay seniors were present :— Rev. John Daniel, president ; Rev. Joseph Hodgson, vice-president ; Rev. William Poynter, prefect of studies ; Rev. Thomas Smith, professor of natural philosophy.

"In this meeting,"—I again quote from Dr. Douglass —"the resolves of November 26th were explained and confirmed. It was resolved that Messrs. J. Daniel, Thomas Smith, John Bew, President of Oscott, and Thomas Cleghorn, one of the professors at St. Edmund's, should go over to Flanders and France to see into the state of our Colleges and other property, report their opinion of the same and be ready to take possession of the same after the signature of the definitive treaty."

After some delay this resolution was carried into effect, and the above named set out on May 19th, 1802. Bishop Stapleton also accompanied them. He had been suffering

---

[1] It will be observed that the Western district was unrepresented. As has been already remarked most of their Clergy were regulars, and consequently they had less interest in Douay than the others. It seems that there were never more than one or two Western students there.

for some time past from fits of drowsiness, bordering on stupor; but before starting he spent a day at Shooter's Hill, from which he derived great benefit, and after a good night's rest, set forward the next morning, says Bishop Douglass, in good spirits. This was Wednesday, May 18th. The following day he arrived at St. Omer, and on the Friday he transacted business as usual. In the evening the illness returned on him, but his condition was not considered serious enough to detain Messrs. Daniel and Smith, who left for Douay on the Saturday morning. During the day Bishop Stapleton became so much worse that medical aid was called in, and a consultation between three doctors resulted in a determination to try the effect of opening a vein, which operation they performed on the Sunday morning. "Better symptoms then appeared," writes Bishop Douglass, "but the stupor continued, and at the half-past ten at night he expired, without a groan. God's Holy Will be done! May he rest in peace."

Dr. Stapleton was well known at St. Omer, and the Church of St. Denis, where the funeral service was held, was crowded with people, the municipality sending a special deputation of their own body to represent them. The interment took place afterwards, in the cemetery attached to the ancient Church of St. Martin-au-Laert, about a mile outside the town.[1]

The death of Bishop Stapleton was a great blow to the Midland district and to the Catholic Church in England. It need hardly be added that St. Edmund's owes him a special debt of gratitude, as one who took a chief part in its foundation. He was not a great scholar, but he had thoroughly sound judgment and great powers of organization and government.[2] He was also a man of singular piety,

---

[1] The Church of St. Martin-au-Laert was rebuilt between thirty and forty years ago, and many of the graves were removed to make room for the new church. Dr Stapleton's was one of this number. A mural tablet records the fact of his having been buried there.

Bishop Stapleton's servant, Jones, afterwards came to Old Hall, and became the college shoemaker. His daughter, Mary Jones, was dairymaid for over fifty years, and will be remembered by old Edmundians. She died in 1883.

[2] The following extract from a letter of Dr. Poynter to Bishop Douglass, dated August 9th, 1796, is strong testimony of Dr. Stapleton's governing powers, coming as it does from one who was living under him:—"It

and, to use Dr. Milner's expression, of "unimpeachable orthodoxy and morality." He left most of his property to St. Edmund's and his crozier is preserved in the museum.

Messrs. Daniel and Smith, who had left St. Omer for Douay the day before Dr. Stapleton's death, went on from thence to Paris, where they were joined a little later by Dr. Bew and Mr. Cleghorn. It was necessary for them to obtain an *arrête* to authorize them to take possession of the English College, and therefore the title deeds, which had been taken to Paris by the authorities at the time the Revolution broke out, had first to be discovered. Dr. Bew was successful in obtaining possession of the Paris Seminary, and they stayed there during the long negotiations which followed.[1] There was far more at stake than the colleges themselves. Most of the ecclesiastical funds belonging to Douay had been invested in French securities, and the efforts to obtain compensation for these occupied most of the time. Mr. Cleghorn had to return to St. Edmund's and Dr. Bew to Oscott before the end of the summer; but Mr. Daniel stayed in Paris, "waiting," says Bishop Douglass, "for better times." He was assisted at first by Mr. Smith, and later on by Dr. Brewer, President-General of the Anglo-Benedictines, Mr. Tuite, Dr. Barrett, and ultimately by Dr. Poynter. The restitution of the English College was opposed at Douay, and for some time nothing was done. When Buonaparte was in power he was by no means friendly to the English, and united all the British establishments under a single administrator, the

---

gave me the highest pleasure," he wrote, "to perceive that your Lordship was satisfied with the manner in which the college is conducted, which I beg leave to say is, under the blessing of God, in greatest part to be ascribed to the vigilance, firmness and economy of our President, who has certainly acquired great knowledge in the art of government in colleges from the long experience he has had. And I am the more sensible of the good effects of our present government from what I experienced the last two or three years at Douay, under a government less firm and less vigorous."

[1] There are several old letters and documents in the Westminster archives, from Mr. Daniel, Mr. Smith, and others, describing the progress of these negotiations, and all the facts here stated are given on their authority. The letters are very full, but unfortunately only some out of many have been preserved, and they do not supply a continuous account, there being on some occasions intervals of several years without anything.

Rev. Francis Walsh, an Irishman. By his consent Douay College was let on a long lease as a spinning factory, and it gradually fell into ruin. Thus Dr. Brewer writes, after his visit in 1803 :—

"The Culte at Douay is not yet organized. Priests cannot obtain their scanty salaries; the ancient hotel of Jacques Gilmot is still standing. The College Church is filled with hay, which has been stowed in since Mr. Daniel went to Paris. The Infirmary is a frightful ruin. . . . The Refectory is spoiling fast."

In the year 1805 Pope Pius VII. was in Paris and Messrs. Daniel and Tuite were presented to him. Bishop Douglass writes that "His Holiness showed particular attention to them, and held Mr. Tuite's hand in his own for several minutes."

Mr. Tuite returned to St. Edmund's, leaving Mr. Daniel still in Paris as before. The negotiations dragged on for another ten years, and were still uncompleted at the time of the fall of the Empire.

We must now return to the internal history of St. Edmund's during Dr. Poynter's presidency. The first thing we have to chronicle is the compulsory raising of the pension on account of the price of provisions. On February 1st, 1801, Bishop Douglass writes in his Diary :—

"The harvest having failed throughout the kingdom on account of the wet season, the price of bread has gradually risen, and this day the quartern loaf costs 6*d*."

The following circular letter was addressed to the parents of all the students of the college :—

"The Administrators of St. Edmund's College beg leave to represent to those Parents and Guardians who have honoured them with their confidence, that the extraordinary pressure of the present time and the unexampled dearness of every article of life, particularly of wheat, have reduced them to the painful alternative, either of raising their terms for a limited period, or of considerably diminishing the conveniences and comforts which the students enjoy. This latter plan, they are convinced, would meet with the general disapprobation of their friends. They have, therefore, adopted a resolution which is fully justified by the necessity of the case, of making an addition of £6 6s. 0d. to the annual pension of each student. This temporary demand, which is to commence on the 15th day of April, 1801, and to continue till wheat has fallen to the price of £4 per quarter, must be approved by all who take into consideration the peculiar hardship of the present calamitous period. However painful it may be to resort to this expedient, the Administrators have the fullest assurance that the necessity of the measure will not admit of a doubt, and under this impression they venture to appeal to the good sense and candour of their numerous and respectable friends.

"WILLIAM POYNTER, President."

The next event of internal importance was the conferring of the honorary degree of D.D. on the Vice-President, the Rev. W. H. Coombes. The following account is from Bishop Douglass's Diary :—

"February 3rd, 1802.—On this day I invested Mr. William Henry Coombes, Vice-President of St. Edmund's, with the cap and ring, the insignia of his new dignity conferred by the Pope &c. in the Hall of St. Edmund's College.

[Here follows a copy of the Brief.]

"Accordingly, this morning (February 3rd) the Professors and Divines being assembled, I went to the Hall in my Episcopal dress, and, seated in an arm-chair, opened the business to the gentlemen who were seated before me, spoke a few words on the honour done to our College by the promotion &c. &c., begged Mr. President to be so obliging as to read the Diploma or Brief to the gentlemen. This done, I requested Mr. Coombes to step forward and make the Profession of Faith, which being finished, I rose and put the cap on his head and the ring on his finger, (while he was still kneeling before me) with an appropriate form of words, viz : Pursuant to the orders received from Rome &c. &c. wished him a long life to enjoy, &c. and closed with 'May this honour granted to you, the first Professor of Divinity in St. Edmund's College, be a prelude to future grants,' &c. Mr. Coombes is here called the first Professor, because appointed by me first in order of time and before Mr. Poynter came to England.

"The ceremony was somewhat solemn, and the congratulations of the President, Superiors, Professors, and Divines, were true and hearty."

A year after this, Dr. Poynter was elected Coadjutor to Bishop Douglass, and at the same time Dr. Milner's appointment took place as Vicar Apostolic of the Midland District. The consecration of the two new bishops followed, one a week after the other, Dr. Milner's taking place at Winchester on May 22nd, and Dr. Poynter's at Old Hall on the 29th. On the latter occasion, Dr. Milner preached his first episcopal sermon. The officiating bishops were Dr. Douglass, Dr. Gibson, and Dr. Sharrock, and all the vicars apostolic of England being thus brought together, advantage was taken of it to hold a meeting or quasi-synod.

It appears from letters of Bishop Gibson and others that it had been intended for some years past to arrange such a meeting as soon as circumstances would allow; but no favourable opportunity had presented itself, and it had been put off from year to year. One reason for this had been the long vacancy in the Midland district. This was now filled up, and the occasion being otherwise suitable, the meeting was at last held. It was the first attempt on the part of the vicars apostolic at anything of the kind; but after some discussion it was decided that, as it was not canonically a synod, it would not be necessary to send the resolutions to Rome for confirmation, and they would, therefore, have no strict binding force beyond that attaching to a circular letter from the bishops.

The proceedings were opened at Winchester on May 23rd when Bishop Douglass said Mass *De Spiritu Sancto*, at which the other bishops assisted. They then assembled for the deliberations, which lasted altogether five days, the first part being at Winchester, and the last part at Old Hall.

Several secular priests were invited to attend as "Theologians," but the only religious order represented was the Trappists, then settled at Lulworth. The minutes of the discussions, in Dr. Poynter's writing, are among the college archives, and the resolutions arrived at will be found printed in full in the Appendix.[1] A perusal of them will bring forcibly to mind the progress which Catholicism has made during the present century.

We have next to speak of Dr. Poynter's chief work for the material improvement of the college. This was the building of what were then known as the "New Chapel and Refectory."[2] The temporary chapel in use till then had been very insufficiently furnished, and Dr. Poynter's first idea was to fit it up properly, for which purpose he sent out the following appeal for funds, dated St. Edmund's College, August 10th, 1803:—

"The President and Administrators of St. Edmund's College beg leave to acquaint their friends that they have taken the resolution of furnishing a considerable apartment in their house, in which the divine mysteries have hitherto been celebrated, and of giving it completely the form of a chapel. For this purpose, it is their intention to procure an organ, to purchase becoming ornaments for the altar, and to embellish the whole apartment in a neat and elegant style. To meet the expense of this undertaking, and to carry the plan into full effect, the President and Administrators resort to the benevolence of their friends, and solicit their pious contributions. They entertain a well-grounded hope, that an ardent desire of ensuring respect to the house of God, and of adding splendor to the practice of religion, will excite approbation, and attract support."

In response to this appeal, sufficient money was subscribed to do more than was first intended, though not enough to carry out the original plans for church and refectory. These were therefore abandoned, and in their place were substituted the two buildings alluded to, which were far less

---

[1] See Appendix E.
[2] The present senior study place and library respectively.

costly, not only on account of their smaller size, but also because in each case two of the four walls required were already built.[1] At the same time, what was afterwards known as the "Church Playroom" (now the "Bounds Playroom" and "Chess-room") was erected, and over it the "Poets' Dormitory," which consisted of eight small private rooms.[2]

These additions were begun in 1804 and completed the following year. Mr. Taylor did not approve of the new buildings, and refused to have anything to do with their erection. He urged that the roof would have to be pitched so flat that the rain would not be kept out by the slates, and prophesied that it would eventually destroy the building and communicate dry rot to the main part of the college. His views were not listened to, and as Mr. Bangs, the local builder, undertook to do the work at a low rate, it was put in hand. The whole cost amounted to 1550*l.*, a very moderate sum, all things considered.

The general appearance of the "Old Chapel" is familiar to many living Edmundians. The altar stood at the north end, the sanctuary being still discernible by the raised floor and vaulted roof. Behind the altar stood a picture, generally understood to represent St. Edmund, but in reality a copy of the celebrated picture of St. Andrew Corsini, in the Palazzo Corsini at Rome.[3] The chapel was entered by the double doors underneath the organ gallery, which are now fastened up. The entrance in use at the present day then led to the sacristy, which was in the place now occupied by the passage at the end of the Ambulacrum. Over one of these doors stood the picture of St. Charles Borromeo, which is now over the door of the "New Chapel."

The boys all knelt facing the altar, but there were stalls for the divines and priests, and the old black "eagle"—now at St. Thomas's Seminary—stood in the middle of the choir. In front of the stalls on each side stood a large iron bookstand,

---

[1] That on the north side of the college was only partially built. See last chapter.
[2] The other four rooms were added much later.
[3] This picture is now in the sacristy of the present chapel.

on which the plain chant books were placed. These stands, the work of a Puckeridge blacksmith, rough as they were, served their purpose, and prevented the necessity of the singers continually coming out to a central lectern. Some of the old boys used to tell how they went down in a party to Puckeridge in the year 1805, while the chapel was building, and carried the lecterns home upon their shoulders. The refectory was first used on the Exhibition Day of 1805, and after the holidays, on the Feast of the Assumption, the chapel was solemnly opened. The blessing was performed by Bishop Douglass, and the first High Mass was sung by Dr. Coombes.

The institution of the college medals dates from the same year; those who have obtained them in later times may notice that the date 1805 is on them, and that they represent the college in the state in which it was at that time. The following account of their institution is in Dr. Coombes's writing in the Prefect of Studies' book:—

"In order to excite a spirit of emulation and to promote the cause of learning, a medal of virgin silver has been this year struck, on the front of which appears a representation of the College, and on the reverse are seen the figures of Religion and Science, with the motto 'Religioni ac Bonis Artibus.' Three medals of this description are to be annually presented, one to the greatest proficient in the art of speaking, the second to that student in Rhetoric who, on an average calculation, shall have gained the superiority over his schoolfellows in his exercises in the Latin, Greek, English, and French languages. The third is to be presented to the student in Poetry who shall have gained the same superiority."

The first medals were awarded on June 19th, 1805; two to the Hon. Valentine Browne (Lord Castlerosse), and the third to Richard Horrabin. The ceremony of the presentation is thus described:—

"The person who is to receive the medal is first to read, at the discretion of the President of the Exhibition, some of the literary performances which have procured him the distinction.

He is then to walk between two attendants, appointed for the purpose, to the President of the College, to make his obeisance, and to receive the medal suspended on a ribbon, which is to be put about his neck. After making a respectful bow to the President and company, he is to be reconducted by his attendants to his place. One of the attendants, who are called clerks of the house, is to read the attestations which are to be given to the gentlemen who have received medals."

In this same year, also, one or two entries in the college books occur which are connected with the public events of the time, and are interesting for that reason. One of these

COLLEGE MEDAL.

occurs in the procurator's accounts, where it is chronicled that wine was provided for the professors one day in November, in honour of the great victory of Trafalgar. Another records the giving of special faculties to Dr. Poynter as Vicar-General of the Midland district; the reason assigned being the apprehension of an invasion from Napoleon Buonaparte, in which case everything was arranged for the students and professors to retire to Cambridgeshire or Huntingdonshire, so as to be further from London. The year before an order had been sent for all in the college above a certain age to serve their time in the Hertford militia. An appeal was lodged against this, which was heard at Hertford on January 18th, 1804, and was apparently successful, so far as the students in Holy Orders were concerned. Lastly, as connected with the internal history of St. Edmund's, the entry which records the arrival of Thomas Griffiths, then a boy of fourteen years of age, on January 5th, 1805, should not be overlooked.

Dr. Poynter did not resign his position as president on becoming Bishop, but continued for ten years to discharge the duties of both offices, and no special changes took place at this time. Mr. Tuite had ceased to be prefect, and after managing the Preparatory School for a year, had been summoned to Paris on business connected with the colleges, as we have seen. On his return he resumed his post as procurator, which he retained till he left the college; his successor at the Preparatory School being the Rev. Lewis Havard, who had been recently ordained. The Rev. Joseph Kimbell was prefect for three years, and after him the Rev. Robert Varley for five.

The aged administrator of the college and Dean of the Chapter, Rev. John Lindow,[1] came in 1805 to end his days at St. Edmund's, and died the following year on December 5th. He was buried at Standon, where a corner of the churchyard was reserved for Catholics. There his tombstone may be seen at the present day, near those of Dr. Poynter's father [2] and Mr Potier's mother, who both died in the neighbourhood.

Mr. Potier continued as parish priest till the year 1810. During the last two years he lived at Puckeridge, where he opened what he termed a small preparatory school for six young gentlemen under twelve years of age.[3] In

---

[1] John Lindow, son of James Lindow, was born in the parish of Ulverston, Lancashire, in 1729. He was sent by Bishop Challoner to Douay, where he took the College Oath in September 29th, 1761. After his ordination, he went on the London Mission. In 1770 he was elected an Archdeacon of the Old Chapter, and he succeeded the Rev. Peter Brown, on his death in 1794, as Dean. He resided with Bishop Talbot at Castle Street, and afterwards with Bishop Douglass, till he retired to Old Hall in 1805.—"Gillow's Dictionary," vol. iv., M.S.

[2] Dr. Poynter's father had a farm near Hadham, where he died in 1808. His other son, the younger brother of the Bishop, farmed the college lands for many years.

[3] The house Mr. Potier had was one almost opposite the turning to Standon, now used as Mrs. Cottam's shop.

October, 1812, he removed to Shefford, in Bedfordshire, taking his boys with him. He remained there the rest of his days, and died there on March 31st, 1823. His body was brought back to Old Hall and laid beside that of his mother in Standon churchyard, where the following quaint inscription may still be seen :—

> Sacred to the memory of
> REVD. JOHN POTIER
> Who departed this life March 31st, 1823,
> Aged 66 years.
> Calm and meek, benevolent and kind,
> There are but few such left behind.
> Requiescat in pace.

We have now to speak of the gradual decline of St. Edmund's as a lay college. In the early years of the present century, it was the chief place of education for the Catholic nobility and gentry. Since Dr. Poynter's time it has never held this position, and after the year 1818, when Dr. Griffiths was appointed President, its character became chiefly ecclesiastical; indeed, from that time until the divines left in 1869, the number of lay students was always small. At the present day the lay and church students are numerically almost equal; but owing chiefly to the greater number of church students in the upper part of the house, their influence always preponderates. This is clearly recognized in the constitutions and government of the college. The interests of the lay students are not neglected, but they are never allowed to interfere with those of the church students.

All this presents a striking contrast with the St. Edmund's of Dr. Stapleton and Dr. Poynter, but not an unfavourable one. The college was founded by Bishop Douglass chiefly and primarily for the education of the clergy, and the large proportion of lay students had always been a grave disadvantage, though it was considered an unavoidable one. Dr. Poynter felt this all along. In a letter written in 1803, he says, plainly, that Old Hall cannot "pretend to say that it has not felt the bad effects of the want of a more considerable number of candidates for the ecclesiastical state," and he speaks of church students being "often discouraged and sometimes laughed out of their vocation by the young gentlemen of the world." "All who have had experience in Colleges," he continues, "must feel the advantages, I might almost say the necessity, of having such a number of candidates for the Church that they may have the preponderance in the College; where it is not so, it will be extremely difficult to inspire or support the ecclesiastical spirit, and to preserve those for the Church who come with a good vocation."

Many years afterwards, a priest who had received his education at St. Edmund's at the time of which we are speaking, wrote in a similar sense, and his words may fairly be taken as a sample of what was felt by the church students of that period. "Upon the whole," he writes, "the time I spent at St. Edmund's remains still a sunny spot in my memory. It had, however, one great drawback for me. I became by God's great and undeserved grace a Catholic at the age of twenty-four, and went to St. Edmund's with all the fervour of a convert, dreaming of and desiring nothing so much as Church services and a real religious life. Now at that time, things were not well regulated for students destined for the Church. We were all mixed with future Lords, Earls, and Dukes, and other lay students, who, at the end of each vacation, used to return full of London news and London pleasures, and I got more harm than good from such conversation."

Although the final result of the change was to remedy much that required it, it was not brought about designedly, and the college was involved in debt and difficulty during the time of transition. The beginning of the troubles is traceable to the election of Dr. Poynter as coadjutor-bishop, which threw so much additional work upon his shoulders that the interests of the college suffered. As time went on, and Bishop Douglass advanced in years, he became more and more infirm, and the share of his work which devolved on Dr. Poynter became larger. The London district being a very large one, he was necessarily away on visitation and other business during a great part of the year, and was not able to give as much attention to the college as its interests required. During his periods of absence, he left very little power in the hands of Dr. Coombes, the vice-president, and none of the greater punishments were allowed to be administered until his return.

It has been said, that at this point he ought to have resigned his post as president. This remark brings out the fundamental difficulty of the case. It is quite clear that Dr. Poynter only kept to his position because he was firmly convinced that there was no one else at all capable of filling it, and that it was a less evil to be away during a great part of the year than to be absent altogether. Subsequent events go far towards bearing out this view.

The enemies of the college were not slow to make its state a subject of remark and gossip. It was reported that the president was always away, that in his absence there was no one capable of keeping order, and that the whole place was in a state of material and moral neglect. There were said also to be so many foreigners, that the spirit of insubordination was very prevalent, and that it was not a fitting place for the education of priests.

These rumours frequently reached Dr. Poynter's ears. He alludes to them in a long letter written in 1808, wherein he attempts to show that they are devoid of foundation. "I have for many years been accustomed," he wrote, "to hear of vague and unsupported clamours against the College; indeed, it has long been the tone to speak against it. This has been very injurious to us in many respects. . . . I had all along disregarded the obloquy which was reported to me, partly because it was vague and unsupported by any authority, partly because it was so evidently false that I was convinced it would be best refuted by facts. I could scarce ever prevail on any who were so much prepossessed against Old Hall to come and see the true state of things."

It is only fair to Dr. Poynter to mention that on more than one occasion, when those who were most prejudiced against St. Edmund's came and spent a certain time in the college, they went away with changed views. One distinguished instance was that of Dr. Wilkinson, at one time Vice-President at Douay, and afterwards Dr. Stapleton's predecessor in the presidency at St. Omer. He came to St. Edmund's in 1802, and stayed several weeks, being specially commissioned by Bishop Sharrock, of the Western District, to inquire into the truth of the prevalent reports. At the end of his visit, he declared himself satisfied, and said that he had never seen discipline better observed at Douay in Douay's best days than it was at Old Hall. So also when Mr. Edward Blount was sent on a similar errand by Lady Shrewsbury and Lord Dormer, who were anxious about their children's welfare, he sent them a good report of the state of the college.

Lastly, Dr. Poynter's own testimony may well be added, from the letter quoted above. Speaking about the ecclesiastical students and their course of education, he writes :—

"We have twenty very promising subjects for the Church.[1] Of these two are subdeacons, five in minor orders. The others are in the different classes of Rhetoric, Poetry, etc. Our ecclesiastical students are, in general, at the head of their respective classes; they edify the others by their piety and good example, and we may say have gained an ascendancy in the College. They follow the same exercises of piety here as we did at Douay. They have a daily Meditation before Mass, they daily assist at the Adorable Sacrifice, have prayers and instructions twice in the evening. The greatest part of our ecclesiastical students go to Communion every Sunday. We have an annual retreat, besides the retreats previous to Holy Orders.

"As to their studies in Divinity, and in the classes previous to Divinity, I will make this assertion, that there was nothing taught at Douay which is not taught at Old Hall, and that many things are taught at Old Hall preparatory to the mission which were not taught at Douay."

About the general discipline of the house, he says, "I will add from my own knowledge and experience in both places,

[1] Out of a total of seventy-eight at that time; exclusive of some thirty or forty "children" in the Preparatory School.

that the rules of discipline are better observed at Old Hall than they were during the twenty years I was at Douay; and that there is more submission and obedience here than there was there." "Our rules," he concludes, "are those of Douay, accommodated to our situation."

After making all allowance for exaggeration and inaccuracy, however, it is impossible to escape the conclusion that during the latter part of Dr. Poynter's presidency the college was not in a good state. We know this on the authority of more than one who was at the college at that time, and there was furnished by the great disturbance of 1809—to be described presently—conclusive evidence of the prevalence of insubordination among the students.

The first sign of the coming troubles was the departure of the vice-president, the Rev. William Coombes, who left on May 11th, 1808. The Rev. Lewis Havard likewise went about this time, leaving Dr. Poynter the only remaining member of the "Trente-deux." Both losses were much felt at the college. Dr. Coombes on leaving returned to his own district, and was temporarily appointed to the mission of Shepton Mallett in Somersetshire. The temporary appointment gradually became permanent, and he remained there for nearly forty years. "I was sent here for a fortnight," he used to say when quite an old man, "and that fortnight, Sir, has not yet expired." During the latter part of the time he was a frequent visitor to the neighbouring monastery of Downside, where he was a great favourite. He lived to be one of the last survivors of those who had said Mass at St. Gregory's Monastery at Douay, which formed an additional bond of union between him and the Downside Community. He was esteemed a good preacher and was often asked to deliver the sermon on special days at Downside. During the Christmas holidays, and at other times, he used likewise to help in the amusements and recreations. He was particularly fond of singing a Greek translation which he had made of "Rule Britannia." The last year of his life he spent in retirement at the monastery, where he died on November 15th, 1850.

The new vice-president at St. Edmund's was the Rev. Francis Tuite, and if the current rumour be accepted Dr. Poynter intended shortly to resign the presidency in his favour. He does not appear, however, to have been fitted even for the post of vice-president, and much of the trouble which followed his appointment must have been due to his mismanagement. Mr. Varley, who was still prefect, was hardly more successful in winning the affections of the students, and hence during the periods when Dr. Poynter was away from the college it did not go on at all smoothly.

Matters culminated in a great disturbance in the year 1809, which has left its mark permanently on the college and on its history. A full narrative has been left us by three different people, Mr. Jones, Mr. Tuite and Dr. Poynter himself, and it is therefore possible to form a fairly just estimate of what was afterwards commonly spoken of among the students as " The Great Affair."

The disturbance was led up to by two or three events which sound trivial and even childish, but they were rather the occasion than the cause, and they could not have had the effect they did, had there not been great underlying discontent ready to show itself at the slightest provocation. Dr. Poynter was away at the time giving Confirmation in Hampshire, and the troubles began with the refusal of a play-day by Mr. Tuite, on the ground that there had already been one that week. This was on Friday, October 6th, 1809. At the same time one of the " poets " received a note for a thrashing, to be carried to Mr. Varley, the prefect. Till recently this had been regarded as a punishment to be inflicted only on small boys, as was the case at Douay and is in modern days at St. Edmund's. Mr. Tuite, to whom Dr. Poynter allowed more power in his absence than he had to Dr. Coombes, had himself usually acknowledged this, but on more than one occasion recently he had, for special reasons, and with Dr. Poynter's approval, broken through the tradition. This was a point on which the students seem to have felt very strongly. The cause assigned for the punishment on this occasion was absence that morning from meditation, which the student said was due to illness. The note was not delivered to the prefect.

The next day an equally trivial but more amusing incident occurred. A student who had a glass of port wine in the prefect's room every morning, going as usual to fetch a new bottle from Mr. Tuite, received from the latter some Lisbon wine instead, the port having been all used. This displeased the youth, and he went down and distributed the wine amongst his companions. The bottle was then filled with water, corked up, and placed in Mr. Varley's room. On being questioned, the youth denied all knowledge of the bottle having been filled with water, but his statement was not believed, and he was ordered to be thrashed.

The students who had been disorderly all the Friday had returned in the evening to their duties, and it seemed as if the affair would end here; but the following day, Saturday, when the boy last referred to was ordered to be thrashed, they broke out into open rebellion. A party of them, numbering about thirty, left the college, walked as far as Waltham Cross, and there put up at the inn. According to the account they afterwards gave, they knew that they were doing wrong, but had no intention of carrying things so far as they afterwards did. Had Dr. Poynter been at home, they said, respect for him would in any case have prevented them, but with his continued absence and the prospect, according to report, of his early resignation, they thought that now was the time to emphasize the fact that they had grievances which required remedying. They therefore drew out a letter to Mr. Tuite, which was despatched to the college by a special messenger. It ran as follows:—

"SIR,—From the discontent so generally prevalent amongst the students, we have been under the disagreeable necessity of having recourse to these measures; and to obtain a promise of a total remission of punishment of any kind, and better treatment, is the motive which actuates us to address these few lines to you. Should this be complied with, we will immediately return to the college and to our duty. But if not, it is our firm resolution not to return to the college, and to persevere in the measures we have adopted. Think not this the impulse of a moment, nor the idle boast of inexperienced youth. Our means are equal to our perseverance and more than may be imagined, and our perseverance is such as will ensure success. We rely upon your honour for no equivocation concerning punishment, and that your answer will include that of Dr. Poynter. It will be needless to except any individual in the remission of punishment, as there is not one who has taken a more active part in it than another. We solicit a clear and unequivocal answer to every article contained in the above. If we receive an answer suitable to our expectations, we shall comply with your desires. In case you should think it necessary to have a personal interview, we shall receive you with respect; but should your intentions be to enforce our return, they will be totally useless, as in that case we shall oppose force to force. Our words of honour are given not to deviate from any particular of the above.

"Waltham Cross, 5¼ of the clock.
"October 7th, 1809.

"P.S.—Should any letters have arrived for the absent students, they will esteem it a favour to have them forwarded by the bearer of this."

Here follow the signatures of the "fugitives."

It is needless to say that Mr. Tuite was unable to accede to the proposed conditions. He was thoroughly alarmed, however, and, not knowing what to do, he requested Mr. Cleghorn to proceed to London without delay, to call on Bishop Douglass, and having ascertained where Bishop Poynter was, to follow him and beg him to hurry back immediately. In the meantime the Chief Constable at Ware was communicated with, and he wrote to the "fugitives" as follows :—

"GENTLEMEN,—It is with much concern that I inform you that Mr. Tuite has applied to me to interpose the authority of the law, to restore at Old Hall Green that subordination and obedience so essential to the existence of that Seminary, and of Society in general. But, Gentlemen, not having forgot the days of youth, when by myself and associated, numberless irregularities have been committed, proceeding entirely from inconsideration and a redundance of the fire of youth, and which have been prevented from extending to a length that might have produced serious consequences by the kind advice of more experienced friends, I take the liberty to offer you mine on the present occasion, which is that with the same unanimity with which you have fallen into error, you exhibit one of the principal traits of a great mind, that of acknowledging an error, and return immediately to your studies, await patiently the return of Doctor Poynter, and if any grievances exist, I will pledge my honor he will redress them to the satisfaction of your cooler consideration. I flatter myself that your good sense will render it almost needless for me to represent to you what must be my conduct if you refuse the advice I have offered and persist in disobedience. I must appoint (as I have ample power to do) constables to any number I find necessary, with the assistance of whom I should shortly take into custody a mob of the most disorderly and ignorant of the people.

"I leave you to reflect how painful it must be to many respectable [people] that such measures should be resorted to, to bring to a sense of duty young men of enlightened understandings and honourable connexions. Trusting you will receive what I have said as it is meant, I remain

"Your humble servant,

"B. DICKENSON.

"Ware, October 9th, 1809."

This letter did not have the effect anticipated. Some indeed of the students came back on the Sunday evening; but a considerable number, driven to desperation, determined on extreme measures. Thinking that their only way to escape from the power of the district constables was to get into another county, some went towards London, while those who had enough money started in the opposite direction, with the idea of making for Scotland.

Mr. Tuite now communicated also with the Rev. John Jones, the college agent in London, and he, together with

Mr. Angelo, the father of one of the boys, after a short search found the London section of the "fugitives" and induced them to return, subject to certain conditions. These were first, that they should not be punished till Dr. Poynter had returned and heard what they had to say; secondly, that there should in any case be no "partial expulsions," i.e. that they should all be expelled or none; and thirdly, that if Dr. Poynter, when he came back, did not agree to these conditions, Mr. Jones should conduct the "fugitives," back to London and leave them *in statu quo*. The party drove down to the college without delay, and arrived on the Monday evening, Mr. Tuite being glad enough to accept provisionally the terms proposed.

This much settled, Messrs. Jones and Angelo again set out, the same night, in pursuit of the other party, who were supposed to be making for Scotland. They soon got on their track, and after posting all night and following them through Buntingford, Royston, Arrington, and Huntingdon, finally caught them up about five o'clock the following morning at a little village called Stilton, where they had rested for the night and were asleep at the inn. They took possession of their room, therefore, and great was the astonishment of the youths when they came down to breakfast to find their unlooked-for visitors. A consultation ensued similar to that which had taken place in London, and the boys withdrew to consider the situation. Some wanted to give their pursuers the slip and start off a second time, but wiser counsels in the end prevailed, and they consented to return on the same conditions which the others had accepted. The party therefore started homewards, and reached the college that evening about nine o'clock.

Dr. Poynter had by this time returned, and he took a very strong view of the case, refusing absolutely to recognize the conditions proposed. The next morning he saw each of the students individually, and told them that while he was then, as always, willing to examine into any cause they might have of complaint, their conduct would not be excusable even if such causes existed, and that of course they would have to be punished for what they had done. After a long consultation with the vice-president, he determined on expelling immediately the three chief instigators, and sent there and then for a post-chaise to convey them to London. It now remained to be seen how much influence these three really possessed over the rest, and in the event eight others left the college the same day of their own accord. The remainder settled down to work again, no doubt heartily ashamed of what they had done.

The people who profited most by the whole affair were the inn-keepers and chaise proprietors. They evidently took in the situation and saw what class of people they had to deal with. They gave unlimited credit, but when the bills came in the charges were exorbitant. For example, we find in one case :—

|  | £ | s. | d. |
|---|---|---|---|
| Bill at Stilton . . . . . . | 5 | 19 | 7 |
| Chambermaids, Boots &c., and a pair of stockings, dressing, &c. . . . . . | 1 | 17 | 6 |

and for the next day, in addition to a great deal which had been paid for in ready money by Mr. Jones, the following :—

|  | £ | s. | d. |
|---|---|---|---|
| Return to Huntingdon from Stilton and to Arrington, 9 pair horses, 15 miles . . | 9 | 0 | 0 |
| Sundries, Postboys, Hostlers, Waiters . . | 2 | 0 | 10 |
| From Arrington to Buntingford, 13 miles . | 2 | 18 | 6 |
| Sundries, &c. . . . . . . | 1 | 4 | 6 |
| Postboys from Arrington to Old Hall . . |  | 15 | 6 |

We also find such items as "Glass broken and expenses on the road, 10s. 0d."; "An umbrella lost, £1 1s. 0d."; and others of the same kind.

When it was all over, Mr. Angelo and Mr. Jones were far from satisfied at what had taken place. They considered that the conditions agreed to had not been kept; for the penances had been administered before the grievances had been examined into. Mr. Angelo therefore sent a circular to the parents of the different boys, inviting them to meet at his house on a certain day, there to hold an inquiry on the matter. He was thus proposing that they should form themselves into a sort of self-constituted court of appeal, and to this Bishop Poynter strongly objected. "When the terms of a College, with the nature of its government are known," he wrote, "if any parent does not approve of them, he is at liberty not to place his son there;" but the idea of a council of parents, and especially a self-appointed one, to try and govern the college over the president's head, he considered subversive of all discipline and order. He therefore went himself to London and called on all the parents, and, after explaining his views, told them that if they wished to attend Mr. Angelo's meeting, he would that day send their boys home to them; "for," he said, "I would rather lose thirty students than have so many discontented boys encouraged by their parents."

Mr. Jones's sympathies were on the whole with Mr. Angelo, though he regretted the proposed meeting. He considered that they had both done their best to adjust matters at the college, having been especially asked to do so by Mr. Tuite, on an occasion of emergency, and that they had received no thanks from Dr. Poynter for their exertions, but rather the reverse. After some correspondence he resigned the college agency, and his resignation was accepted. This took place about a week before Mr. Angelo's meeting. When the day of the meeting came only a few attended, and they were all parents of the boys who had already left the college. Whether any conclusion was arrived at, then or subsequently, we are not told; but the whole affair had its effect on the prospects of St. Edmund's. Ushaw had been opened the previous year, and no doubt that helped to make Old Hall decline.[1]

The college itself was now outwardly quiet and orderly, and the natural reaction succeeded the exciting events recounted; but there was still a good deal of discontent below the surface. "We are at length outwardly tranquilized," wrote one of the church students, "though inwardly disgust and disaffection are still very prevalent, nor do I think it will

[1] Ushaw College was commenced in 1804 and opened in July, 1808. Only one of the actual "fugitives" was admitted there, and this was a special case which Bishop Gibson undertook to explain to Dr. Poynter. Several others applied for admission, both at Ushaw and Oscott, but were refused. One or two were allowed, under very strict conditions, to return to St. Edmund's.

ever be otherwise during the administration of that unfortunate man [Mr. Tuite]; but Dr. Poynter most likely has his reasons for retaining him. . . . We are in our playroom most miserably dull, as the defection is principally there." [2]

The resignation of Messrs. Tuite and Varley was a natural consequence of the above events. Mr. Tuite was a painstaking and careful man: he afterwards rendered good service for many years as Vicar-General of the London District, and helped much in the matter of reclaiming the colleges in France and winding up the affairs of Douay, of which he was the last nominal president; but he does not seem to have been fit for the position he held at St. Edmund's, and was probably not sorry to exchange it for a missionary life. Mr. Varley, on the other hand, still remained at the college; but a change for a time to the easier life of a professor was not unwelcome to him.

Dr. Poynter's third vice-president was the Rev. Joseph Kimbell, one of Dr. Stapleton's first students, and the new prefect was the Rev. Joseph Stapleton. In this manner the college went on for another two years, before the death of Bishop Douglass on May 8th, 1812, made further changes necessary, and Dr. Poynter's presidency came to an end.

The obsequies of Bishop Douglass took place at Lincoln's-Inn-Fields on May 15th, the Mass of Requiem being sung by Bishop Poynter, his successor. A specially interesting feature in the ceremony was the presence of many of the French clergy who were still in London, and who owed so much to Bishop Douglass when they first came over during the Revolution, nearly twenty years before. Many of them had worked under him for years on the London mission, conspicuous among them being the well-known figure of the Abbé Carron, founder of the Somers Town mission. There were also no less than six French bishops in the sanctuary.

---

[2] That is the "poets' playroom." The "fugitives" were all lay students, and some of them belonged to the oldest Catholic families in the country.

The Absolutions were given by the English Vicars Apostolic and the Bishops of Aire and Angoulême, this being the first time that a vicar apostolic had been buried with full episcopal rites in London.

The funeral sermon was preached by the Rev. Lewis Havard, who alluded to St. Edmund's as the most important work set on foot during the episcopate of Bishop Douglass. He spoke as follows:—

"The main object of his solicitude was the perpetuation of the sacred ministry. His most ardent prayers were offered to Heaven, and his most earnest wishes were ever expressed for the prosperity of that establishment which boasts him for its founder . . . . He considered St. Edmund's College as claiming his first, his fostering concern, because it is the only remaining nursery from which the faithful of this district can expect an adequate supply of spiritual instructors . . . . It is to St. Edmund's College that we all look for successors in our arduous and most painful labours. If our pastor could have had a favour to ask of us with his dying breath, it would have been that we should take this institution under our most anxious care; and if he be now arrived (as we hope in God he is arrived) at his crown in Heaven, his zeal for religion is concentrated in fervent supplications for the prosperity of St. Edmund's College."

A few days later a second Dirge and Requiem were celebrated, this time in the French chapel in King Street, Portman Square. Bishop Poynter again sang the Mass, and the English Vicars Apostolic were present, as well as very many of the French bishops and clergy, the French ambassador and many of the distinguished French laymen then in London.

It now remains to enumerate some of the most distinguished sons of St. Edmund who were educated at Old Hall during the first twenty years of the existence of the college. Of the original students from Douay and St. Omer, several afterwards attained celebrity. Bishop Walsh has already been mentioned, and we shall come across his name again later on. Bishop Penswick was at St. Edmund's only about eleven months, and though he had been under Dr. Poynter at Douay, he was never under him at Old Hall. The Rev. Lewis Havard, who stayed on several years after his ordination, as a professor, and afterwards returned again to teach theology, became known later on as a preacher. His funeral sermons for Bishops Douglass and Poynter were both printed. The Rev. Edward Peach is still remembered in the Midlands as the founder of St. Chad's, Birmingham. The Rev. Joseph Birch was afterwards President of Sedgley Park, as were also Revs. Joseph Bowdon and George Rolfe, who came later. Lastly may be mentioned the Rev. Joseph Kimbell, who came with Dr. Stapleton from St. Omer. His appointment as Vice-President of St. Edmund's has already been alluded to, and he afterwards succeeded Dr. Poynter as President.

Among those who came during the early years of the present century, we find three future presidents, the Revs. John Rolfe, Richard Newell and Thomas Griffiths, the last named of whom was afterwards Vicar Apostolic of the London District, to whom, indeed, St. Edmund's owes more than to any other man, living or dead. There were also two other ecclesiastical students at that time, who may justly be reckoned among the most eminent that St. Edmund's has ever had. One of these was the Rev. Mark A. Tierney, the learned editor of "Dodd's Church History of England." He came first to St. Edmund's as a student in 1810, and, after his ordination in 1818, he remained for a time as a professor. The other was the Rev. Daniel Rock, the celebrated archæologist, author of the "Church of our Fathers," "Hierurgia," etc. He went through his "humanities" at St. Edmund's; but went to Rome for his theology. The name of William Tilbury, who laboured for nearly fifty years as a missionary at Rio de Janeiro, and on his death left a large legacy to the college, should likewise be mentioned; and last, but not least, that of Thomas Doyle, the well-known Provost of Southwark and founder of St. George's Cathedral, who came just at the end of Dr. Poynter's reign, and lived to be one of the last survivors of those who had been under him. He died in 1879.

Turning now to the laymen who were at the college at this time, the first to be noted is John Talbot, great-nephew of Bishop James Talbot, and afterwards the well-known saintly and charitable Earl of Shrewsbury, who did so much for Catholicity in the Midland district. He had been a student

JOHN TALBOT, SIXTEENTH EARL OF SHREWSBURY.

for a year or two at Stonyhurst, but came for his higher studies to St. Edmund's. He gained distinction in his work and carried off the medal in his Rhetoric year. The prize poem which he wrote on that occasion, and which he recited on the Exhibition Day, received the unusual honour of being printed, and the original manuscript is among the College archives.¹ He succeeded his uncle as sixteenth Earl of Shrewsbury in 1827, and lived about twenty-five years afterwards.

The following testimony to his sanctity in after life is given by Bishop Ullathorne:—"As Lord Shrewsbury's private history comes out, it shows what a saintly man he was. His love of purity all his life was remarkable, as well as his spirit of poverty. No servant in the house had his room so poor as was the private room of the Earl—a picture of St. Francis of Assisi; old-fashioned common paper; faded, worn-out curtains; no prospect from the windows; the commonest painted deal furniture and common earthenware, with an old broken-down chest of drawers. It was as poor as any convent cell could be."²

Another eminent Edmundian layman of this period was Arthur Clifford, grandson of the last Lord Aston. The first part of his education was received at Douay, and he was there when the college broke up. After the imprisonment, he came to St. Edmund's to complete his studies, and he forms an interesting additional bond of connection with Standon Lordship. From Old Hall he went to Edinburgh to study medicine, but he does not seem to have taken to that profession. He lived for a long time in Paris and edited Galignani's newspaper. Among his other literary works may be named the "State Papers and Letters of Sir Ralph Sadler," "Tixall Letters," "Tixall Poetry," "Collectanea Cliffordiana," etc. He died at Winchester in 1830.

Besides the above may be named Henry Howard, afterwards thirteenth Duke of Norfolk, grandfather to the present duke; Valentine Browne (Lord Castlerosse), afterwards second Earl of Kenmare, and his three brothers, Thomas, William, and Michael, the last named of whom was wounded in the battle of Waterloo;³ Charles Petre, son of Robert

---

¹ The poem is entitled "Alma," and contrasts the peaceful holiday of their college home with the troubles their predecessors at Douay went through during the French Revolution, within the memory of many of those present. The literary merit of the piece is not great.

² Letters of Archbishop Ullathorne, p. 26.

³ According to a traditional story, Michael Browne was picked up on

Edward, tenth Lord Petre (his mother being a sister of Bernard Howard of Glossop, who was the father of the Henry Howard at St. Edmund's); Thomas Stonor, third Lord Camoys; and James Everard, tenth Lord Arundel of Wardour. In addition to these, the families of Fitzherbert, Brockholes, Selby, Blount, Eyre, Dease, Ffrench, Walmesley, Vaughan, Eyston, Ferrers, Mostyn, Stapleton, Dormer, Stonor, Tichborne, Berkeley, etc., were all represented by one or more students.

Many of these names, and others as well, remain a lasting tribute to the work of Dr. Poynter, and we cannot conclude this chapter better than by quoting the words of Lewis Havard, one of his pupils both at Douay and at St. Edmund's, testifying to the universal esteem and respect which he always inspired. "It is almost needless," he said, "to dwell on his conduct in the arduous office either of Vice-President or of President of the College. There was no alteration in him; the same unassuming and unambitious Christian modesty, the same humility without baseness or degradation (all who have known him can bear testimony that he was the most humble of the humble), the same piety, the same edification, the same zeal for the spiritual and literary improvement of his pupils, the same punctuality and order, I would almost say the same military precision and regularity of discipline, were exhibited with cool, collected, and steady perseverance. He was beloved and respected; it would not be correct to add that he was feared. For the veneration and esteem in which he was held were such that they precluded the introduction of fear, and seldom, very seldom, was it requisite that this lowest motive in human conduct should operate on the minds of his inferiors."[1]

the field of Waterloo by a French soldier, who was an Edmundian, and recognized him from his memory of old college days.
[1] Funeral Sermon, p. 14.

## CHAPTER X.

### THE TRANSITION PERIOD.
#### 1813—1818.

*The decline of St. Edmund's continues—Its causes—Most of them traceable to the loss of the Douay funds—Dearth of missionaries—Bishop Poynter's efforts on behalf of Ecclesiastical Education—Further changes at St. Edmund's—Rev. Thomas Griffiths, Vice-President—He builds the Parish Chapel—Resignation of Rev. Joseph Kimbell—Appointment of Dr. Bew—Establishment of "Ecclesiastical Seminary" at the Old House under Mr. Griffiths—Resignation of Dr. Bew—Critical state of the College.*

ON the death of Bishop Douglass, Bishop Poynter became Vicar Apostolic of the London District. For a while, he endeavoured to continue as President of St. Edmund's, but it very soon became clear that the two offices were incompatible, and he formally retired from the presidency at Midsummer, 1813. The fact of his leaving materially quickened the decline of Old Hall as a place of education for the Catholic laity. He had been looked on by every one as the most capable man at the college, so now that he no longer took a personal part in its management, it was but natural that its prospects should sink at a greater pace than before. A clear token of this is that the names of the new students no longer included those of the many well-known Catholic families formerly represented at the college.

Unfortunately, this decline was not limited to the lay element. Ecclesiastical education also had fallen very much below its earlier standard. During the first years of the college's existence, the Douay theological traditions were strictly adhered to. The professors were Douay men, the old "Dictates" were used as a class book, and great attention was paid to the preparation of the divines for their

St. Edmund's College, from the "Catholic Gentleman's Magazine," 1818.

exhibitions and defensions, exactly as had been done at Douay.[1] As time went on, owing to the loss of the funds and the withdrawal of the Northern and Midland students, the number of divines became so small, and the competition so reduced, that the defensions lost their interest, and were soon abandoned altogether. The natural result ensued. When the next generation came on—that is after the departure of Dr. Coombes, for Bishop Poynter was too much occupied to teach theology—it became evident that no efficient professors had been trained up to replace those who had gone before.

Another most important cause of the lowering of the standard of ecclesiastical training, was the great dearth of priests for the mission, which was being felt more and more every day. This also had its origin in the loss of the Douay funds, and the consequent paucity of students, on account of which the number ordained year by year was far below what was required to replace the losses by death and other causes. This may be verified by statistics. In each year's Directory is given an obituary list of English priests who had died since the last issue. If these are balanced against the ordination lists at St. Edmund's,[2] it is easily seen that the number of missionaries was not only not increasing at the rate it ought, but in many years it actually diminished. Thus, between 1800 and 1815, no less than 177 deaths are recorded. Allowing for a few of these being colonial priests, and taking the average of the secular clergy in the London district at its approximate number at one-third of that in the whole of England, we see that the number of deaths to be credited to the London district could not have been much less than fifty. During the same period, the priests ordained at St. Edmund's numbered only seventeen. And in addition to the losses by death, must be counted also the loss of many of the French refugee priests, some of whom had

---

[1] The disputations held at St. Edmund's used to be printed, and copies o them are still extant. There are none of later date than 1811.

[2] St. Edmund's was practically the only source for the supply of the London mission at that time. A priest was occasionally sent from Valladolid or Lisbon, but only rarely.

rendered important service to the London mission at a critical time, and who had either already returned to France or were likely to return in a few years.

This conclusion is supported by a comparison of the report of the district, which Bishop Challoner sent to Rome in 1773, before the arrival of the French priests, with that sent by Bishop Poynter forty-two years later, when most of them had gone back and when the English mission once more depended on its own resources. In the former, there were said to be 120 priests all told,[1] and they had to look after an estimated Catholic population of 24,000. By Bishop Poynter's time, the Catholics had increased to 69,000, an increase of more than 180 per cent.; and yet the missionaries had during the same time fallen from 120 to 88.[2]

Bishop Poynter had foreseen this state of things from the first, and had already set himself to do what was possible to meet the difficulty. He explains his views and what he had been able to accomplish, in a letter to a London priest, dated October 19th, 1807, from which the following is an extract:—

"It is a known fact, that in consequence of the subversion of our Colleges in France (we fear now for those in Lisbon and Spain), and of the loss of the greatest part of the means which we possessed of educating ecclesiastical students, all our four districts, and particularly the Western, have reason to be alarmed at the sad prospect of a great want of clergymen to succeed those who are now employed in the work of the sacred ministry. I have all along felt the necessity of making every exertion to repair our losses, and to provide a due supply for the mission. It was my wish to see all the four districts united in this common cause and supporting one

---

[1] In the same report, Bishop Challoner says there were 90 priests on the London missions, and 55 in the country, which would give a total of 145 instead of 120.

[2] See Brady's "Catholic Hierarchy," pp. 169 and 190. The statistics are not altogether satisfactory, as no distinction is made in Bishop Poynter's report between the secular and regular clergy. It appears from a similar document three years later, that the proportion of seculars was greater than in Bishop Challoner's time; but it must be remembered that Bishop Challoner's report was sent before the suppression of the Jesuits, who should therefore be counted among the seculars in making a comparison.

common College.  The advantages of this would have been great indeed.  Besides other advantages, which are obvious, what a saving there would have been in expenses for masters, servants, taxes, &c.  How many more hands would have been spared for the mission.  But this union could not be effected, and it seems that there are to be three Ecclesiastical Seminaries, Old Hall, Crook Hall, or Ushaw, and Sedgley Park.[1]  We know not what may be the views of Providence in this, and what benefits may ultimately result from this division.  But considering the present state of the mission in England and its finances, I cannot help thinking that one College would have been sufficient for all at present, and of course that it would have been better for the general good to have had but one.  However, as it seems to be determined that there shall be one for each of the three districts, the London, Northern, and Midland (for you may be sure that Bishop Milner will exert himself to carry his own plan into execution), I think that this circumstance should determine the clergy of each district to direct their zealous endeavours, in the first place, to the support of their own Seminary; and when a sufficient provision is made for the education of such a number of ecclesiastical students as will answer the demands of their own district, it will then become their charity to step forward for the relief and support of others.  I do not know whether you have been informed that, feeling the distresses of the London District, we have laid the foundations of a fund for the education of ecclesiastical students, which we hope will in the end prove very beneficial.  Our plan is never to touch the principal, but to nourish and increase it by the addition of all monies applicable to this purpose.  We shall

---

[1] At the time this was written, Oscott was still under the "Old Government," a committee of laymen, who were joint proprietors of the college.  Bishop Milner had therefore determined to educate his church students at Sedgley Park.  The following year, the Oscott Committee found themselves in such difficulties financially, that they were glad enough to allow Bishop Milner to take the college over, on the condition of his accepting the liabilities at the same time.  These amounted, according to a letter from Bishop Milner to Bishop Douglass, to over 600*l.*; but he accepted the conditions, and on the Feast of the Assumption, 1808, St. Mary's College, Oscott, was formally founded as the Seminary of the Midland district.

employ the annual interest in the education of as many as it is adequate to support. At present it is growing like a sinking fund. Some of our Professors at St. Edmund's and other friends have engaged to contribute such a sum annually as their circumstances will permit. Several give ten pounds a year. From the 12th November, 1805, till this time I have collected £263 6s. 6d., with which I have purchased in the Navy 5 p. c. £276 14s. 4d. stock. Having thus begun, I wish to make our intention public, and to engage the respectable clergy of the London District to recommend this important object to the charity of their friends, and to apply to it such sums as they judge themselves authorised by the intentions of pious donors. I know of no object of charity equal to this. . . . I am persuaded that Bishop Gibson will not educate his ecclesiastical students at Ushaw cheaper than we do. We wish to economise as much as others; but there is a certain medium to be observed in all things. If I were to enter into details, and to explain to you what St. Edmund's has contributed by its savings towards the support of the ecclesiastical students it has hitherto educated, you would be much surprised. It is only by our numbers that we have been enabled to support them."

By the time that Bishop Poynter became vicar apostolic, the ecclesiastical education fund had attained considerable dimensions, and in 1815 he made a public appeal for assistance, which was well responded to. The accumulation of money, however, took time, and many years elapsed before the number of clergy was sufficiently restored and the supply equal to the demand.

The dearth of missioners affected St. Edmund's in two ways. On the one hand, it became impossible to supply the college with the professors required, in order to carry on its work efficiently; on the other hand, it was often necessary to ordain a student before his time, at the expense of his theological training, owing to the pressing needs of the mission. No one felt the evil of this more keenly than Dr. Poynter; but the need was urgent, and he had no choice. He wrote in this sense to Mr. Kimbell in 1815. "My most painful distress at present for want of priests," he said, "is beyond conception. Greenwich, Woolwich (dreadful want), St. George's-in-the-fields, where, I fear, we shall lose Mr. Griffiths, and Mr. Bramston cannot support the fatigue he has to go through, Virginia Street,[1] Gosport &c. . . . Our distress is not ordinary, and therefore ordinary difficulties and inconveniences are not to be regarded." And again, "I beg you to consider what a priest is now to the London Mission, and to know that I am now under the greatest anxiety and pain of mind on account of the state of some congregations." With such considerations before him, Dr. Poynter said that for the present they must be content to turn out good strong hard-working priests, with a minimum of cost and a minimum of time, and to look forward to the next generation, who, he hoped, would recover the Douay funds, to restore the ecclesiastical training to its true level. These funds were never in fact recovered, and there was no theological revival for many years.

The changes necessary on Dr. Poynter's departure from St. Edmund's were effected quietly enough. The Rev. Joseph Kimbell became President, with the Rev. Thomas Varley as Vice-President, the Rev. Joseph Stapleton remaining as Prefect. The traditions established during the last few years continued without material alteration, and there seems to have been as much discontent as formerly.

Mr. Kimbell's term of office lasted three and a half years. From one or two letters of his which have been preserved, we can get a general idea of the state of the college during that time. Thus, for example, writing to Dr. Poynter on March 9th, 1814, he says: "The boys are in pretty good order, and I hope will continue so. I am obliged to keep a tight hand upon them, and to give them no playdays and very little extraordinary pocket-money." It seems, however, that the "tight hand" was not sufficient to maintain discipline, which became far from good. Rumours to this effect frequently reached Dr. Poynter's ears, as appears from his

[1] Virginia Street was the antecedent of the present Commercial Road Mission.

letters, and Mr. Kimbell was so conscious that the college was not prospering under him, that in the year 1816 he intimated his willingness to resign. Dr. Poynter did not at that time accept his resignation, but induced him to continue under certain conditions.

In the summer of 1816, therefore, further changes took place, the chief of which was the departure of Mr. Varley, the vice-president. On leaving the college he was appointed to Warwick Street, where he remained till the year 1819, when he went out to the newly-revived English College in Rome. The Roman climate did not suit him, and he returned a short time afterwards, and retired to Hales Place, Canterbury, where he died on June 27th, 1821, at the comparatively early age of forty.

The new Vice-President was the Rev. Thomas Griffiths, who, since his ordination two years before, had been Master of the Preparatory School. He had also been appointed "Parish Priest" in 1815, and this office he retained. His successor at the preparatory school was the Rev. Daniel Picquot. At the same time the Rev. John Rolfe, who had been engaged in teaching for four years, left the college, and was appointed to Virginia Street: the Rev. Mark Tierney—the future historian—became Professor of Mathematics and Plain Chant; and the Rev. Joseph Daniel, Procurator. A little later on, the prefect, the Rev. Joseph Stapleton, also left, and was succeeded by the Rev. John White.

The only one of the above alterations which Mr. Kimbell seems to have regretted, was the removal of Mr. Rolfe. He wrote in this sense to Dr. Poynter. "Thus, my Lord,". he said, "although I am very sorry to be deprived of so valuable a hand as Mr. Rolfe, I am still in hopes that we shall brush on, and by the assistance of Heaven, we shall prosper. All the Masters who have the minor employments of the house seem to undertake the work with alacrity. . . . I am persuaded that Mr. White will bring [his class] on well, as he has a good name among the students for teaching, and I cannot doubt but he will apply to literature as he applies to every other branch of science, with the greatest zeal."

It now remained to be seen whether under the new circumstances Mr. Kimbell would be more successful in the management of the college. By the end of the year it was evident that such would not be the case, and when he sent in his resignation for the second time it was accepted. He left on February 11th, 1817. No immediate arrangements could be made to fill his place, as Dr. Poynter was absent on the continent. For the time being, Mr. Griffiths as vice-president, took charge of the internal government of the house; but he did not feel himself competent to undertake the management of the finances, and for this purpose Mr. Rolfe was recalled. He arrived on February 21st, when Mr. Daniel, the procurator, left, and with his departure Mr. Kimbell's administration came to an end.

Before taking leave of this period, one or two material developments of the college property may be mentioned, such as the setting up of the post-office at the college lodge [1] in 1813, and the purchase of " Riggory's Farm " two years later. The cost of the latter was 6000*l*. Another farm was likewise rented, known as "The Hole," in the draft lease of which the following very curious condition is to be found:—

" And also that in case at any time during this demise, the said premises or any part thereof shall be damaged by any riot in consequence of the same premises being attached to a Catholic College, or occupied by a tenant of the Catholic persuasion, he the said William Poynter, his Executors or Administrators, shall and will, in a reasonable time afterwards, repair and make good all such damage which shall so happen to be done, at his and their own costs."

In commenting on this, Mr. Kimbell says that he is " willing to allow that the case of a riot is not very probable;" but nevertheless, he proceeds seriously to discuss what would happen if it did occur. " Should it take place," he says, "we shall be in the most awkward situation. For at the same time it is most likely that the College and

---

[1] This is the old lodge, which was burnt down a little later. The present lodge was built by Dr. Griffiths.

Riggory Farm would be destroyed by the same mob. We should therefore have to make good the loss at a time when we should not have the means of providing for our own subsistence." Ultimately Dr. Poynter called attention to the fact that, by the law of the land, damage done by rioters was made good at the public expense, and the condition was not insisted on. It is hardly necessary to add that no rioters or mob ever came to the college.

The rebuilding of the chapel of the preparatory school, which was still used for the Catholics of the neighbourhood, was also set on foot during Mr. Kimbell's presidency, the new edifice being what is now known as the "Parish Chapel." It was considered a great improvement on its predecessor, from which some idea may be gathered of the small amount of accommodation at the old one. The building of the new chapel was due to the energy of the Rev. Thomas Griffiths, the necessary money being got together by a subscription among the old students and friends of the college. In his appeal, the special motive Mr. Griffiths urged was the want of accommodation for the Catholics of the district, from which it is clear that he regarded it primarily as a parish chapel, though it was also used by the students of the preparatory school. The doors into the old college are still visible, but they have not been opened for many years. The chapel itself is built in a plain, square style, with a gallery or organ loft at the end opposite the altar, a plan on which most Catholic chapels were built at that date. The interior decorations were plain, and the whole was devoid of beauty, but it answered its purpose.

Five months elapsed after Mr. Kimbell's departure before his successor was appointed. The Exhibition Day took place on June 18th, and a fortnight afterwards the unexpected announcement was made that Dr. Bew, the founder of Oscott, at that time on the mission at Brighton,[1] was to be President

---

[1] Dr. Bew went to Brighton when he retired from Oscott in 1808. His predecessor, Abbé Mouchel, one of the French emigrés, was virtually the founder of the mission. He began in 1804 in a room in Middle Street, afterwards moved to Margaret Street, and lastly to a house in High Street. This latter continued to be used till 1835, when the present

of St. Edmund's. The following is a copy of Dr. Poynter's circular:—

"Dr. Poynter feels a sincere pleasure in announcing to the Catholic Public the appointment of Dr. Bew to the important and dignified situation of President of St. Edmund's College at Old Hall Green. From the lively interest which every friend to science, virtue and piety, must take in the prosperity of that Establishment, Dr. P. confidently expects this appointment will meet with the full approbation, and cordial concurrence of the Clergy, and Catholic Nobility and Gentry of the United Empire: and he anticipates the most beneficial results from the co-operation of their kind and strenuous endeavours to promote and render permanent the beneficial influences of an Establishment, so essential and so dear to the interests of the Catholic Religion in this country.

"The talents and estimable qualities of Dr. Bew, as likewise his experience acquired by having long respectably filled a similar situation, are so well known and so highly appreciated, that to dwell on them must be wholly superfluous. He has Dr. Poynter's full and unqualified confidence, and no doubt will win and secure the good-will and affections of the Students in the College."

"Castle Street, Holborn, July 14th, 1817."

Dr. Bew's presidency only lasted a few months, but was not uneventful; indeed, the circumstances which occurred during that short time led to some of the most important events in the annals of the college. The chief of these was the separation of the church and lay students, which now for the first time took place.

It will be remembered that one of the chief reasons alleged by Bishop Gibson against making Old Hall a general ecclesiastical college for all the country, was the preponderance of the lay element there; and its later history would certainly seem to bear out the objection. By the time that Dr. Bew was president, the number of lay students in the upper classes was considerably diminished; but in the lower

church in Bristol Road was opened. The Rev. E. Cullen, the priest there then, and for more than thirty years, was a well-known Edmundian.

part of the house they still formed the large majority. After some consideration, it was decided to separate them entirely from the ecclesiastical students. The younger church boys, therefore, were removed to the old house, where an "Ecclesiastical Seminary" was established under the care of the Rev. Thomas Griffiths; while the lay students, together with the church students in the "poets' playroom" and the divines, remained at the college.

The Diary of the new seminary opens as follows:—

"The Ecclesiastical Seminary was begun 2nd of September, 1817, under Rev. T. A. Griffiths and Rev. H. Riley, Deacon, with the following students from the College."

(Here follows a list of students, thirteen in number, in the classes of Grammar and the Second and Third of Rudiments.)

"£80 had been given to the College for the purpose of making such alterations as should be judged necessary for fitting up the Seminary. It was expended in making a staircase to the study-place and playroom, opening doors, &c."

During the next few weeks the number of students increased to about twenty. The first new boy to arrive was Bernard Jarrett, who was later on Vice-President of the College, and lived to be the last survivor of the "Seminary" students. His first arrival is thus chronicled:—

"1817.—September 8th.—Bernard Jarrett came to the Seminary. Born in London 3 March, 1805. He was strongly recommended and very promising for his virtues and tractable dispositions. He began Latin in the Third of Rudiments."

As soon as the seminary had been fairly started, Dr. Bew began some repairs and improvements in the college which were much needed. Amongst other little alterations may be mentioned the construction of the procurator's office, which was made by partitioning off the end part of the passage, and a corresponding room at the end of the prefect's gallery was fitted up as a little chapel. This latter was afterwards used as "the book room," and for a long time after it served this latter purpose it continued to have the form of a chapel, and the Blessed Sacrament was transferred there every night for safety.

The repairs at the college were not proceeded with for any length of time. It appears that Dr. Bew had not realized the state of the finances before embarking on fresh expenses, and when he began to see how things really were, and learnt the amount of debt left by his predecessors, he was greatly discouraged. He went to London on October 9th, just three months after his appointment, and told Bishop Poynter that it was impossible for him to carry the place on. He complained that he had been kept in the dark and had not been informed of the financial position of the college, and, in short, he considered that he had not been treated well. Bishop Poynter succeeded in persuading him to return for a time; but the difficulties in which the college seemed now irrevocably sunk had their natural effect on the public mind, and a further decrease in the number of students took place at Christmas. This and many other things weighed on Dr. Bew's spirits, and affected his health so much that he found it necessary to retire from the presidency at the end of the year. Dr. Poynter was at this time again away in France, and no permanent re-arrangement of St. Edmund's could take place till his return. The Rev. John Rolfe was therefore made President *pro tem.*, and he carried on the college till the following midsummer. Dr. Bew returned to his old mission at Brighton for a few months only, and then accepted the easier post of chaplain at Brockhampton, Hants, where he ended his days in quiet and seclusion. He died on October 25th, 1829.

No allusion to the above events is made in the Seminary Diary, which proceeds to the results of the Christmas examinations and the enumeration of the students for the new term as if nothing unusual was happening. The list after Christmas shows twenty-three names.

The next entry of interest records the completion of the parish chapel :—

" 1818.—March 12th.—The new Chapel was blessed with

the name of St. Edmund by the Rev. T. A. Griffiths, by leave of Dr. Poynter, who was in Paris."

In the meantime, Mr. Griffiths was trying to introduce a thoroughly ecclesiastical spirit into his little community at the seminary, and during the next few months he made two important steps in advance towards this end. The first of these was the introduction of the monthly conferences, or half-day retreats, which have been kept up to the present day. He describes them thus in the Diary:—

"1818.—April 4th.—The Ecclesiastical Conferences began, to be repeated every Saturday afternoon before the first Sunday in each month. To begin at three o'clock, continue till 6¾. The sermon, meditation, spiritual reading &c. to be all on the same subject. This Conference was on the Advantage of Ecclesiastical Conferences once a month."

The second step alluded to was the institution of cassocks for the church students. Mr. Griffiths thought, not without reason, that the wearing of the ecclesiastical dress would help, as it did in foreign seminaries, to keep the students in mind of their vocation and would have a real influence on their conduct. Hitherto, no one had ventured to wear a cassock except in chapel. "Church dress for Church use, Sir," Dr. Poynter used to say, and he himself went about in a dark brown coat. The Rev. Joseph Silveira used often to describe the astonishment produced the first time Dr. Poynter walked from his room to the chapel in his cassock in 1817.

The church students appeared in their cassocks for the first time at the Seminary Exhibition, on June 23rd, 1818.[1] Dr. Poynter also wore his; but the professors did not take to

---

[1] The cassocks introduced at this time were in two parts, and the skirts were removable when the students played games. The collars fitted round the neck, and the Roman collar was then unknown. About forty years later, they were abolished in favour of cassocks similar to those now worn by divines and philosophers; and at the same time the Roman collar was adopted by all the church students. The present form of "Propaganda Cassocks" dates from Mgr. Patterson's time. They were first worn in 1871. The gowns introduced by Dr. Griffiths were worn by professors and divines, and they lasted till the departure of the latter in 1869. The priests towards the end of Dr. Griffiths' time began to wear plain cassocks under their gowns; but the modern cassocks, with capes, did not come into use till about 1855.

them at that time, for almost immediately afterwards the gowns were introduced and the ordinary priest's dress became the trencher and gown.

The day after the Seminary Exhibition, that at the college took place, and a week later the crisis arrived. Three professors left, and it became a question, both for financial and other considerations, whether the college could be carried on any longer. "By whatever cause St. Edmund's College has been lowered in public esteem," wrote the Rev. J. Jones, of Warwick Street, "the event is a misfortune as deeply to be deplored as it is severely felt." And again, "A failure so complete, so nearly bordering on bankruptcy in its finances, . . . . must have some very deeply rooted cause, and that notwithstanding repeated attempts have been made to reform the cause, is at the present moment as fruitful of discontent as it has been heretofore."

The saving of the college and its restoration to a sound state, financially and otherwise, was due to one man—the Rev. Thomas Griffiths. The account of his work as president will be given in the next chapter.

## CHAPTER XI.

### THE PRESIDENCY OF DR. GRIFFITHS.

### 1818—1834.

Dr. Griffiths appointed President—The Lay Students at the Old House—A year later they are transferred back to the College—Institution of the " Lay Bounds "—St. Edmund's once more in a flourishing state—List of the chief students—Description of the College under Dr. Griffiths—Visit of Ambrose Lisle Phillips and Kenelm Digby—" Mores Catholici" written at Old Hall—Death of Mr. Cleghorn—Consecration of Bishop Bramston—Death of the Rev. John Daniel—Fate of the Colleges of Douay and St. Omer and final loss of the Douay funds—Rev. F. Tuite last titular President of Douay—Death of Dr. Poynter—Catholic Emancipation—Standon Inclosure Act—Dr. Griffiths appointed Coadjutor of London District—He succeeds Bishop Bramston as Vicar Apostolic.

THE difficulty which confronted Dr. Poynter at the beginning of the midsummer holidays of 1818 was the same which he had met with ever since he had first thought of retiring from St. Edmund's. Where was a new president to be found? The experience of the last few years was not encouraging, and did not point to an easy answer to the question.

Though the main difficulty was the same as before, however, the circumstances had altered considerably. For some years the character of the college had been steadily undergoing a change. Owing chiefly to Dr. Poynter's exertions, and the progress of the ecclesiastical education fund, the number of church students had almost doubled within ten years, and since the negotiations for the restoration of the Douay money seemed at that time likely to be brought to a successful issue, there was every prospect of a further increase. On the other hand, the number of lay students had during the same period shown a falling off, and instead of their being six or seven to one as

St. Edmund's College, from the "Catholic Miscellany," 1826.

Page 224.

formerly, by the year 1818 they had become practically equal in number to the church students, each amounting to about forty.

With these facts in his mind, Bishop Poynter came to a bold decision. After going through the figures in detail, he found that by means of the strictest economy, and by considerably reducing the establishment, the college might be supported by church students only. He determined therefore to profit by the present crisis to close it as a lay establishment. At the same time he transferred the seminary to the new building, and established St. Edmund's as a purely ecclesiastical college, appointing the Rev. Thomas Griffiths President. This involved the dismissal of from twenty to thirty lay boys. Those in the lower classes were allowed to remain, but were removed to the old house, where they had no intercourse with the church students at the college. A change such as this could not be effected without ill-feeling in some quarters, and several angry letters were written by old Edmundians and others. Dr. Poynter, however, had his answer ready to hand. The very people who were loudest in their complaints had already anticipated him by sending their sons elsewhere. Had they continued to support the college, he said, the present step would never have been rendered necessary. If there were reason for complaint, the cause rested not with him but with themselves.

Mr. Griffiths—or Dr. Griffiths, as he soon became—was only twenty-seven years of age when he was appointed president, having been born in London on June 2nd, 1791. He was brought up in his early years in the established religion, but the example and prayers of his mother had their effect, and, while still quite a boy, he declared himself a Catholic, and was received into the church at St. George's-in-the-Fields. After his conversion he showed signs of extraordinary piety, and every morning he walked to church at an early hour in order to have the privilege of serving Mass. This so displeased his father that it is said he used to keep him without his boots in the morning; but his efforts were unavailing, as young Griffiths thought nothing on such an occasion of walking through the streets barefoot.

The early piety of the youth soon attracted the attention of the clergy of St. George's, particularly of Dr. Bramston, who recommended him to Bishop Douglass as a candidate for the priesthood. On being accepted, he came to St. Edmund's on January 5th, 1805, as has been already stated.

During his school days, he showed no unusual ability; but he was unremitting in his application to his work, and by means of steady perseverance, added to good retentive faculties, succeeded in keeping well abreast of his class fellows. He did not earn the medal either in Poetry or Rhetoric, but he gained several prizes and became a fair scholar. Throughout the whole of his student's life at St. Edmund's he was the cause of edification. "His mild, humble, and cheerful disposition," says his biographer,[1] 'made him a favourite with all during his college career. He was a model to all from his humility, his piety, his attention to study, and his exact obedience to every college rule." He had been a priest only four years when he became President of the College, and the difficulties and responsibilities inseparable from the post were in his case largely increased by the critical state of the college. Dr. Poynter was not mistaken in his estimate of him, however, and lived to congratulate himself on his choice. "It would be unnecessary to enter here," says a writer in the "Catholic Directory,"[2] "into the circumstances that then rendered the presidency of St. Edmund's College a station of great difficulty and labour, one that required great and persevering energy of mind, united with a disposition that could win the minds of others. These qualities were found in the new president. For more than fifteen years he governed the college, and by his prudence, labour, and parental care, gained the affections of his students and raised the college to be, what it is to be hoped it will long continue to be, an abode

---

[1] The Rev. Edward Price, in *Dolman's Magazine* for September, 1847, p. 201.
[2] "Catholic Directory" for 1843, p. 128.

of piety and learning, and a nursery of truly apostolical priests."

The necessary arrangements having been completed, Mr. Griffiths and his students moved across to the new college on August 1st, 1818. The following is the record in the Seminary Diary:—

"1818.—July 31st.—The Ecclesiastical students removed most of their things to the College, having been informed that they were to remove to the College on the 1st of August.

"August 1st.—The Ecclesiastical students went to the College for Last Prayers, in their cassocks, 28 in number; all the Lay Students having been dismissed the house."

The Diary now commences afresh as that of the college:—

"St. EDMUND'S COLLEGE.

"August 1st, 1818.

"The Secular Students having been all dismissed, it began solely as an ecclesiastical establishment, with the students who had come over from the Seminary and those ecclesiastical students who were in Philosophy, Rhetoric, and Poetry. The Preparatory School continued as a Lay Establishment."

Next follows a list of professors and students. There was no vice-president, but the duties of that office were temporarily discharged by the prefect, the Rev. J. White. The Rev. Lewis Havard returned to the college to teach philosophy, with a view to taking the divinity later on; for there were so few divines that it was not thought worth while to form a class for the first year, and they therefore attended philosophy lectures. The Rev. Mark Tierney, who was ordained the following month, became Prefect of the Lay Establishment. In addition to these, Mr. Brannan, a layman, who had been at Old Hall since the early part of Dr. Poynter's time, remained as a professor, assisted by Mr. Abbott, also a layman. Mr. Cleghorn, who was too old for work, continued to reside at the college as a "Convictor."

The students numbered exactly forty, of whom ten were in Philosophy. The others were distributed through the classes of Rhetoric, Syntax, Grammar, and the Rudiments. The Diary continues as follows :—

"At 7 o'clock, High Mass was sung by the Right Rev. Dr. Poynter, after which the list of students was read by the Rev. J. White, for the Rev. Mr. President. After Breakfast a whole Playday was granted according to the Rules. The next three whole study days in the rules were playdays for the new President."

Nothing of note happened during the next few months, but the following year further changes were made in the constitution and arrangements of the college, which then assumed a form that remained unaltered for more than forty years. The chief change was the closing of the Old Hall and the transfer of the lay boys to the college. They were still separated from the church students in play-time and in the dormitories, but attended the same classes. The lay playroom and lay bounds were therefore established at this time. The former was where the chemical laboratory now is, and the bounds extended over about a third of what is now the "pleasure ground." The present parlour was the lay study place, and the old parlour was next door.

The church students inhabited the north end of the house, and were given what had formerly been known as the "great bounds." The poets and divines shared it with them, the "divines' bounds" being that part at the upper end beyond the cross walk level with the "ball place." The "divines' bounds" were "out of bounds" for all those below divinity.

The "church playroom" was a single large room, covering the whole space now occupied by the "bounds playroom" and "chess room," there being then no partition between them. At the further end stood a cupboard, in which were kept the books of the "church library," as there was no separate room set apart for the purpose. The "poets' playroom" and library were in the same place as they are at the present day, and the "divines' playroom" was where the physical science room now stands; the ecclesiastical study place being next door.

It is interesting to note, amongst other economies necessitated by the new state of affairs, that the glass was taken out of the windows of the divines' rooms and of the ambulacrum, so as to lessen the window tax, and was replaced by wooden shutters. The windows remained in that state till the tax was reduced in 1823. According to Canon Last's account, the shutters did not close properly, and let in the wind and weather, but not the light, so that it became impossible to use the rooms for studying in except in the middle of summer. The students, however, seem to have got accustomed to their hardships, and to have put up with them as cheerfully as did the first divines from Douay when lodged in the "Ship."

The presidency of Dr. Griffiths lasted nearly sixteen years, and marks the period of the complete regeneration of St. Edmund's, both financially and otherwise. As the internal state of the college improved, confidence was gradually restored, and the increased number of students bears witness to its improved condition.

Dr. Griffiths' first vice-president was the Rev. John White, who was appointed to that office in 1819; his place as prefect was taken by the Rev. Joseph Siddons, then just ordained. A year later he gave way to the Rev. Richard Newell. The Rev. Mark Tierney left the college about this time, and the Rev. Lewis Havard a little later, after which Dr. Griffiths taught the divines. He also acted as procurator after the departure of Mr. Tierney, who had filled the post for a year, but the Rev. John Clarke, a divine in minor orders, became assistant procurator, and succeeded to the office on his ordination in 1825.

In 1824 Mr. White resigned the vice-presidency and was succeeded by the Rev. Richard Newell, but the prefects about this time followed each other in rapid succession—the Revs. James Holdstock, Edward Ewart, John Welch, William Woods, and Charles Threllfall. In 1830 the last-named became Parish Priest, which post he afterwards retained for eight years, while a little later, the Rev. James Whelan, then a deacon, became Procurator, and the Rev. William

Hunt, well known afterwards as Provost of Westminster, undertook the prefectship.

A few only of those who were students at St. Edmund's under Dr. Griffiths are still alive. At the time of writing, the Rev. Charles King, who came to the college on August 1st, 1823, is the oldest living Edmundian. Canon Bower and Canon Fryer, who arrived together on October 3rd, 1826, stand next in order. Rev. Henry Telford (March, 1827) follows, and after him Mr. William Bower, who lives at the college, and whose connection with it dates back to September, 1827. Bishop Weathers came ten months later, and of the others there now remain Canon Applegath, Judge Stonor, Dr. George Weathers, and possibly one or two others.

Among the students at that time who are now dead, we may notice the names of Charles Baggs, afterwards Rector of English College, Rome, and then Vicar Apostolic of the Western District; Edward Hearne, some time Vicar-General of Westminster; Edward Cox, for eleven years President of St. Edmund's, and later on Vicar-General of Southwark; George Rolfe, Bernard Jarrett and John Maguire, future Vice-Presidents, the last of whom left his valuable library to the college; John Telford, afterwards Procurator; Joseph Silveira, well known for many years as priest of Lincoln's-Inn-Fields; John Mount, for forty-five years priest of Southampton and Canon of Southwark and Portsmouth.

Among the laity three names may be especially mentioned. The late Lord Petre came to the college in 1832, and remained four years. He lived till comparatively recently, and his memory is still known and respected by all English Catholics as that of a model layman and as a pattern of charity and piety. His brother, the late Mr. Henry Petre, came and left with him, and was also well known for his admirable qualities. The third name is that of the late Mr. Charles Corney, one of the founders of the Edmundian Association, and for thirty-five years its treasurer; and he also was widely known and respected in after life.

The following description of St. Edmund's under Dr. Griffiths is given by Mr. William Bower:—

WILLIAM BERNARD,
Twelfth Lord Petre.

"I came to St. Edmund's on September 24th, 1827. My father drove me down from London, and though it is now more than three score years ago, every incident in the journey is quite fresh in my memory, for my going to College was the realization of my earnest longings since I was quite a child. Our first stoppage was at Waltham Cross, that souvenir of a pious Queen in the ages of Faith. At that time it was greatly defaced; but it was some time afterwards restored to its original form. Our second halt was at Ware, then famous for the large bed, and known to all boys by John Gilpin's involuntary ride. Thence we went on to Wade's Mill [1] and had a rest at the "Feathers'," then one of the very best roadside inns in England, with stabling for at least a hundred horses. Those who know it now as little better than a large ruin, can form no idea of the continual bustle and noise inseparable from one of the chief stages of the old post roads. Twelve coaches changed horses there daily and many a chaise and four turned out there for the Newmarket Races. It was famed also for a raven, the original of Barnaby Rudge's, whose skill in imitating the drawing of corks was admirable, as was his knowing look and hoarse call of 'Coach coming, bustle about!' which I then and often afterwards thoroughly enjoyed.

"From Wade's Mill we went on to Colliers' End, not by the present embankment, which was not made till some years later, but down a steep descent and up a stiff hill. It was then that the first view of the College came before us, the long roof forming the sky line, unbroken by any tree save one, a very high poplar which was long a land-mark in the county, even now bearing aloft its withered limbs in the middle of what is now the cricket field.[2]

"The present Lodge of the College was not then built—it was in fact put up a few years later whilst I was at St. Edmund's—and as we did not notice the entrance gate, we

---

[1] Wade's Mill is traditionally pointed out as the place where St. Thomas à Becket fell into the water when out hawking as a boy. See Father Morris' "Life of St. Thomas," p. 10.

[2] The old poplar was blown down in the storm of October, 1891.

drove up the lane, entered the grounds by the Farm, and following the road round a large circular grass plot, arrived at the front door. A servant met us and led us up to the President's room. There I was introduced to Dr. Griffiths, whose kind greeting, " I am to be your father now," made an impression on me which still lasts.

"In appearance Dr. Griffiths was the very picture of neatness; his hair cut quite short and powdered white, gave a contrast to his closely-shaven grey face. He wore spectacles, and had on a University gown; and when showing us round the house, wore a mortar-board cap. The College dinner being over, we had some refreshment in the Bishop's room, and then Rev. William Woods, the Prefect, introduced me to my companions, the two who were to have the play-day with me,[1] and my father drove off.

"I was a student at St. Edmund's on and off for ten years, before my weak health forced me to leave England for a milder climate. We always held a high place among the Catholic Colleges, acknowledged as the first and chief successor of old Douay. On one occasion, I think in 1828 or 1829, a student from another of our Catholic Colleges, who had carried off the first prize there, both in Poetry and Rhetoric, came to St. Edmund's, and though he had already passed through both classes at his former college, he was beaten by one of our own students, of which we were very proud.

"Even in games St. Edmund's was well thought of. Lord Grimston, afterwards Earl of Verulam, once petitioned the President for three of our cricketers to play for the county in some important match. These were William Hunt, the future Provost, who was considered the best bat in Hertfordshire, Matthew Ryan, our crack bowler, and Joseph Alberry the wicket keeper. In those days, it seems to have been considered out of place for clerical students to contend in public matches, and Dr. Griffiths would not hear of it. But

---

[1] It was then, as now, the custom to give a new boy in charge of two other students, who had the play-day with him the day after his arrival, and were expected in return to look after him for his first few days at the college.

our great game was Cat, and there was always in those days more enthusiasm exhibited at the latter game than even at the best House Cricket Matches.

"The daily life at St. Edmund's sixty years ago was very like what it is now, though the arrangement of the hours was somewhat different. Dr. Poynter was still alive when I came, but he was in failing health and died a few months afterwards. He confirmed me in London in 1826, but I never saw him at the College. His Coadjutor and successor, Bishop Bramston, was well known to all of us and was a frequent visitor. He had a kind and genial presence, a boy's heart, though burdened with many years. No visit passed without an hour or so in the play-room amongst us, whom he called his dear, very dear children.

"The stream of converts from Anglicanism had not commenced at the time of which I am writing, and the very few who did come over then required extraordinary courage. One of the Edmundians, John Tilt, who became a priest and was for short time Prefect, was the son of one of the earliest clerical converts, who astonished and doubtless shocked many of his congregation when at the evening service at his London church he announced his intention, after serious study and earnest prayer, of joining the Church of Rome. I met him afterwards in Paris, where he was employed by Louis Philippe in the College of Henri Quatre. He had previously held the same appointment under Charles the Tenth.

"Mr. Ambrose Lisle Phillips, afterwards Mr. De Lisle, also spent a considerable time at the College soon after his conversion, and received Confirmation in the old Chapel at the hands of Bishop Bramston. He came from Cambridge, and with him came another well known convert, Mr. Kenelm Digby, then known to us only by his " Broadstone of Honour." He presented to the College copies of portraits of many of the Popes, which hung in the old Refectory and were afterwards transferred to the new one. His well known "Mores Catholici" was written at St. Edmund's, and the opening of that book is in fact a description of one of the College services."

We may now take in order the chief events of interest

which occurred during the presidency of Dr. Griffiths. The death of Mr. Potier, in 1823, has already been alluded to. Less than two months after his funeral at Standon, another link with the past was severed by the death of Mr. Cleghorn, the last of the Doullens prisoners left at Old Hall. For the last five years of his life he was past work, and being a most kind and charitable man, he spent most of his time in distributing clothing and other alms to the poor of the neighbourhood, by whom he was known as "the Good Man of Odey Green." He had always prayed he might die without giving any trouble, and he was heard in a remarkable manner, for his death took place with great suddenness.

It appears that to the last he kept a horse at the college, and used to ride sometimes as far as London, in which case he would make an early start. It was on one of these occasions that he left his room at a quarter past six on a bright summer morning of June, 1823, equipped for his ride. As he went down stairs, he was taken suddenly ill. Two students who happened to be passing on their way down to their morning meditation, took him back to his room and called Dr. Griffiths. The latter saw at once that he was in a dying state, and lost no time in anointing him. He had scarcely time to finish before Mr. Cleghorn, who had never recovered consciousness, calmly expired. He was buried in a leaden coffin under the sanctuary of the "Old Chapel," his being the first interment at the college. Subsequently, all those who died there were buried in the same way, and when the vaults of the "New Chapel" were completed, the coffins were removed there. Mr. Cleghorn's remains therefore now lie under the present church, and his name is on the memorial tablet in the ante-chapel. He left a considerable amount of money to the college, and Masses are still said for him every year.

A fortnight after the death of Mr. Cleghorn, on the Feast of SS. Peter and Paul, the consecration of Dr. Bramston, as Bishop of Usula and Coadjutor to the London District, took place. Bishop Poynter himself performed the ceremony, assisted by Bishops Collingridge and Baines. Dr. Bramston

BISHOP BRAMSTON,
Vicar Apostolic of London District, 1827-1836.

Page 235.

was a convert, and had been a lawyer in early life.[1] After his conversion he studied divinity at Lisbon, and soon after his ordination he was sent on the mission at St. George's-in-the-Field's, where he first knew Dr. Griffiths. Later on he became vicar-general to Dr. Poynter, whom he accompanied to Rome in 1814-15. Dr. Poynter on that occasion petitioned for Dr. Bramston as coadjutor, but his wish was not granted till eight years afterwards, by which time Dr. Bramston had reached the age of sixty-one.

On the 3rd of October of the same year, the Rev. John Daniel died in Paris, where he had been ever since he left England in 1802. Here we may pause to consider the last chapter in the history of the Colleges of Douay and St. Omer, and the ultimate fate of the buildings. We have seen how Buonaparte had placed all the British establishments in France under a single administrator. After his fall, a petition for the restoration of the colleges and property was addressed to the King of France by the Bishops of Great Britain and Ireland, which had the desired effect. By an *ordonnance* dated January 25th, 1816, the union was dissolved, and the colleges declared restored to their respective owners. The lease of the college at Douay had still eighteen years to run, and Mr. Daniel could not enter into possession; but he received henceforth an annual rent of f. 2500 (100*l*.). On the expiration of the lease it was sold to the French Government for the sum of f. 80,000, or about 3200*l*.[2] The price sounds at first a very moderate one, but the college was probably by that time in a very dilapidated condition. The sale was effected in 1834, and since then has served as barracks for soldiers.

---

[1] Dr. Bramston always liked a joke, and one of his favourite sayings was, that being a Popish priest grafted on a Protestant lawyer, he ought to be a match for the devil.

Another well-known story is told of him, that a lady once came to see him to secure his interest in arranging a marriage between her daughter and a friend of the bishop, and that, through ignorance of his name, she called him throughout "Mr. Brimston." Having listened to her with great patience, the bishop answered quietly: "Madam, I see you are making a mistake. My name is not *Brimstone*, and I have nothing to do with making *matches*."

[2] See "Le Collége Anglais de Douai pendant la Revolution Française," par M. l'Abbé Dancoisne, Introduction, p. li.

With respect to St. Omer, a settlement was come to at the same time. The annual rents were paid over to the administrators or trustees, who were the Revs. Francis Tuite and John Yates, with Mr. Cleghorn. It was at one time proposed to make it into a covered riding-school, but this idea was afterwards abandoned, and it continued to be used as a military hospital. In 1834 negotiations were entered into for its purchase by the French Government, and it was valued at f. 250,000 (10,000*l.*). Four years later the sale was completed. On the 27th of September, 1840, a further and final claim of f. 27,900 (about 1100*l.*) was paid over, and the college became the property of the French Government.[1]

The question of the restoration of the funded property was not so easily settled. In the end the French Government paid over a large sum to meet the claims of all British subjects for their losses during the Revolution, and, on their part, the English Government deputed three commissioners to adjudicate the different claims. Those on behalf of Douay were duly put before them in 1818 by Dr. Poynter, who acted for Mr. Daniel in virtue of a power of attorney. The claim seems to have been confounded by the commissioners at first with that of St. Omer,[2] and the fact that the latter had been a "Royal College," in receipt of a yearly pension from the King of France, and subject to his control, according to its constitutions, is probably what gave rise to the idea that Douay College also was to be considered a French establishment. To confute this theory Dr. Poynter drew up a memorial,[3] and later on, at the request of the commissioners, a formal declaration was signed by the vicars apostolic, and confirmed by Mr. Daniel, that the funds, when recovered, should be expended entirely in England and not in France.

Further delays occurred, and much correspondence passed on both sides. In the midst of it came the death of Mr. Daniel; but this contingency had already been provided for by the election of the Rev. Francis Tuite as his coadjutor,

---

[1] Piers, "Le Collége Anglais de Saint Omer," p. 26.
[2] See *Catholic Magazine*, February, 1831, p. 54.
[3] See Appendix G.

with right of succession, at his death, as titular president. The negotiations were, therefore, not delayed, and Dr. Poynter continued to act, now on behalf of his old vice-president, Mr. Tuite.

According to a tradition at St. Edmund's, Dr. Poynter was asked by Mr. Canning to give a detailed description of the nature and object of the Douay funds. Dr. Bramston's experience as a lawyer led him to suspect the motives of this request, and he recommended Dr. Poynter not to answer the question. The latter, however, took an opposite view, and wrote fully, mentioning burses for the education of priests, funds for the endowment of the libraries and for the printing of the Theological Defensions, and foundations for masses. At first it appeared as if he were right, and the money seemed on the point of being paid over. He was congratulated by Mr. Canning on his success, but at the eleventh hour a decision in the opposite sense was arrived at by the commissioners, and the claim was rejected. The plea on which the decision was based was, that the purposes described by Dr. Poynter being, by the law of England, illegal and "superstitious," the College was not carried on with the sanction of the British Government, and must be considered to have been a French establishment, and, therefore, not to come within the province of the commissioners.[1]

An appeal against this decision was taken before the Privy Council, but without success. Lord Gifford delivered judgment on November 25th, 1825, in the following terms [2]:—

---

[1] This traditional account may be compared with the *Catholic Magazine* for February and March, 1831, and will be found to be consistent with what is there given. Had Dr. Poynter been more reticent, it is hardly likely that any different decision would have been arrived at in the end, the main object of Douay College being well known.

What became of the Douay money is not certainly known. The common Catholic tradition asserts it to have been spent in paying for the Pavilion at Brighton, which was erected for George IV. when Prince of Wales. (Gillow, vol. ii. p. 15.) Another account says that it went towards the furnishing of Windsor Castle. (*Catholic Magazine*, February, 1831, p. 52.) Both these stories have been denied, and all that is certain is that the Catholics never received the money.

[2] *Catholic Magazine*, February, 1831, p. 53.

"In considering this question, it is necessary to attend to the nature and object of these establishments, and to the intent and meaning of the treaties under which the indemnity is asked. Now the institutions in behalf of which the claims are made, although their members were British subjects, and their property derived from funds constituted by British subjects, were in the nature of French corporations; they were locally established in a foreign territory because they could not exist in England; their end and object were not authorized, but were directly opposed to the British law; and the funds dedicated to their maintenance were employed for that purpose in France, because they could not be so employed in England; and if other circumstances were wanting to fix their character, it appears that these establishments, as well as their revenues, are subject to the control of the French Government; and the conduct of that Government since the restoration of the monarchy, shows that if all had been suffered to remain entire during the period of the Revolution, the monarchical Government would have taken the whole under its superintendence and management. We think, therefore, that they must be deemed French establishments."

When the above sentence was delivered, Dr. Poynter's counsel, Sir James Macintosh, wished to bring the matter before the House of Commons, but was dissuaded from doing so lest the cause of Catholic emancipation should suffer, and the matter therefore ended. A few years later, such moneys as had survived the general wreck were handed over to the vicars apostolic, and the affairs of Douay College were finally wound up. The Rev. Francis Tuite was the last to hold the title of president, and on his death, in 1837, the diaries and other Douay papers became the property of the London district, of which he was vicar-general.[1]

Dr. Poynter survived Lord Gifford's decision exactly two years. It is said that the grief caused by the loss of the funds notably accelerated his death.[2] His last visit to the

---

[1] See Preface to "Douay Diaries," p. v., and *Catholic Magazine*, December, 1831, p. 684.

[2] One of his last works for his district was the introduction of the clergy

College was in Holy Week of 1827, at which time he looked already much broken. His illness was a long and very painful one; the disease being tumour in the stomach, brought on by over-work. He bore it throughout with the greatest patience, and after receiving all the rites of the Church, calmly expired on the evening of November 26th, 1827.

The funeral obsequies took place on December 11th, at Moorfields, then a new church, which Dr. Poynter himself had solemnly opened less than seven years before. Bishop Bramston officiated, and the ceremonies were conducted by the Rev. Matthew Ryan of St. Edmund's, all the servers being Edmundians. A sermon was preached, and afterwards printed by Dr. Poynter's old pupil, the Rev. Lewis Havard. The body was placed in the clergy vault at Moorfields, where the following inscription may now be seen:—

> Gulielmo Poynter Ep. Hal. et. V.A.L., Hoc Marmor Coadjutor Clerusque dolentes posuere. Obiit A.D. 1827, aet. 66.
> Nullum diem prætermisit, quo non aliqua præclara fidei pietatis atque innocentiæ argumenta præstiterit. Requiescat in pace.

The same evening his heart, which he had left as a legacy to St. Edmund's, was brought down to the College by Bishop Bramston and Dr. Griffiths. The next day Pontifical High Mass was celebrated in the college chapel for the repose of his soul, after which the *De Profundis* was chanted while two of the professors deposited the case containing the heart beneath the foot of the altar, where the priest stands to

retreat, which took place for the first time in July, 1826. The order of the day has been preserved, and is worth reproducing, as it gives us a sketch of an old-fashioned retreat before they were formally preached by one man as now. All rose at 6 a.m., and from 6.30 to 7 a Meditation was made from Challoner. The bishop then said Community Mass, after which there was free time for half an hour. Prime and Tierce were next recited, followed by a short reading out of sacred scripture, and then breakfast. At nine o'clock a Meditation was made out of Bourdaloue; and at a quarter to ten Dr. Poynter preached a sermon, which was the only thing in the way of preaching throughout the retreat. At half-past eleven Sext and None were recited, and another three-quarters of an hour's Meditation from Bourdaloue formed the conclusion of the morning's work. After dinner nothing took place till four, when Vespers and Compline were recited, after which there was half an hour's Meditation and an hour's retirement. Next came Matins and Lauds, followed by supper. Night prayers were at nine o'clock.

begin Mass, this being the spot which Dr. Poynter had chosen when alive. The case was made in the shape of a heart, covered with purple velvet, and in front was a brass plate bearing the inscription which he had himself written :—

<blockquote>
In hoc Collegio Catholico<br>
fidei Seminario<br>
unde nunquam fuerat<br>
avulsum cor suum<br>
testamento<br>
reponi mandavit<br>
Illmus ac Revmus Gul.Hal.V.A.L
</blockquote>

Within two years after Dr. Poynter's death, the long-hoped-for Bill for Catholic Emancipation was passed. It received the Royal Assent on April 13th, 1829. The occasion of the passing of the Act was celebrated at St. Edmund's in a private manner, as it was considered advisable to avoid any display.

A year after this another Bill passed through Parliament which, although of merely local interest, concerned St. Edmund's so closely that Bishop Bramston used to say that it was as good as a present of 2000*l.* to the college. This was the "Standon Inclosure Act," promoted by Mr. Plumer Ward, Lord of the Manor of Standon, and one or two others. It received the Royal Assent on May 29th, 1830, and provided for the exchange of certain common and other lands in the parish of Standon, the details of which were to be settled by a commissioner appointed for the purpose. Mr. Anthony Jackson, the commissioner, sat at the Bell Inn, Puckeridge, on September 27th, 1830. Dr. Griffiths attended on behalf of St. Edmund's, and an agreement was come to by which some land near Standon was exchanged for some fields in front of the college, its appearance being thereby greatly improved.

The last event to chronicle during the presidency of Dr. Griffiths is his own Consecration as Bishop. After the death of Bishop Gradwell, who had been coadjutor to Bishop Bramston, the latter had petitioned for Dr. Griffiths to succeed him, and, his request being granted, the Consecration took place on October 28th, 1833. Five bishops were present, Bishop Bramston performing the ceremony, assisted by Bishops Penswick and Walsh. Bishop Baines preached, and Bishop Briggs also was present in the sanctuary. It was in one sense a day of great rejoicing at St. Edmund's, in that the dignity had been conferred on the President of the College and on one so universally loved and esteemed; but on the other hand there was not wanting a strong admixture of regret, inasmuch as the promotion would probably require his retirement from the college at no distant date. In the event, this took place within six months, Bishop Bramston's feebleness of constitution rendering it imperatively necessary that his coadjutor should reside in London, and in April, 1834, Dr. Griffiths formally resigned the presidency of the college into the hands of Dr. Newell. Thus closed the period of nearly sixteen years, which may be looked on as the most prosperous St. Edmund's has ever had.

Bishop Bramston survived only two years after this. He died at the priest's house at Southampton, whither he had gone for rest and change, on July 11th, 1836. His body was taken to London and buried in the clergy vault at Moorfields. Bishop Griffiths succeeded as Vicar Apostolic, and during the remaining eleven years of his life his zeal and charity had a larger and more important field of work than when he was President of St. Edmund's. He continued his interest in the college, and one of the chief works of his episcopate was the erection of the new chapel. Of this and his other works as bishop we shall speak in the next chapter.

## CHAPTER XII.

### ST. EDMUND'S COLLEGE DURING THE EPISCOPATE OF BISHOP GRIFFITHS.

#### 1833—1847.

*Dr. Newell, Rev. John Rolfe and Dr. Cox successive Presidents—List of students—The* Edmundian *magazine—Welcome given to the Queen when passing the College in 1843—Plans for new Chapel—Visit of Pugin—His answer to the Address presented to him—Foundation stone of the new Chapel—Oxford Converts—Canon Oakeley and Dr. Ward—Society of St. Vincent of Paul established at the College—Charles Lynch drowned skating—Philip Weld drowned at Rye House—The "Weld Ghost Story"—Death of Bishop Griffiths.*

THROUGHOUT his episcopate, Bishop Griffiths was a frequent visitor to the college, and for several years he used to drive down almost every week to spend his Sunday in the country and refresh himself after his week's work. To the end of his life he continued to take an active interest in the management of the college.

Dr. Newell held the office of President for about three and a half years. His first Vice-President, the Rev. Bernard Jarrett, only remained a short time before leaving to join the Society of Jesus, in which he spent the rest of a long life, dying at Beaumont in 1890. He was succeeded as Vice-President by Dr. Maguire; but after Dr. Newell's departure at the end of 1837, the Rev. John Rolfe was recalled from Moorfields, and the Rev. Edward Cox from Chelsea, the former becoming President and the latter Vice-President.

The Prefects during this time were the Revs. Edward Hearne, John Tilt and John Telford. When the Rev. John Rolfe left in 1840, Dr. Cox became President, with the Rev. George Rolfe as Vice-President, and the Rev.

BISHOP GRIFFITHS,
President 1818-1834;
Vicar Apostolic of London District, 1836-1847.

William Weathers as Prefect. Three years later, the Rev. George Rolfe also left, the Rev. William Weathers became Vice-President and Procurator, and the Rev. Henry Telford Prefect. This arrangement lasted through the remaining eight years of Dr. Cox's presidency, except that at the end the Rev. Frederick Rymer was Prefect.

If we turn to the list of students, we find many names which are still familiar to us. Archbishop O'Callaghan, Bishops Butt, Danell, Luck, Virtue; Mgrs. Crook, Crookall, Gilbert, Giles, Goddard, McCarthy; Canons John and James Bamber, Henry Rymer, Mount, Doyle, Bans, Oakeley, Bagshawe, Bowman, Kyne, Thomas Luck, Purcell; Rev. Robert Whitty, S.J., now English Consultor of the Jesuits; Revs. Edmund and Albert Buckler, now Dominicans; Revs. Edward Keogh and Thomas Gloag, who afterwards joined the Oratorians; Revs. Robert Butler, Thomas Dillon, and Edward Lescher, who became Oblates; Revs. Frederick Rymer, D.D., Alfred Dolman, Alfred White, William I. Dolan, Edmund Tunstall, Edmund Pennington, Francis Stanfield, are only a few out of many that might be mentioned. Among the laymen who were students at this time several have also become known. Mr. James L. Molloy, the composer, and his brother, Bernard Molloy, M.P., Mr. John S. Smith, now English Consul at Munich, Richard and Thomas Walmesley, Ambrose and Everard De Lisle, Lawrence Dolan, Horace Rymer, and Philip Weld may be specially mentioned.[1]

During his short term of office, the Rev. John Rolfe did much towards improving the college grounds. The common and other lands, which had been acquired a few years before under the "Standon Inclosure Act," were thrown into the park and the whole laid out under the superintendence of Mr. Joseph Knight, of Chelsea. The oaks in front of the

[1] A traditional story may be told here, though it really belongs to a later date, about a practical joke played by Colonel Vaughan, of Courtfield, when a boy at St. Edmund's. It is said that one Tuesday afternoon, having ascertained that the president was out for a walk, he came running into the Bounds, shouting "Hours off!" Every one believed him, including the prefect, with the result that when the time for evening study came, they all remained in the cricket field. The mistake was not found out till it was too late to rectify it. The youth was penanced; but he remained the most popular boy in the college for a long time afterwards.

college had by this time grown to a fair size; other trees and shrubs were planted, and the hedges between the fields removed. At the same time the carriage approach was remodelled. Formerly the road from the lodge led up to the main entrance of the college, in front of which it formed a large ring, enabling carriages to turn by driving round it. This was now abolished and the road continued past the old chapel, curving round thence till it made a junction with the "College Lane," at the spot known ever since as "the White Gate."

Dr. Cox, who succeeded Mr. Rolfe, was President through the remaining seven years of the episcopate of Bishop Griffiths, and for four years afterwards. This includes a period which forms an important landmark in the history of Catholicity in England. Two events stand prominently out. The first is the crisis of the "Oxford Movement," which was followed by the conversion of such men as Cardinal Newman, Cardinal Manning, Father Faber, Dr. Ward and others who afterwards took a leading part in Catholic affairs. The second, of no less importance, is the restoration of the Hierarchy; but as this took place after the death of Dr. Griffiths, we shall speak about it in the next chapter.

The period of Dr. Cox's presidency was also important as regards the internal history of the college. He and Bishop Griffiths worked together throughout in perfect unity for the good of St. Edmund's, and it was whilst Dr. Cox was President that Pugin came down and the new chapel was planned out and executed. When Dr. Cox left, though it had not been formally opened, it was in such an advanced state that little more required to be done. It is perhaps not too trivial to add that it was during the presidency of Dr. Cox that the college was placed in railway connection with London, and that the last coaches disappeared from the high road.[1]

Many of these events are alluded to in the old volumes of

---

[1] The following list of "Coaches which pass by the Lodge of the

the *Edmundian*, which first appeared in the early part of Dr. Cox's presidency, and it is the mention of such contemporary events which gives them their chief interest, for the contributions themselves are not of high literary excellence.

In the third volume of the *Edmundian* is an account of the welcome given to the Queen and Prince Albert, when they passed by the college on October 25th, 1843. They were on their way from Windsor to Cambridge, whence they were to go on to Wimpole Hall, the seat of the Earl of Hardwicke. As soon as it was known that they would pass along the high road, great preparations were made for a display of Catholic loyalty. A triumphal arch was erected outside the lodge, and at the hour when the Queen was expected, Dr. Cox, together with the professors and students, assembled to greet her. The professors and divines wore their gowns, and on the opposite side of the road the members of the newly-formed college band [1] were grouped together in readiness to

---

College," appears in the advertisements of St. Edmund's under Dr. Griffiths:—

"Union (Cambridge) which leaves the White Horse, Fetter Lane, Holborn, every morning at 9 and goes through Bishopsgate Street.

"Telegraph (Cambridge) which leaves Ditto every morning at half-past 9, and goes through Islington.

"Tallyho (Cambridge) which leaves Piccadilly every afternoon at 2, calls at the Swan with Two Necks, Lad Lane, and goes through Bishopsgate Street.

"Safety (Cambridge) which leaves the Bull, Whitechapel, at half-past 2, and goes through Bishopsgate Street."

The fare by coach to the college was seven shillings and sixpence, outside; hence the expression among the students, "to give a boy seven and sixpence" as a polite way of expressing his being expelled.

The "Eastern Counties Railway Company" was formed in 1836, and the line was built as far as Bishop's Stortford within a year or two; but the extension to Cambridge was deferred through want of funds. Broxbourne was then the nearest station to the college. The *Edmundian* for September 3rd, 1841, chronicles the projected branch to Ware and Hertford, which was opened the following year. The Buntingford coach continued to run till the opening of the Standon branch in 1863, by which time the "Eastern Counties Railway" had become the "Great Eastern." The old Shoreditch station was used till 1875, when Liverpool Street was opened.

[1] The College Band was first formed about the year 1842, the chief promoters being James Danell, afterwards Bishop of Southwark, and William Dolan, now priest at Holloway. Dr. Crookall was at that time in Rome. He took a leading part in the band after his return.

There was a full orchestra, with both brass and string instruments, and

play "God save the Queen." When the royal carriage was seen in the distance, however, the excitement was so great that everything else was forgotten. All the musicians joined in the general cheering and waving of hats, and not one of them played a note.

It was said that on reaching Buntingford, the Queen enquired who had erected the arch, and who had formed the group assembled at the lodge gates; and that on being informed that they were members of a Catholic College, she showed considerable interest. Encouraged by this, the professors boldly proposed to present an Address on her return journey. There was no time to be lost. An address was at once prepared, and the vice-president, the Rev. William Weathers, wrote to the Lord Chamberlain to know if they might be allowed to present it; but apparently in those days this was too much to expect for a Catholic College. The following is the answer that was received :—

"Wimpole Hall, October 27th, 1843.

"SIR,—I have received the commands of the Queen to inform you that Her Majesty is well convinced of the loyalty and zeal of the students of the Catholic College of St. Edmund's; and that the arrangements made by them on Wednesday last for greeting Her Majesty and Prince Albert on their road to Cambridge were duly observed and much admired. But as it is desirable that Her Majesty should not be delayed on her return to Windsor to-morrow, the Queen will dispense with the presentation of any address.

"I have the honour to be, Sir,

"Your obedient and humble servant,

"DELAWARR.

"Lord Chamberlain."

the most elaborate music was attempted, including operatic overtures, Mozart's, Haydn's and Beethoven's Symphonies, and the like. The following is given by one of the members as the composition of the band; but the players named were not all in it together at any given time. Some came a little later when others had left. Moreover, the list is not complete, but it includes all the most prominent members.

CONDUCTOR: James Danell. STRING INSTRUMENTS: *First Violin*,

The students had therefore to be content with a demonstration similar to that given before. This time it was rather better arranged; for the royal party being prepared, orders were given for the speed to be slackened at that part, and they drove slowly by, while the band this time kept their presence of mind and played the National Anthem.

Two years afterwards, the jubilee of the present college was celebrated,[1] and though the festivities were of an unpretending nature, the jubilee year was made the occasion of an event of the greatest importance, namely the laying of the foundation stone of the new chapel.

The inadequacy of the old chapel had long been felt. It had been built and furnished by Dr. Poynter early in the century, and was a great advance on anything previously existing. But it had served its time and the numerous consecrations of bishops and other interesting functions which had taken place in it, served each time to emphasize more and more the need of a better and worthier chapel, in which such ceremonies could be properly carried out. The following quotation from Canon Oakeley's "Priest on the Mission,"[2] written many years later, expresses what most Edmundians felt at that time:—

"The first Ordination which I witnessed after I was a Catholic," he writes, "was in the old chapel of St. Edmund's

---

James McQuoin. *Second Violin*, Jeremiah McCarthy. *Viola*, John Crookall. *Violincello*, Robert Mount. *Double Bass*, John Connolly. WIND INSTRUMENTS: *Flute*, William Dolan. *Bassoon*, Joseph Bans. *Hautboys*, John Riley and John Smith. *Clarionets*, Edward Taylor and Daniel Santry. *Cornopeans*, Frederick Holmes and Thomas Trowbridge. *Trombone*, Alfred Fryer.

[1] It should be noted that there has been a certain amount of confusion as to the date which is to be considered as that of the formal foundation of St. Edmund's College. Not that there is any doubt as to the facts. The original foundation, as described by Bishop Douglass, was on November 16th, 1793; but the new constitutions were not drawn out and signed till 1795. Dr. Poynter, who was still in prison at the earlier date, always reckoned the formal foundation to have taken place in 1795, and this date appeared for a time in the advertisements of the college. Dr. Douglass, on the other hand, on more than one occasion, dwells on the fact that St. Edmund's existed before Dr. Poynter's arrival, and was in reality founded in 1793. If this view be adopted, the jubilee in 1845 can be considered as that of the present building.

[2] p. 2.

College, in the year 1846. Those who remember that chapel will bear me out in saying that neither its construction nor its appendages were such as to enhance the dignity of the sacred offices celebrated within its walls; and now that it has been replaced by one far more spacious and far better calculated to give effect to the worship of the Church, I may make this remark without the least risk of offence. Indeed, I make it only with the view of bringing out in all the greater prominence, the greater intrinsic majesty and beauty of the Office to which I refer, and of paying a just tribute to the reverence and devotion with which all holy solemnities were there carried out. In the case to which I allude, the celebrant was the late Right Reverend Dr. Griffiths, whose truly paternal manner of administering the Ordination rite, was more than an ample compensation for the want of external accessories to its celebration."

Although the ceremonies had been always carried out with great care at St. Edmund's, however, it would not be true to say that they had been performed with rubrical correctness. Many French customs and traditions which had come over from Douay still survived. Others were of English origin, and had come down from the days of the Penal Laws. Both would alike grate on the feelings of those who had studied in Rome and seen the ceremonies properly performed there. Thus, for example, Benediction was given with the Ciborium, except on great feasts; but the Ciborium was placed upon the throne, and the same ceremonies were used as for Benediction with the Monstrance. Again, when Dr. Griffiths took part in the High Mass, as he very often did on Sundays, he used neither throne nor faldstool, but knelt at a prie-dieu in the middle of the choir. Nevertheless, he used to bless the incense and perform other episcopal rites as if he had been in the sanctuary. It should, moreover, be noted that processions outside the chapel had never been ventured on till Dr. Cox's time, and the idea of an open-air procession, such as now takes place every year to the parish chapel on Corpus Christi, had hardly even occurred to any one throughout England. The *Edmundian* for 1843 records the first pro-

St. Edmund's College, with proposed New Chapel, 1845.

cession round the Ambulacrum on Palm Sunday, which seems to have been regarded as a striking novelty.[1]

The first step towards reforming the ceremonies was to provide a better chapel, and this had long been one of Dr. Griffiths's great desires. All the money which he was able to collect during his episcopate he laid aside for this object, and by the aid of the legacies from the Rev. Francis Tuite, Mr. Charles Blundell and others, which fell in during this time, he was enabled to make a commencement in the year 1845.

At the time when the new chapel was planned, the "Gothic Revival" was proceeding in England, and the elder Pugin was at the height of his reputation. He visited St. Edmund's in November, 1842, and an address was read to him on behalf of the professors and students, to which he afterwards sent the following characteristic answer:—

"London, Feast of St. Francis Xavier, 1842.

"MY DEAR FRIENDS,—The shortness of my stay at St. Edmund's College having prevented me from making a suitable acknowledgement to the kind address you presented to me, I take an early opportunity of expressing the great satisfaction which I have received from this un-

---

[1] While on the subject of the Church services, a few words about the music will be in place. The introduction of plain chant when the college was founded, has been alluded to in a previous chapter. St. Edmund's was at that time probably the only place in England where plain chant was systematically used. Thirty years later, when Dr. Newell was choir-master, some simple harmonized masses were sung, and about 1832 he introduced some Italian ones, by Zingarelli, Casali, and others, which Dr. Wiseman had sent from Rome. In 1833, the latter also sent Vittoria's *Turba* for the Passion, and Palestrina's *Reproaches* for Good Friday, to the Rev. Charles Newsham, then choir-master at Ushaw, asking him to forward them to Old Hall, but they appear to have been considered at that time too difficult to perform. A few years later, with Dr. Crookall, then a divine, as choir-master, and the Rev. William I. Dolan, still a boy, as organist, more elaborate things were attempted than before; but the performance of the Mass known as "Mozart No. XII." so alarmed every one that for a time Dr. Griffiths insisted on universal plain chant. This did not last long, however, and when Dr. Crookall came back from Rome he gradually established a regular musical tradition which has lasted ever since. Many of his best known pieces were written at St. Edmund's for the college choir, among which may be mentioned his *Lauda Sion, Justorum Animæ, Missa Quadragesimalis, Te Deum, Missa Brevis et Dulcis*, for Holy Saturday, and *O Doctor Optime*, written for the first High Mass of the Rev. William Dolan.

expected testimony of your kind feelings towards me, not so much on personal grounds, but as the evidence of your views respecting the great revival of Catholic art. You may be assured, my dear friends, that it is the bounden duty of all Catholics throughout the world, but especially in our native land, to forward with all possible energy the restoration of Christian architecture. It is not a mere question of taste, or of abstract beauty and proportion, but it has far higher claims on our veneration as the symbolism of the antient faith. Viewed in this, its true light, ecclesiastical architecture cannot fail to receive from those who are destined to the sacred function of the priesthood that consideration which it deserves. From you, therefore, who will at some future period minister at these very altars which are now erecting under the sanction of your respected bishops (at St. George's and other churches), this testimony of the feelings you entertain on this important subject is most gratifying to me.

"There is but one sentence in the whole address which did not afford me sincere pleasure. I allude to the epithet of fame referring to my labours. This savours of paganism. Architectural fame belongs rather to the Colosseum than the Cathedral. It would be a fearful and presumptuous attempt in any man to exalt himself by means of the temples of God. It is a privilege and a blessing to work in the sanctuary. The majesty of the vast churches of antiquity is owing to the sublime mysteries of the Christian faith and the solemnity of its rites.

"The ancient builders felt this. They knew the small share they could claim in the glories they produced, and their humility exceeded their skill. How unbecoming then would it be for any man at the present time to exult where works are after all but faint copies of antient excellence. God has certainly permitted me to become an instrument in drawing attention to long-forgotten principles, but the merit of these belongs to older and better days. I still enter even the humblest erections of Catholic antiquity as a disciple to the school of his master, and for all that is produced, we must cry in most bounden duty, 'Non nobis, Domine, non nobis, sed nomini tuo da gloriam.'

"Recommending myself to your prayers and exhorting you to take every opportunity of informing yourselves in Catholic art,

"I remain, your devoted friend,

"✠ A. WELBY PUGIN."

At the time of Pugin's visit it was arranged that the new chapel should be entrusted to him, and he began forthwith to draw out plans. Most of his drawings have been preserved, though much of what he designed was never executed through want of funds. He regarded the Rood Screen as one of his very best, and used to say that he looked forward to the day when the whole choir inside the screen would be filled with divines, and when the boys would be outside in a nave to be afterwards built.

The new chapel was begun on September 17th, 1845. Six weeks later, the foundation stone was formally laid by Bishop Griffiths, on the anniversary of his consecration, Dr. Cox preaching on the occasion.

The date of the beginning of the new chapel coincides almost exactly with the crisis of the Oxford Movement. Dr. Ward became a Catholic the same month that it was begun, and Dr. Newman followed within a few weeks. During the following years numerous other conversions took place from among the Anglican clergy. Owing chiefly to its proximity to London, St. Edmund's saw a great deal of the new converts, who frequently visited the college for the Sunday to see the Catholic ritual carried out. Several of them afterwards studied theology there, preparatory to their ordination to the priesthood.

Among those who visited the college, the name of Dr. Newman claims first mention, though he only came once and was never intimately connected with it. On his arrival an address of welcome was read by Dr. Crookall, then Vice-President, to which he made a suitable reply, and when in 1869 the centenary of Old Hall was being celebrated, he wrote expressing his warm interest in St. Edmund's and its work.

Two other leaders of the movement were much more closely connected with the college, namely William George Ward and Frederick Oakeley. Their first visit was paid when they were Anglicans, and many still alive remember the feeling of curiosity with which their arrival was watched by the students and professors. They came one afternoon, together with Mr. George Tickell, also one of the Tractarians, and spent several hours at the college, Dr. Cox showing them round. All three afterwards became Catholics. Mr. Tickell joined the Society of Jesus; but the other two both came to St. Edmund's. Mr. Ward, who was then married, built himself a little house inside the college grounds—the present St. Hugh's Preparatory School—while Mr. Oakeley took his place amongst the professors, and attended the theological lectures.

When Mr. Oakeley arrived at the college, the first impression he created was one of disappointment. The Rev. William I. Dolan, who was student at the time, writes in this sense:—

"We had heard so much of the Oxford converts and of the ritual of the 'Tractarians,'" he writes, "that we expected to find Mr. Oakeley fall in at once with the ordinary routine of our services. We were, therefore, rather surprised when we found him more or less bewildered by the whole thing. He made one or two curious mistakes, which we were not slow to notice and to make fun of. For example, the first time that he saw a High Mass, when the Priest, Deacon, and Subdeacon said the *Confiteor* in turns, he thought that they were disputing with each other as to what should be done next, and as to the proper rubrics. Again, the first week that he was at the College, he caused great amusement when, on finding a boy 'kneeling on the gallery,' and being told that it was a 'penance,' he accepted this as meaning a Sacramental Penance, and thought that the boy must have been confessing some very grievous sin.

"When we got to know him, we soon forgot these little mistakes. He mixed with us all as if he was one of ourselves, and became a leading spirit in the house. At one time he created quite an enthusiasm for Ecclesiastical functions and ceremonies, and we found him so unassuming and at the same time so thorough and genuine that we learnt to respect him very highly, and were always ready to take up anything that he might propose.

"Amongst the things he took up with zest may be mentioned some missionary efforts among the people in the country, which had already been begun by the Divines. The Society of St. Vincent of Paul was established about this time,[1] and from it our labours took their rise. From visiting the poor in their houses, we gradually developed into assembling them at a common meeting place, and a little chapel was

[1] The introduction of the Society of St. Vincent of Paul into England is due to an Edmundian layman, Mr. C. J. Pagliano, sometime Vice-President of the Edmundian Association. In 1845, Mr. Horace Rymer, also an Edmundian, came down to St. Edmund's to establish a conference, which was one of the very earliest established in England. Some doubts were at first expressed whether it could be properly affiliated to the society, as the members were ecclesiastics. For a time, therefore, the St. Edmund's Conference worked independently, and for this reason, the formal establishment in the records of the society is dated 1854, by which time it had been decided that ecclesiastical students could lawfully become "Brothers." From the time of its first foundation, the meetings have been regularly held every Sunday evening, and the work of visiting and relieving the poor has been carried on without intermission. The management has been always entirely in the hands of the students, originally the divines, but after their removal, the "First Division" or senior students. The advice of the parish priest is of course always taken; but he takes no direct part in the management of the conference.
The following details are taken from a paper read before the Society in London in July, 1892, by the Rev. Edmond Nolan:—
"From 1845 to 1869, when the conference was suspended for about five months, through the removal of the divinity students to the seminary at Hammersmith, there are on record the minutes of one thousand and six meetings of the conference. At the fourth meeting a letter was read from the president and secretary-general to the effect that St. Edmund's was to be numbered among the London conferences. The minutes of the fifty-ninth meeting remind us of a new tie between St. Edmund's and Oxford. This was the coming of Ward and Oakeley, and these were followed later on by Bampfield and Oxenham. At this meeting Mr. Frederick Oakeley, afterwards the well known Canon Oakeley, was elected a member. The lists of the office-bearers tell us that many priests, afterwards well known, received their first lessons in the charitable visitation of the poor as members of this conference. Thus they record that Mr. John Butt, now the Bishop of Southwark, was secretary in 1848 and president in 1849; Mr. Daniel Gilbert, now provost and vicar-general of Westminster, was treasurer in 1851; Mr. Edward Keogh, afterwards superior of the London Oratory, was secretary in 1853; Mr. Robert Butler, late superior of the Oblates of St. Charles, was president in 1855."

established in a barn at Nasty,[1] where we preached on Sunday afternoons. Mr. Oakeley's sermons were very successful, to judge by the results, for there were numerous conversions. Some of those who became Catholics at this time are still among my parishioners at Holloway."

Dr. Ward's name has long been identified with the college, not only as a great benefactor, but even more in connection with the professorship of dogmatic theology, which he held

OLD HALL HOUSE (NOW ST. HUGH'S PREPARATORY SCHOOL).

for a considerable time. Reasons have already been given why the study of theology had declined at St. Edmund's. Mr. Ward appears to have done much to restore it to its true level. The present Archbishop of Westminster, for some years Vice-President of the College, speaks as follows of the results of his professorship:—

"The result, on the whole, of the intercourse between Ward and the divines, was the creation of an enthusiastic appreciation of theology, and more hard study was done under Ward's

[1] A little village near Great Munden Church.

inspiration and guidance than, perhaps, had ever been done before. The combination of moral and dogmatic teaching which he introduced, and his own intense devotedness to the truths he taught, raised men's minds above themselves, and introduced them into the regions of almost a new estimate of life and the possibilities which were opening before them."

To this day, Mr. Ward's old pupils retain lively recollections of gratitude for what they learnt under him, and in recognition of his services the Holy See presented him with the honorary degree of Doctor of Philosophy.

Besides those who studied under him, Dr. Ward is well remembered by all at the college at the time as a constant attendant at all the liturgical services. His prie-dieu in the "New Chapel" was on the epistle side, under the present memorial window, and at High Mass and Vespers it was always occupied. For a long time also it was customary for all those in sacred orders to recite matins and lauds every evening after night prayers, and at this voluntary devotion Dr. Ward seldom failed to be present.

The mention of converts calls to mind an amusing story about another of them, the Rev. George Pringle, in connection with the matriculation examination of the then recently instituted London University.[1] Mr. Pringle came to the

---

[1] The University of London was set on foot in December, 1837, and St. Edmund's was one of the first of the Catholic colleges to be affiliated. According to the original regulations, it was necessary for a candidate for a degree to produce a certificate of having passed through the requisite course of instruction at a college recognized by the Senate. St. Edmund's became authorized to issue such certificates by its affiliation and by a special warrant of June 8th, 1840. The first Edmundian students to matriculate were James Danell, afterwards Bishop of Southwark, and Henry Rymer, Canon of the same diocese, who passed in 1840. Four years later, Mr. Lawrence Dolan took his degree and became the first Edmundian B.A.

The custom of sending students up for degrees has not continued uninterruptedly. Difference of opinion has existed as to the advisability of making the course of studies at the college fit in with the syllabus required at London, and in particular the wisdom of allowing the large amount of modern philosophy, which was formerly a compulsory subject, to be studied by church students at so young an age, has been freely criticized. For a long time only a few were sent up, and for many years no one at all. In recent times, the philosophy has been made an optional subject, and the course has been worked more systematically, especially during the presidency of Mgr. Fenton, when the Rev. William Lloyd was prefect

college in 1846 to teach classics. Towards the end of the following June, he was away in London, ostensibly on business, but in reality going through the matriculation examination. This latter fact would probably have escaped observation, except that he took the first exhibition in classics, entitling him to 30*l.* a year for two years, and an official notification of his success was sent to the president of the college, to his great astonishment.

Before closing this chapter, we have to chronicle two accidents which occurred within about five years of one another, by which in each case a promising student lost his life. The first of these was Charles Lynch, son of Mr. W. Lynch, of Great Russell Street, London, who came from Oscott to St. Edmund's after the midsummer holidays of 1840. Six months after his arrival, he was drowned whilst skating at "Hull," a place on the River Rib, not far from Hammel's Park, under circumstances described thus by the Rev. Henry Telford, the prefect in charge of the party:—

"There was severe frost in January, 1841. At the beginning of the month, the River Rib was frozen near Braughing, and we skated above the mill. Near the wooden bridge the river is narrow. Lynch wore a cloak buttoned down the front. The ice broke under him at about three o'clock in the afternoon of January 7th. His cloak was cumbersome, his hands and arms were not free, and the cold was intense. I was at some distance off when I saw him go in. The ice was much broken between the place where I was and where the accident happened, so I got on to the bank and ran to his assistance as fast as I could; but when I got to the spot, he was in no way visible. A short ladder was at hand, and I put this into the

of studies. In 1885, ten matriculated, five passed the intermediate arts, one the intermediate science, and five took their B.A. degrees. So far as numbers are concerned, this is the best year the college has had.

The highest places taken from St. Edmund's at matriculation have been as follows: In classics, George Pringle, 1st in 1847; John Rees, 4th in 1844; John Wallace, 4th in 1858; William Howe, 5th in 1859. In Mathematics, Frederick Rymer, 5th in 1841; William Giles, 7th in 1847; John Bamber, 8th in 1847: and in General Honours, Arthur Doubleday, 7th in 1883; Thomas Scannell, 11th in 1874; Francis Ross, 21st in 1890; Thomas Inwood, 26th in 1874. In all, 113 have matriculated, of whom 55 have proceeded further.

river and climbed down it. I pulled the body to me with a hooked stick; but when we got him out he was quite dead, having been apparently frozen to death by the cold. He was about fourteen years of age and was considered a good boy. He had been to the Sacraments very shortly before his death."

An inquest was held at the college on Saturday, January 19, when a verdict of "Accidental death by drowning whilst skating" was returned.

The other death alluded to was that of Philip Weld, the circumstances connected with which have gained notoriety in connection with a famous ghost story. Descriptions have appeared in several periodicals in this country, in America, and recently also in Australia, in each of which full details have been given. In many cases these details have differed very materially from each other and from the truth, while in one or two instances incidents have been described quite unlike anything which really happened. The account given below may be taken as trustworthy in all particulars. The events as they occurred at the college are given on the authority of the Rev. Henry Telford, who was prefect, and his description is corroborated by several who were students or professors at the time, while the circumstances of the apparition at Southampton are given by Miss Weld herself, who was an eye-witness of what happened.

Philip Weld, brother of Monsignor Weld, of Isleworth, and nephew to the Cardinal of that name who died in 1837, was the youngest son of Mr. James Weld, of Archer's Lodge, Southampton. He came to St. Edmund's in 1841, and from the first was a well-conducted and amiable boy, much loved by his companions and superiors. He had been at the college nearly five years when he met with his death, under circumstances thus described by Mr. Telford:—

"The accident occurred on the Thursday in Easter Week, 1846. On that day Philip asked leave of me, as Prefect, for some six or seven lay students to go to Hertford. The leave was granted, and it was arranged that the dinner for the party should, for their accommodation, be ordered for four

S

o'clock. Hertford lies about seven miles south-west of Old Hall. Ten miles south from the college, on the east bank of the Lea, stands the Rye House, the scene of the plot against the Royal brothers, Charles II. and James Duke of York. This interesting spot is now a well-known resort of boating parties in the summer months.

"It appears that the students had induced the master, to whose care they were confided,[1] to take them to the Rye House instead of to Hertford. Without the knowledge of the superiors, they had arranged that a conveyance should be in waiting for them on the road, and they took their seats in high spirits, with fine weather and a day of pleasure before them. They reached their destination soon after eleven, and a very few minutes later were enjoying their sport on the River Lea.

"All went well till the afternoon, when the time came for setting out homewards. It was nearly three o'clock and Philip petitioned for one row more. Leave for this being granted, they went some little way up the river, but when they finally turned back, through an unlooked-for movement of the boat, Philip was thrown out into the river. The water only reached up to his waist and no immediate danger was apprehended. Joseph Barron, who was one of the party, offered to reach him an oar, but he refused it, saying, 'Row the boat over to me.' These were his last words, for he immediately sank and never rose again. It was afterwards found that when he had fallen from the boat he had alighted on the verge of a deep layer of clay at the bottom of the river, which, yielding under his weight, held his feet in the tenacious soil, and he lay stretched at the bottom of the river beneath the bank. Drags were procured, but they failed to grapple the body as it lay in its protected position.

"The master sent the students home immediately, and directed Joseph Barron to announce the painful fact to Dr. Cox, whilst he remained to superintend the endeavours to raise the body. The President briefly informed me of

---

[1] Mr. John Connolly, who afterwards joined the Redemptorists. He died at their house at Perth on August 12, 1871.

what had occurred and himself hastened to the river side. He remained there till nightfall, but had to return to the college while the body remained beneath the water. Next morning he repaired early to the scene, and had the satisfaction of finding that the body had been recovered. The Master of Enfield Lock had lowered the river; the movement of the water had shifted the body and placed it where the drags were able to grapple it, and they drew it to the surface."

Dr. Cox did not return to the college that day, but proceeded by train to London and thence to Southampton, to break the news to Philip's father. On his arrival, he went first to the priest, the Rev. Joseph Siddons, whose name we have already come across among the prefects under Dr. Griffiths. When he had told him what had occurred, they both drove together to Archer's Lodge to inform Mr. Weld, Mr. Siddons undertaking to act as spokesman.

Before they reached the entrance to the grounds, they met Mr. Weld walking towards the town, according to his custom at that time of day. Dr. Cox immediately stopped the carriage, and Mr. Siddons began thus: "It has seemed good to Almighty God, Mr. Weld, to call your son to Himself by the same element which first conveyed to him grace." Mr. Weld's answer took them both by surprise, and as it contained his account of the apparition of his son, it shall be given as Miss Weld describes it. According to her, he spoke as follows:—

"You need not say one word, for I know that Philip is dead. Yesterday afternoon I was walking with my daughter Katherine and we suddenly saw him. He was standing on the path at the opposite side of the turnpike road, between two persons, one of whom was a youth dressed in a black robe. My daughter was the first to perceive them, and exclaimed, 'Oh, papa, did you ever see anything so like Philip as that is?' 'Like him!' I answered, 'why it *is* he!' Strange to say, my daughter thought nothing of the circumstance beyond that we had seen an extraordinary likeness of her brother. We walked on towards the three figures.

Philip was looking with a smiling, happy expression of countenance at the young man in a black robe, who was shorter than himself. Suddenly they all seemed to me to have vanished; I saw nothing but the countryman whom I had before seen. I, however, said nothing to any one, as I was fearful of alarming my wife. I looked out anxiously for the post the following morning; to my delight no letter came (I forgot that letters from Ware came in the afternoon), and my fears were quieted. I thought no more of the extraordinary circumstance until I saw you in the carriage outside my gate. Then everything returned to my mind and I could not feel a doubt but that you came to tell me of the death of my dear boy."

"The reader may imagine," continues Miss Weld, "how inexpressibly astonished Dr. Cox was at these words. He asked Mr. Weld if he had ever before seen the young man in the black robe at whom Philip was looking with such a happy smile. He answered that he had never before seen him, but that his countenance was so indelibly impressed on his mind that he was certain that he should know him anywhere at once."[1]

After his interview with Mr. Weld, Dr. Cox hastened back to the college to make arrangements for the funeral. In the meantime an inquest had been held and a verdict of "Accidental death by drowning" duly returned. The body was then removed to the college, where it arrived late at night. When the day of the funeral arrived, a solemn Requiem Mass was sung by the President, and Philip's remains were laid under the sanctuary of the "Old Chapel,"

---

[1] The above account was written by Miss Weld a year or two before her death, to be placed before the "Society for Psychical Research." The following additional particulars were elicited in private correspondence:—

Q. "Did you, as well as your father, think the disappearance strange?"
A. "No. I thought no more about it!"
Q. "Did your father, before Dr. Cox spoke to him, look upon the apparition as significant of some mishap to his son?"
A. "Yes; he thought much about it and was very anxious for the arrival of the letters the next morning, but did not speak of the matter till afterwards. He had frightened my mother so much on a former occasion that he had promised never to speak of such things again."

close to the heart of Bishop Poynter. The apparition described above was the subject of much conversation among those who attended the funeral, as well as among the superiors and students of the college. Mr. Weld himself was there, and was particularly anxious to see whether he could recognize amongst the students, or others, the young man whom he had seen with Philip, and he looked round as he passed out, to see whether any resembled him, but without success, and he left without having had any light thrown on this part of the story.

The sequel to the above is as curious as the former part. It shall be given again in Miss Weld's own words :—

"About four months afterwards, Mr. Weld and his family were on a visit to his brother, Mr. George Weld, at Leagram Hall, in Lancashire. He went, with his daughter, to the neighbouring village of Chipping, and after attending a service at the church, they called on the priest, the Rev. Father Raby. They waited in the parlour for some little time before the priest came, and amused themselves by looking at the framed prints on the walls. Suddenly Mr. Weld stopped before a picture which had no name written under it that could be seen (as the frame concealed it), and exclaimed, ' That is the person whom I saw with Philip. I do not know whose likeness it is supposed to be, but I am certain that that is the person whom I saw with Philip.'

"The priest entered the room a few moments later and was immediately questioned about the print. He answered that it was a likeness of St. Stanislaus Kostka. Mr. Weld was much moved when he heard this ; for St. Stanislaus was a Jesuit who died when quite young, and Mr. Weld's father having been a great benefactor to that Order, his family were supposed to be under the particular protection of the Jesuit Saints. Also, Philip had been led of late by various circumstances to special devotion to St. Stanislaus. Moreover, St. Stanislaus is supposed to be the particular patron of drowned men, as is mentioned in his life.

"Father Raby presented the picture to Mr. Weld, who of course received it with the greatest veneration, and kept it until his death. His wife valued it equally, and when she died it passed into the possession of the daughter who saw the apparition with him, and she has it now in her possession."

When the "New Chapel" was completed, the body of Philip Weld was moved, along with others, and placed in vaults under the sanctuary, where it now lies. Nearly over it, in the east end of the choir, a slab to his memory is let into the pavement, with the following simple inscription :—

> Pray for the soul of PHILIP WELD; who was accidentally drowned on the 16th day of April, 1846, aged 17 years.
> Jesus, mercy; Ladye, help.

In the meantime, the walls of the "New Chapel" were rising, and it was roofed in by the autumn of 1846. The interior, however, took much longer to finish than had been anticipated, and Dr. Griffiths did not live to see the completion of his work. His health had been for some time failing, and he paid his last visit to the college in the month of July, 1847, when he went through the Clergy Retreat. "He was much shattered," writes his biographer ;[1] "he walked feebly and was terribly altered in look. He was then all but blind. The sight of one eye had for a twelvemonth left him; the vision of the other was failing daily . . . . [When] I expressed my regret at the trial he was about to undergo in the approaching operation on his eyes, he good-humouredly rebuked me, saying it would be no trial at all; he should be glad of it; his being shut up in a dark room would give him more time to pray and meditate. He bore his threatened blindness with the most unruffled patience and equanimity. It was the will of God; that was enough for him."

A short time before his death, Bishop Griffiths had the happiness of receiving his father into the Church, at the advanced age of eighty-four. He did not survive long afterwards. His death was very peaceful, the acute suffering which he had previously gone through having ceased

---

[1] The Rev. Edward Price, in *Dolman's Magazine* for September, 1847, p. 205.

for the last two or three days of his life. When he was anointed by Dr. Cox, he made the characteristic remark that his only motive for fear was that he had no fear. Though his illness had been a long one, its fatal termination came somewhat suddenly. A few days before, he directed his vicar-general, the Rev. Edward Norris, to write to Rome to petition for the appointment of a coadjutor, the three names suggested being the Revs. William Hunt, John Rolfe, and Edward Cox. The letter was still in the house when he passed away on August 12th, 1847, and a postscript was added recording the mournful event.

The funeral took place at Moorfields on Friday, August 20th, and was attended by five bishops and about 120 of the clergy. Bishop Ullathorne sang the Mass, with Dr. Cox as assistant-priest, and the ceremonies were conducted by the Revs. George Rolfe and Thomas Bowman. The sermon was preached by Dr. Maguire, after which five absolutions were given and the body was deposited temporarily in the clergy vaults, pending the completion of the "New Chapel" at St. Edmund's, where it was afterwards buried under his present monument in the "Griffiths Chantry" or Chapel of St. Thomas.

## CHAPTER XIII.

### THE NEW CHAPEL.

Negotiations for the restoration of the Hierarchy—Bishop Walsh appointed first Archbishop of Westminster—He dies before the arrangements are completed—Dr. Wiseman becomes Cardinal Archbishop—Dr. Weathers President of St. Edmund's—The "New Rules"—Description of the new Chapel—Consecration and opening in 1853—Additions since the opening—The Windows—The Lady Chapel—The Scholfield Chantry—Church plate and furniture—Names of Donors.

THE death of Bishop Griffiths was a great blow to St. Edmund's. His whole heart and soul had been in the college, and as long as he ruled the London district everything possible was done to further its good. Although his nominal successor, Bishop Walsh, was an Edmundian, one of the few survivors of Dr. Stapleton's first students, he had been away from St. Edmund's nearly half a century, and had lived all that time in another district, and when he came to London, he was too old and infirm to take an active part in the management of affairs. Dr. Wiseman really ruled the district, first as "Pro-Vicar," before Dr. Walsh's appointment, then as Coadjutor, and lastly, after Dr. Walsh's death, as Vicar Apostolic. He had never been a student at St. Edmund's, and it was hardly to be expected that he would show the same interest in the college as Dr. Griffiths had done. The change was at once apparent, and in no way more so than in its effect on the progress of the new chapel. As long as Dr. Griffiths lived, no anxiety was felt as to the building money, and the work proceeded steadily without intermission. Now all was changed. Everything had to be paid for by Dr. Cox as it was finished, and as a result the concluding stages took much longer than would otherwise have been the case.

CHOIR OF THE "NEW CHAPEL."

In the meantime, a great change was coming over Catholic England, and one that had been long hoped for. Dr. Poynter, in his letters to Rome, had more than once expressed his conviction of the necessity of the re-establishment of the Hierarchy as soon as it could be safely done, and more recently Bishop Griffiths had written strongly in the same sense. The first movement in the desired direction was the division of England into eight instead of four vicariates in 1840; but every one felt that this was only a step, and the appointment of bishops with ordinary jurisdiction was anxiously awaited. A brotherhood was formed, calling themselves the "Adelphi," of which Dr. Rock, an old Edmundian, was an influential member, their object being to promote by every means in their power the re-establishment of the English Hierarchy. Within three months after the death of Bishop Griffiths, the Vicars Apostolic met by direction of Propaganda, to draft a scheme for the division of England into dioceses, and as a result of this meeting, Bishops Wiseman and Sharples went to Rome to negotiate matters. At first it was proposed to make Bishop Wiseman the first Archbishop; but after some deliberation, Propaganda decided at a meeting held on July 17th, 1848, that it should be Bishop Walsh. To this decision they adhered, notwithstanding Bishop Walsh's protests on the score of his health. "Whether living or dying," they said, "he shall be the first Archbishop."[1]

When affairs were in this state, the negotiations had to be postponed on account of the Revolution in Rome. As soon as peace was restored, the question again came to the front; but in the meantime Bishop Walsh had passed away. He died on February 8th, 1849, at the age of seventy-two years, and lies buried in the Cathedral Church of St. Chad, Birmingham, of which he was the founder, and in which a stone monument has been erected to his memory.

Dr. Wiseman now succeeded to the London District, and when the negotiations for the hierarchy were brought to a conclusion in September, 1850, he was named first Arch-

[1] Brady's "Catholic Hierarchy," pp. 336 and 356.

bishop of Westminster, and at the same time created Cardinal. A little later Dr. Grant was appointed to the See of Southwark, and St. Edmund's became subject to two bishops.

About this time Dr. Cox resigned the presidency of the college, and he was shortly afterwards appointed Vicar-

BISHOP WALSH.
Vicar Apostolic of Midland District, 1826-1840; of Central District, 1840-1848; and of London District, 1848-1849.

General to Dr. Grant. He was succeeded at St. Edmund's by Dr. Weathers, with Dr. Crookall as Vice-President, the Rev. Frederick Rymer as Prefect of Studies, and the Rev. Henry O'Callaghan—the present Archbishop of Nicosia—as Prefect of Discipline. Under the new régime, very considerable alterations took place in the method of life at the college, which were collectively known as "the New Rules." The daily distribution of hours was modified and assumed practically the shape which it has at the present day. The list of playdays was remodelled; the "Title Playdays" were clearly defined, and any playday not a "Title" was henceforth known as a "Grace Playday." The old "Greek Playdays" were abolished; but, on the other hand, the "First Thursdays" of the winter months were introduced.[1] At the same time the date of the summer holidays was changed. From about the year 1830, when the church students were first allowed home, the holidays began after the feast of St. John the Baptist, and lasted till the end of July; under the new rules, the students remained for the feast of SS. Peter and Paul, and returned in time for the feast of the Assumption. This arrangement lasted till 1883, when Mgr. Fenton put it a month later, and this arrangement is still in force.

The old Douay "Pedagogue" system, which had been in disuse for more than thirty years, was likewise revived under the "New Rules." The boys used to be with their "Pedagogues" during the "hours,"—i.e. six till half-past-seven—at which time the professors had their dinner; but the arrangement was not successful, and a few years later the "Pedagogues" were once more abolished and the professors dined again in the middle of the day.

[1] The arrangements for the food were also changed. Edmundians of that time will be familiar with the word "Cart-wheel," a name given by the students to a sort of currant pudding, which came at the beginning instead of the end of dinner. After the introduction of the new rules, it was changed, and ordinary pudding at the end of dinner substituted.

I am told by Edmundians who were at the college in early days that the food, though rough, was always good and plentiful. A story is told in illustration of this. It is said that more meat used to be served at dinner than the boys cared to eat, and it was a common practice for them to fasten what they left under the edge of the table, by means of one of the steel forks then in use. There it remained safe till supper-time, and those who had had sufficient foresight, were provided with a meat supper. All went well till one unfortunate day, when a dog entered the refectory between dinner and supper. He soon smelt out the numerous pieces of meat and made short work of them. In so doing, he betrayed the trick. Henceforth the prefect was on his guard. It is needless to add that the dog had a rough time of it afterwards, if ever it appeared among the boys.

Another novelty introduced at this time was the present form of morning and night prayers. These were taken for the most part from a Roman Prayer-Book, called the "Veni mecum," the work of translating them being undertaken by Dr. Crookall and Dr. Ward. They were not, however, printed till nearly ten years later, when the first edition of the college prayer-book[1] was published.

After many delays and disappointments, the new chapel

HIGH ALTAR.

was at length ready to be opened in the spring of 1853, but it was still far from finished. The design for carving the stone work of the sanctuary, including the sedilia, which Pugin had estimated at 640*l.*, was abandoned, and in order to build the reredos and high altar, a subscription had to be raised among the clergy of the South of England. The ceiling of the sanctuary was decorated according to Pugin's designs by two divines, Mr. Virtue, now Bishop of Ports-

---

[1] This refers to the book containing the college prayers only. A general prayer-book, edited specially for the students of St. Edmund's, had been brought out in 1843.

ROOD SCREEN.

mouth, and Mr. White, the present missionary rector of Holy Trinity, Brook Green.

Pugin himself did not live to see the church opened. Had he done so he would have deprecated the erection of the organ on his rood loft as a sort of desecration, and all the more so, since it was the gift of Dr. Ward, of whom he had by this time the lowest possible opinion. There had been a time when he had great expectations of the Oxford converts; but many of them had now declared themselves openly against Gothic architecture, and this was an unpardonable offence in Pugin's eyes. He wrote to Dr. Cox in 1850, lamenting over Dr. Ward's fall. "I assure you," he said, "that if I had known that Mr. Ward would have turned out so badly, I would never have designed a respectable house for him. He ought not to be allowed to reside in the vicinity of so fine a screen. I would assign him a first floor opposite Warwick Street Chapel. Who could have thought that the glorious man whom I knew at Oxford could have fallen so miserably low? It is very sad." To Dr. Ward himself he wrote more strongly still:—"I can only say, that the less we have to do with each other in future the better, for I must plainly tell you that I consider you a greater enemy of true Christianity than the most rabid Exeter Hall fanatic." It is said that Dr. Ward's remark on reading this letter was, "I knew Pugin was strong in rood screens: I didn't know he was so good a hand at rude letters."[1]

The following account of the new chapel is taken from the *Tablet*:—[2]

"The new College chapel is erected at the east angle of the former chapel, and is approached by a cloister leading from the College. It is in the geometric decorated style of English architecture, and was designed by the late Mr. Pugin. It consists of ante-chapel and choir, separated by an elaborately carved double stone screen, under which are two altars, dedicated to St. Peter and the Holy Doctors, and SS. Charles

---

[1] See "William George Ward and the Oxford Movement," p. 153.
[2] May 28th, 1853, p. 341.

Borromeo and Aloysius. The tracery at the back of the screen is filled with stained glass, and the lower portion with plate. In the spandrils are six quatrefoils filled with most exquisitely carved bas-reliefs, representing the Marriage of the Blessed Virgin, the Annunciation, the Salutation, the Holy Nativity, the Presentation, and the Coronation of the Blessed Virgin Mary. Above the screen is a light open parapet of trefoiled lights, surmounted by quatrefoils. Above this appears the great rood, with Mary and John, the cross being most elaborately carved, and, as well as the figures, relieved with painting and gilding. Altogether this screen may be safely pronounced the most beautiful modern work of the kind in the kingdom.

"Passing through the centre arch of the screen, one is struck by the admirable dimensions of the choir, and the eye is irresistibly attracted to the great east window, of geometric tracery, with seven lights. The whole of this window is filled with stained glass, consisting of full-length images of Our Lord, His Blessed Mother and St. John, SS. Peter and Paul, St. Andrew and St. David, and the holy Patrons of the College, SS. Edmund and Thomas of Canterbury, Venerable Bede and SS. Gregory, Augustine, and St. John Chrysostom. This window is certainly one of the best which has been produced by Messrs. Hardman, whether the correctness of the drawing, or the effective translucency of the glass, or rich colouring be regarded. The high altar, the gift of the Clergy of the dioceses of Westminster and Southwark, is of stone, divided by highly decorated pillars into three equal portions, in which are bas-reliefs of our true High Priest offering up Himself, and on either side two of His types, Isaac and Melchisedech. Above the altar rises a handsome reredos of niches filled with Angels bearing emblems, the whole surmounted by an impending canopy. Above the tabernacle is an open throne for the Blessed Sacrament, the pinnacles being Angels, and the top is surmounted by the emblematic pelican feeding her young with her own blood. On either side of the choir are three rows of oak stalls, the uppermost having an impending canopy running along the whole length ;

CARDINAL WISEMAN,
Vicar Apostolic of London District, 1849-1850;
Archbishop of Westminster, 1850-1865.

these stalls will accommodate 150 students. The choir is lighted by ten three-lighted windows, five on each side. Above the screen is an organ of great power, made by Bishop, of London, and presented to the chapel by W. G. Ward, Esq.; it is divided into two parts so as not to interfere with the rood. In the ante-chapel spaces are enclosed for altars; the one which first attracts the eye on entering the chapel contains the altar tomb of the founder of the chapel—the late venerable Bishop Griffiths, who is represented reclining on the tomb in full Pontificals. Above the altar is a stained glass window representing his patrons, St. Thomas Apostle and St. Thomas of Canterbury. The other altar will be dedicated to Our Blessed Lady. On the north of the ante-chapel are large sacristies, with rooms above. Such is a faint description of this most noble chapel, so much needed, without which, indeed, so important an institution as the seminary and lay college of two great dioceses could not be considered complete."

The consecration of the new chapel took place on Whit Monday of 1853. The chapel and high altar were consecrated by Cardinal Wiseman, the two small screen altars by Bishop Grant. On Whit Thursday the church was solemnly opened, Bishop Grant singing the Mass in presence of Cardinal Wiseman, who preached the sermon. The ceremonies were conducted by the Revs. D. Woollett and J. Wheble. Dr. Crookall led the choir and the Rev. William I. Dolan presided at the organ, Haydn's Third (Imperial) Mass being the one selected. In the afternoon, the Bishop of Northampton (Dr. Wareing) gave Benediction, when Dr. Crookall's " Te Deum " was sung for the first time.

Forty years have elapsed since the solemn opening and the chapel is appreciably nearer completion. A few words on the principal additions since it was first used will be in place here.

### THE WINDOWS.

The windows of the choir are now all filled with painted glass, the last two having been put up for the centenary celebration of 1893. Out of the ten windows, seven are due to the Edmundian Association,[1] and these shall be described first.

The four in the sanctuary represent scenes of the life of St. Edmund. Three of them were erected according to designs of Messrs. Hardman in 1870, in memory of the centenary of Old Hall kept the previous year. This is recorded by the following inscription :—

Anno sal. rep. MDCCCLXIX celebrata fuit centenaria hujus collegii commemoratio, adstitit insignis corona antistitum, sacerdotum, alumnorum, Deo O M gratias agens, pia lætitia gratulabunda, omnia bona fausta feliciaque auspicans. Ad perpetuam rei memoriam Societas Sti Edmundi hoc munus dilecto patrono gratulantes dicaverunt. Gaudet in cœlis patronus, clientibus idem sit thronus.

The subjects are divided in the same way as Cardinal Wiseman's well-known hymn, "O Beate mi Edmunde," to which allusion will be made presently. The first window represents three scenes in the boyhood of the Saint—his praying whilst the monks at Abingdon are chanting their office, his vow to the Blessed Virgin when he took the ring off his own finger and placed it on that of the statue at Oxford; and

---

[1] The Edmundian Association was formed about forty years ago. It originated as a cricket club, but soon developed into the "Edmundian Club," and was established as the "Edmundian Association" in 1853. By the rules then drawn out, the president of the college is always president of the association, and there are two vice-presidents, one clerical and one lay. The clerical vice-president at present is Mgr. Goddard, who has held the office since 1887. His predecessors were Canons John Bamber, Last and O'Neal, and the Rev. Frederick Rymer. The lay vice-president is Mr. Lawrence Dolan, who succeeded his father in 1874; and before Mr. Lawrence Dolan, senior, came Mr. C. Pagliano, who was the first to hold the office. The first treasurer, Mr. Charles Corney, continued in office for more than thirty years, till his death in 1886. He was succeeded by Mr. Field Stanfield, the present treasurer. There have been four secretaries, Messrs. Horace Rymer, A. C. Ryan, Field Stanfield, and the Rev. Bernard Ward.

The association was well patronised by the old students, and the annual meetings at Richmond and elsewhere have been numerously attended. At the beginning, most of the surplus funds were divided in prizes or scholarships. A special examination was held every year at the college by Canon Oakeley, who sent in a formal report of the studies. As time went on, and the funds at the disposal of the committee increased, more was done for the material structure of the college. Amongst other gifts due to the Edmundian Association, besides the seven stained-glass windows alluded to, may be mentioned the memorial chapel at the end of the "new wing," and the furnishing of the library and physical science room.

his mother's present to him and his brother of two hair shirts while they were setting out to study at Paris. The second window gives the leading events of the priesthood of the Saint; how he first taught mathematics, how then his mother appeared and told him to cease studying geometrical figures, and to give himself instead to such as these—drawing at the same time three circles, which she marked with the names of the three Persons of the Blessed Trinity, adding, "These are the figures which must now occupy your mind"; and in the third light is represented his sermon out of doors during a storm when, in answer to his prayer, all those around him remained untouched by the rain. In the third window, he is represented as Archbishop of Canterbury. The first light shows him reforming a monastery that had become relaxed; in the second he is occupied as bishop in works of charity, and finally he is placed before us crossing the Channel on his way into exile.

The fourth window is of a different character. The glass is by Meyer, of Munich, the designs by Mr. Purdie, architect. It was given thirteen years after the others and represents the closing scenes in the life of St. Edmund, his death and his entrance into glory. In the centre light he is shown looking down from Heaven and blessing St. Edmund's College underneath.

We will next follow the windows below the sanctuary on the Gospel side of the choir. The first is the "English Martyrs' Window," given in 1887, in memory of their beatification. It represents those who were beatified standing in a crowd before the throne of God, with the Blessed Virgin leading them on one side and St. John the Baptist on the other. Blessed John Fisher is there, as well as Blessed Thomas More, Blessed Margaret, Countess of Salisbury, Friar Forrest, the Carthusian Monks and others.

The last two windows on that side are commemorative of the Centenary Celebration of 1893. One is the "Douay College Window," and shows the three patrons of Douay, who are also the "Minor Patrons" of St. Edmund's, namely, St. Thomas of Canterbury, St. Gregory the Great, and St.

T

Charles Borromeo. Underneath a scene is depicted of the missionaries leaving Douay for England during the days of persecution, and the following inscription records the connection between Douay and Old Hall :—

> Alumnos Duacenses, Dei ipsius ducis providentia ac benignitate, anno salutis MDCCXCIII, DIE XVI$^{MO}$ Kal. Dec., huc quasi in montem sanctificationis suæ inductos, Sti. Edmundi Societas, lucem anniversariam pie agens centesimam, sic illustrare voluit.

The other window is the "Founders' Window," in memory of the founders of the college, Bishops Douglass, Stapleton and Poynter. Above are represented their patron Saints St. John of Beverley, St. Gregory Nazianzen, and St. William of York; below are the kneeling figures of the founders and the representation of the benediction service at the formal inauguration of St. Edmund's College in 1793, The following is the inscription :—

> Festo die anniversario domus nostræ denuo institutæ, in seminarium evectæ sacerdotii, divo Edmundo dedicatæ, annis centum expletis, conditorum imagines, ne unquam obscuretur memoria, filii devotissimi consecramus.

There remain to be described the three windows on the Epistle side of the choir. The one nearest the sanctuary is the "Good Shepherd Window," in memory of Dr. Cox and the Rev. John Rolfe, former presidents of the college. In the centre is Our Lord as the Good Shepherd, and in the side lights are represented Dr. Cox and Mr. Rolfe praying before their patron Saints, St. Edward and St. John respectively.

Next beyond the Good Shepherd window is one in memory of Dr. Ward, given by his children in 1883, the year after his death. His three patrons, David, St. Peter, and St. Paul, are above, and below is the kneeling figure of Dr. Ward himself, the position being so chosen that it is immediately above where his prie-dieu used to be.

The last window on the Epistle side, nearest the screen, is the "Crimean Window," in memory of three English priests who lost their lives in the Crimean war. Two of these, the Revs. Denis Sheehan and Michael Canty, were Edmundians; the third, the Rev. John Wheble, was an Oscotian, but a benefactor to St. Edmund's. In the three lights are represented their three patron Saints, and below are scenes in the life of a chaplain during the war, first ministering to the soldier before battle, then attending one who is dying, and lastly, being helped himself by one of the soldiers when he is dying.

Besides the three mentioned above, five other Edmundian priests went through the campaign and survived. These were the Rev. James Doyle and Joseph McSweeney, who have since died, and the Rev. John Butt, now Bishop of Southwark, the Rev. John Bagshawe, Canon of the same diocese, and the Rev. H. Clark, still alive.

Of Canon Bagshawe it is said that he was talking with Bishop Grant, and the latter told him that he did not like to ask anyone to go to the Crimea, as the chances were very great against coming back alive ; that the Rev. John Butt had volunteered to go and he was waiting for someone else to do the same. Father Bagshawe argued that there would be nothing unreasonable in asking anyone to go, as such risks were only what every priest ought to be prepared for at any time. Dr. Grant said nothing then ; but a few days afterwards, Father Bagshawe received a pencil note from him late one night, with simply these words: "Will you go to the Crimea? if so, call on me to-morrow morning." The next day he started with the Rev. John Butt. They landed at Scutari, opposite Constantinople, on the Asiatic side, and after seeing Father Cuffe, who was in charge of the barrack hospital, it was arranged that Father Bagshawe should go on to the front, and a little later Father Butt followed him.

During the winter Father Butt was seized with the fever which killed so many during the war, and was in an unconscious state for three weeks. He was anointed by Father Sheehan and his life was despaired of. One day Colonel Vaughan, the father of the present Archbishop, came to see him in his tent with Colonel—now General—Sir Arthur Herbert. They had been talking on their way about miracles, and on leaving the tent Colonel Herbert said that it would certainly be a miracle if Father Butt recovered, and added that he had ordered a coffin to be made for him, as a mark of respect, for he did not wish him to be rolled up and buried in a blanket, as was done in the case of the common soldiers. Father Butt, however, got through the crisis of the disease, and on recovering consciousness, the first question he asked was whether he had been anointed. He was told that Father Sheehan had anointed him some days back, but that now he himself had been struck down by fever and was not expected to live through the night. On hearing this, he said that he must go at once to see him, but at this the men only laughed, for he had not strength enough to raise his hand, and Father Sheehan was at the other end of the camp, more than a mile off. He insisted so strongly, however, that at last eight men consented to carry him across the snow, which was thick upon the ground, on the mattress on which he had lain for the past three weeks. They formed themselves into two parties of four each and took turns in carrying, and after nearly an hour's exposure to the intense cold, Father Butt was safely carried into Father Sheehan's tent.

Father Sheehan was still conscious, but had evidently not much longer to live. The two priests were laid side by side, and one heard the other's confession and gave absolution. The sacrament of Extreme Unction presented greater difficulties, on account of Father Butt's extreme weakness. A Catholic soldier was therefore called in to assist him, and taking his hand, he lifted it to the Holy Oil and thence to Father Sheehan's forehead, where he had just strength enough to make the sign of the cross, and pronounce the words. Father Sheehan then said that the Blessed Sacrament was hanging before him in his coat, but he was too weak to receive the Holy Communion, and shortly after he died. Father Butt waited till the end, after which he was carried back to his tent in the same way that he had come, but bearing the coat containing the Blessed Sacrament.

## THE LADY CHAPEL.

On the north side of the ante-chapel, opposite the Griffiths Chantry, is the Lady Chapel. It was built in 1861, at a cost of 550*l*., and was a present from the three brothers Luck, all of whom were students at the college. The eldest, Thomas Luck, is now a Canon of Portsmouth; the second, John, is Bishop of Auckland, New Zealand; and the third, Francis, is a Benedictine priest in his brother's diocese.

The designs for the Lady Chapel were drawn by Mr. Edward Pugin, and the work was carried out under his superintendence. The chapel is in two parts. The inner one contains the altar and is built on the spot which was destined for the steeple of the church. The reredos represents the Holy Family, with their cousin St. John the Baptist. Below, in front of the altar, are carved representations of the three kings at Bethlehem and the flight into Egypt respectively.

The outer part of the Lady Chapel projects into the transept and is surrounded by a stone screen, in the upper part of which are lilies of the valley, emblems of Our Lady's purity.[1] This part is now used as a Chapel of the Relic of St. Edmund. The relic consists of an entire bone from the left leg, known to anatomists as the *fibula*. It was obtained by Cardinal Wiseman, by the kindness of Mgr. Bernadou, Archbishop of Sens, from Pontigny, France, where the body of the saint is preserved, the authentication being dated October 24th, 1853. It was brought to Old Hall for veneration, but was not left there permanently till the present reliquary had been completed,[2] seven years later. The solemn enshrinement took place on the feast of St. Edmund, 1860, for which occasion Cardinal Wiseman wrote his well-known hymn, the opening words of which have been placed round the upper part of the screen surrounding the altar of the relic :—

> O Beate mi Edmunde,
> Sic pro me ad Filium Dei
> Cum Maria preces funde,
> Ut per vos sim placens ei.

The hymn is divided into three parts, which refer to the

---

[1] The statue of the Blessed Virgin was put up at an earlier date, before the Lady Chapel had been contemplated.

[2] The reliquary, which is of Italian design, was exhibited in the Roman Court, at the International Exhibition of London, 1862.

youth, priesthood, and episcopate of St. Edmund respectively. It is used in all processions of the relic, and a third part is sung as a novena on the nine days preceding the feast of the saint in November. The two tunes to which it is sung were written by Dr. Crookall and Dr. Weathers.

The altar in front of the relic was not erected for more than ten years after the arrival of the relic itself. An inscription records that it was given in fulfilment of a vow. The circumstances are thus related in the College Diary:—

"On Sunday, November 12th, 1871, a student named Cecil Heathcote was so seriously injured by falling over a bench in the bounds that his life was despaired of. The President [Mgr. Patterson] administered him, and going into the chapel, before the Relic of St. Edmund, made a vow of an Altar to the Saint, for the recovery of the youth, who was so ill that for several hours it was thought every moment would prove his last. The Relic was carried to the infirmary and applied to the youth's lips and forehead (he being apparently unconscious) and shortly afterwards a change for the better set in. The next morning the doctor, Mr. George Covey, of Puckeridge, not a Catholic, was amazed to see the change, and, both then and many times afterwards, expressed his belief that it was unaccountable except, as he expressed it, on the supposition of ' our fellows' prayers.'"

The new altar was erected the following year and was consecrated by Bishop Weathers. Cecil Heathcote himself was present at the ceremony, having been restored to perfect health.

### THE SCHOLFIELD CHANTRY.

Outside the main chapel, at the end of the cloister leading to the south transept, is a small but very beautiful chapel, commonly known as the Mortuary Chapel, more properly called the Scholfield Chantry. Mr. Edward Scholfield, who is buried underneath, was half-brother to the member of Parliament of that name, who sat for many years for Birmingham. Upon his death his widow was anxious to raise a monument to his memory, and it was practically arranged that it should be at Fulham, when the Rev. Frederick Rymer, who was the priest there, was recalled to St. Edmund's as Vice-President. At the suggestion of Mr. Edward Pugin, the Chantry was erected there instead.

Like the Lady Chapel, it is in two parts. The outer one is above the tomb of Mr. Scholfield. Four steps lead up to the inner part, which contains the altar. The walls are all carved in stone, representing the spiritual and corporal works of mercy. The altar piece shows the Crucifixion below and the Ascension above, the reredos being at the same time surrounded by the different emblems of the Passion of Our Lord.

## THE CHURCH PLATE AND FURNITURE.

The best Gothic monstrance was designed specially for the present chapel by the elder Pugin. The one in ordinary use was given by the Rev. Thomas Horrabin, after the robbery of the old one in 1799. The chalices include gifts from four old Edmundians, Bishop Griffiths, Bishop Weathers, the Rev. William P. Tilbury, and the Rev. Henry Nutcombe Oxenham. There is also a very small chalice, which tradition asserts to have come from Douay College, and which undoubtedly dates back to the middle of last century.

Most of the brasses have already been alluded to. They are in memory of the Rev. William Paul Tilbury; Napoleon and Constantine Lowe, two brothers who died at the college within four years of one another; Philip Weld and Joseph McFaul. There is also a large brass in the middle of the west wall, recording the names of all those buried under the chapel, put up by the Edmundian Association in 1886.

The four silver candelabra, which stand in the sanctuary, were given by Mgr. Patterson in 1871. The brass "eagle," or lectern, is the gift of the late Mr. Robert Roskell, afterwards the head of the celebrated firm of jewellers, Hunt and Roskell, of New Bond Street, who was a student at St. Edmund's. The two silver sanctuary lamps were given by Mr. Alfred Luck and Mgr. Patterson respectively. The furniture of St. Thomas's Chapel was given by Mrs. Ward; that of the

Lady Chapel, as well as the statue of St. Joseph, by Mrs. Thompson, for many years housekeeper to the Ward family; the two additional oak stalls, rendered necessary by the increase in the number of students, and the Gothic Paschal candlestick by the Rev. Bernard Ward; the old Paschal candlestick, now matched with another and placed before the shrine of St. Edmund, by Canon Bamber; the statue of the Sacred Heart by the Rev. Edward Watson, and the candlesticks on the Rood Screen by the Marchioness of Londonderry, Mgr. Patterson, the Rev. William Lloyd (afterwards Vice-President), Mr. Everard Green, and Mr. E. Granville Ward, formerly students of the college, and the Rev. Father Coffin, then provincial of the Redemptorists, and afterwards Bishop of Southwark, respectively.

Finally, among the donors of vestments, may be mentioned Cardinal di Rende, Archbishop of Benevento, a former student at the college, Mr. Alfred Luck, Dr. Ward, Mgr. Crook, the Rev. Cyril Shepherd, the Rev. John Jones, of Warwick Street, and the Rev. Douglas Hope.

St. Edmund's College (Modern).

## CHAPTER XIV.

### LATER REMINISCENCES.

*This chapter not a continuous history—Three main events—Establishment of St. Thomas's Seminary by Archbishop Manning in 1869, and consequent changes at St. Edmund's—Fourth Provincial Council of Westminster held at St. Edmund's College in 1873—Pilgrimage to the shrine of St. Edmund at Pontigny in 1874—Sermon by Archbishop Manning—His last gift to St. Edmund's sixteen years later—His death—The third Archbishop of Westminster, Dr. Vaughan, formerly Vice-President of St. Edmund's—Conclusion.*

WITH the opening of the "New Chapel" we enter on the modern period of St. Edmund's. Those who have been presidents since that time are still amongst us, and the events which have happened are fresh in the memory of many living Edmundians. It seems, therefore, a fitting point to end this sketch of the history of the college.

Within the last forty years, however, there have been changes of radical importance. The St. Edmund's of Dr. Griffiths and Dr. Cox differs materially from the St. Edmund's of to-day, and a final chapter tracing the connection of the past with the present is necessary for completeness. For obvious reasons, a connected history of the period must be left to a future writer, and I shall confine myself here to the description of three leading events, all within my personal recollection, which will be sufficient to indicate the general course of the change and will be also otherwise of interest. These are, the establishment of St. Thomas's Seminary, the Fourth Provincial Council of Westminster held at St. Edmund's in 1873, and the pilgrimage to Pontigny in the following summer.

The origin of the idea of founding St. Thomas's Seminary takes us back a little more than a quarter of a century.

Cardinal Wiseman died on February 15th, 1865, and his successor, Mgr. Manning, was appointed in the following June. Within a few months of his appointment, it became known that he thought the time had come for the establishment of a seminary as defined by the decrees of the Council of Trent, and that St. Edmund's would cease to be a theological college. He announced his intention on the Exhibition Day of 1868, and St. Thomas's Seminary, Hammersmith, was opened in August the following year.

The new Seminary was opened exactly one hundred years after Bishop Talbot had first established his "Academy" at Old Hall Green, and before their departure, the divines took part in celebrating the centenary of that event. Dr. Weathers had already resigned the presidency, having gone to Rome as Theologian for England, in preparation for the Vatican Council, but he returned in time to be present as a visitor. His successor, as President, was Dr. Rymer, who had been Vice-President under him for seven years. A large gathering of clergy and laity, old Edmundians and others, joined in the festivities, which lasted three days. On the first day, Tuesday, June 8th, a cricket match was played between the Past and Present, resulting in favour of the latter team. The second day was devoted to athletic sports, and the third to the planting of the jubilee trees and the distribution of prizes. An interesting lecture on the History of the College, prepared by Canon Doyle, was read by the Rev. Isaac Goddard, the Vice-President.[1] A special centenary ode, composed by Canon Oakeley, was recited by Wilfrid Ward, then a student at the college, and a second one was written by the Rev. Francis Stanfield. A cantata was likewise sung, with words by Thomas Hood the younger, set to music by Mr. J. L. Molloy. The Archbishop presided throughout, and among those present were Bishops Clifford, Amherst, and Morris; Mgrs. Weathers, Patterson, and Virtue; Canons Bamber, Crookall, Gilbert, Last, and Henry Rymer; the Duke of Norfolk, Sir George

---

[1] This lecture has recently been published by the Edmundian Association, together with a full account of the centenary celebration.

Bowyer, and the oldest Edmundian, Mr. Alvavo Camera, whose recollections of the college dated back to the year 1806.

St. Thomas's Seminary may be well considered—as Cardinal Manning called it—a colony of St. Edmund's. The President of St. Edmund's became Rector of the Seminary, and nearly all the first superiors and students were Edmundians. Many customs and traditions were taken from St. Edmund's, and the theological library, which included many of the old Douay books, was moved bodily from Old Hall, and forms the greater part of the present seminary library.

The work of St. Thomas's was at first carried on in Cupola House, Hammersmith, and three houses adjoining, all of which had been in Catholic hands since very early days. Cupola House was the country residence of the Portuguese Ambassador, and the other houses were inhabited by a community of nuns of the Institute of Mary, who shared with the old Convent of the same order at York, the honour of being the only nuns in England during the penal days. The foundation of the Hammersmith Convent took place during the reign of Charles II., and was due to the piety of Catharine of Braganza. It is alluded to by Miss Strickland [1] as follows :—

"Catharine's devotion to her own religion had prompted her to bestow a part of her royal manor at Hammersmith to found a convent for nuns, but secretly, because of the penal statutes, which prohibited every institution of the kind. The tradition of the present Benedictine ladies of the convent at Hammersmith is that Catharine of Braganza first sent for a sisterhood of nuns from Munich, whom she established in that house, which was supposed to be a boarding school for the education of young ladies of the Roman Catholic persuasion. They did not venture to wear the conventional dress and veil, or any distinctive costume, but contented themselves with a strict observance of their vows and the rules of their order. They were in some peril and considerable alarm during the persecution caused by the perjuries of Titus Oates and Bedloe, but escaped attack. If the queen

[1] "Queens of England," edition 1877, vol. iv. p. 466.

had been suspected of founding a convent in England, there is no telling to what extent popular prejudice would have been excited against her and her *protegées*. They were the first nuns who settled in England after the accession of Queen Elizabeth."

At the time of the French Revolution, the old community had dwindled down to three in number, and when the Benedictine nuns from Dunkirk arrived in England, in May 1795, the Hammersmith Convent was handed over to them. Here they remained till 1863, when they moved to their present abode at Teignmouth, and the Hammersmith Convent became the property of the Westminster diocese. Six years later it was converted into a temporary seminary, and it served that purpose till the year 1879, when the present spacious building was ready for use. The chapel was added six years later. Nearly two hundred priests have been ordained from St. Thomas's since it was first set on foot.

The establishment of the seminary involved many changes at St. Edmund's, which was henceforward to be carried on without the divines. The system of the college was not changed abruptly. There was a large class of philosophy still left, and for a time they did much of the work of supervision formerly done by the divines. Gradually, as years have gone by, much of this has been altered. In some years there were too few philosophers to replace the divines. This has been especially the case lately, since the withdrawal of the Southwark and Portsmouth students, and at the present day most of the supervision is done by the professors.

At the time of the centenary, the "lay bounds" had already been discontinued for some time ; but the lay playroom and library still survived. When the divines left, the church and lay students were once more reunited, as they had been in old days, and the lay playroom, after an existence of exactly half a century, was abolished. The house was henceforth divided into two "divisions." The upper classes, or "first division," consisting of all those in the "poets' playroom "[1] were given

---

[1] The philosophers, who had before used the divines' room, were henceforth in the "first division."

the use of the "front field," while the "second division" received the old "church bounds." A great improvement in the appearance of the college was effected by the change. The "lay bounds" were thrown into the "pleasure ground," and additional trees and shrubs were planted, which are now well grown and give a much more pleasant outlook from the windows at the back of the college.

The Fourth Provincial Council of Westminster was held at St. Edmund's four years after the centenary. During those four years, the appearance of the college, both inside and out, had been greatly improved. This was due to the energy and taste of Mgr. Patterson, now Bishop of Emmaus, who was appointed President in 1870, and retained the post for ten years. Space will not permit the enumeration of all the works which he put in hand during that time for the material improvement of the college. The decoration of the chapel and ambulacrum, the complete renovation of the library and refectory,[1] the laying out of the terraces in front of the college, the new kitchen and offices, are only some out of many that might be mentioned. The college now no longer looks like a "Priest Factory," and since the ivy planted by Mgr. Fenton has grown and the flower boxes have been put in the

[1] That is, the present refectory, in the "New Wing," still so called, though it has been standing more than thirty-five years. It was erected mainly by the expenditure of a legacy of 3000*l*. left to the college by Miss Nutt. A further donation was promised by M. de Zulueta, Count de Torre Diaz, with certain restrictions as to the manner in which it was to be spent. The plans were drawn out chiefly under his direction by Mr. Parker, agent to the Duke of Bedford. According to the original design, there was to have been a library at the further end, with a passage leading thereto along the north side of the refectory. Owing to want of funds, this idea was temporarily abandoned, and the part intended for the passage thrown into the refectory, which thus extended right across the wing. When the plans were first put into the hands of Mr. Myers, the builder, he refused to construct it, on the plea that the span of the roof was too great to be safe, considering the immense weight above it. Mr. Parker therefore revised the plans, adding extra tie rods, and Mr. Myers consented to put it up, though not without some protest. His fears afterwards proved well founded, and several hundred pounds had to be spent a short time ago to prevent it falling in. The refectory was first used in 1858. It was redecorated in 1871. The walls were pannelled, the oak gallery was put up, and the ceiling was painted with the arms of the Pope, the Queen, the Archbishop of Westminster, the Bishop of Southwark, Cardinal Allen and St. Augustine.

windows, the front in summer-time looks as bright as can be desired.

In recalling the ceremonies of the Synod of 1873, a comparison is at once suggested. Just seventy years earlier, in the same College of St. Edmund, a similar meeting or quasi-synod had been held, the first of the kind attempted by the vicars apostolic. The contrast between the two scenes is an instructive commentary on the progress of Catholicity during the present century.

In 1803 the synod consisted of four vicars apostolic and one coadjutor. Bishop Gibson, the senior bishop, presided and around him sat Bishops Douglass, Sharrock and Milner, and Bishop Poynter, the President of the College. One solitary religious order was represented by Father Walmesley, Superior of the Trappists at Lulworth, and the only church service was a Low Mass, said by Bishop Douglass, at which the others assisted.

At the Synod of 1873, Archbishop Manning presided, and was surrounded by twelve bishops of the restored hierarchy. Two Colonial Bishops were likewise present and the religious orders included the Benedictines, Dominicans, Jesuits, Passionists, Redemptorists, Fathers of Charity, Franciscans, Capuchins and Servites. For the business of the synod, four "congregations" were formed, according to the proper Ecclesiastical Law, for dealing with matters connected with Liturgy, Discipline, Ecclesiastical Life and Education respectively, and the sittings of each extended through the greater part of three weeks.

The formal opening took place on Wednesday, July 23rd. High Mass was sung, at which all the bishops and others assisted, the ceremonies being conducted by the Rev. John Rouse, Vice-President of the College. The procession started from the ambulacrum, and passing out of the front door on to the terrace, entered the church through the mortuary chapel. "The *coup d'œil*," says the *Tablet*, "was in reality very striking. Before the shrine of St. Edmund of Canterbury the whole procession paused for a moment and knelt. As the lengthened train of mitred prelates and of religious and dignified clergy moved down the beautiful cloister of St. Edmund's, along the esplanade in front, and reached the stately Gothic church by the western entrance, few sights of Ecclesiastical splendour more magnificent have been witnessed in England during the last three centuries." At the end of High Mass, a sermon was preached by the Bishop of Birmingham (Dr. Ullathorne), immediately after which the business of the synod was commenced.

The sessions lasted till Monday, August 11th, inclusively, and the following day the synod was brought to a formal termination. The final sermon was preached by Archbishop Bede Vaughan, then coadjutor to Archbishop Polding of Sydney. After High Mass, the Archbishop of Westminster gave his solemn blessing and the synod was over.

The only memorial of the event now at the college consists of one of the inscriptions of welcome which were at the side of the front door :—

D.O.M.<br>
Pio Papæ IX<br>
Ecclesiæ jurium<br>
Custodi et vindici fortissimo<br>
Seni majestate verendo<br>
Vincto Jesu Xti<br>
Annos augeat Deus<br>
Diuque tam<br>
Orbis Catholici votis expetitum<br>
Triumphum largiatur.

D.O.M.<br>
Archiepiscopo nostro<br>
Et Metropolitano<br>
Qui gregis factus est forma<br>
Cum episcopis et patribus<br>
Orthodoxis<br>
Athletis Christi fortibus<br>
Pastoribus veris<br>
Fausta omnia<br>
Et hic et in Æternum.

Dr. Ward was at Old Hall during the synod, and it was practically his last connection with the college. The rest of his life was spent in the Isle of Wight, and his house at Old Hall was converted into a preparatory school for younger boys before entering the college. For several years it was popularly known among the students as "Ward's," but its official name was "St. Hugh's." When it was in full working order, the accommodation there, added to that at the college, made a total of over one hundred and twenty. This number was reached under Father Akers in 1882 and again under Mgr. Fenton four years later.

The organization of the synod did not exhaust Mgr. Patterson's energies. The following year he got up a public pilgrimage to the Shrine of St. Edmund at Pontigny, which was joined by about three hundred and fifty old Edmundians and others. The nature and object of the pilgrimage is best explained by the following letter, which was read in all the churches of the archdiocese :—

"Archbishop's House, August 18th, 1874.

"REV. AND DEAR FATHER,—On Tuesday the first of September, a Pilgrimage to the Shrine of St. Edmund of Canterbury at Pontigny will leave England. The purpose of this act of devotion is to make intercession for our Holy Father according to his intentions; for the whole Church, especially in countries where its pastors are under persecution; for the peace of the Christian world, now menaced everywhere by anti-Christian revolutions.

"It is, moreover, an act of loving veneration to St. Edmund, one of the chief Patrons of our clergy, and special Patron of our oldest College for the training of Priests: and further, it is a public homage to the laws and liberties of the Catholic Church, in defence of which St. Edmund died in exile.

"I therefore invite you and your flock to join in this intercession, and I hereby give leave for a triduum on Friday, Saturday and Sunday next, with Benediction of the most Holy Sacrament and Exposition on one of those days. You may add such prayers as you see fit to use: and I request you to explain the intention of the Pilgrimage in preaching.

"A petition for a Plenary Indulgence has been made to the Holy Father for those who join in this act of devotion: to which I invite all who are able.

"I remain, Rev. and dear Father,

"Your affectionate servant in Christ,

✠ "HENRY EDWARD,

"Archbishop of Westminster."

The Abbey Church of Pontigny, now more than seven centuries old, stands in the middle of the flat country of Burgundy, ten miles from Auxerre and six miles west of St. Florentin station, on the main line from Paris to Lyons. "The traveller who finds his way to this once again obscure

SHRINE OF ST. EDMUND, PONTIGNY.

spot, whether he approach it from the north or the south, from Troyes or from Auxerre, beholds at a distance on a slightly rising ground, the still imposing mass of the conventual church. Simple and wholly devoid of ornament, like all the Cistercian churches in the architecture of the twelfth century, it has three peculiarities which, united, produce the most singular effect. These are its long plain line of high-pitched roof of slate, unbroken to the eye by battlement or finish of any sort; the absence of all tower or bell turret; and, above all, the uniformity of its style, the whole nave, choir, sanctuary, and transepts, having been raised at one time, by one effort and on one and the same plan. It is, perhaps, one of the most perfect monuments remaining of the original and rustic spirit of Citeaux."[1]

The interior of the church is plain but grandly proportioned, one of the earliest examples of pointed architecture in Europe. The reliquary containing the body of St. Edmund can be at once seen, apparently above, but in reality some little way behind the high altar. It consists of a richly-ornamented *chasse*, supported by four large angels. It is approached from behind by a wooden staircase, from the top of which the body can be seen through four small windows of crystal glass. The present reliquary dates back only to the middle of last century, but it is in the same position as the one first erected, when, on the formal promulgation of the bull of canonization, the saint's relics were exhumed on June 9th, 1247. A large concourse of people from near and far, including many from England, assisted at this, the first translation of the relics, and the feast is kept annually at Old Hall, by a special privilege.

Down to the end of the last century Pontigny remained a great centre for pilgrimages. It was just seven days' journey from England, and formed a convenient halting-place on the road to Rome or Compostella.

During the great Revolution the monastery shared the fate of other such houses in France, and but little now remains of the old abbey. The church, however, escaped destruction,

---

[1] "Lives of the English Saints," edited by Newman: St. Edmund, p. 77.

and, what is more remarkable, the body of St. Edmund remained untouched. It is said that one of the revolutionists actually climbed up, axe in hand, to destroy it, but was seized with a sudden fear and came down, and that after this, none of the others ventured to injure it.

For half a century afterwards Pontigny was deserted, except by the few inhabitants of the small village which had grown up around, and a single priest who ministered to them. In 1843 what remained of the abbey was bought by Mgr. de Cosnac, Archbishop of Sens, and under his direction Père Muard [1] founded a new congregation of "Oblates of St. Edmund," whose double work should be to protect the shrine of St. Edmund, and to help the Archbishop of Sens, by missions and other works. The new congregation was formally installed on September 29th, 1852; it quickly increased in numbers, and now has several branch houses, one of which is at Mont St. Michel, Britanny. It was the Oblates of St. Edmund, under their present superior, Père Boyer, who gave hospitality to the English pilgrims in 1874.

The pilgrims travelled from London by special train and boat throughout, and reached St. Florentin station at half-past one on the afternoon of Wednesday, September 2nd. Immediately on alighting they formed themselves into a procession in the following order:—

Lord Edmund Howard, bearing the banner of the pilgrimage, followed by about fifty pilgrims.

The Earl of Gainsborough, bearing the banner of St. Edward, Patron of the Archdiocese of Westminster, followed by more pilgrims.

The Hon. and Right Rev. Mgr. Stonor, and two other prelates.

Mr. Francis Clifford, bearing the banner of St. Edmund's College, followed by the President (Mgr. Patterson), Professors and students of the College.

The Rev. Lord Archibald Douglas, bearing the banner of

---

[1] See his Life, edited by Healy Thompson.

CARDINAL MANNING,
Archbishop of Westminster, 1865-1892

St. Thomas of Canterbury, followed by the Rector (Bishop Weathers) and students of St. Thomas's Seminary.

After a walk of about two hours, the Abbey church of Pontigny came into view. Some delay now occurred caused by a very tragic event. Père Barbier, the Procurator of the Monastery, who had prepared everything for the reception of the pilgrims, was seized with a stroke of apoplexy and died. His death cast quite a gloom over the village, where he was greatly respected. The body was visited the next day by all the pilgrims, who showed great sympathy with the community in their loss.

After the delay mentioned, the procession was seen coming out from the abbey, a reliquary containing the arm of St. Edmund being carried by four men, behind which walked Archbishop Manning, followed by some hundreds of Frenchmen from the surrounding country. All knelt to receive the Archbishop's blessing and, the two processions having joined, went through the village into the church.

In the evening, Vespers of St. Edmund were sung by Archbishop Manning, and few of those present will forget the effect of the three hundred and fifty voices, singing together, without accompaniment and without books, the old Venetian "Ecce Sacerdos magnus," to which they were so accustomed at the college. The following day, High Mass was sung by the Archbishop of Chambéry, in the presence of the Archbishop of Sens. After the Gospel, Dr. Manning preached a sermon, taking his text from 2 Cor. iii. 17, "Ubi Spiritus, ibi libertas." He said:—

"Never, till the latest day of my life, shall I forget this pilgrimage of England's sons, bearing the banner of St. Edmund to Pontigny, visiting the land hallowed by the memory of St. Germanus, St. Hilary and St. Martin, and scenes so dear to the Archbishop from whom I derive the Pallium that I wear. Though the line be interrupted, and though I cannot claim the virtue or the sanctity or the merit of these Saints, I claim the same Faith, and the same authority and jurisdiction which was conferred on them, by the visible Head of the Church who gave authority to the first

Archbishop of Canterbury. When I saw that great Church of France come to meet that little Church from England, torn and thinned in its ranks, but the same victorious army still, I felt that those who came to welcome them, had met the sons of Confessors and Martyrs, and I felt that the smallest number of such a descent is dignified. St. Irenæus, founder of the See of Lyons, has left us the words 'Ubi Ecclesia, ibi Spiritus,' 'Where the Church is, there is the Holy Ghost'; there is all truth and all liberty ; there is the power of the keys. If you know the truth, 'The truth shall make us free ;' free from all earthly creeds, from all human teachers, from all royal and imperial despotism.

"In this Abbey of Pontigny, in this chapel there on my right, St. Thomas of Canterbury received a vision of Our Blessed Lord, Who said to him, 'Thomas, the Church shall be glorified in thy blood and I shall be glorified in thee.' Here St. Edmund prayed, fasted and offered the Holy Sacrifice for the liberties of the Church in England, and for noble, Catholic, charitable France. With an energy and beauty which comes from the Holy Ghost, St. Edmund preached. In one discourse he said, 'If you truly love and serve God, every hair of your head shall be glorified.' St. Anselm, St. Thomas and Stephen Langton, are dear to France, and they were noble champions for the liberties of the Church, but St. Edmund specially is in our hearts to-day. As the Metropolitan Archbishop of England, he had the glorious duty of bearing testimony of the liberty of the Church, for after the See of Peter, I claim for the See of Canterbury this glory and privilege of thus bearing witness.

"What is the liberty of the Church ? It is the supreme and sole authority for choosing the priest who is to officiate, and him who is to be over the flock and the sole authority to give that man authority to bind and loose. Legislators and law-givers can lay no hand on this. This power belongs exclusively to the Church. It is a liberty given by God. All other liberties, political and social, co-exist with this liberty of the Church. Our Saxon Forefathers maintained these liberties for the Church, they passed into our laws, were enacted in our statutes, and Royal oaths confirmed them before the King ascended the throne. I will not mention the names of those who broke their faith. I name only those who defended the liberties of the Church. They were the noblest of Englishmen, the most glorious of our land, and if I said the most glorious Martyrs of any land, my tongue and my thought would not err. St. Thomas died for this liberty, and the Church has chosen St. Thomas as the Patron Saint of the Ecclesiastical liberty.

"But he who is specially before our minds and hearts to-day is St. Edmund. Why is he here? A weak and unjust king kept vacant Bishoprics and Abbacies, to please the cupidity of creatures and courtiers and parasites. The discipline of the Church had relaxed; the clergy were disorderly, the people following in their path; the Cathedral Churches were paralyzed. Edmund refused to endure these things in silence. He obtained from the Sovereign Pontiff the power to fill every vacant see and benefice, if the Patron should not exercise his rights within six months. In the very moment when victory seemed sure, by some cause the Pope's decree was suspended in its operation. His heart was broken; his enemies fell on the See of Canterbury and robbed it on every side. He assembled the Bishops of his province, who unanimously joined in excommunicating the offenders. They however despised the excommunication, and Edmund did, as Our Lord did, when threatened by those who hated Him—he withdrew in peace that he might not increase their guilt. From a high hill he gave his parting blessing to England with that right hand reposing here, which was carried in procession yesterday. When he arrived here, he was sick and an exile, and, in a hospitable house not far off, he departed to a better life. On the very day he had promised in prophesy he was brought back hither, and here for six hundred and forty years his body has reposed in honour. Neither the animosity of Huguenots nor the infidelity of the Revolution has violated this shrine. God's providence has protected him who stood up for those imperishable liberties.

"Six hundred years ago a king of France, with Archbishops of France, and our English St. Richard of Chichester, the loving friend of Edmund, were present at the translation of St. Edmund's body. Tens of thousands camped around him here. Since that day no such sight as this of to-day has here been seen, no such testimony of honour to the glorious St. Edmund, who here gives his name in Holy Baptism to so many children. One hundred of our priests, and priests of the Irish clergy also, for our Church is all one, and many thousands of our brethren, priests and laymen of France, following our little band, make this a day of glory for France and England. Would to God that England could enjoy it equally! Although in the precedence of charity and spiritual need England in our prayers should come first, our first prayer to-day shall be for France. We pray for the peace of France, and for the consolidation and perfect unity of this great people, for the guidance of Catholic France, the grand French Church, with Hierarchy unbroken, foremost whenever danger needs or charity demands her. If for a moment shadowed by a passing cloud, the great Church of France is wide and fair like its plains, lofty like its hills, united indissolubly with St. Peter, and Peter is founded on the Rock. We pray for the Bishops and priests of England, that they may unite in themselves the sweetness and fortitude of St. Edmund with the courage and strength of St. Thomas, for strength without sweetness is cruelty. Edmund was sweet and also strong, because he was a Saint. Thomas was strong and also sweet, because he was saintly too. We pray for sweetness and fortitude, courage and gentleness, to do well whatever may be laid upon us, and to persevere in the path of piety. We pray for the flock of England, and that each one may carry, like Evangelists into their families, the sweetness and fortitude of St. Edmund.

"We pray for England, dear to us, though England, alas! in one sense does not claim to belong to us. England owes a fourfold reparation. First to Jesus in the Blessed Sacrament of His love, for England has cast down His altars and desecrated His Divine presence in the Blessed Eucharist; but thanks be to God, England with the instinct of men born again in Baptism, has been lavish to restore with exquisite art and costly skill the material structure of her ancient Cathedrals. Is not this the dawning of a brighter day? Is not this the sweeping of the house and the preparing of the chamber for the Master and His coming? Secondly, England owes reparation to the Ever Blessed and Immaculate Mother of God for having struck out in part her glorious name from the Calendar, taken away her Festivals and torn her beads from the hands of her children. England has refused to give her that title of Blessed which in the inspired words of her own prophecy she declared that all nations shall call her, and she has been deprived in our land of the filial piety due to the Mother of God, our Saviour. God grant that England may become again the dowry of Mary! Thirdly, England owes reparation to the Vicar of Christ for having lifted up the heel against his authority when England broke away and fell from Catholic unity; but we hope for England's recovery, for what natural power cannot do supernatural grace may accomplish. Fourthly, we owe reparation to God the Holy Ghost. Separation from the Holy See was outward, but there was an inward separation of the spirit first. "Ubi non est Spiritus, ibi servitus et omnis error." The Holy Ghost is not with divisions. If England will not seek the blessing of restoration, we must lovingly bear her in our arms as the infant to the font, and answer for her, and God will do the rest. Let us answer for the future of England in the plenitude of charity. If Englishmen could be brought to love one another, they would be brought to believe the same thing. We must pray for all Christendom, for the Vicar of Jesus Christ, and for the world in its desolation, which modern error and modern civilization has drawn off from the unity of the Faith. How long it may remain desolate, we know not; it may be till the world is purified and until God has taken chastisement of His people.

"My task is almost done. I must not detain you; for a multitude who have come to greet us with a loving welcome cannot understand the strangeness of my speech. My last words, therefore, shall be these. St. Edmund has here a glorious and majestic sanctuary, which for six hundred years has remained inviolate; pardon me if I say St. Edmund remains here the possessor of Pontigny. St. Thomas, alas! is not the possessor of Canterbury, for his shrine has been ignominiously despoiled and destroyed with a mockery of law. Now a little church is rising in Canterbury the one speaking record of St. Thomas in that place. In Rome there is a Church of St. Thomas, but it was wrecked in the beginning of this century, I need not say how. The Holy Father has watched over it with anxious, loving care, and one whom you know has devotedly laboured for its restoration. For five years he was assailed by sickness. He has now been restored to health, and his first thought on his recovery was for the Church of St. Thomas. Only the sanctuary remains to be built. We owe it to St. Thomas that it should be done. St. Edmund will not grudge if an honour that he does not need himself be given to a brother whom he loved so well. St. Edmund received two visions from St. Thomas. Once here, in this Abbey Church of Pontigny, when St. Edmund would have kissed his feet, Thomas forbade him, saying that before long he should kiss his face in glory. Again, in a vision in his Church at Canterbury, St. Thomas showed St. Edmund his head and placed his hands on the wounds there where the sacred anointing had been. I ask you to make an offering to him whose crown St. Edmund would have shared. If all were to give something, the whole work would be finished at once. It will be the offering of St. Edmund to the Church of St. Thomas, and we will lay it at the feet of the Vicar of Jesus Christ, Pius IX., the Confessor for the liberties of the Church of God."

The year after the Pontigny Pilgrimage, Dr. Manning was made a Cardinal, and he lived to rule his diocese another seventeen years. Throughout his episcopate he was a regular visitor to Old Hall, and seldom an exhibition or feast of St. Edmund passed without the college being favoured with his presence, till the last four years of his life, when his age and infirmity made him a prisoner in London. In 1890 he celebrated the jubilee of his episcopate, and the celebration is especially memorable to Edmundians, as he made it the occasion of a handsome present to the college. A testimonial was presented to him, amounting to nearly eight thousand pounds, and at the presentation an address was read by the Duke of Norfolk, as the representative of the Catholics of England. In his reply, the Cardinal announced how it was to be spent. "My desire," he said, "is to die as a priest ought, without money and without debts. As the time cannot be far off, I make my will *in procinctu*, as it is called, girded for battle, as a soldier going into the fray, and I take you all to be my witnesses. My purpose is to devote your generous offerings in the following way and order." He then went on to enumerate various charitable objects, including the foundation of a "Jubilee Burse" for the education of an ecclesiastical student, the foundation of a bed in the Accident Ward of the London Hospital, an offering to the restoration of his titular Church of St. Gregory on the Cœlian Hill in Rome. He concluded as follows:—

"Lastly, there is a residuary legatee, to whom all that remains ought to go. I have weighed the claims of persons and of works and of institutions. I have tried to find what would draw the fullest sympathy of the largest number and of the most domestic brotherhood of my clergy and laity. There is no person who fulfils these conditions. The works of the diocese are a multitude, and they have their provision and their poverty. What could I do without a miracle among so many?

"There is, however, one representative of our forefathers under the Penal Laws, older than the restored Church in England. It has already kept an informal anniversary of its hundred years. It will soon keep its formal centenary. It is the surviving link between the Vicariates and the Dioceses. To this institution which stands out alone, uniting the past and the present, whatever remains of your generous offerings shall go: I mean the venerable and beautiful College of St. Edmund of Canterbury at Old Hall. Hundreds of devoted priests have come out from its walls to live and die in the labours of charity, both in the old Vicariate of London and now in the Dioceses of Westminster, Southwark, and Portsmouth. Many still are living, united in brotherhood, though scattered in their fields of pastoral work. They cherish loving memories of their boyhood and youth under the oak trees and the roof of St. Edmund's. They also, both near and afar off, with many of our most devoted laymen, will not, I hope, think that I have erred in making this last bequest."

The money left to St. Edmund's was spent in substantial repairs, which the building stood greatly in need of, after the wear and tear of nearly a hundred years. The whole of the roof was renewed, a hot-water heating apparatus was added to the refectory and the rooms and dormitory in the "New Wing," and fresh wood-work for the window frames was put up throughout the house. These repairs were still in progress when Cardinal Manning died on January 14th, 1892.

The third Archbishop of Westminster has now been elected in the person of Dr. Herbert Vaughan, and once more, after a lapse of forty-three years, St. Edmund's is ruled by a bishop who may be called an Edmundian; for though Dr. Vaughan received no part of his education at St. Edmund's,[1] he was Vice-President for six years, from 1855 till 1861,[2] and therefore is thoroughly acquainted with the spirit and traditions of the college. He presided at the Edmundian dinner for the first time as Archbishop, at the Grand Hotel, on July

---

[1] Though never a student at St. Edmund's, Dr. Vaughan attended Dr. Ward's lectures for a considerable time, and his name appears in the testimonial presented to him by his old pupils on his retirement in 1858.

[2] During his vice-presidentship Dr. Vaughan also served the mission at Hertford, going over every Sunday and returning in the evening. It was during this time that he built the present Church and Presbytery there.

On one occasion, when he was returning, as usual, in the College dog-cart, he was stopped between Hertford and Ware by a man, who presented a pistol at him and demanded money. Dr. Vaughan succeeded in getting out of the cart on the other side, and going round, attacked the man from behind with his whip; whereupon the latter got into the cart and drove off in the direction of Hertford, leaving Dr. Vaughan on the road with his whip. He did not drive very far; for when Dr. Vaughan reached Hertford on foot, he found his horse and cart in the station yard, the man having taken the train and made off.

CARDINAL VAUGHAN,
Bishop of Salford, 1872-1892; Archbishop of Westminster, 1892.
*(From a photograph by Russel & Sons, Baker Street.)*

5th, 1892, and his health was proposed by the President, Mgr. Crook, who had been a divine under him at the college.

In his reply he said that he should never forget that he was an Edmundian, for he had spent what he could. not but regard as the most important years of his life, those which immediately succeeded his ordination, under the roof of St. Edmund's. When a few weeks later he visited the college for the Exhibition Day, he said that he felt like coming home, so strong were the associations and memories attached to the college. Though it was thirty years since he had been there as vice-president, the place and its traditions were still fresh in his memory, and many of the faces which he saw around him, both on the Exhibition Day and at the Edmundian dinner, were familiar as those of former students under him. He promised that he would be a frequent visitor to St. Edmund's, and that he would do all in his power for its prosperity. He hoped that the time was not far distant when the college would be again unable to hold all the students who would wish to come there, and that further building would once more become necessary.

On 16th of August, 1892, Archbishop Vaughan received his Pallium at the London Oratory from the hands of Archbishop Stonor, the Papal Legate. It was the first time for three hundred years that such a ceremony had been performed in London, and many Edmundian priests and laymen were present to assist at the investiture of their former vice-president. All will join in wishing that Dr. Vaughan may long be spared to work for the Diocese of Westminster and the Catholic Church in England, and that his good wishes for St. Edmund's College and its welfare may continue to be realized.

THE END.

# APPENDIX A.

## Rules and Customs of Standon School.

(THE following is a copy of a document preserved at St. Edmund's, and the rules were probably drawn out soon after the establishment of the school in 1753. The handwriting is unknown; but there are several corrections and additions written by the Rev. Richard Kendal, the "Chief Master.")

1. From ye first Sunday after Easter, to ye first of October, ye Scholars are call'd at Six in the Morning on all days, except Sundays and Holy days, when they are called at 7, and on School days ye rest of the year at 6½. They are allowed no more than a Quarter of an Hour to dress in, unless it be on days they change their Linen, viz. on Sundays and Thursdays, when they are allowed a qr. of an hour longer.

2. As soon as they are come down stairs, they are to wash themselves, during which time the Master yat called them, is to attend them, and see them comb'd, silence being observ'd while each learns his Catechism; It is the Housekeeper's and housemaid's business to comb them, who are always to be ready, and not make ye children waite for them. From ye 1st of Novr. to ye 25th of March, they are allow'd a Fire in ye School in combing time, which is to be lighted as soon as they are call'd: the Fire ought to be greater or lesser according to ye nature of the Weather, Number of Scholars, &c.

3. After they are comb'd, they all go up to the Chappel to say Morning Prayers, & it is required of the Master yt call'd them yt he be present ye whole time, to see yt they be read leisurely and distinctly by a good Reader and to prevent Irreverence of any kind. As soon as Morning Prayers are ended, one of ye Priests begins Mass, at which ye whole family, it were wish'd, could assist and all are to be accountable to the chief Master for their Neglect. The Master there present is to see yt they behave with a becoming Respect and make a right use of their Books or Beads, and that all hurry in ye Chappel and particularly about ye Altar, in serving at Mass be laid aside, yt a respectful Genuflection at comeing into or going out of ye Chappel and at every passing before ye Altar be always made.

4. As soon as they come down from ye Chapel, they go directly to Breakfast, which must always be ready for them, which consists chiefly of boiled milk and milk pottage, &c., but such as have a real aversion to either, may be allowed something else. No one is to be absent from Meals without leave.

5. Breakfast being ended, on Notice given by ye Bell, which it were to be wish'd could always be at 8 o'Clock, all repair to School, on School days, to say their Lesson in some Catechism suitable to their Age & Capacity, as 1st ye Doway Abstract, with Mr. Gother's Instructions for Children,

2ndly, Fleury's Historical Catechism, 3rdly, Tuberville's &c., with the Chief Master's Approbation. The short Abridgement of ye Christian Doctrine is indeed ye Catechism in use for Children very young.

6. After ye Catechism Lesson is said, each Scholar is to have his Task set him, in English, Latin or Greek, about which he is to be employed till 12 o'clock, tho' they are allowed a quarter of an hour's play at 10 o'clock, that they may not be too long at their studies at once; a Lesson in English is always read by every young Gentleman in ye morning, though he reads very perfect. In cold weather they may be allow'd a fire in ye School till noon, & whenever it is so cold yt a fire is thought necessary by ye chief Master, whoever has a great Coat (as all ought to have) must wear it at his Studies, & must hang it up when he putts it off, upon one of ye Pins in ye School, yt it may not be thrown about, otherwise let him forfeight a halfpenny to ye Poor for every omission, when found out, the same to be said of Hatts, Handkerchiefs, Gloves & Books whether in Chappel, School, Study Place or Garden.

7. At 12 exactly all meet in ye dining Room, where Grace being said by one of ye Scholars in an audible Voice, every one sitts down according to his Class; one of ye Masters ought always to be there the whole time and are all desired to have an exact Eye upon ye Scholars to see yt they behave in such a manner as is expected from Gentlemen's children, yt they do not talk at all, unless to ask for anything they may have Occasion for, as Bread, Beer, &c. yt they don't throw their Victuals about, but eat what is given them, yt they eat Bread with their Meat, &c. As 'tis ye chief Master's Duty to see nothing comes to Table but what is wholesome & good in its kind, so neither are ye Scholars to be suffer'd to refuse eating what is sent them under Pretence of natural Antipathy or Aversion, without very good Proofs of this or that kind of Food disagreeing with them &c. One of ye Ends of sending Children to School being to break them of Nicety in their Diet. And here ye House-keeper must take special Care yt ye Cook be ready *exactly* as ye Clock strikes 12, since the Children are to come *directly*, at yt time to dinner, where every thing is to be in readiness for them, yt they may not lose their time alloted for their Recreation, nor every thing be put out of order by her delay. After Dinner they recreate till 2 o'Clock, but all violent Exercise such as drawing one another in ye Cart &c. ought not to be allow'd in very hot weather, especially so soon after dinner. In Recreation time they are not permitted to throw Sticks or Stones on any account, and those who break ye Windows are to pay for them out of their Pocket Money, & if the Author is not to be found out they are to be charg'd to them all. They are not to take hold of each other's Cloaths for fear of tearing them, nor to go out into ye open air without a Hatt or Cap on, nor to be out in ye Rain, nor to lie on ye Ground when 'tis damp, as 'tis presumed to be in all Months yt have ye Letter R in ye Name, as January, &c.

8. At two o'clock on School Days all go to ye Study place, no one being allow'd to play or loiter after ye Bell has rung to this or any other duty of ye House, where they are to be under ye Care of ye Writing Master till 5, and from 5 to 6 they are to be under ye care of one of ye other Masters and to learn Geography or ye like.

9. At 6 o'clock, ye Master, whose business it was to attend ye Scholars yt day, is to ring the Bell for Evening Prayers, consisting of ye Litany of ye Saints, ye Rosary or Bona Mors with ye Night Exercise & Reflection or Meditation for ye following Day, all which are to be read leisurely and distinctly by ye ablest Readers amongst ye Scholars in their Turns (ye whole Family being present) nor are any of ye Rest to be excused from answering slowly and distinctly, if able. From ye Chapel all go down

quietly to Supper, which consists of Bread and Butter, or Cheese. Applepy once a week most part of the year and Milk sometimes in ye Summer.

10. From ye 1st of Novr. to ye 25th of March they are allowed a fire in ye School from Supper till bed time, which is to be prepared and got ready while they are at Supper. In Recreation time after Supper, while they have Fire, they are not to play out of Doors ; If ye weather be severe, either before ye 1st of November or after ye 25th of March, they may be allowed fires sooner or later than ye usual time, Leave being obtain'd of ye chief Master. From ye 1st of June to ye 1st of 7ber, they recreate after Supper till half an hour past 8, but ye rest of ye year only till 8 o'Clock. They are allow'd a Draught of Smal Beer at 4 o'clock from ye 1st of May till ye 1st of Septr. and in extream hot Weather ye same at 8 in ye Evening, with Leave.

11. At ye Sound of ye Bell, all go quietly to their Chambers, & after a short Prayer said on their knees, by their own Bed Side, undress themselves modestly, without romping, noise or going into each other's Chambers, & it is always one of the Masters Business to be present while they are undressing, to keep them in order, &c. Care must be taken yt every Scholar has in the coldest Weather at least 2 Blankets or a large one doubled, and a Quilt. All talking after they are put to Bed or before they are call'd in the Morning is strictly forbidden.

12. On Sundays and Holy days Mass is said at 10 o'clock, & some Spirituality ought always to be read, or preach'd to ye congregation on those Days, either before or after Mass. Moreover on Sundays and Holy days before Mass the Scholars meet to hear Spiritual Books read for the space of an hour, one of ye Masters being present all ye while to keep them in order, & to rectify Mistakes yt may be made in reading by them, & above all to prevent their Reading so fast as they do, which is not only a Discredit to the School, but a great Impediment also of that Instruction and Edification that would acrue to themselves and hearers by Gods Grace, from ye contrary Practice and it were to be wish'd ye Serv'ts were also present. The first Lecture should be out of some Book yt contains an Exposition of ye Catholick Doctrine in a catechistical way. The 2nd should inculcate and enforce Morality, such as the Instructions of Youth. The 3rd may be historical, such as ye Life of our Lord Jesus Christ, ye History of ye Bible, ye Saints Lives, &c. no more than ye last half hour ought to be spent in reading ye above mentioned or like pious Histories. The Master here would do well to make them give an Account of what is read by asking them Questions, particularly if he perceives them negligent and don't seem to mind, and punish them for their neglect; he may likewise, if he thinks it propper, instruct them in their Catechism or tell them of their faults &c. in hopes of amendment. On holy days except the feasts of Christmas and ye Epiphany, one hour ought to be employ'd in their Studies, as yt of Geography or ye like. Care must be taken that they make little noise on Sundays in their Recreation time for fear of givving Scandal, for which reason Nine Pins, Drawing ye Cart about &c. are forbid, as also whistling or singing.

13. At half an hour past two at ye latest, all meet in ye Chappel to assist at Vespers, to which all must answer slowly and distinctly yt can, and keep together, and such as cannot, must learn it as soon at least, as they begin to make Latin. Serveing of Mass ought to be learnt sooner, so 'tis required yt they serve by weeks in their Turns, but only one at a Time, unless when one begins to serve Mass at first he may have an Assistant. The Rest are not to answer, but mind their own Prayers. The Server at Mass must speak distinctly and articulate every Sylable, go

gently and quietly about ye Altar, making always a becoming Genuflection whenever he passes by it. Vespers and Complin being said, as also ye Litany of ye Saints, Ave Maris Stella, De Profundis, and Exaudiat, all in English (except when ye B. Sacrament is exposed, which is always done on every 1st Sunday in ye month & ye most solemn Festivals) & ye Night Exercise; the whole is concluded on all Sundays with an Explication of ye Doway Catechism, by one of ye Priests for about half an hour. From ye time they come down from ye Chappel till 6, they are allowed Recreation and may walk out if they chuse it, & ye weather permits, yt is if it be neither too hot nor dirty nor stormy &c., all which is to be left to ye Judgment & discretion of ye chief Master, whose Leave is to be asked, if at home. In extreame hot weather, with his leave, they may bathe now and then, with a handkerchief tied round their Waste and a Master always with them, to see that they behave modestly & do not venture into deep places, &c.

14. They may also walk out once a day on Recreation Days, if ye Weather permits, as above. Accordingly, as soon as ye Bell has rung, for walking, all come to meet ye Master at ye dineing Room door, where they are to waite his coming, who is to go out with them, for they are never suffer'd to go out without a Master to inspect their Conduct. No Scholar is to be exempted from going out with ye Rest, but for *very good reasons*, such as Indisposition, &c., Air and Exercise being very conducive to health, but all climbing of Trees, breaking down wood or Hedges, all stroling out of Sight of ye Master are strictly forbid, and care must always be taken to bring them home in due time and all together.

15. No Scholar is permitted to go into any part of ye house without express leave from a Master nor out of Bounds at any time without some Masters leave, let ye pretence be what it will, & if he does, he must expect to suffer in proportion to what his fault deserves, without hopes of Impunity. The Scholars are not allowed to dig holes in the play place, as being liable to make them fall, &c. tho' they may be allow'd a spade to dig their own Boarders towards ye raising of Sallads, &c., provided what they buy of Seeds for this intent be paid for out of their weekly allowance of pocket Money, which is given them once a week or fortnight by one of ye Masters: no debts to be contracted by borrowing of one another or &c.

16. There are 4 Vacations in ye Year viz. Christmas, Shrovetide, Easter and Whitsuntide. Ye Christmas Vacation begins on Christmas Eve & ends on ye 12th day; The Shrovetide Vacation begins on Quinquagessima Sunday and ends with Shrove Tuesday. Easter Vacation begins on Wednesday in H. Week & ends on Easter Tuesday. Whitsuntide Vacation begins only on Corpus Christi & ends on Monday, ye fourth day after ye 4 weeks from Corpus Christi day are expired. On all working days in ye Xmas and Whitsuntide Vacations, ye Scholars study at ye rate of an hour and a Quarter each day & all yt go home have proportionable Tasks set them & as ye end of these is to hinder them from forgeting what they have already learn'd they ought to relate thereunto.

17. Besides Tuesdays & Thursdays Afternoons, their weekly playdays, extraordinary Recreation may be granted them now and then, as and when ye chief Master thinks propper, but never a whole day is to be granted upon any Account whatsoever.

18. While their Cloathes which they wear on the Week days are mending, they are not to wear their best suit, but rather a great Coat or Night Gown, especially in ye Study place, for fear of Ink falling upon them, as

has often happen'd, & if ye weather be very cold, they may wear their great Coat or night Gown over their best suit; They ought always to have a pair of Shoes & Stockings fit to put on as occasion may require, besides those on their feet, which they must always change once a week and as often as they get wett on their feet, to prevent catching cold.

19. It is ye chief Master's business to see yt they write neither too often nor too seldom to their Parents, Relations and other Friends. It also belongs to him to appoint ye days for approaching ye Sacraments, which ought to be once every Month. Moreover he is to appoint a day for Composition or strivving for places once a month at least. There ought always to be 2 general Examens in the Year, one before Christmas and ye other before Whitsuntide & those yt bring good Exercises & give a good Account of what they have learnt, may be allow'd half a days play as the chief Master shall think they deserve, while ye rest are not only to go to school, but be punished by whiping, stoppage of Money &c. according to what their past Idleness shall be judged deserving of. Yet for this or any other faults I would have ye Rod made as little use of as possible, & desire the diligent may always be encouraged by a little more play when ye others are at their studies, by a larger allowance of Pocket Money &c. which Parents on such occasions 'tis presumed will never be against; besides there are several little punishments may be thought on for ye Indolent, such as making them study on their Play days, lessening their allowance of Pocket money, making them sit and be served last at table &c. &c. which things may probably have a better effect, particularly as ye Children are mostly young, than that of ye Rod, but when this is to be *necessarily* made use of, I require yt ye Master do not inflict it on his own Scholar, if for School affairs at least, but yt he send him to be punished by ye other Master to prevent any heat or warmth yt may possibly be occasioned, but no Lay Person is ever on any account to lay hands upon them without ye Chief Master's consent.

20. On all Saturdays after Supper one of the House Maids is to wash ye Children, and one of ye Masters ought to look in upon them to see they behave as they should do, & on Sunday mornings they are to be powder'd. After dinner and supper and at other times of Recreation they are not to be left to themselves, but the Masters in their turns ought to visit and overlook them from time to time, to prevent several accidents they are liable to for want of an Overlooker. They are neither to give nor sell each other anything of value without leave. While ye snow lies on ye ground they are not to go into it, much less make Snow-balls or ye like. They are always to make a Bow to ye Master, &c. as often as they go in or out of a Room where he is (ye Chappel excepted) also when any of ye Masters or Strangers appear in the House or out of the house they are all to take their Hatts of, and are to continue so till they are order'd to put them on, and are never to speak to any one but in ye same manner, & whenever anything is given them or they present anything to another, it must always be done with a Bow; and they are never to give an answer but with ye Word Sir or Madam at ye end of it, as Yes Sir, No Sir; Yes Madam, No Madam. Also great care should be taken of ye Childrens walking with their Toes out, yt they sit upright at their studies, writing &c. and yt they in no ways grow awkward in their behaviour and carriage. Their Hair should be cut once a month, heads shaved once a fortnight and their Feet wash'd once a Month. They are allowed Mince Py thrice between All Saints and Candlemass; also Plum Cake for Supper on ye 12th night, they paying for it.

# APPENDIX B.

## NARRATIVE OF THE ESCAPE FROM FRANCE OF THE REV. WILLIAM HENRY COOMBES,[1] PROFESSOR OF DIVINITY IN ST. EDMUND'S COLLEGE, OLD HALL GREEN.

> Forsan hæc olim meminisse juvabit.—*Virgil.*
>
> An hour will come, with pleasure to relate
> These sorrows past, as benefits of fate.—*Dryden.*

ON the 10th of October, 1793, a cruel decree, by which the subjects of his Britannic Majesty resident in France were stripped of their property and imprisoned, was framed by the rulers of that country. The pretext, which served to cloak this inhuman proceeding, was the supposed indignity shown to the French nation in the person of Beauvais, one of the representatives of the people. This man was said to have been put to death by the English at Toulon; and, as Barrere stated in his report to the Convention, not to have suffered like a freeman, but to have been hanged like a slave. After the recapture of Toulon, Beauvais was found alive and in good health. It then appeared that his conduct had exposed him to the resentment of his countrymen, and that he had been indebted for his safety to the generous protection of the British officers. Impressed with the noble behaviour of the enemies of his country, he set off for Paris, with a full determination to make known the humanity of the English towards him; but he was dispatched on the road by the secret orders of the Committee of Public Safety.

The decree framed in consequence of an impudent and malicious falsehood was immediately carried into execution. The subjects of his Britannic Majesty were deprived of their effects, taken into custody, and left to depend, for the common necessaries of life, on the generosity of the Great Nation. Disliking the thoughts of a painful imprisonment, unable to calculate the consequences of this cruel treatment, and deprived of the

---

[1] The Rev. W. H. Coombes was born at Meadgate, Somersetshire, on May 8, 1767. In 1779 he entered Douay College as a student, and after passing through his course, was ordained priest in 1791, after which he stayed on as professor of Rhetoric. The account here given of his escape on the seizure of the college two years later is reprinted from the "Catholic Directory" of 1800. On reaching England, Dr. Coombes came to St. Edmund's, where he taught theology from 1793 till 1808. He was also vice-president from 1801 till he left. The last part of his life was spent on the mission at Shepton Mallett, Somersetshire. In 1849 he retired to Downside, where he died on November 15th, 1850.

means of serving my friends any longer, I thought it time to concert measures for my personal safety, and to secure a speedy and honourable retreat.

Having formed my resolution of escaping, I left on the 12th of October, 1793, the English College at Douay, in which I had been Professor of Rhetoric; and before the arrival of the Commissioners, who were directed to execute the decree of the Convention, I stole from the town unperceived by the guards. I immediately repaired to the country house belonging to the College, situated in the village of Esquerchin, about three miles from Douay. My design was to spend the evening in that place, and, after taking proper measures for my escape, to leave it the next morning. Scarcely had I reached the village of Esquerchin, when I was met and accosted by a stranger, whom I considered as a tutelary angel sent from heaven to assist me in my distress. Perceiving me to be an Englishman, he asked me if I had no apprehension of appearing so publicly at so critical a time. I informed him that I was then meditating my escape, and was repairing to our country house for that purpose. After a short pause he addressed me to the following effect: "Sir, if you hope to succeed in this hazardous undertaking I will suggest to you an excellent plan. Proceed to the village of Esquerchin, endeavour to obtain a passport from the Mayor, and direct your course to Mons, where you will be in the vicinity of the allied armies. I am personally connected with one of the proprietors of the coal-pits in those parts, and to conceal the object of your journey you may be the bearer of a commission for coals to a considerable amount. Relate your story privately to my friend and mention my name; he will understand the rest." I accepted the commission, thanked him for his kindness, and we parted. Pleased with my new character of a coal-merchant, as I thought it an excellent disguise, I proceeded in high spirits to the country house, prepared everything for my escape, and fixed my departure at four o'clock the next morning. The prospect appeared to me sufficiently cheering, and I was adjusting my little affairs with philosophic calmness, when suddenly my plan was defeated, and my hopes frustrated.

About six in the evening, as I was entering my apartment in the country house, I was followed by the Mayor of the village. I turned round to salute him; he answered my salute with a republican frown. Immediately there appeared a commissary of the district of Douay, and an officer in the national uniform. I was informed that I was their prisoner. The officer conducted me into the court, laid his hand on his sword, and told me in an angry tone that he knew me to be the President of the house; that I was to collect together the young men, whom he had seen straying about the village, and inform him where our effects lay, and that this was to be punctually performed at the hazard of my life. I assured him that I was but a private individual in the house, unauthorized to assume any command, and that, consequently, I could transmit no orders to the young men of whom he spoke; that as to the effects I believed that everything valuable had been taken away, and that nothing remained, which he might easily discover by examining the different apartments. He appeared greatly dissatisfied with this answer, and repeated his menaces, assuring me that he had surrounded the house with forty armed guards, and that nothing remained for me but to comply with his orders. I replied, that as I was an innocent and a helpless prisoner in his hands, he might do with me what he pleased, but that I was unable to give him any farther satisfaction as to the particulars he had mentioned. I civilly invited him to take some refreshment, telling him I thought that the best method of adjusting matters between us. His republican fierceness was by this time considerably abated; he accepted the invitation, and became easy and familiar.

After this followed the solemn ceremony of putting the national seals on the doors of the different apartments in the house. I was desired to attend. We visited the rooms, on which the Commissary fixed the seals; the Mayor wrote the minutes of the proceedings, and the officer attended to give a solemn sanction to the business. All the valuable effects had been before removed; and little remained to be secured for the nation but decayed bedsteads, tattered curtains, and old chairs. A comical solemnity accompanied the scene. The Mayor, who wrote the account of the proceedings, would sometimes distinguish the doors by mentioning the points which they faced; the Commissary, who professed not to know the north from the south, would then insist that the doors should be distinguished in the minutes by the colour of the paint. A singular debate would often take place on those occasions, which could be terminated only by the interposition of the Officer. In the course of these researches my attendants desired to see the cellar, where they found a store of excellent wine. They treated themselves with such a quantity of it as produced no small degree of merriment; and prudently reserved what remained for some future day of mirth. To conceal it with more security they ordered me in the name of the law to retire.

After having placed the national seals on all the apartments of the house, these citizens, whose wisdom had been observably enlarged by the fumes of the wine, addressed me in a solemn manner, and charged me, in the name of the nation, to inform them if any other place remained unsealed. I replied that the only places of that description which occurred to me, were certain necessary apartments at the bottom of the court, and that if they thought proper to place the national seals on them, they might proceed thither. This proposal occasioned much diversity of opinion. The Mayor very gravely held the measure to be unnecessary. The Commissary, on the contrary, maintained with great force of lungs, and all the strength of rustic eloquence, that necessary places ought to be sealed as well as other apartments, and seemed shrewdly to suppose that the discovery of some concealed treasure would reward their search. Many weighty reasons were urged on both sides, when the Officer, appearing to consider this scene as a violation of the national dignity, interposed and put an end to this curious and entertaining debate. The Commissary, awed by his authority, addressed me in these words: "Citizen, there is no farther room for deliberation." After the conclusion of this business, which lasted the greatest part of the night, I was conducted to Douay, about seven o'clock in the morning, in the company of some of the students, and joined my friends in the prison of the Scotch College. My plan of assuming the character of a coal-merchant, and the other adventures which ensued, excited much merriment.

Of my stay in the Scotch College, a house which, by the forms of republican justice, had been taken from some of his Majesty's subjects, and converted into a prison for honest men, I have very little to relate. My friends and myself were confined there but four days, during which time many of us were stowed together in the same room. The beds on which we reposed in the night were converted into seats in the day; we ate, we drank, we slept in the same apartment. On the fourth day of our confinement (October 16th) orders were issued by the department of Douay to send us to the citadel of Doulens in Picardy. On hearing this news I was fully determined to attempt my escape. About two o'clock in the afternoon of the same day we were conveyed from the prison at Douay, under a guard of cavalry. It happened, fortunately, that the officer who commanded the detachment of guards, was the same person who had taken me into custody at our country house at Esquerchin. With this man, whom I knew by the name of Citizen George, I was become familiar. He gave me many assurances of kindness, pitied my misfortunes and those of my friends, and entreated me to tell him if he could do me any service. Without discovering to him my intention of attempting my escape on the road, I thanked him for his goodness: from his behaviour I had reason to think that, were I missed, I should not be pursued by his orders. Full of my design, I frequently left the waggons in which we were conveyed, went from one waggon to another, walked by the side of the Officer, conversing familiarly with him. Often did I attempt to conceal myself behind the thickets, or in places remote from public view, but was as often prevented by the vigilance of the guards. I looked into every corner, I surveyed every lurking-hole with the most diligent observation, but without effect. I now began to despair of executing my design, when, by the blessing of the Almighty, to whose bounty I am indebted for peculiar protection at this, as well as at every other period of my life, a favourable moment came, of which I availed myself with the utmost alacrity.

It was evening; the waggons were at some distance from each other, and the attention of the guards was, of course, more divided; or, what is more probable, their vigilance was considerably relaxed. We had just entered a village situated at the bottom of a considerable declivity; while some of the waggons advanced, and by the irregularity of the road were soon out of sight, the rest were gently proceeding down the hill. I embraced this happy moment, alone and unperceived retired to a poor habitation on the side of the road, and begged the favour of enjoying the comfort of a fire. A poor, honest woman, the wife of a day-labourer, and her aged parent gave me a kind reception; the door was shut, and I seated myself by the fire.

Here I remained in some agitation, while the prisoners and guards were passing by the door; fortunately no one entered the house at this critical moment, when I might have been easily discovered. The name of this village is St. Laurent, it is but a small distance from Arras, at which place the prisoners soon arrived. The gates of that town were shut at an early hour, and I was relieved from the apprehension of being pursued. After I had been in this house for some time, the husband of the good woman who had so kindly received me, returned home from the labours of the day. He sat by me and spoke in a civil and obliging manner. My dress, my appearance, my conversation, and particularly the depression of spirits which I betrayed, naturally attracted his attention, and excited him to propose such questions as I was unwilling to answer. I was, however, questioned so closely that I felt the necessity of giving some account of my situation. Perceiving in the countenance of this poor day-labourer a peculiar air of honesty and candour, I ventured to ask him if I could with confidence reveal to him a secret which involved my personal safety? He generously replied: "Speak without fear, I will never betray you." I then informed him of my real situation, and of that of my friends, and of the purpose for which I had taken refuge in his house. I represented my distress to him in so pathetic a manner that his commiseration seemed greatly excited, and he promised to give me all assistance in his power in my perilous situation. I thanked him for his generous behaviour, and told him that I begged only the favour of staying a little longer in his house, and of having some directions about the road which I designed to take.

About ten o'clock the same night, I left the house of this hospitable man, in very high spirits, and walked to the village of Esquerchin, which I reached about two in the morning. My intention was to repair to the house of an honest man, who had always shown me a great personal regard; but being disturbed by a very general barking of dogs, I thought it prudent to leave the village and wander about till daybreak. I then returned to the house of my friend in order to awaken him, and solicit his help. While I was waiting in much agitation at the door, a young man, whom I had never before seen, came to me from the opposite side of the road. His appearance afforded me much uneasiness, as I was unable to judge whether he was a friend or a foe. My embarrassment, however, was soon removed by the kindness with which he assisted me to awaken the good people of the house. The wife of my friend immediately undertook to conduct me to Flers, a village at the distance of about two miles. There others resided, on whose active and benevolent exertions I could safely depend. On the road to Flers my guide cautioned me to walk at some distance from her that, in case of accident, we might not both be taken. I obeyed her injunction; but the haziness of the morning and the shortness of my sight exposed me to danger, for seeing before me a woman, whom I mistook for my guide, I advanced to her as she was entering a house and discovered her to be a stranger. This accident threw me into some perplexity, as I knew not the house to which I was going, and I thought it dangerous to make any enquiries. I however found the necessity of asking for the place, and was conducted to it, where I found my guide and her friends in much alarm, as they knew not what was become of me.

After the agitation of the preceding day, and the fatigue of the night, I found myself sick and feverish, but sleep and refreshment soon revived me. To prevent all danger of discovery, it was necessary to remain in a retired apartment, from which the daylight was excluded. Such was my distress in this particular, that I was obliged to place myself in the chimney in order to have light to recite the divine office. About evening I received intelligence that a member of the College, the Rev. Mr. Devereux, had effected his escape from the guards in a similar manner, and that he lay concealed in a neighbouring village. I obtained a guide and went to join him. While we were talking of our adventures, another member of the College, the Rev. Mr. Rickaby made his appearance. He had eluded the vigilance of the guards by retiring behind a mow, and naturally repaired to that part of the country where our connections lay. As we were three in number, we were better able to animate each other to bear our distress with fortitude. We spent that night and the next day in the house of an honest farmer, in the most retired and secret manner. In the night of the 18th of October, we made an attempt in the company of this farmer and another peasant, to proceed to the Austrian frontier. The canal which flows between Lille and Douay was necessarily to be passed; but the bridges were guarded and the stream was not fordable. In this perplexity we depended upon the chance of finding a boat, which used to be stationed in a certain part of the canal for the convenience of travellers. We directed our course to that place; but to our astonishment the boat was removed, and a stranger was standing on the spot to which we were going, as if he had purposely taken that station to disconcert our plan. Apprehensive that intelligence of our design might be communicated to the administrative bodies of Douay, we fled at the appearance of this stranger, over marshes and dreary and pathless fields, and returned to the house of the farmer in great depression of spirits.

The next day (October 19) a report prevailed that the village was suspected of harbouring emigrants, and that Commissioners were expected from Douay to take cognizance of the affair. Our host was alarmed; we were unwilling to expose him or his friends to danger. After some deliberation we agreed to retire to a loft in a barn at some distance from the house. This narrow receptacle was nearly filled with straw, and room was scarcely left for the reception of three persons. Besides, the barn was double, and one part of it belonged to people distinguished by a spirit of democracy, who were employed at the time in thrashing their corn. We were cautioned to preserve a profound silence for fear of a discovery. To this forlorn place we retired, taking for our support a jug of ale, bread and apples; here we spent a long and tedious day in silence, in darkness, and in sorrow. A great source of our perplexity was that those democratical persons, who were thrashing corn in the adjoining part of the barn, might, in the interval of their labour, hear our whispers, and the noise which we made in eating our hard apples. But we providentially remained in great security; and when night approached took more effectual measures than before to forward our escape. We advanced to a part of the canal, where we found remnants of a broken bridge, there we fixed across the stream a ladder, over the rounds of which we walked to the opposite side. Our principal difficulty was now subdued, and we proceeded with much confidence to a part of the French Netherlands which was then in the possession of the Allied Armies. One hazard, however, remained, which consisted in eluding the vigilance of the republican patroles on the frontier. Our guide inadvertently conducted us within half a furlong of the guard-house, in which soldiers were stationed. This was indeed a moment of distress. The least noise would have betrayed us. We walked along in the utmost trepidation and the most profound silence, and in about half an hour were pronounced to be in a place of security. This, as may easily be conceived, afforded us the most heartfelt joy. It was about four o'clock in the morning of the 20th of October, 1793, when this fortunate event took place. We after that surrendered ourselves to the Austrian patroles at Coutiche, and were conducted to General Kray, the commanding officer at Orchies, who treated us with civility, and gave us a guide to Tournay. Thus, after the anxiety, the difficulties and dangers of three days and four nights, we reached a land of religion and hospitality.

"Hic labor extremus, longarum hæc meta viarum."—*Virgil*.

"Such was the term of all my labours past,
And here my lengthened wanderings ceased at last."

# APPENDIX C.

## EXTRACTS FROM THE LAST DOUAY DIARY.

Containing the lists of Professors and Students, made by Dr. Poynter, the Prefect of Studies, during the last year of the College's existence, and the final entries made in the prison at Doullens.[1]

N.B.—Those who were afterwards at St. Edmund's or Crook Hall are marked (E) and (C) respectively.

### CATALOGUS PRO DIE 1 OCTOBRIS, 1792.

#### SENIORES.

   R.D. Joannes Daniel, Præses.
   R.D. J. Hodgson, V.P. and S.T.P.
(E)  D. Gul. Poynter, S.T.P. et Præf. Stud.
   D. Tho. Smith, Phil. Prof.
   D. Bened. Rayment, Phil Prof..
   D. Joseph Beaumont (Hunt), Procur.
   D. Tho. Stout, Præf. Gen.
   D. Jac. Newsham, Prof. Rud.

#### PROFESSORES.

(E) D. Gul. Wilds, Sac.    D. Jac. Lancaster, Diac.
  D. Jac. Haydock, Sac.  (E) D. Joan. Lee, Diac.
(E) D. Gul. Coombes, Sac.   Georgius Simpson.

#### *Theologi.*

   D. Gul. Davies, diac, 4 an. alum.
   D. Gul. Croskell, diac, 3 an. alum.
(C) D. Tho. Berry, subdiac, 3 an. alum.
(C) D. Rob. Blakoe, subdiac, 3 an. alum.
   Mag. Joannes Woodcock, 4 an. alum.
   —— Georgius Taylor, 4 an. alum.
(E) —— Jac. Delaney, 3 an. alum.
(C) —— Joannes Bell, 2 an. alum.
   —— Joannes Baines, 3 an. alum.
(E) —— Gul. Beacham, 3 an. alum.
   —— Nicholas Woodcock, 3 an. alum.
   —— Jac. Worswick, 3 an. alum.

---

[1] The Prefect of Studies' Book, or Last Douay Diary, was brought by Dr. Poynter to St. Edmund's. It is now kept, with the other Douay papers, among the Westminster archives at the Oratory.

　　　　　　Mag. Car. Thompson, cler. 3 an.
　(E) ——— Robertus Freemont, 2 an. alum.
　　　——— Joan. Dowling, 2 an. alum.
　(E) ——— Joan. Law, 2 an. alum.
　(C) ——— Joan. Lingard, 1 an. alum.
　(E) ——— Fris. Bowland, 2 an. alum.
　　　——— Christopher Dalin, 2 an. alum.
　(E) ——— Edwardus Peach, 1 an. alum.
　(E) ——— Joannes Devereux, 1 an. alum.
(E & C) ——— Car. Saul, 1 an. alum.

### Physici.

| | |
|---|---|
| (E & C) Ricardus Thomson. | (E & C) Eduardus Monk. |
| (E) Joannes Clarkson. | Joseph Montgomery. |
| (E & C) Thomas Gillow. | Timotheus Duggan. |
| (C) Thomas Haydock. | Joannes Hall. |
| (E) Thomas Cook. | Joachim Oliveira. |

### Logici.

| | |
|---|---|
| (E) Ric. Broderick. | (E & C) Georgius Haydock. |
| Jac. Harrison. | Joan. Canning. |
| (E & C) Thomas Penswick. | (E) Gul. Lucas. |

### Rhetores.

| | |
|---|---|
| (E) Lud. Havard. | Car. Sims. |
| (C) Joan. Rickaby. | Maur. O'Connell. |
| And. O'Callaghan. | Dan. O'Connell. |
| Gul. Barry. | |

### Poetæ.

| | |
|---|---|
| (E) Arth. Clifford. | Lud. Clifford. |
| (C) Joseph Swinburne. | Joan. Bates. |
| Gul. Stourton. | (E) Joan. Eldridge. |
| Nich. Kirwan. | Georg. Aylmer. |
| (E) Thomas Pitchford. | Joan Frankland. |
| Steph. Phillips. | Edw. Beck. |
| Ric. Davies. | Francis Hay. |
| (C) Thomas Lupton. | |

### Syntaxiani.

| | |
|---|---|
| (C) Thomas Dawson. | Rob. Dale. |
| Vincentius Eyre. | (C) Joan. Bradley. |
| Joan. Smith. | (C) Thomas Storey. |

### Grammatici.

| | |
|---|---|
| (C) Joan. Penswick. | (C) Mat. Forster. |
| Thomas Bray. | Petrus Flanagan. |
| (E) Gul. Veal. | Henricus Boithamon. |
| (C) Thomas Cock. | Jac. Teebay. |

*Appendix.* 313

*In Prima Classe Rudimentorum.*

Laur. Teebay.
Vincent Oliveira.
(E) Joan. Bulbeck.

Thomas Brennan.
Jac. Arkwright.

*In Secunda Classe Rudimentorum.*

Edmundus Costello.
(C) Robertus Gradwell.
Albertus Boithamon.
Robertus Lopez.
**Christopher** Galway.

Augustinus Amarigo.
Georgius Strickland.
Thomas Murphy.
Michael Langton.

*In Tertia Classe Rudimentorum.*

Joseph Fountain.

CATALOGUS PRO DIE 1 OCTOBRIS, 1793.

SENIORES.

R.D. Joannes Daniel, Præses.
R.D. J. Hodgson, V.P. et S.T.P.
(E)   D. Gul. Poynter, S.T.P. and Præf. Stud.
D. Tho. Smith, Phil. Prof.
D. Jos. Beaumont, (Hunt), Procu.
D. Tho. Stout, Præf. Gen.
(E)   D. Gul. Wilds, Phil. Prof.

PROFESSORES.

(E) D. Gul. Coombes, Sac. secessit in itinere Oct. 16, 1793.
D. Jas. Lancaster, Diac. abiit Oct. 12, 1793.
(E) D. Joan. Lee, Diac. abiit Oct. 12, 1793.
D. Gul. Croskell, Diac.

*Theologi.*

(C) D. Rob. Blakoe, 4 an. Subdiac. evasit Nov. 24, 1793.
(C) Mag. Joan. Bell, 3 an. alum.
—— Jac. Worswick, 4 an. abiit Oct. 12, 1793.
—— Car. Thompson, 3 an. evasit Jan. 18, 1794.
(E) —— Rob. Freemont, 3 an. alum. evasit Aug. 4, 1793.
—— Joan. Dowling, 3 an. alum.
(E) —— Joan. Law, 3 an. alum. abiit Oct. 12, 1793.
(C) —— Joan. Lingard, 3 an. alum.
(E) —— Fran. Bowland, 3 an. alum.
(E) —— Edw. Peach, 2 an. alum, secessit Aug. 4, 1793.
(E) —— Joan. Devereux, 2 an. alum, secessit Oct. 16, 1793.
(E & C) —— Car. Saul, 2 an. abiit Oct. 12, 1793.
(E & C) —— Ric. Thomson, evasit Nov. 24, 1793.
(E & C) —— Tho. Gillow, abiit Oct. 12, 1793.
(E & C) —— Ed. Monk, secessit Oct. 16, 1793.
—— Joan. Clarkson, evasit Nov. 24, 1793.

### *Physici.*

(E) Ric. Broderick.
Jac. Harrison.
(E & C) Tho. Penswick, abiit Oct. 12, 1793.
Joan. Canning, evasit Jan. 16, 1794.
(E) Gul. Lucas, evasit Nov. 24, 1793.

### *Logici.*

(E) Lud. Havard.
(C) Joan. Rickaby, secessit in itinere Oct. 17, 1793.
Car. Sims.

### *Rhetores.*

(E) Arthur Clifford.
(C) Jos. Swinburne.
Steph. Philips, evasit Jan. 15, 1794.
Ric. Davies.
(C) Tho. Lupton, evasit Jan. 16, 1794.
(E) Joan. Eldridge, evasit Jan. 16, 1794.
Fran. Hay, abiit Parisios, Nov. 16, 1793.

### *Poetæ.*

(C) Tho. Dawson, evasit Jan. 16, 1794.
(C) Joan. Bradley, evasit Jan. 16, 1794.
(C) Tho. Storey, evasit Jan. 16, 1794.

### *Syntaxiani.*

Tho. Brady, relictus Duaci ob infirmitatem.
(C) Joan. Penswick.
(E) Gul. Veal, evasit Jan. 16, 1794.
(C) Tho. Cock, evasit Jan. 16, 1794.
(C) Mat. Forster.
Hen. Boithamon, abiit Parisios, Oct. 16, 1793.

### *Grammatici.*

| | |
|---|---|
| (E) Joan. Bulbeck. | Jac. Arkwright. |
| Tho. Brannan. | (C) Rob. Gradwell. |

*In Prima Classe Rudimentorum.*

Alb. Boithamon, abiit Parisios Oct. 16, 1793.

*In Secunda Classe Rudimentorum.*

---

*In Tertia Classe Rudimentorum.*

Jac. (*sic*) Fountain.

Die 12 Octobris, anni 1793, omnes, tum Superiores, tum Scholares, quotquot erant domi, ad Collegium Scotorum tamquam **ad carcerem**, comitantibus hominibus armatis, educti sunt, inibi arcte conclusi usque ad diem 16 Oct.: vi deinde translati sunt ad arcem Dourlensem (Dourlens) ubi varia passi, adhuc libertatem expectant, Oct. **1**, 1794.

CATALOGUS EORUM QUI HAC DIE 1 OCTOBRIS, 1794, IN INTERIORI ARCE DOURLENSI PRO COLLEGIO DEGUNT.

Joan. Daniel.
Jos. Hodgson.
(E) Gul. Poynter.
Tho. Smith.
Jos. Beaumont.
Tho. Stout.
(E) Gul. Wilds.
Geo. Simpson.
Gul. Croskell.
(C) Tho. Berry.
(E) Jac. Delany.
Joan. Dowling.
(E) Ric. Broderick.

Jac. Harrison.
(E) Lud. Havard.
Car. Simms.
(E) Arth. Clifford.
Lud. Clifford.
(C) Jos. Swinburne.
Ric. Davies.
(C) Joan. Penswick.
(C) Mat. Forster.
(E) Joan. Bulbeck.
(C) Rob. Gradwell.
Tho. Brannan.
Jac. Arkwright.

Jos. Lopez, liberatus Oct. 23, ad Col. Franco-Audomarense abiit.
Aug. Amarigo, liberatus etc., ut supra.
Mic. Langton, liberatus etc., ut supra.
Tho. Murphy, liberatus, etc., ut supra.
Jos. Fountaines.
Tho. Brady, relictus Duaci pie obiit Oct. 30, 1794.

Die 27 Novembris, 1794, reducti sumus ab arce Dourlensi ad Collegium Hibernorum Duaci, ibique arcti conclusi.

Die 25 Februarii, 1795, Duaco Angliam versus profecti sumus. Die 2 Martii, 1795, patrium littus libero jam pede pulsavimus.

# APPENDIX D.

## FIRST ATTEMPT TO RECLAIM THE FOREIGN COLLEGES.

Extract from the Diary of Bishop Douglass:—

"1796.—December 19th.—Mr. Baynes (formerly a student at Douay College and now an inhabitant of Lisle) breakfasted here this morning and told us that Douay College was offered for sale, but that Monsieur Warrington, the Commissary at War, sent a petition to the Committee at Paris, praying that the English College might be preserved for a Magazine for corn and that his petition was granted. It is now employed for the keeping of Corn, Bedding, Blankets and other Baggage for the Army. Almost all the partitions of the Students' Rooms are thrown down. The books of the Divines' Library and Philosophical Instruments and books, and the marble Tabernacle are kept in the College of Anchin under the care of a man who has the title of Librarian. He adds that the Shoemaker and other servants have behaved ill and carried off many goods out of the College, on the pretence that they were given to them by the Superiors before their going to Dourlens.

"1797.—May 27th.—The French Agent for Doway College has written over for a Superior of the College to go over to take possession of the College; promising on his part to procure a passport for the Superior's admission into France. Mr. Poynter is the person Mr. Daniel has fixed upon. Mr. John Strickland has obtained possession of the Seminary at Paris. The same notice has been sent to the Superiors of the other establishments, Scotch, and Irish, and English.

"1797.—June 21st.—Messrs. Tuite and Cleghorn will sail from Dover for Calais this evening, to go to St. Omer. *Vide* May 27th. Mr. Barrow, an ex-Jesuit, has possession of Liege College or Seminary. The Dominicans have obtained possession of their house at Bornheim. Messrs. Daniel and Smith are to go to Douay.

"1797.—June 26th.—Messrs. Tuite and Cleghorn arrived at Calais on the 22nd and were well received by the magistrates, but not permitted to go into the country (to St. Omer's) till Passports arrive from Paris."

Letter from Dr. Poynter to Bishop Douglass, dated Old Hall Green, August 19th, 1797:—

"MY LORD,—Having lately transmitted to Bishop Gibson, at his Lordship's request, some account of the information received from Messrs. Tuite and Cleghorn, I flatter myself that I shall do an acceptable service to your Lordship, if I address to your Lordship a few lines on the subject. These Gentlemen inform us that they have been very kindly received at St. Omers, and particularly that the municipality of the town has shown itself very favourable to them in giving them all encouragement and assistance in the recovery of their property. They have restored to them the private effects belonging to the President and other gentlemen of the

College and furnished them with all the papers and other deeds that could be found to enable them to secure the common property of the College. Mr. Cleghorn mentions that by a letter received from M. Deprez, our agent at Doway, he is informed that the municipality of Doway is very differently affected in our regard. That they wish not to see us return and that some are bent on the sale of our College. Messrs. Tuite and Cleghorn have not yet received their passports to go to Paris, but they are assured they shall have them very soon, and the delay is caused by the changes and confusion that have taken place in the ministry. By a letter received three days ago, Mr. Tuite says that Godin, the agent at Paris, writes to Mr. Doullens, their agent at St. Omers, that the delay they experience is only caused by the changes at Paris; that the decree is in their favor, that he waits the sanction of the Directory. Now Mr. Tuite observes that this (which is rather obscurely expressed) cannot be understood of their pasports, for the sanction of the Directory would not be required for them, since the Ministre de Police is authorized to grant them; besides this letter is addressed to M. Doullens, who had written to claim the College of St. Omers, so that there is reason to think that it relates to the recovery of their College. Mr. Cleghorn mentions that the municipality has employed an Architect to value the damages that have been done to the College by the fury of the Revolution, and that he estimated them at 3000*l.* sterling; that many of their friends assured them they would be indemnified. Mr. Cleghorn and Mr. Tuite have lately paid a visit to the Nuns at Aire, and were happy to find them all very well. Mr. Cleghorn mentions that it is his opinion and that of some intelligent friends, that it will be extremely useful, if not necessary, to obtain some clause to be inserted in the Articles of Peace for the restoration of all our property. But it is a very delicate matter to determine the expression so as to include all and not to run counter to some of their constitutional decrees. This is a subject on which several letters have passed between Mr. Stapleton and Mr. Smith, who both of them very well understand the constitution and decrees as far as they affect our affairs. Mr. Stapleton expected Mr. Smith here before this; after an agreement with him about the form of the expression, he intended to do himself the honour to wait on your Lordship, to lay it before your Lordship and deliberate on this common cause. Bishop Gibson informs me that Mr. Daniel was to meet him and Mr. Smith at York last Wednesday or Thursday, when they would endeavour to come to some decision on measures to be taken in this critical situation of the Colleges. Mr. Sharrock informs me by a letter this morning that he has had the honor of speaking to your Lordship on the subject of a clause in our favor. He mentions the term Corporate Bodies. But we apprehend that that term would not suffice without some qualification, as Corporate Bodies are not acknowledged in the Republic. Besides, we must not forget the property in France which may stand in the name of individuals in the funds or elsewhere. If your Lordship should wish to receive any further information on the subject, Mr. Stapleton would be happy to communicate all in his power. I beg leave to conclude now, as Mr. D'Ancel is in a hurry. Mr. Stapleton begs leave to unite in most humble respects to your Lordship, with your Lordship's

"Most obedient and humble servant,

"W. POYNTER.

"Old Hall Green,
"August 19th, 1797.

"All unite in best respects and compliments to Mr. Barnard, Mr. Lindow, and Mr. Horrabin."

The following is again from the Diary of Bishop Douglass :—

"1797.—September 20th.—On this day arrived for Dinner from France Messrs. Tuite and Cleghorn. The three members (Jacobins) of the Directory, viz., La Ravillere Lepaux, Rewbel, and Barras having gained the army, surrounded the Councils and arrested Barthelemy, a director (Canot, the other Director, escaped), and all those of the Council of 500 who voted for the return of the priests and seemed to favour Royalty, among whom was my friend Camille Jourdain, of Lyons, who made the motion for the return of the priests, Merlin of Douay, and Francois of Neufchateau being chosen in the place of Barthelemy and Canot, members of the Directory, and the Revolution was completed. The negotiation for peace was broken off, Lord Malmesbury returned on this day to London, and the Minister of Police at Paris wrote to the Municipality at Calais to order Messrs. Tuite and Cleghorn to return to England by the first vessel.

"They dined with me to-day, and say that the College of St. Omer's is totally stript, that nothing remains of the building besides outward walls, the staircases and windows. It had been used for a hospital. That the priests who don't take the oath of hatred to kings, &c., are ordered to quit the territory of the Republic in 15 days, under pain of being treated as Emigrants and shot. That the Grand Vicars not knowing what advice to give, leave the priests to their own consciences, and that many orthodox priests have taken the oath, that many others are quitting France, and that all the little private oratories in private houses in which the orthodox priests used to say Mass, are now shut. When will the Revolution and these evils end?"

# APPENDIX E.

## RESULT OF THE DELIBERATIONS

Of the R.R.V.V.A.A., of the four districts, in a synod held at Winchester, May 23rd, 24th, and 25th, and continued at Old Hall Green, May 30th and 31st, 1803.

### On the Sacraments.

That all converts to the Catholic Faith who have been baptized by Sectaries or Ministers out of the Catholic Church within the space of thirty years, or from the year 1773, shall be baptized conditionally, except in cases where there is sufficient proof that the baptism was duly administered. This decision is to be inserted in the instructions annexed to the formula of faculties.

That it is advisable that children be brought to the Chapel to be baptized, unless it be attended with danger to the child or some considerable inconvenience.

That the baptismal water be blessed as soon as convenient, after the holy oils are received.

That the ceremony of having Sponsors in Confirmation is not observed in England.

That the rule of conduct delivered by Bishop Challoner in 1759, declaring that Catholics should first be married by a Catholic priest before they go to the Protestant minister, is to be observed in all the Districts.

That great caution be taken to prevent all superstition in the use of blessed wine given for the hooping cough, that missionaries rather confine themselves to those things which are strictly approved by the Church.

### Discipline.

That the strictest precautions are recommended with respect to foreign Priests, asking permission to say Mass.

That the practice of saying certain prayers in English before Mass on Sundays and Holidays, where the ceremonies permit it, is approved of. That it is very desirable that some approved prayers should be uniformly adopted for the four Districts, and be brought into use as far as can prudently be done. That in the meantime it is most prudent not to express any disapprobation of the different forms of prayer, now in use, but, if consulted, to recommend the approved prayers found in the Garden of the Soul and the Double Manual.

That it is desirable that approved lessons containing the authentic histories of the edifying lives of our English Saints should be compiled and inserted in their offices with due authority.

That the missionaries be exhorted to interest their congregations in the great and necessary work of providing for a succession of ministers of Religion, and to invite their people to concur by contributions, charitable donations, or pious legacies in enabling the Bishops to educate young men to the ecclesiastical state.

That a course of Divinity be composed for the use of our Seminaries and of the mission in general, by the Professors of Old Hall Green, of Crook Hall and of Actonburnel, with the assistance of some experienced missionaries, that the same should be recommended to the study of the clergy on the mission.

That the R.R.V.V.A.A. petition the Pope to grant their Lordships leave to confer Academical degrees on those of the clergy whom they shall judge worthy of these honours.

That the clergy be and are forbidden to go to plays *sub reatu peccati mortalis*, and under pain of suspension *ipso facto* for the secular clergy: which is to be inserted in the instructions annexed to missionary faculties.

That it is desirable that the missionaries would have power to grant leave to Catholics to give meat to Protestants, when entertained by Catholics, and when it cannot be refused without considerable inconvenience.

That the expediency of petitioning an abrogation of the ecclesiastical law enjoining abstinence from meat on Saturdays be further considered, and that inquiry be made concerning the practice of other countries.

That inquiry be made whether the conditions of all the indulgences be the same in all the Districts.

That the business of Pawnbrokers, when confined to the limits and rules prescribed by the Legislature, is not unlawful.

That a case be drawn up, and the Judges be consulted on the nature of the obligation of the law against smuggling.

That the instructions annexed to the formula of missionary faculties be revised and augmented with the additional clauses agreed to.

That the following are spiritual grievances to which Catholics are subject in England :—

1. The invalidity of the certificate of a Catholic Clergyman respecting the marriages of Catholics.
2. That Catholic soldiers, sailors and others, his Majesty's Catholic subjects of various descriptions, are forced to attend Protestant service on Sundays and on other occasions; that they are not at liberty on those days to unite in worship with those of their communion, even when their civil and military duties to his Majesty leave them free.
3. That the possession of Ecclesiastical property belonging to Catholics is legally insecure.

## APPENDIX F.

LETTER OF DR. POYNTER TO DR. BEW, PRESIDENT OF OSCOTT, ADVOCATING A UNION AMONG THE DISTRICTS TO FORM A SINGLE GENERAL COLLEGE.

"Old Hall Green, August 31st, 1803.

"DEAR SIR,—The ways and means of effectually providing for the mission in our present distress, and the still more distressful prospect that lays before us have been the frequent subject of my thought and conversation. Who can consider the number of the priests whose names appear in our obituary every year, and the small supplies which the mission receives, or has reason to expect from our Colleges in their present state without being alarmed? Doway, Paris and Rome at present yield nothing at all. Lisbon and Valladolid promise little (indeed Valladolid nothing for several years); Old Hall Green in its present state cannot promise more than at the rate of one a year; Crook Hall not much more. Oscott at present has two ready for orders. I do not understand that the mission can depend on Stonyhurst for a regular supply. The religious houses are reduced to the lowest state. From this it must appear evident that the resources of the mission are very inadequate to its wants. To support the establishment of the mission a constant supply of ten priests a year is necessary; but where are they to be found? In the present deficiency I think that the most effectual means should be employed to furnish an adequate number of labourers for this vineyard, and it appears to me that the most effectual would be as perfect an union of our Colleges as can possibly be formed. I know that Bishop Berington was desirous of having one Clergy College established for the four Districts, and he declared that if the other three Districts would accede to it, he should most readily agree. At present I see no prospect of engaging Bishop Gibson to unite in the plan, but I observe that the other three Bishops are desirous of it. Bishop Sharrock, indeed, acknowledges that he has little or nothing in his hands to contribute towards it; he is in singular distress. Although the effects of the proposed union will not be so extensive without the conjunction of the North, yet I am persuaded that the three districts, London, Middle, and West, will derive the greatest advantages from it, and that it will prove an effectual means of procuring an abundant supply of missionaries for them. The economy of the education is certainly a very considerable advantage; but I consider that this economy will appear not only in our being able to educate the Ecclesiastics at a cheaper rate (since where the number is greater, each individual may be maintained at a smaller expense), but likewise in our saving many for the Church who are often discouraged and sometimes laughed out of their vocation, where they are overpowered by the young Gentlemen of the World. It is of consequence that in a house destined for the education of Ecclesiastics, a very considerable number of the students should be of that description; they will then support and encourage one another in the trials they have to sustain; they will apply to their studies with more emulation and success; they will diffuse a general spirit of piety and religion which will animate them to ardour and perseverance in their vocation. All who have had experiences in Colleges must feel the advantages, I might almost say the necessity, of having such a number of candidates for the Church that they may have the preponderance in the College; where it is not so, it will be extremely difficult to inspire or support the Ecclesiastical spirit, and to preserve those for the Church who come with a good vocation. Neither Old Hall nor Oscott can pretend to say that they have not felt the bad effects of the want of a more considerable number of candidates for the Ecclesiastical state, nor can we expect ever to succeed in such a manner as to produce a sufficient supply for our Districts, unless they be collected in a greater number. But this cannot be done so as to answer our purpose, as long as we are two separate houses. We shall never collect a sufficient number in either house to produce the effect. On the article of economy I might add the advantage of saving masters, expenses of servants, &c., which will occur to a person accustomed to the details of a College.

"I will add, as an advantage, that in the system of the proposed union, our clergy would become more united and better acquainted with one another; they would be brought up in the same religious sentiments and principles which would contribute to promote that concord and harmony which we wish to see established. Although in different houses they would not differ in Faith, yet they might be brought up in certain diversities of opinion which are connected with practice, and which it must be an advantage to do away by having our young clergy educated in the same principles and sentiments, and in such as are recommended by their Bishops. I am far from thinking of introducing those scholastic questions which have divided universities; the great doctrines of religion now claim all the attention of theologians. But in this country, where we live among those who assume the liberty of thinking and speaking as they please on religious matters, it is of great consequence that our Divines should be well instructed in the doctrine and language of the Church, and they should be directed to follow one uniform rule in practice. It is well known that many of our missionaries differ too much in certain practical points in which it is to be desired that they should be united. To this I trust our proposed union will greatly contribute.

"But a very particular advantage which I have in view is that the Nobility and Gentry, seeing the Bishops uniting their influence and endeavours to provide a succession of missionaries, will come forward in a more generous and liberal manner to enable them to carry it into execution. We have not the means of educating such a number as is absolutely requisite to supply the wants of the mission. But I am persuaded that when the Bishops and their clergy unite in supporting and recommending one common establishment from which their Districts are supplied, the spirit of the Catholic body will be roused, and opulent Catholics will contribute generously to the support of so necessary a work.

"It is an important cause, and if some vigorous measures be not adopted for its success, our Districts will soon see their clergy sadly diminished, many Gentlemen's families and congregations will soon be without Pastors. The Bishops will recommend it to the charity of the opulent part of their Districts and will exhort their clergy to recommend it to their respective congregations. I hope to see them all united in promoting it with zeal. Surely every Pastor solicitous for the salvation of his flock must be concerned at the idea of leaving it without the means of instruction and spiritual assistance after his death, which must be the case of many congregations unless we provide for a succession. Now I am persuaded that this general spirit of contributing to this great cause will be more effectually roused by a union of the three Bishops in recommending one establishment. I am persuaded that, instead of having three free places for the Midland District, each of the three Districts will have nearly the proportion of ten or twelve. Does it not appear to you, Sir, that we have a great reason to expect a far more abundant supply for our Districts from this proposed union than from our Colleges in a separate state as they are at present? So great will be the advantage of having a greater number of candidates for the Ecclesiastical state collected together, and such will be the effect of an union on such as are enabled to contribute to its support. I flatter myself that the supporters of Oscott would readily agree to transfer the maintenance of the three destined for the Middle district to any other place where the Bishop, in union with his brethren, should judge proper to educate them in the proposed plan.

"I have hitherto explained my ideas of the advantages of an union only relative to the education of Ecclesiastics for the three Districts, in which I have no other view or motive than the prospect and desire of relieving the mission in its great distress by more effectually providing for a succession of labourers. But as to anything further, viz. the total coalition and union of the two houses in one, that is to be considered rather in another light. It appears indeed clear, that one large house is sufficient for all the English young Gentlemen who are, or probably will be in both; in that case many expenses would be reduced by an union. Fewer masters would be necessary (of course, more spared for the mission), expenses of servants, taxes, &c., considerably diminished. But we cannot remove young Gentlemen of fortune or those who pay for their own education, as we can others who are educated for the mission. This deserves consideration and may be determined one way or the other by circumstances with which I am not acquainted. I can only say, that if such a plan should appear to Bishop Milner and you and to the supporters of Oscott conducive to the general good, I should be very happy to show every mark of esteem and distinction to any Gentlemen who should come from Oscott to St. Edmund's. In this case the whole system of studies and discipline should be maturely considered and agreed to by the Bishops and others concerned, and what is agreed to be vigorously pursued.

"I have here proposed to your consideration my views and ideas concerning the effects of an union between our Colleges. As far as it relates to the education of those who are preparing for the Ecclesiastical state, I think it so necessary that neither District can entertain a hope of providing for itself without it. If it appear to you in the same light as it does to me, I doubt not you will readily accede to it. I consider it as the most effectual means of relieving the three districts in their pressing wants, which I believe no man feels more than Bishop Milner. If any plan be proposed more conducive to the end we have in view, I shall be happy to concur in it.

"I beg leave to assure you, Sir, &c.

"WILLIAM POYNTER."

# APPENDIX G.

## EXTRACT FROM BISHOP POYNTER'S MEMORIAL TO THE BRITISH COMMISSIONERS ON THE DOUAY CLAIMS.

To the Honourable Commissioners of his Britannic Majesty at Paris, appointed to liquidate the claims of British subjects on the French Government.

The MEMORIAL of the Right Rev. William Poynter, Bishop of Halia, Vicar Apostolic at London, in behalf of the claim of the Rev. John Daniel, a British subject, President of the English Secular College of Douay.

SHEWETH :—

THAT your Memorialist, who is deeply interested in the success of the Claim of the Rev. John Daniel, now before the Honourable Commissioners, has been informed that a question has been raised, whether the Rev. John Daniel, as representing the English Secular College at Doway, is included in the description of British Subjects who according to the terms of the Treaty of the 13th May, 1814, and of the Convention of the 20th Nov., 1815, are entitled to claim indemnities from the French Government, through the Honourable Commissioners, for property confiscated or sequestered in consequence of decrees in France since the 1st January, 1793, most respectfully begs to be allowed to offer some observations which may tend to place the subject in its true light, and to show that the right of Mr. Daniel, as representing the English Secular College at Doway, to the benefits of the Treaty and Convention, cannot, reasonably, be called in question.

In order to place the subject in its true light, your Memorialist begs to state the nature and condition of the establishment of this College, for which Mr. Daniel is claimant, and also to give a short account of the calamities and losses it has suffered since the 1st Jan., 1793, in consequence of French Decrees against British Subjects and British Property; observing,

1°. That this College was founded in the Town of Doway, in 1568, when Flanders was under the Dominion of Spain.

2°. That its eminent Founder was induced to establish it in a foreign realm, not from preference or choice, but from necessity at the time, and, as he declared in his Apology for the Seminaries, addressed to Cecil, Lord Burleigh, merely because he could not then, as a Catholic, have a place of education, nor even enjoy secure existence in England, adding that if his country would grant him security at home, he would transfer his Seminary thither immediately.

3°. That this College was established for the education only of English

Catholic Subjects, who as soon as they had completed their studies, or finished their course of Professorship, returned to England.

4°. That all Lands, Houses and Goods of every description, belonging to this College, were purchased, built and acquired with British Money and that the College did not derive any portion of its Property from France.

5°. That this College was never connected with any French establishment or institution; that it was not incorporated in the University of Doway, neither was it subject to the Rector or Masters of the University, nor to any board of superintendance or administration in France.

6°. That the Presidents of this College, all subjects of his Britannic Majesty, and not naturalized in France, were neither chosen nor presented nor nominated or appointed by any person, power or authority, civil or ecclesiastical, in France.

7°. That they were not responsible for the government or administration of the College to any French authority whatsoever; being subject only in matters *merely spiritual* (such as Preaching, Administering the Sacraments &c.) to the jurisdiction of the Diocesan Bishop, according to the general laws of the Catholic Church.

8°. That in the government of the College, all authority was, by the constitutions, subordinate to the President: "A strict obedience is to be observed, according to the subordination appointed by the President, who is absolute in his power; and though obliged to advise with the seniors, yet he is not tied to a majority, but may act independently." See Dodd, Vol. iii. p. 256, Records of Doway College.

9°. That only the President could give a power of attorney to receive the *Rentes sur l'Etat*, and other monies due to the College; that the possession of the whole of the property belonging to the College was invested in the President, who alone, by the constitutions had the sole absolute administration of it.

10°. That this College, merely existing on French soil, as an isolated English Establishment, foreign in every respect to France, to which neither the Members nor Superiors were ever bound by any oath or promise of allegiance, had continued from its beginning to the period of the French Revolution in the free exercise of its government, and of the administration of its property, independently of any authority of superintendence or administration in France.

11°. That early in the French Revolution, when the National Assembly decreed the suppression of French Establishments of Education, and seized the goods of those establishments as national property, it respected this as a Foreign Establishment, although it called for and seized all the Title Deeds of this College, as well as those of other British Houses of Education, to examine whether all the property held by them was of British origin: that whilst the French authorities took that portion of the property of some other British houses which was derived from France, leaving the same houses in possession of the rest, as British property, they left the President of Doway College in possession of the whole of the property belonging to this establishment, confirming his rightful possession of it as British Property, according to the Law of the 7th Nov., 1790, and the Decrees of the 8th and 12th March, 1793, in which the future modifications alluded to evidently do not relate to the property, but to the mode of education which the superiors of these foreign houses of education were free to reject.

12°. That the Superiors of this College as well as of the other British Establishments, maintained their independence of the new laws made at the beginning of the Revolution by claiming the rights of foreigners. That the Civic Oath was never taken by them. That the following Arrête which was at last obtained from the Assemblée Nationale 14 June, 1791, settled the point in their favour: "L'Assemblée Nationale par l'organ de son Comité Ecclesiastique ordonne que les Supérieurs Étrangers ne sont pas des fonctionnaires publics Ecclesiastiques ; que l'on ne peut exiger d'eux aucun des points exigibles des Nationaux ; que le Département doit leur procurer paix et protection. Etant evident qu'on ne peut pas être en même temps étrangers et natifs, il est également qu'on n'est pas tenu aux formalités exigibles des uns et des autres ; il est donc constant que les lois relatifs aux Ecclesiastiques François ne peuvent pas atteindre les Etrangers ; ils ne doivent pas se rendre inhabiles à succéder dans leur pays, ni s'assujettir à aucun serment, aucune formalité que puisse devenir un titre de proscription chez eux." Moreover, that the Superiors of the English Catholic establishments in France claimed as foreigners under the treaty of navigation and commerce of 26th September, 1786, their exemption from any obligation of attending the public ceremonies of Divine Service in the churches or elsewhere, and their privilege of performing the exercises of religion privately in their own houses without molestation. That this claim of the English Catholic Establishments to the benefit of the Treaty of Navigation and Commerce in that respect was acknowledged and confirmed by the answer of the Comité Ecclesiastique to the Directory of the department du Pas de Calais à Arras, 14 June, 1791, of which a copy is annexed.

13°. That in December, 1791, when in virtue of a severe decree ordering all Ecclesiastics who had not taken the oath (*non-assermentés*) to appear personally before the Directory, the Superiors of the five British houses in Doway were peremptorily summoned to appear within a limited time. One Superior was deputed from each house to the Directory They all remonstrated strongly that being foreigners they were not to be classed either with the " Prêtres Assermentés " or with the " Prêtres non Assermentés," being at most " Fonctionnaires Publics " of their respective countries, now *in* France but not *of* France. That the five deputies of the British Houses were politely dismissed with an assurance that a due regard should be paid to their remonstrance. That the next morning a favourable message was sent to each of the five British Houses.

14°. That the Rev. John Daniel was duly appointed President of the English Secular College of Doway in the beginning of the year 1792.

15°. That in the month of February, 1793, commissaries, accompanied by a detachment of national guards, proceeded to put the public seals on all the effects in the College.

16°. That on the 10th of October, 1793, a Decree was passed in the National Assembly, ordering that all the moveable and immoveable property, and all the goods of every description in France belonging to the English, Scotch, Irish, Hanoverians, and in general to the subjects of the King of Great Britain, should be confiscated for the Property of the Republic, and that these goods should immediately on the receipt of this Decree be seized and put into the hands of the Managers of the National Domains. Also ordering that all the English, Scotch, Irish, Hanoverians, and in general all the subjects of the King of Great Britain, actually on the territory of the Republic, should instantly, on the receipt of this Decree, be put in a state of arrestation, and that the seals should be put on their papers. That the punishment of ten years imprisonment should be inflicted on any public functionary who should be convicted of negligence in the execution of this Decree. That the decree was sent into the departments by couriers extraordinary.

17°. That on the 12th October, 1793, the Rev. John Daniel, President of the College, and the present claimant; the Rev. Joseph Hodgson, Vice-President and now Vicar-General of the London district; the Rev. William Poynter, your Memorialist, then Professor of Divinity, now Bishop Vicar Apostolic in London; the Rev. Thomas Smith, 1st Professor of Philosophy, now Bishop Coadjutor in the North; the Rev. William Wilds, then 2nd Professor of Philosophy, now Chaplain in the Bavarian Chapel, London; the Rev. Thomas Stout, then General Prefect in the College, now Pastor of a Congregation near Alnwick; the Rev. Joseph Beaumont, Procurator (or Bursar) of the College, now Pastor near Bath, with several Scholars, altogether in number forty-seven, were suddenly summoned at eight o'clock in the evening, and conducted immediately by an armed force from the English College to the Scotch College in Doway; that they were all confined there as prisoners till October 16th, together with seven English Benedictins; that on the 16th October they were all conducted by an armed force to Arras, and on the 17th October were conducted in like manner to the citadel of Dourlens, in Picardy; that twenty-two of the company having effected their escape, the rest, thirty-two in number, including the English Benedictins, were confined in this citadel thirteen months, during which they suffered great distress and extreme hardships; that in the month of December, 1794, they were all permitted to return from Dourlens to Doway, where they were again shut up under still closer confinement in the Irish College for three months longer; that leave having been obtained by the exertions of the Rev. Mr. Stapleton, then President of the English College at St. Omer, for all the Superiors and Students of the English Houses in Douay and St. Omer to return to England, they all hastened to their native country and arrived at Dover on the 4th of March, 1795,[1] after having lost all their property in France and suffered imprisonment and most extreme hardships, *because they were British subjects*, in execution of the Decree of 10th Oct., 1793.

18°. That as soon as the Rev. John Daniel, President, with his Professors and Scholars, were put into confinement, the doors of the College were thrown open for three days, during which part of the furniture was sold, the rest of the goods that could be easily moved and carried off was plundered by the mob. That the libraries were soon after removed, and now do not exist. That the country house of the College in the village of Esquerchin and the lands at Coutiches and Bersée were sold. That the building of the College itself was in a short time, after Mr. Daniel and his Professors and Scholars were put into arrestation, converted into a military hospital, and was employed as such for about ten years; that it was afterwards let on a long lease (of about 27 years) to a cotton manufacturer, by Mr. Walsh, an Irishman, appointed by Buonaparte, Administrator General of all the British Establishments. That the offices and outbuildings of the college have been demolished, and the partitions and interior distributions of the apartment have been so changed that it is no longer fit for the purposes of a college.

19°. That the *rentes sur l'état*, which the President of the College was in the receipt of in the year 1792, were sequestered in the execution of the decree of 10th Oct., 1793, and that they are still withheld from Rev. John Daniel, who claims them with their Arrears through the British Commissioners.

20°. That in short, from the time of his arrestation on the 12th Oct.,

---

[1] This is a slight error. The actual date was March 2nd, 1795.

1793, in consequence of the Decree of the 10th of the same month, the Rev. John Daniel has suffered the loss of his College and all the property belonging to it by confiscation or sequestration in execution of the same decree against all British subjects. That he still remains deprived of the whole, except merely the property of the house, which was restored to him by an order of 26 Jan., 1816, into which nevertheless he cannot enter till the expiration of the lease, but for which he has received an annual rent of 2500 francs since the date of that *Ordonnance*. That such are the calamities and losses which have been brought on the Rev. John Daniel as President of the English Secular College of Douay, by execution of the Decree of 10th Oct., 1793, *because he was a British Subject and the Head and Representative of a British Establishment and of British Property.*

21°. That Buonaparte, by a Decree dated 28 floreal, an 13 (18th of May, 1805,) with declared political views hostile to England, formed one British United Establishment, by connecting together houses of education in France, which belonged to the English, Scotch, and Irish Catholics; that he appointed Mr. Walsh, first Administrator General of the new United Establishment and of all the English, Irish, and Scotch property in France, which he could collect together, as the remains of the property formerly possessed by those houses. That Buonaparte instituted a Board of Superintendance (Bureau de Surveillance), to which he subjected the administration of his United Establishment.

22°. That the British Catholic Archbishops and Bishops protested against this act of the usurpation of the rights of the legitimate Superiors and Administrators of their Colleges and Seminaries in France, and this invasion of their respective foreign property and demanded justice; but in vain.

23°. That on the 21st June, 1814, the signature of His Most Christian Majesty was obtained to an *Ordonnance*, by which the above Decree of Buonaparte of 28 floreal, an 13, was confirmed, and Mr. Ferris, an Irishman, was named Administrator General of all the English, Irish, and Scotch Colleges and Seminaries in France ; and that on the 30th Oct., 1815, the signature of the King was in like manner obtained to another *Ordonnance*, forming in the terms of the former *Ordonnance*, a *Bureau Gratuit de Surveillance Générale*, and continuing the same system of the violation of the rights and property of the respectful lawful superiors.

24°. That on the remonstrance made to the King by Archbishop Everard, Bishop Cameron, and your Memorialist, Bishop Poynter, in the names of all the Catholic Archbishops and Bishops in Ireland, Scotland, and England, His Most Christian Majesty was pleased to issue an *Ordonnance* on the 25th Jan., 1816, by which the union of the British Establishments was dissolved and Mr. Ferris was removed, and the separate possession of the moveable and immoveable property which had not been sold, belonging to the different British houses, was restored to the respective superiors, who, in the 6th Article, were acknowledged by name. That the Rev. John Daniel recovered nothing more by the effect of this *Ordonnance*, than a claim to the future rent of his college at Doway, which had been let on a long lease by Mr. Walsh. That conceiving that under the terms moveable property might be understood the Rentes sur l'Etat, and wishing to save the inconvenience of the delay attending the liquidation of the great number of claims in the hands of the Honourable Commissioners, your Memorialist applied to the French Treasury in March, 1816, to have Mr. Daniel inscribed on the Great Book for the amount of these *Rentes* and their Arrears, in execution of the *Ordonnance* of the 25th Jan., 1816; that the answer given was, that under the terms moveable property, the *Rentes* were not understood, unless expressly specified. That your Memorialist then obtained an order from the King to the Minister of Finance to proceed to the liquidation and inscription of these *Rentes*, &c.; that the Minister of Finance answered your Memorialist that this order must be ineffectual, as by the Treaty and Convention (to which the *Ordonnance* itself of the 25th Jan. referred) the liquidation and inscription of these *Rentes* must be done by the Commissioners appointed for that purpose. That notwithstanding, a letter was afterwards sent from the Treasury to the French Commissioners, recommending to them to accelerate the liquidation of the claims of the Rev. John Daniel.

25°. That on the 17th Sept., 1817, the King's signature was again obtained to a new *Ordonnance*, grounded on considerations and informations which in no manner regard the English Secular Houses of Doway and Paris, by the articles of which *Ordonnance* the *Bureau Gratuit de Surveillance* is brought into activity again, is invested with new powers over the British Establishments, is authorized to demand of the Superiors the state of their accounts, to take from them the money they have in hand, except what is judged by the Bureau necessary for current expenses, to interfere in the discipline of the Houses and even to make regulations for them. That the Minister of the Interior is authorized by the order to suspend or remove the Superiors who do not conform to these Articles and to propose to the King the appointment of others.

26°. That your Memorialist, sensible that, as a Catholic Bishop, and as a British Subject, he could not consent to this *Ordonnance*, entered his protest to the French Government against it, as a violation of the independent government and administration of the English Secular College of Doway and of the English Seminary at Paris, enjoyed and exercised by the superiors of these English Houses, to the period of the French Revolution; that he has protested against the subjection of these Foreign Establishments to the *Bureau Gratuit de Surveillance* and called for the revocation of all the Decrees, *Arrêtes* or *Ordonnances* made from the beginning of the Revolution, injurious to the independent rights and interests of these Foreign Establishments. That in his remonstrance to the Minister of the Interior, dated Dec., 1817, your Memorialist observed to his Excellency that the considerations in the preamble on which the ordonnance was grounded were utterly void of foundation, at least inasmuch as they regarded the English Secular College at Doway and the English Seminary at Paris. Your Memorialist expressed his observations in these terms: "Le considérant parle des Supérieurs-Majeurs chargés autrefois de diriger ces Etablissemens sous l'Autorité Royale; et aussi d'une Commission de Magistrats pris dans le sein du Conseil d'Etat, à laquelle étoit confiée depuis longues années le surveillance de cette administration. J'ai l'honneur de représenter à votre Excellence, qu'il n'y a jamais eu de Supérieurs-Majeurs chargés de diriger ces Etablissemens de Douay et de Paris, sous l'Autorité Royale, et aussi que la surveillance de l'administration de ces Etablissemens, loin d'avoir été confiées depuis longues anneés, ne l'a jamais été à aucune Commission de Magistrats pris dans le sein du Conseil d'Etat, ni à aucun Bureau de Surveillance en France."

27°. That your Memorialist having shewn that this secular College of Doway, for which the Rev. J. Daniel is Claimant, is completely English in every respect, and that all the property belonging to it was confiscated or sequestered as *English property*, in execution of the decree of 10th Oct., 1793, now presumes to express his confidence that no reasonable objection can be brought against the claimant, Rev. John Daniel, a British-born Subject, and as President sole Representative of all this British property, but that he will be admitted to the full benefit of the Treaty and Convention. As the Treaty and Convention were expressly made to secure indemnities from the French Government for the subjects of his Britannic Majesty, who have been injured by the effects of Decrees of confiscation and sequester in France, since the 1st Jan., 1793, it is lawful to contend that all such subjects of his Britannic Majesty are included against whom there is not a clear exception expressed in the terms of the Treaty and Convention.

. . . . . . .

Your Memorialist begs, with all due respect, to submit the above Statement, Observations and Answers to your fair consideration, and has the honour to subscribe himself, Honourable Gentlemen,

Your humble and obedient servant,

(Signed)   W. POYNTER, Bp. of Halia, V.A. at London.

Paris, Jan. 27th, 1818.

# APPENDIX H.

### PRESIDENTS OF DOUAY COLLEGE.

1568—1588. Cardinal Allen.
1588—1599. Rev. Richard Barrett, D.D.
1599—1613. Rev. Thomas Worthington, D.D.
1613—1641. Rev. Matthew Kellison, D.D.
1641—1645. Rev. George Musket.
1646—1651. Rev. William Hyde, D.D.
1652—1670. Rev. George Leyburn, D.D.
1670—1676. Rev. John Leyburn.
1676—1682. Rev. Francis Gage, D.D.
1682—1688. Rev. James Smith, D.D.
1688—1714. Rev. Edward Paston, D.D.
1715—1738. Rev. Robert Witham, D.D.
1739—1750. Rev. William Thornburgh, D.D.
1750—1770. Rev. William Green, D.D.
1770—1781. Rev. Tichbourne Blount.
1781—1790. Rev. William Gibson.
1790—1792. Rev. Edward Kitchen.
1792—1793. Rev. John Daniel.

The Rev. John Daniel continued titular President till his death in 1823, when he was succeeded by the Rev. Francis Tuite, who died in 1837, and was the last to hold the title of President of Douay.

### PRESIDENTS OF ST. OMER.

After the College was handed over to the Secular Clergy.

1762—1763. Rev. Henry Tichbourne Blount (*pro tem.*).
1763—1766. Hon. and Rev. Thomas Talbot.
1766—1773. Rev. Alban Butler.
1773—1787. Rev. William Wilkinson.
1787—1793. Rev. Gregory Stapleton, D.D.

### "CHIEF MASTERS."

At Silkstead, Twyford, Standon, Hare Street, and Old Hall.

#### *Silkstead.*

1685—1692. Rev. Augustine Taylor.
1692—(about) 1695. Rev. William Husband.

*Twyford.*

(About) 1695— . Rev. Edward Taverner.
1726—1732. Rev. Francis Fleetwood.
1732—1736. Rev. Joseph Gildon.
1736—1745. Rev. John P. Betts.

*Standon and Hare Street*

1753—1769. Rev. Richard Kenda

*Old Hall.*

1769—1792. Rev. James Willacy.
1792—1793. Rev. John Potier.

### ST. EDMUND'S COLLEGE.
#### PRESIDENTS.

1793—1795. Rev. John Potier (*pro tem.*).
1795—1801. Very Rev. Gregory Stapleton, D.D.
1801—1813. Right Rev. Bishop Poynter, D.D.
1813—1817. Very Rev. Joseph Kimbell.
1817—1818. Very Rev. John Bew, D.D
1818—1834. Very Rev. Thomas Griffiths, D.D.
1834—1837. Very Rev. Richard Newell, D.D.
1838—1840. Very Rev. John Rolfe.
1840—1851. Very Rev. Edward Cox, D.D.
1851—1868. Right Rev. Mgr. Weathers, D.D.
1868—1870. Very Rev. Frederick Rymer, D.D.
1870—1880. Right Rev. Mgr. Patterson, M.A.
1880—1882. Very Rev. George Akers, M.A.
1882—1887. Right Rev. Mgr. Fenton.
1887. Right Rev. Mgr. Crook.

#### VICE-PRESIDENTS.

1795—1801. Rev. William Poynter, D.D.
1801—1808. Rev. William Coombes, D.D.
1808—1810. Rev. Francis Tuite.
1810—1813. Rev. Joseph Kimbell.
1813—1816. Rev. Robert Varley.
1816—1818. Rev. Thomas Griffiths.
1819—1824. Rev. John White.
1824—1834. Rev. Richard Newell.
1834—1836. Rev. Bernard Jarrett.
1836—1838. Rev. John Maguire, D.D.
1838—1840. Rev. Edward Cox.
1840—1843. Rev. George Rolfe.
1843—1851. Rev. William Weathers, D.D.
1851—1855. Rev. John Crookall, D.D.
1855—1861. Rev. Herbert Vaughan, D.D.

---

[1] The office of vice-president was formally introduced on the reconstitution of St. Edmund's in 1795. From 1793 to 1795 Dr. Coombes acted as "Second in authority and respect," and was the superior of the Divines; but did not at that time take the title of vice-president. There was likewise no regular prefect or procurator before 1795.

## Appendix.

1861—1868. Rev. Frederick Rymer.
1868—1870. Rev. Isaac Goddard.
1870—1877. Rev. John Rouse, D.D.
1877—1880. Rev. George Akers, M.A.
1880—1882. Rev. William Smullen.
1882—1887. Rev. William Lloyd.
1887—1889. Rev. William Traies, M.A.
1890. Rev. Bernard Ward.

### Prefects.

1795—1798. Rev. John Law.
1798—1800. Rev. Francis Tuite.
1800—1802. Rev. J. C. D'Ancel.
1802—1803 { Rev. Francis Tuite. / Rev. Walter Blount.
1803—1806. Rev. Joseph Kimbell.
1806—1810. Rev. Robert Varley.
1810—1816. Rev. Joseph Stapleton.
1816—1819. Rev. John White.
1819—1820. Rev. Joseph Siddens.
1820—1822. Rev. Richard Newell.
1822—1825. Rev. James Holdstock.
1825—1826. Rev. Edward Ewart.
1826—1827. Rev. John Welch.
1827—1828. Rev William Woods.
1828—1830. Rev. Charles Threlfall.
1830—1833. Rev. William Hunt.
1833—1834. Rev. Bernard Jarrett.
1834—1836. Rev. Edward Hearne.
1836—1839. Rev. John Tilt.
1839—1840. Rev. John Telford.
1840—1843. Rev. William Weathers.
1843—1848. Rev. Henry Telford.
1848—1851. Rev. Frederick Rymer.
1851—1851. Rev. Michael Canty.
1851—1856. Rev. Henry O'Callaghan.
1856—1861. Rev. Thomas McDonnell.
1861—1865. Rev. Charles Bell.
1865—1866. Rev. James R. Browne.
1866—1868. Rev. William Lloyd.
1869—1869. Rev. Edward Redmond, D.D.
1869—1872. Rev. John Brenan.
1872—1873. Rev. William Lloyd.
1873—1874. Rev. John Brenan.
1874—1876. Rev. Peter Kernan.
1876—1877. Rev. William Herbert.
1877—1879. Rev. William Smullen.
1879—1881. Rev. John O'Meara.
1881—1882. Rev. Edward Ryan.
1882—1884. Rev. Bernard Ward.
1884—1884. Rev. John Boase.
1884—1884. Rev. John Watson.
1884—1885. Rev. Bernard Ward.
1886—1891. Rev. William Davies.
1891. Rev. Frederick Hopper.

## PROCURATORS.

1795—1798. Rev. Francis Tuite.
1798—1800. Rev. John Law.
1800—1810. Rev. Francis Tuite.
1810—1815. Rev. Richard Horrabin.
1815—1817. Rev. Joseph Daniel.
1817—1818. Rev. John Rolfe.
1818—1819. Rev. Mark Tierney.
1819—1824. Rev. Thomas Griffiths.
1824—1830. Rev. John Clarke.
1830—1832. Rev. Charles Threlfall.
1832—1839. Rev. James Whelan.
1839—1843. Rev. George Rolfe.
1843—1851. Rev. William Weathers.
1851—1852. Mr. Henry Reilly.
1852—1856. Rev. Henry Telford.
1856—1861. Rev. Edmund Tunstall.
1861—1878. Rev. William McAuliffe.
1878—1879. Rev. Edmund Tunstall.
1879—1880. Rev. Joseph Palmer.
1880—1883. Mr. Thomas Inwood.
1883—1885. Rev. Edward St. John.
1886—1887. Rev. Arthur Byrne.
1888—1891. Rev. Charles Turner.
1891. Rev. William Davies.

## PARISH PRIESTS AT OLD HALL.

1769—1792. Rev. James Willacy.
1792—1810. Rev. John Potier.
1810—1815. Rev. Richard Horrabin.
1815—1818. Rev. Thomas Griffiths.
1818—1819. Rev. Louis Havard.
1819—1824. Rev. John White.
1824—1827. Rev. John Hutchison.
1828—1830. Rev. John Clarke.
1830—1838. Rev. Charles Threlfall.
1838—1839. Rev. George Rolfe.
1839—1840. Rev. William Crook.
1840—1842. Rev. Patrick O'Dwyer.
1842—1845. Rev. John Geary.
1845—1848. Rev. John Ainsworth.
1848—1849. Rev. John Larkin.
1849—1851. Rev. Walter McAvila.
1851—1859. Rev. Alfred Dolman.
1859—1861. Rev. William A. Johnson, D.D.
1861—1864. Rev. Thomas Parkinson.
1864—1864. Rev. John Wyse.
1864—1865. Rev. Charles Bullen.
1865—1871. Rev. Robert Swift.
1871—1874. Rev. Charles Collingridge.
1874—1875. Rev. Henry Joyner.
1875—1876. Rev. Anthony Glattfelter.
1876—1878. Rev. Philip Gun Munro.
1878—1879. Rev. Joseph Redman, D.D.

1879—1882. Rev. John Noonan.
1882—1883. Rev. Alfred Roche.
1883—1883. Rev. James Horan.
1883—1884. Rev. Daniel O'Sullivan.
1884—1885. Rev. John H. Pape.
1885. Rev. Charles Jones.

## CARDINALS, ARCHBISHOPS, AND BISHOPS CONNECTED WITH ST. EDMUND'S.

In the following list, those marked with an asterisk were only connected with Old Hall as proprietors. The others were all superiors or students at the college.

*His Eminence Cardinal Wiseman, Bishop of Melipotamus, 1840—1850; V.A. London, 1849—1850; Archbishop of Westminster, 1850—1865.
*His Eminence Cardinal Manning, Archbishop of Westminster, 1865—1892.
His Eminence Cardinal Vaughan, Bishop of Salford, 1872—1892; Archbishop of Westminster, 1892.
His Eminence Cardinal di Rende, Bishop of Tricarico, 1877—1879; Archbishop of Benevento, 1879.
The Most Rev. Henry O'Callaghan, Bishop of Hexham, 1888—1889; Archbishop of Nicosia, 1889.
Right Rev. Charles Baggs, Bishop of Pella and V.A. Western, 1844—1845.
*Right Rev. James Yorke Bramston, Bishop of Usula, 1823; V.A. London, 1827—1836.
Right Rev. John Butt, Bishop of Melos, 1885 (January); Bishop of Southwark, 1885 (June).
Right Rev. Gonzalo Canilla, Bishop of Lystra, and Vicar Apostolic of Gibraltar, 1881.
*Right Rev. Robert Aston Coffin, Bishop of Southwark, 1882—1885.
Right Rev. James Richard D'Ancel, Bishop of Bayeux, 1827—1836.
Right Rev. James Danell, Bishop of Southwark, 1871—1881.
*Right Rev. John Douglass, Bishop of Centuriæ and V.A. London, 1790—1812.
*Right Rev. Thomas Grant, Bishop of Southwark, 1851—1870.
Right Rev. Thomas Griffiths, Bishop of Olena, 1833; V.A. London, 1836—1847.
Right Rev. Thomas Jumentier, Bishop in France about 1815.
Right Rev. John Luck, Bishop of Auckland, 1882.
Right Rev. James Laird Patterson, Bishop of Emmaus, 1880.
Right Rev. Thomas Penswick, Bishop of Europum, 1824; V.A. North, 1831—1836.
Right Rev. William Poynter, Bishop of Halia, 1803; V.A. London, 1812—1827.
Right Rev. Gregory Stapleton, Bishop of Hiero-Cæsarea, and V.A. Mid., 1801—1802.
*Right Rev. James Talbot, Bishop of Bertha, 1759; V.A. London, 1781—1790.
Right Rev. William Weathers, Bishop of Amycla, 1872.
Right Rev. John Virtue, Bishop of Portsmouth, 1882.

## Bishops Consecrated at St. Edmund's.

Right Rev. Gregory Stapleton, Bishop of Hiero-Cæsarea, March 8, 1801.
Right Rev. William Poynter, Bishop of Halia, May 29, 1803.
Right Rev. Bernardine Collingridge, Bishop of Thespia, October 11, 1807.
Right Rev. Thomas Smith, Bishop of Bolina, March 11, 1810.
Right Rev. James Yorke Bramston, Bishop of Usula, June 29, 1823.
Right Rev. Thomas Weld, Bishop of Amycla, August 6, 1826.
Right Rev. Daniel McDonnell, Bishop of Olympus, March 25, 1829.
Right Rev. William Morris, Bishop of Troy, February 5, 1832.
Right Rev. Thomas Griffiths, Bishop of Olena, October 28, 1833.

# INDEX.

Abbott, Mr., 227.
Acton Burnell, 150, 152.
Adelphi, the, 265.
Aire, 151
    Bishop of, 205.
Akers, Rev. George, 287.
Alberry, Joseph, 232.
Albert, Prince, 245.
Allen, Cardinal, 3, 5, 50 *seq.*, 285.
Amherst, Bishop, 282.
    Rev. William J., 42, 119.
Amiens, Bishop of, 62, 84.
    Peace of, 180.
Ancona, 178.
Angelo, Mr., 201 *seq.*
Angoulême, Bishop of, 205.
Ankerwycke Park, 165.
Applegath, Canon, 230.
Archbold, Robert, 176.
Archer's Lodge, 257, 259.
Arras, 64, 66, 79, 80, 85, 86, 90, 91, 93, 97.
Arrington, 201, 202.
Association, Edmundian, 272, 279, 282.
Aston, the Lords, 19, 22, 208.
Atkinson, Rev. Matthew, 4.
Auckland, Bishop of, 277
Auxerre, 288, 289.

Backhouse, Margaret, 11.
Baddesley Green Academy, 41.
Baggs, Bishop, 230.
Bagshawe, Canon, 243, 275.
Baines, Bishop, 234.
Bamber, Canon James, 243, 280, 282.
Bamber, Canon John, 243, 255, 272.
Bampfield, Rev. George, 253.
Bangs, Mr., 188.
Banister, *see* Taverner.
Bans, Canon, 6, 243, 247.
Barbadoes, 12.
Barbier, Père, 291.
Barnaby Rudge, 231.

Barnard, Rev. James, 23, 26, 107, 137, 157, 160, 165, 168.
Barratt, Dr. Richard, 56.
Barrett, Dr., 183.
Barron, Joseph, 258.
Barrow, Rev. John, 161 *seq.*
Bates, John, 85.
Bath, 102.
Bayeux, Bishop of, 117.
Beauchamp, William, 100, 102, 104, 108, 146.
Bedford, Duke of, 285.
Bedhampton, 128, 135.
Benevento, Archbishop of, 280.
Bennett, Martin, 105.
Berington, Bishop, 124, 135, 136, 151, 159, 160, 179.
Berington, Rev. Joseph, 40.
    Rev. Thomas, 13.
Bernadou, Archbishop, 277.
Bernard, *see* Husband.
Bertha, Bishop of, *see* James Talbot.
Bethune, 86, 95.
Betts, Rev. John P., 13 *seq.*
    Dr. John, 14.
Bew, Rev. John, 118, 119, 181, 218 *seq.*
Bianchini, Mgr., 10.
Birch, Rev. Joseph, 64, 117, 146, 206.
Birmingham, 40, 206.
Bishop, Dr., 5.
Bishop's Stortford, 104, 245.
Blakesware, 32.
Blakoe, Robert, 84.
Blount, Sir Walter, 31.
    Edward, 195.
Blundell, Charles, 249.
Borgia, Cardinal, 179.
Boulogne, Bishop of, 62, 63.
Bourdaloue, 239.
Bowdon, Rev. Joseph, 296.
Bower, Canon, 230.
    William, 230.

z

Bowland, Francis, 102, 104, 108, 146.
Bowman, Canon, 243, 263.
Bowyer, Sir George, 282.
Bradley, John, 85.
Brady, Mazière, 122, 131, 137, 212, 265.
Brady, Thomas, 77.
Braganza, Catherine of, 283.
Bramston, Bishop, 157, 215, 226, 233, 237, 240, 241.
Brand, Mrs., 34.
Brannan, Mr., 227.
Braughing, 256.
Brettargh, Rev. Richard, 92.
Brewer, Dr., 183.
Brighton, 218.
Bristow, Richard, 53, 55.
Broadstone of Honour, 233.
Brockhampton, 129, 221.
Broderick, Richard, 120, 146, 165.
Brook Green, 269.
Brown, Rev. Thomas, *alias* Weatherby, 6, 7.
Brown Mostyn, 91.
Browne, Rev. Peter, 13, 17.
    Michael, 208.
    Thomas, 208.
    Valentine, 189, 208.
    William, 208.
Broxbourne, 245.
Bruges, 61.
Brussels, 81.
Buckler, Rev. Albert, 243.
    Rev. Edmund, 243.
Bulbeck, John, 120, 128, 146.
Buntingford, 39, 201, 202, 245, 246.
Buonaparte, 183, 190, 235.
Burke, Mr., 26.
Butler, Rev. Alban, 26, 51, 62.
    Arthur, 38.
    Charles, 26, 28, 42, 62.
    John, 38, 129, 167.
    Rev. Robert, 243, 253.
    Thomas, 38.
Butt, Bishop, 174 *seq.*, 243, 253.

CALAIS, 77, 95.
Cambridge, 1, 19, 233, 245, 246.
Camera, Alvavo, 282.
Camoys, Lord, 209.
Campion, B. Edmund, 53, 54.
Canford House, 247.
Canning, John, 85.
Canning, Mr., 237.
Canterbury, 293, 296.
Canty, Rev. Michael, 254.
Carlton Hall, 62.
Carron, Abbé, 204.
Casali, 249.
Castlerosse, Lord, 189, 208.

Castle Street, 47, 97, 136, 157, 181, 191, 219.
Catherine of Braganza, 283.
Cavrois, 64.
Centuria, Bishop of, *see* Douglass.
Challoner, Bishop, 15, 21 *seq.*, 31, 35, 41, 43, 102, 212, 239.
Chambéry, Archbishop of, 291.
Charles II., 13, 258, 283.
Charles X., 233.
Charles Edward, 15.
Chauncy, 18, 21.
Chelsea, 242, 243.
Cherbourg, 117.
Chester, Dr., 90.
Chichester, 294.
Clarke, Rev. John, 229.
Clarke, Rev. H., 275.
Clarkson, John, 75, 86, 102, 105, 146, 165, 227.
Claughton, 161, 162.
Cleghorn, Thomas, 51, 91, 137, 146, 147, 168, 169, 181, 211, 227, 234, 236.
Clifford, Arthur, 31, 146, 165, 208.
    Bishop, 282.
    Francis, 290.
    Miss, 173.
    Thomas, 31.
Clutterbuck, 34.
Coelian Hill, 297.
Coffin, Bishop, 280.
Colliers' End, 11, 231.
Collingridge, Bishop, 234.
Colwich, 12.
Commercial Road, 215.
Compostella, 289.
Connolly, Rev. John, 247, 258.
Constantinople, 275.
Cook, Thomas, 49, 81, 100, 102, 146.
Coombes, Rev. William H., 51, 78 *seq.*, 97, 99, 100 *seq.*, 112, 113, 115, 116, 145, 175, 173.
Coombes, Rev. William (senior), 111, 124.
Cork, Bishop of, 175, 179.
Corney, Charles, 38, 88, 89, 91, 230, 272.
Corney, John, 38.
Cosnac, Bishop, 290.
Covey, Dr., 278.
Cox, Rev. Edward, 230, 242 *seq.*, 264, 266, 269, 274, 281.
Crimea, 274.
Crook, Mgr., 6, 243, 280, 299.
Crookall, Mgr., 243, 245, 247, 249, 251, 268, 271, 278, 282.
Crook Hall, 50, 51, 58, 97, 109, 112, 114, 115, 117, 124, 131 *seq.*, 140,

150, 156 *seq.*, 161, 179, 180, 185, 186, 189, 194, 196, 197, 213.
Cuffe, Rev., 275.
Cullen, Rev. E., 219.
Cupola House, 283.

D'ANCEL, Bishop, 157, 121, 146, 147, 165.
Dancoisne, Abbé, 143, 235.
Danell, Bishop, 243, 245, 246, 255.
Daniel, Rev. John, 61, 69, 72, 77, 83, 84, 92, 96, 97, 124 *seq.*, 131, 154 *seq.*, 164, 168, 181 *seq.*, 235 *seq.*
Daniel, Rev. Joseph, 216, 217.
Deane, Rev. Thomas, 8.
Debra, Bishop of, *see* Challoner.
Delaney, James, 102, 146.
Delawarr, Earl of, 246.
De Lisle, Ambrose Phillipps, 233.
    Ambrose, 243.
    Everard, 243.
Devereux, John, 49, 80, 97, 99, 100, 102, 146.
Dickenson, Constable, 200.
Digby, Kenelm, 233.
Dillon, Rev. James, 41.
    Rev. Thomas, 243.
Dodd, *see* Tootell.
Dolan, Lawrence, 243, 255, 272.
    Rev. William I., 243, 245, 247, 249, 252, 271.
Dolman, Rev. Alfred, 243.
Dormer, Lord, 195.
Douay, English College, 2, 3, 9, 14, 23, 25, 28, 31, 35, 37, 44, 45, 47, 49, 50 *seq.*, 65 *seq.*, 96 *seq.*, 125 *seq.*, 178, 180 *seq.*, 195 *seq.*, 205, 208 *seq.*, 232, 235 *seq.*
Douay, Irish College, 69, 93.
    Scotch College, 69, 72.
    Benedictine Monastery, 69, 77, 93, 150, 196.
    Catechism, 30.
    Diaries, 54, 56, 141.
    Rules, 56.
    University, 53.
Doubleday, Rev. Arthur, 255.
Douglas, Rev. Lord Archibald, 290.
Douglass, Bishop, 17, 44, 45, 49, 50, 78, 81, 84, 86, 96 *seq.*, 122 *seq.*, 152 *seq.*, 178 *seq.*, 210, 213, 226, 247, 274, 286.
Doullens, 66, 67, 76 *seq.*, 96, 97, 101, 104, 106, 142, 150, 234.
Dover, 95.
Downside College, 83, 150, 196.
Doyle, Rev. James, 274.
    Canon Thomas, 243, 282.
    Provost Thomas, 206.
Dresden, 278.

Dumont, 82.
Dumourier, General, 77.
Durham, 47, 109, 115.
Dyneley and Ashmall, 28.

EDGBASTON, 40.
Edinburgh, 208.
Edmundian, the, 47, 245.
Eldridge, John, 77, 85, 102, 146.
Elizabeth, Queen, 18, 52, 284.
Emmaus, Bishop of, 285.
Enfield Lock, 259.
Equerchin, 35, 47, 62, 77, 78, 80, 81, 85, 86, 96.
Erskine, Mgr., 130 *seq.*, 154, 157, 169.
Everard, James, 209.
Ewart, Rev. Edward, 229.
Exeter College, Oxford, 53.
Eyre, Rev. Thomas, 97, 112, 114, 116, 132, 133, 141, 160, 161.

FABER, Rev Frederick W., 244.
Farquharson, Rev., 72.
Fenton, Mgr., 255, 287.
Fernyhalgh, 161, 162.
Finchley, 38, 43.
Fingall, Earl of, 13, 17.
Fisher, B. John, 273.
Flass Hall, 97, 98.
Fleetwood, Rev. Francis, 12, 13.
Flers, 80.
Ford, Thomas, 53.
Forrest, Friar, 273.
Freemont, Robert, 76, 102, 113.
Frene, 102.
Fryer, Alfred, 247.
    Canon, 230.
Fulham, 297.
Furneux, Pelham, 35.

GAINSBOROUGH, Earl of, 290.
Galignani, 208.
Gateshead, 133.
George I., 26.
Gerdil, Cardinal, 159.
Ghent, 86.
Gibson, Bishop, 60, 97, 106, 107, 109, 111 *seq.*, 125, 126, 131, 152, 154, 181, 186, 203, 214, 219, 286.
Giffard, Bishop, 8 *seq.*
    Rev. Andrew, 10.
Gifford, Lord, 237.
Gilbert, Mgr., 243, 253, 282.
Gildon, Rev. Joseph, 13.
Giles, Mgr., 243, 255.
Gillow, Rev. Henry, 98.
    Rev. John, 133, 161.
    Rev. John, D.D., 69, 77.
    Joseph, 5, 7, 52, 69, 103.

Z 2

Gillow, Rev. Thomas, 69, 71, 97, 102, 113 *seq*.
Gilmot, Jacques, 184.
Gilpin, John, 231.
Gloag, Rev. Thomas, 243.
Glossop, 209.
Gloucester, 47.
Goddard, Mgr., 243, 272, 282.
Goldwell, Bishop, 4.
Gordon Riots, 37, 43.
Gordon, Rev. J. F., 59, 109.
Gosselin, Martin Haddesley, 32.
Gother, Rev. John, 23.
Gradwell, Bishop, 140, 157, 240.
Grant, Bishop, 256.
Gray's Inn, 15, 28.
Green, Everard, 280.
    Rev. William, 59.
Greenwich, 215.
Gregory XIII., 54.
Griffiths, Bishop, 56, 139, 191, 192, 206, 215 *seq*., 225 *seq*., 242 *seq*., 265, 279, 281.
Grimston, Lord, 232.

HADHAM, 18, 191.
Halia, Bishop of, *see* Poynter.
Haly, Rev. John, 179.
Hamburg, 178.
Hammel's Park, 35, 256.
Hammersmith, 44.
    Convent, 283, 284.
    Seminary, 3, 281 *seq*.
Harcourt, Collége d', 117.
    Colonel, 165, 166.
    John, 165.
Hardman, Messrs., 270.
Hardwicke, Earl of, 245.
Hare Street, 34 *seq*.
Harvey, Father, 12.
Havant, 128.
Havard, Rev. Lewis, 50, 52, 120, 146, 165, 179, 191, 196, 206, 209, 227, 229, 239.
Hay, Bishop, 109.
Haydock, 52, 60, 72, 88, 92, 114, 160.,
    George Leo, 102 *seq*., 114 *seq*., 157.
    Thomas, 157, 160.
Hearne, Canon, 230, 242.
Heathcote, Cecil, 278.
Henri Quatre, 233.
Henry VIII., 18, 57.
Herbert, General Sir Arthur, 275.
"Hermitage," the, 2, 35, 105, 106, 149, 171, 174.
Hertford, 10, 104, 190, 257, 258.
Hierocæsarea, Bishop of, *see* Stapleton.
Higginson, Mr., 151.
Hodgson, Rev. Joseph, 76, 90, 94, 99, 141, 144, 150, 151, 162, 165, 168, 181.
Holdstock, Rev. James, 229.
Hole Farm, 217.
Hollingworth, John, 36.
Holloway, 245, 254.
**Holmes**, Frederick, 247.
**Hood, Thomas**, jun., 282.
Hope, Rev. Douglas, 280.
Hormead, 34.
Horrabin, Richard, 189.
    Rev. Thomas, 65, 124, 157, 159, 162, 174, 279.
Howard, Bernard, 209.
    Lord Edmund, 290.
    Henry, 208.
Howe, William, 255.
Howlett, John, 253.
Huguenots, 293.
Hunsdon, 18.
Hunt, Provost, 230, 232, 263.
Hurst Castle, 4.
Husband, Rev. William, *alias* Bernard, 7.
Husenbeth, Provost, 41, 179, 180.

INGATESTONE, 31.
Inwood, Thomas, 255.
Ireland, Rev. William, 20.
Islington, 245.

JACKSON, Anthony, 240.
Jacobins, 70.
Jacobite Rising, 14, 15.
James I., 19.
    II., 3, 4, 5, 8.
    Duke of York, 258.
Jarrett, Rev. Bernard, 220, 230, 242.
Jenison, John, *see* Potier.
Johnson, Dr., 7.
Jones, Rev. John, 197, 200, 223, 280.
    Mary, 182.

KENDAL, REV. HUGH, 28.
    Rev. Richard, 22, 28, 34.
Kenmare, Earl of, 208.
Kent Street, 27.
**Keogh**, Rev. Edward, 242, 253.
Kildare, 176.
**Kimbell**, Rev. Joseph, 146, 191, 204, 206, 214, 215.
King, Rev. Charles, 230.
Kingston, 27.
King Street, 205.
Kirk, Rev. John, 37, 180.
Kirkham, 159, 181.
Kitchen, Rev. Edward, 61.
Knight, Joseph, 243.
Kyne, Canon, 243.

LANCASTER, Rev. James, 97.
Langton, Stephen, 292.
Lartington, 157.
Last, Canon, 6, 229, 272, 282.
Law, Rev. John, 97, 100, 102, 108, 145, 147, 179.
Lawson, Sir John, 109, 111, 126, 132.
Lea, River, 258.
Leagram, 261.
Lee, Rev. John, 51, 97, 99, 102, 104, 107, 108.
Leicester, 47.
Lens, 77.
Lescher, Rev. Edward, 243.
Leveson, Joseph, 9.
Lewes, 23.
Lewis, Owen, 53.
Leyburn, Bishop, 5 *seq.*
Liège, 13, 61, 107, 155.
Lille, 80, 151.
Lincoln's Inn Fields, 43.
Lindow, James, 191.
    Rev. John, 124, 135, 137, 146, 147, 157, 191.
Lingard, Rev. John, 114, 116, 124, 161.
Linz, 178.
Lisbon, 14, 102, 170, 211, 212, 235.
Lisle Phillipps, Ambrose, 233.
Lloyd, Rev. William, 255.
Londonderry, Marchioness of, 280.
London University, 2, 255 *seq.*
Longbirch, 179.
Louis XVI., 68.
Louis Philippe, 233.
Louvain, 81, 97.
Lowe, Constantine, 279.
    Napoleon, 279.
Lowell, Mr., 60.
Lowndes, Mr., 167, 168.
Low Walworth, 47.
Lucas, William, 75, 102, 113.
Luck, Alfred, 279, 280.
    Rev. Francis, 277.
    Bishop John, 243, 277.
    Canon Thomas, 243, 277.
Lulworth, 167, 280.
Lupton, Thomas, 85.
Lycett, Rev. Francis, 179.
Lynch, Charles, 255.
    George, 255.
Lyons, 288, 292.

MACAULAY, 8.
McCarthy, Mgr., 243, 247.
McFaul, Joseph, 279.
McIntosh, Sir James, 238.
McLaughlin, Mr., 185.
McQuoin, James, 247.
Magdalen College, Oxford, 8.

Magdalen Lervis, 39.
Maguire, Rev. John, 230, 242, 263.
Manchester, 160.
Manning, Cardinal, 244, 282, 286, 291.
Mansfield, Lord, 41.
Maple Durham, 13.
Marchiennes College, Douay, 53.
Marcolini, Mgr., 10.
Marshall, John, 53.
Martin, Rev. Gregory, 53 *seq.*
Mary, Queen, 18.
Mawhood, William, 38, 43.
    William, jun., 38.
    Charles, 38.
Mellish, Miss, 35.
Mentley, 35.
Merton College, Oxford, 53.
Meyer, 273.
Milkley, 35.
Milner, Bishop, 15, 17, 22, 25, 41, 45, 64, 123 *seq.*, 126, 149, 178, 179, 183, 186, 213, 286.
Molloy, Bernard, 243.
    James L., 243, 282.
Moloney, Rev. John, 27.
Monk, Edward, 97, 102, 113, 115.
Mont St. Michel, 290.
Moorfields, 27, 43, 239 *seq.*, 263.
More, Blessed Thomas, 273.
Morris, Bishop, 282.
    Rev. John, 21, 231.
Mottram, 9, 10.
Mouchel, Abbé, 218.
Mount, Canon, 230, 243.
Moylan, Bishop, 175, 179.
Munden, 254.
Munich, 273, 283.
Myers, Mr., 285.

NAPOLEON I., *see* Buonaparte.
Napoleon III., 75.
Nassau, Rev. John, 178.
Nasty, 254.
Needham, Rev. John Turberville, 14.
Neuville, Francis, 149, 174.
New College, Oxford, 53.
Newell, Rev. Richard, 206, 229, 241, 242, 249.
Newgate, 9, 10, 43.
Newman, Cardinal, 241, 251, 289.
Newmarket, 231.
Newsham, Rev. James, 158.
    Rev. Charles, 249.
Nill, Mr., 86.
Nolan, Rev. Edmond, 253.
Norfolk, Duke of, 19, 75, 208, 282, 297.
Norris, Rev. Edward, 263.
Northampton, Bishop of, 271.
Nutt, Miss, 285.

OAKELEY, Canon, 243, 247, 252 seq., 272, 282.
Oates, Titus, 19 seq., 283.
O'Callaghan, Archbishop, 243, 266.
O'Connell, Daniel, 64, 66.
O'Connell, Maurice, 66.
Olena, Bishop of, see Griffiths.
O'Neal, Canon, 272.
Oriel College, Oxford, 52.
Orrell, Rev. John, 153.
Oscott College, 62, 75, 117, 124, 136, 143, 153, 160, 162, 183, 203, 213, 256.
Osmotherley, 40.
Oxenham, Rev. Henry N., 253, 279.
Oxford, 53, 244, 252, 253, 269.

PAGLIANO, Charles, 253, 272.
Palmer, Mr., 38.
Paris, 14, 68, 74, 94, 117, 181, 183, 208, 233, 288.
Parker, Mr., 285.
Parsons, Father, 51.
Patterson, Mgr., 278, 279, 282, 285, 287, 290.
Payne, J. Orlebar, 22.
Payne, 41.
Paynsley, 13.
Peach, Rev. Edward, 76, 102, 104, 108, 117, 146, 165, 206.
Pennington, Rev. Edmund, 243.
Penswick, Rev. John, 72, 92.
    Bishop Thomas, 69, 72, 75, 97, 102, 114, 115, 241.
Perth, 258.
Petersfield, 128.
Petre, Lord, 42, 209, 230.
    Bishop Benjamin, alias White, 11, 15, 21, 23, 31.
    Charles, 208.
    Henry, 230.
Philips, Morgan, 53.
    Stephen, 85, 86.
Picquot, Rev. Daniel, 216.
Piers, 64, 236.
Pitchford, Thomas, 102, 104, 105, 117, 146, 165.
Pitt, William, 127, 158, 168.
Pius VI., 117, 159.
    VII., 184.
    IX., 296.
Plumer, R., 32.
Plymouth, 100.
Polding, Archbishop, 287.
Pontigny, 277, 288 seq.
Pontop, 112, 114.
Pope, Alexander, 7 seq.
Portland, Duke of, 127, 158.
Portsmouth, 277, 284, 298.
Postlethwaite, Rev. Henry, 39.

Potier, Rev. John, alias Jenison, 39, 47 seq., 99, 145, 146, 149, 172, 191, 192, 234.
Potier, James, 47.
    Mrs., 191.
Poynter, Bishop, 51, 52, 60, 67, 69, 71, 79, 92, 94, 99, 114, 124, 125, 135 seq., 144 seq., 154, 959 seq., 165, 168, 170, 174, 176, 179 seq., 210 seq., 224 seq., 247, 261, 265, 274, 286.
Poynter, William, senior, 191.
Preston, 134, 152, 153.
Price, Rev. Edward, 226, 262.
Pringle, Rev. George, 255, 256.
Puckeridge, 39, 40, 145, 171, 189, 191.
Pugin, A. Welby, 1, 2, 148, 244, 249, 251, 268, 269, 274.
Pugin, Edward, 277, 279.
Purcell, Canon, 243.
Purdie, A. E., 273.

RABY, Father, 261.
Rees, John, 255.
Rende, Cardinal di, 280.
Rheims, 56.
Rib, River, 19, 31, 256.
Richmond (Yorks.), 111, 157.
Rickaby, John, 80, 97.
Riggory's Farm, 217, 218.
Riley, Rev. H., 220.
    John, 247.
Rio de Janeiro, 206.
Robespierre, 92.
Rock, Rev. Daniel, 206, 265.
Roe, Mr., 180.
Rolfe, Rev. George, 216, 230, 242, 263.
    Rev. John, 206, 216, 217, 221, 242 seq., 263, 274.
Rooke, Benjamin, 47.
Roskell, Robert, 279.
Ross, Francis, 255.
Rossall, 52.
Rouen, 156.
Rouse, Rev. John, 286.
Royston, 39, 201.
Rutter, Rev. Henry, 98.
Ryan A. Compton, 272.
Ryan, Matthew, 232, 239.
Rye House, 258.
Rymer, Alfred, 47.
    Rev. Frederick, 6, 47, 243, 255, 266, 272, 279, 282.
    Canon Henry, 243, 282.
    Horace, 243, 253, 271.

SADLER, Sir Ralph, 18, 19, 108.
St. Florentin, 288, 290.
St. George's-in-the-Fields, 215, 225, 226, 235, 250.
St. Germains, 12.

## Index.    343

St. Giles, 27.
St. Hugh's Preparatory School, 1, 2, 252, 254, 287.
St. John's College, Oxford, 53.
St. Laurent, 80.
St. Martin-au-Laert, 182.
St. Omer, 3, 5, 44, 45, 47, 49, 51, 61 *seq.*, 83, 88 *seq.*, 100, 125 *seq.*, 132, 136, 137, 145, 169, 180 *seq.*, 191, 205, 206, 235 *seq.*
Saltmarsh, 10.
Santry, Daniel, 247.
Sardinian Chapel, 43.
Saul, Charles, 47, 102, 104, 115.
Scannell, Thomas, 255.
Scholfield, Edward, 278, 279.
"School-in-the-Garden," the, 2, 149.
Searle, Mgr., 73, 76.
Sedcote, John, 172.
Sedgley Park School, 15, 19, 28, 39, 146, 178, 206, 213.
Sens, Archbishop, 277, 290, 291.
Seville, 9.
Sharples, Dr., 265.
Sharrock, Bishop, 179, 186, 195.
  Prior, 72, 79, 84, 92, 94, 150.
Sheehan, Rev. Denis, 264, 274.
Sheldon, William, 168.
Shepherd, Rev. John, 13.
Shepton Mallett, 196.
"Ship," the, 2, 107, 108, 149, 171, 229.
"Ship" Alehouse, 25.
Shooter's Hill, 182.
Shrewsbury, Earls of, 13, 17, 34, 208, 209.
Shrewsbury, Lady, 140.
Siddons, Rev. Joseph, 229, 259.
Silkstead, 3 *seq.*
Silveira, Rev. Joseph, 222, 230.
Singleton, 133.
Smith, Bishop, 60, 126, 150, 151, 154, 161, 168, 179, 181 *seq.*
Smith, John S., 243, 247.
  Richard, 53.
Somers Town, 204.
Sone, John, 128 *seq.*, 149, 167, 169.
Sorbonne, 117, 146.
Southcote, Sir Edward, 20.
  Rev. P., 21.
Southwark, 206, 289, 298.
  Bishop of, 280, 285.
Southworth, Rev. Richard, 125, 129, 135, 167.
Southworth, Ven. John, 76.
Stacey, 115.
Standon, 11, 15, 18, 21, 39, 192, 240, 245.
Standon Inclosure Act, 243.
  Lordship, 3, 4, 17 *seq.*, 208.

Stanfield, Field, 272.
  Rev. Francis, 243, 282.
Stanstead, 39.
Stapleton, Bishop Gregory, 31, 51, 62, 67, 75, 83, 88 *seq.*, 124, 126, 131 *seq.*, 149 *seq.*, 178 *seq.*, 264, 274.
Stapleton, Rev. Joseph, 215, 216.
  Lady Mary, 134.
  Miles, 134.
  Nicholas, 62.
Stella Hall, 109.
Stilton, 201, 202.
Stonor, Archbishop, 299.
  Bishop, 13.
  Judge, 230.
  Thomas, 149.
Stonyhurst College, 61, 124, 143, 155, 156, 207.
Storey, Rev. Arthur, 109, 112, 132, 134.
Storey, Thomas, 85, 86.
Stout, Rev. Thomas, 85.
Strickland Miss, 283.

TALBOT, Bishop James, 2, 4, 13, 17, 34 *seq.*, 60, 62, 105, 207.
Talbot, John, 206.
  Bishop Thomas, 13, 17, 35, 44, 62, 111, 129.
Taverner, Rev. Edward, *alias* Banister, 7 *seq.*
Taylor, Rev. Augustine, 57.
  Rev. Edward, 247.
Teignmouth, 284.
Telford, Rev. Henry, 230, 243, 256.
  Rev. John, 230, 242.
Thompson, Charles, 85, 86.
  Richard, 75, 81, 102, 115.
  Mrs., 280.
Thorndon, 31.
Thorpe Arch, 126, 106.
Threllfall, Rev. Charles, 229.
Tichborne, Edward, 49, 146.
  James, 49, 146.
Tickell, Rev. George, 252.
Tierney, Rev. Mark A., 31, 206, 216, 227, 229.
Tilbury, Rev. William P., 206, 279.
Tilt, Rev. John, 233, 242.
Tixall, 19, 22, 208.
Tootell, Rev. Hugh, *alias* Dodd, 57, 206.
Torre Diaz, Count de, 285.
Tournay, 81.
Trafalgar, Battle of, 190.
Trent, Council of, 54, 282.
Trieste, 178.
Trinity College, Oxford, 53.
Trowbridge, Thomas, 247.
Troyes, 289.

Tudhoe, 109 *seq.*, 132 *seq.*
Tuite, Rev. Francis, 51, 61, 88, 145, 168, 169, 179, 183, 191, 197, 236 *seq.*, 249.
Tunstall, Rev. Edmund, 243.
Twyford, 3 *seq.*, 17, 35.

ULLATHORNE, Bishop, 208, 263, 287
Ulverston, 191.
Ushaw College, 4, 50, 51, 58, 75, 97, 98, 109, 133, 140, 141, 142, 143, 156, 161, 203, 213, 214, 249.

VALLADOLID, 12, 44, 170, 211.
Valognes, 117.
Varley, Rev. Thomas, 97, 159.
    Rev. Thomas, junior, 191, 197, 215.
Vatican, the, 170.
    Council, 282.
Vaughan, Archbishop Bede, 287.
    Cardinal, 254, 298, 299.
    Colonel, 275.
    Colonel, 243.
Veal, William, 85, 102.
Vendeville, Bishop, 53.
Verulam, Earl of, 232.
Virginia Street Chapel, 43, 215, 216.
Virtue, Bishop, 243, 268, 282.
Voltaire, 14.

WADE, John, 142.
Wade's Mill, 231.
Wallace, John, 255.
Walmesley, Bishop, 98, 100, 111, 118, 119, 135, 136, 152, 159.
Walmesley, Father, 286.
    Richard, 243.
    Thomas, 243.
Walsh, Bishop, 64, 66, 146, 164, 179, 180, 205, 241, 264, 265.
Walsh, Rev. Francis, 184.
Waltham Cross, 198, 199, 231.
Walton, 39.
Wapping, 43.
Ward, Rev. Bernard, 272, 280.
    E. Granville, 280.
    Sir Henry, 32.
    Rev. John, 7.
    R. Plumer, 32, 240.
    Mrs. Plumer, 32.
    Wilfrid, 282.
    Dr. W. G., 32, 244, 251 *seq.*, 254, 268, 269, 271, 274, 287, 298.
    Mrs., 280.
Ware, 1, 39, 231, 260, 298.
Wareing, Bishop, 271.
Warkworth Castle, 8.
Warwick Street Chapel, 43, 269, 280.

Waterloo, Battle of, 208, 209.
Watson, Rev. Edward, 280.
Watts, Mrs., 19.
Wealside, 167.
Weatherby, *see* Brown.
Weathers, Dr. George, 230.
    Bishop, 41, 230, 243, 246, 266, 278, 279, 282, 291.
Welch, Rev. John, 229.
Weld, Mr., 61.
    Mgr., 61.
    Cardinal, 261.
    Philip, 243, 257 *seq.*, 279.
Westminster, Archbishop of, 266, 285, 298.
Westminster, 163, 284, 290, 299.
    Archives, 56, 76, 109, 141, 183.
    Council of, 281, 285.
Wetherby, 126.
Whelan, Rev. James, 229.
White, *see* Petre.
    Rev. Alfred, 269.
    Rev. John, 216, 227.
    Richard, 53.
Widford, 18, 32.
Wilds, Rev. William, 51, 83, 145, 147, 157.
Wilkinson, Dr., 62, 195.
Willacy, Rev. James, 19, 37, 38, 39, 42, 45, 47.
Wimpole Hall, 245.
Winchester, 5, 6, 8, 12, 13, 15, 76, 186, 208.
"Windmill," the, 25.
Windsor, 245.
Wisbech, 5.
Wiseman, Cardinal, 249, 265, 271, 277, 282.
Witham Friary, 13.
Wolverhampton, 40.
Woodham, 134.
Woods, Rev. William, 229, 231.
Woollett, Rev. Daniel, 271.
Worcester, 47.
Worswick, Rev. James, 97.
    Rev. John, 133.
    Rev. Thomas, 133.
Wortham, Hale Young, 35.
Wright, Anthony, 167.
    Thomas, 128, 167.
    and Co., 110.
    Mr., 167.
Wyatt, Rev. Joseph, 6.

YARMOUTH, 178.
Yates, Rev. John, 236.
York, 109, 133, 154, 156, 169, 283
    Duke of, 86.

ZINGARELLI, 249.

www.ingramcontent.com/pod-product-compliance
Lightning Source LLC
Chambersburg PA
CBHW030600300426
44111CB00009B/1055